The Conceptualization of the Inner Life

The Conceptualization of the Inner Life
A Philosophical Exploration

by

Leslie Armour
The University of Ottawa

and

Edward T. Bartlett, III
The Cleveland State University

HUMANITIES PRESS
ATLANTIC HIGHLANDS, N.J.

First published in the United States of America in 1980 by
HUMANITIES PRESS INC.
Atlantic Highlands, N.J. 07716

Library of Congress Cataloging in Publication Data

Armour, Leslie, 1931—
  The conceptualization of the inner life.

  Includes index.
  1. Knowledge, Theory of. 2. Concepts. 3. Perception (Philosophy) 4. Facts (Philosophy) 5. Experience. 6. Collingwood, Robin George, 1889-1943. I. Bartlett, Edward T., joint author. II. Title.
BD181.A68   121   79-275888
ISBN 0-391-01759-4

TABLE OF CONTENTS

Preface

The problem which this book sets out to confront is certainly pervasive: everyone copes, as best he can, with the distinction between his inner life and the world outside. Confusion about how the line is best drawn is common enough to provide a more than decent living for a good many psychologists and psychiatrists.

The problem, which from one perspective is a daily and practical human concern, seems from another perspective a traditional philosophical battle-ground whose territory, one might think, is as well marked out as the field at Gettysburg. There are those who would maintain that the inner world is an epiphenomenon, or even a kind of illusion—that what is real is all "out there" and capable of being described by physics. There are those who would maintain that the outer world is, though not an illusion, at least a "logical construction" out of something ("sense data," or "sensa,") which one might think of as the "stuff" of the inner life. There are those who think that the line somehow develops out of the intersection or interaction of two drastically different kinds of thing. The intention of this book is not, however, to recreate these battles in an attempt to show, as military historians are wont to do, that if one side or the other had moved its troops more effectively, the battle could have been won decisively and the war ended for all time. The intention is not even the more modest one (which has had its vogue in recent times) of showing that the troops of one party were all phantoms, ghostly figures of which the other parties ought not to have been afraid. The aim is, rather, to show that the problem of generating a conceptual structure which will enable us to cope with this crucial human experience is a real and very difficult one, because the concepts which one needs are interrelated in a number of ways. They require us to work rather hard to generate accounts of relations which, quite simply, are not very clear in terms of the conceptual models most commonly employed for looking at the world. The battle, therefore, is rather like the ones which animated Moslems and Christians in their religious wars—the very nature of the

v

problem is apt to make it hard for the disputants to see one another's views as anything but perverse.

The authors hope, indeed, that they have shown that it is *possible* to conceptualize the situation without falling into the logical perils endemic to classical dualism, subjective idealism, and materialism. If that is so, the understanding of the human condition may be just a little easier than it was before. It is all too likely, of course, that the result has been the generation of yet another army to join the traditional dispute; but the surface of the discussion, at least, lies on the level of language, experience, and conceptual construction—leaving, for another day, some of the more ultimate ontological issues. And, even if the quarrel is not resolved, there is hope that something has been added to our insight about some crucial issues: action, intention, the homely notion of thing, the problem of knowledge of persons, and the structure of the situation which led to the drawing of the battle lines.

A work with two authors probably deserves some explanation, though such explanations are apt to be somewhat contrived. Dr. Bartlett and I became involved in the project while jointly directing a graduate seminar at The Cleveland State University—a seminar which forced us to cope with R. G. Collingwood's theory of experience. The questions he posed forced on us some very basic questions about the relations between experience and its conceptualization, and his ghost was much in evidence throughout the work, constantly reminding us that the "givens" of many current philosophical debates are much more subject to question than one might think.

The questions we asked ourselves in order to understand Collingwood developed into answers and another graduate seminar in which, perhaps, we learned more than our graduate students. Their responses to our posing of the problem were often as instructive as our own answers. The combination of our skills and experiences opened possibilities which were not quite open to either one of us alone.

Though both of us were educated in universities in which, at the time, the influence of those philosophical analysts who paid a lot of attention to what was called "ordinary language" was much in evidence, we had gone on through rather different paths. My strongest interest has always been in metaphysics and, amongst the philosophers from whose store of ideas I have borrowed happily, Hegel has figured often. Dr. Bartlett would count himself amongst those philosophers who have tried to take the techniques of the Oxford analysts seriously, but who have tried to extend and improve them as well as to develop clear notions of their limitations. The task in which we found ourselves engaged required both some careful conceptual reconstruction and some careful philosophical analysis, and it turned out that we could learn from one another—though we could not, of course, divide the problem into domains proper to speculation and domains proper to analysis.

For the record, Sections 2.1, 2.3, 4.2, 4.5, 4.6, 4.8, 5.1, and 5.3 are Dr. Bartlett's, while the rest are mine. The reader is not particularly invited to locate two different philosophies, vocabularies, or bags of tricks; the work is meant to be one coherent whole.

We are grateful to our colleagues and our students at The Cleveland State University who have given us help, encouragement, and an environment in which work can be done. Gratitude, too, should be extended to the anonymous editor who made many valuable suggestions and improvements.

Leslie Armour
Cleveland, Ohio
October, 1977

Chapter 1

A Perspective on a Problem

1.1 Some Models and a Metaphor

Everyone is aware of a tension in coping with the boundary line between the world within and the world outside. We all understand how these expressions are used but we are all, like Augustine when he was asked what time was, hard put to express the distinction in words. We are not sure where the line is precisely, and just how one ought to draw it.

We are not at a loss when it comes to specifying its significance. The man who projects too much of his inner world on the world outside is a candidate for the psychiatrist. We know what it is to be mistaken about the line, to face the frustration of being misunderstood or the sharp shock of learning that our neighbours' world is a different place. On the other side, the man who gives up too much of his inner, native country faces the empty frustration of one whose affairs are an echo of someone else's public world and searches, in vain, for the significance.

We know, of course, that "inner" and "outer" are metaphors which cannot, literally, be cashed. One does not peel off the outer layers of a man to find his inner workings. The alternative terminology often preferred by philosophers, "public" versus "private," tends more to specify success and failure at certain enterprises—communication, the keeping of secrets, or whatever—than to clarify the line. But that the metaphors reflect something is not in doubt and, if what they reflect is a grand illusion from which we might be rescued by a suitable philosophical doctrine (materialism or subjective idealism, say?), then it is a very vast and pervasive illusion, and it is by no means clear what it is that would count as rescuing us from it. Indeed, a persistent thesis of this book is that nothing *can* rescue us from it, but that the development of a suitable philosophical program may make it possible for us to understand the line and may very well help us in coping with the daily task of maintaining the boundary. Whether one calls this program a kind of philosophical analysis (which would give it an air of momentary res-

1

pectability in some circles), or a kind of philosophical speculation (which might have the merit of making it sound both mysterious and slightly disreputable), is a matter of indifference.

What we shall be doing, in any case, is clear enough: We shall be looking at some experiences which we have (and which, so far as we know, everyone has), and asking questions about the logic of the concepts and propositions which might be used to render those experiences intelligible. A few of the concepts we shall meet will be technical in the sense that it is mostly philosophers who talk about them; these include the concepts of universal, of intentional object, and of relation. But most of the concepts will be those which serve a great part of the human population more or less continuously; the concepts of seeing, perceiving, dreaming, and imagining are examples; so are the concepts of acting, reacting, willing and deciding (to name one group); and feeling, reflecting, thinking, and imagining (to name another).[1] All of these concepts mark out features of this boundary or that; but, when they are deployed, other features come to mind which make boundary drawing difficult. And these concepts are related to some larger notions—knowing, believing, and valuing for instance—in that some of them are called into play whenever these larger notions are put under question. We shall look at them from the angle of one who wants to know whether there "really is"[2] a "world within" or, alternatively, from the angle of one who wants to know how that world is to be marked out from the "world outside."

In section 1.2, I shall examine more closely just how it is that anyone might think that this kind of quasi-logical enterprise might actually answer some of the questions we pose. But, before I can do that, I must establish just why it is that the questions need to be answered and I shall, in the process, have to put the questions into somewhat sharper focus.

1.12   Someone might say that he simply has no problem of the kind to which we are addressing ourselves. He might very well try to make his point by producing for us a suitable inventory of the things that go on one side and the things that go on the other. But such an inventory would expose or presuppose a principle which led one to put some things on one side and some on the other. For instance, whatever is the proper object of scientific knowledge might be said to belong to the outer world and the rest (if there is a rest) to belong in principle to the inner life. Another answer recommends that we act as nations have when they drew their boundaries—that we employ the principle of power. Whatever I can really control belongs to my world, whatever I have no control over belongs to the outer world. Still another answer derives from the different ways in which criteria for the use of words bear on their client terms. Some expressions like "will withstand 10,000 foot-pounds of continuous pressure at sea level for eleven hours" have criteria which locate them clearly in the world outside. Others like "is now in love with Susan" belong to the private world, for it is only the bearer of the name which precedes the "is" who can tell for sure. In this class belong such expressions as "is a believer in tritheism." The principle is that some expressions are governed by resort to introspection, while others are governed by resort to criteria to which introspection is irrelevant. The former belong to the "world within," the latter to the "world outside."

The proponents of these demarcation schemes usually make two related suppositions. The first is that one might create lists of the contents of the rival domains such that no reasonable person would dispute them. The other is that one can produce a principle which relates the two lists. Now I submit that one can at best arrive at an account of the rival domains after a long philosophical exploration. The reason is not that one cannot carry out the programs of the boundary enthusiasts; indeed, one can carry them out all too easily. The reason, rather, is that in so doing, one covertly pronounces on a host of philosophical issues.

Let us take an example. One might start by saying that the objects of knowledge in our world include both things and feelings. Things have to belong to the outside world and feelings to "the world within." I do not doubt that this is, in some sense, so. I do not doubt, either, that one make a case for believing that "things" are what we have "objective"[3] knowledge of, what we cannot wholly control by simple acts of will. I also think that these criteria could be related to one another and (of course) modified as the exploration went on.

But we can see that this fogs the issue by suppressing a host of philosophical problems. The domain of "things" probably includes motorcars, possibly includes rainbows, and certainly does not include feelings. But in virtue of what do we make these assertions?

The *Oxford English Dictionary* devotes more than three pages to the expression "thing." It has an interesting history which, as it happens, reveals the philosophical issues rather nicely. (No one should leap to the conclusion that the histories of words always, or even often, reveal the philosophical issues. I have no way of knowing whether that is so or not.) The word or one of its cognates (such as *ting, ding,* and so on) appears in all the old Germanic languages. The form *thing* seems first to have appeared in Old Frisian. But in all those languages it first meant a gathering for the purpose of making decisions—a parliament or, less grandly, a gathering of the tribe or of a local jury. Its meaning spread from there to the various objects which attracted the attention of such bodies. Sometimes it meant a crime—the thing which one had done. Then it came to mean whatever it was that was being wrangled over, the object of attention. Thus it came to have its most common current meaning—the kind of object that you might fight over in court, or draft legislation about in parliament. Hence it has to be an object of public attention.

But this leaves very open the philosophical question: Just what counts as a "thing?" It has to be the sort of object which can be investigated, which is not just subject to the willful whim of someone, and which can be talked about in terms of public criteria. But what meets those criteria? Objects, one may say, which have perceptual aspects (so that they can enter into the domain of affairs of those who investigate, act, talk); objects with a certain minimal stability (so that the investigations and criteria can be constructed), and objects which can be reflected in a suitable way in language. But what are those?

Are things, say, atoms and their constituent parts? Perhaps, but those are optional features of our universe of discourse—they enter because we have preferences for certain explanation modes. Is the whole universe a thing? Perhaps, but it is notoriously difficult and perhaps pointless, logically, to talk about "everything." Surely, though, motorcars are things. But one should remember that they are things (in the original legal sense) only rather conditionally—to deal with them, the courts have had to insist upon titles, serial numbers and bills of transfer. And that is because, of course, it is essential to develop criteria for dealing with them. We must remember, when we come to tackle our original boundary dispute, that a man's view of the universe is not just like his knowledge of motorcars and neither is it just like the knowledge he has (or might have) of point-particle phenomena in quantum mechanics.

It would do no harm to remember that, in the development of the idea of the thing, as revealed in the history of the word, it always seemed clear that one had to *do* something in order to locate things. Passive knowledge (the dream of John Locke?) never entered into the story. Just think, to take the simplest case, of what you must do and of what you must know about the world and about yourself in order to tell that *that* really is your motorcar.

It will not prove easier with feelings. True, "feeling" only merits a couple of columns in the *Oxford English Dictionary* and some of that is concerned with activities such as "feeling out" which do not precisely concern us here. Still, notice that it has become, first, the notion of a sensation in general; second, the notion of an emotional condition; and third, the idea of an inner response. Like "sensation" itself, it is charmingly ambiguous in a way which has bred a host of philosophical problems.

On the one hand, it means "what I am aware of when I attend only to the awareness itself and not to its object" and, on the other, it means "the state of affairs objectively present in my mind." In the first sense, I cannot have your feelings and you cannot have mine. If I suggest, in case you have been insulted, that you should let me suffer the hurt feelings in your stead, I am, in this sense, making some kind of logical mistake in the guise of an act of generosity. On the other hand, in the second sense, there is no reason why I shouldn't have your feelings. Lord Brain said that he had no reason to suppose that one person couldn't, for example, feel another's pains—they need only be wired in duplicate.[4] If we are both wired in this way and we have a choice of turning the switch on or off, there is no reason why I should not offer to take the pain this time in your place.

We notice, here, a double ambiguity: A feeling, in one sense, is the subject's awareness; in another sense, it is the immediate object of that awareness. The first is "internal" in the sense of being inseparable from the subject, the second internal in the special sense that the subject has better access to it than anyone else. But there is a second ambiguity. Though "feeling" in the second sense is potentially something that two people could have, or that one person rather than another could have, it is the kind of occurrence which must happen to *somebody*. There seems no sense in imagining a pain which was *nobody's;* it is person-dependent.

But do any of these senses give us a clear notion of the kind of "entity" which belongs to "the world inside?" The answer may be "yes and no." Yes, because we have found occurrences which, in so far as they occur at all, are not "things"; and we have seen some senses of the notion of person-dependence, privacy, privileged access, and so on. But the answer is "no" if we want to be sure that we have found something which belongs properly and only to "the world inside."

For there is a parallel to be found if we develop our notion of "thing" and our notion of "feeling" a little further. "Things," for instance, have their perceptual aspects. If they did not, we would not be able to include them in the scope of our various investigations. But, though every perception is a perception of someone and no perception is the perception of more than one person, that does not make "things" wholly private. To the contrary, the perceptual aspect of things is closely related to our notions of their publicity. But, similarly, feelings have their non-private aspects, too. Having one's feelings hurt is something which happens to one in a context. It can be talked about, understood by others, and, in various ways, shared. Being in pain also has its public context and most (perhaps all) pains have their physical correlates. Something happens to one's neural system when one is hurt physically. Now this event may simply have two aspects. Perceived through one of them it is a neurological event, perceived through another it may be a psychological event. Yet this duality may be hard, even impossible, to sustain. One reason for thinking so is that there is a necessary connection between one aspect of the event and the person in whose life it is an event. But between that person and other aspects of the event there is only a factual connection. Whatever it is that "I" am aware of when I "attend to the awareness itself" is necessarily a part of me; the pain itself is an accidental feature of me. This distinction between kinds of connection suggests a radical distinction between kinds of object. But notice that such distinctions raise philosophical issues, the significance of which is not brought out simply by noticing that "things" belong in one world (given one sense of "feeling") while "feelings" belong to another world. We shall have to investigate.

If we cannot even begin the classification without discovering these major philosophical problems, it is unlikely that we shall find other candidates for the lists which are so obviously qualified as to render the issue really settled and the boundaries effectively drawn.

1.13   It might, however, be suggested that, though we cannot quite succeed in marking out the boundary by calling attention to the obvious criteria or the obvious candidates for the rival lists, we can do it quite well at one remove simply by calling attention to the language.

Here we need to distinguish the proposal about language which figured in the "principles" of the makers of lists whom we encountered in 1.12, and the kind proposal which seems to derive naturally from a casual acquaintance with our language. In the former case, the point was that for various kinds of linguistic expressions there were various kinds of criteria. Some were evidently public and others evidently private. We abandoned that as a "one move" solution because the referents of the expressions seemed not to fall into obvious pigeonholes unless one conceptualized the referents according to the precepts of the philosophical theories being argued for. Here we shall be concerned with the proposal that some departments of language in fact give us a picture of an inner world, while other departments of language give us a picture of an outer world.

Thus, one might say that all of us are familiar with the work done by essentially mental expressions. The language allows us to talk about what people remember, believe, think, imagine, surmise and dream. More importantly, perhaps, it allows us to talk about what people doubt, about what they are wrong about, about what is possible as well as what is actual, and about what could have been but was not. What one sees, hears, smells and tastes is not like what one surmises, is wrong about, or is inclined to believe possible, and it is not like what could have been and is not or what is merely possible. Never mind about the criteria for the use of these expressions, one might say. But the *fact* is that we do use them, and they do mark out two distinct realms. If we can start from an understanding of the criteria and work our way to some understanding of the principle of association then, surely, we can find our way to the solution.

I think that no one will deny that this argument has *some* force. We should be suspicious, say, of a reductive materialist or a subjective idealist whose theory somehow abolishes the boundary by fiat.

The difficulty is that it is by no means clear what is being subdivided here. If we simply look at the language, it divides into ways of talking. We do not talk about possibilities in the way that we talk about things, for instance. Language generalizes and permits us to talk about what is not present. But does this mean that "the mind" runs beyond the outer world? That is one interpretation.

But language is still anchored in experience. Language, as such, is all of one piece. It is composed of words. There are rules governing the words but, as language, the rules are more words. To get the idea of two worlds, we *interpret* the language.

The language is "meaningful" in several senses, but it is important that they not be confused with one another. First, the language is meaningful because it contains or can generate rules which govern the way in which the components go together. That sense is purely internal to the language. Second, it is meaningful because, in some way, it meshes with something which is not (in the same sense at least) simply linguistic. This "meshing" might take the form of a representation. Alternatively, the language might lead us through a pattern of experience so as to "make sense" of it, or it might simply organize our responses to situations.

Language which fails the first test is said to be nonsense or gibberish; language which fails the second test is said to be pointless.[5]

Now all the linguistic "evidence" we have been looking at shows only that people behave as if the language in question passed the first test. But it may not pass the second test and we may be wrong in thinking, even, that it passes the first—for the rules may be so porous that anything will slip through them. (And one might not even know that this was so. For instance, it might be the case that much of the language of Freudian psychologists works in just this way. Since it will mesh with any behaviour, it seems as if there are rules for it when, in fact, there are not. As an example, any act which is not overtly sexual was sometimes said to be a case of sublimation or a case of repression. If the "evidence" that it is not the one counts as evidence that it is the other, the classification is certain to succeed; but, in fact, nothing is being said.)

In any event, we shall need to know much more about the rules governing the language and about what will count toward giving language meaning in the second sense. It is true that there is probably a rough natural law to the effect that language which does not mesh with experience eventually disappears from currency, but even if this is so, we should have to know much more than we do so far about just how this works before we could infer anything from the language itself.

1.14   There is one more consideration about language or, at least, about the logic of language, which promises to set actual limits to any possible solution of the boundary problem. We might call it "the problem of first person propositions." It can be stated, most simply, this way: There are some first person propositions which are true and which cannot be translated, without loss of certainty or change of meaning, into propositions of other sorts. If, for language to be meaningful, we must, ultimately, have meaning in both the senses I mentioned in section 1.13, then this fact entails the truth of some proposition about a distinction between the world within and the objective world.

First person propositions are usually those expressed in sentences which contain the pronoun "I" and make an assertion which, if true, tell us something about the person represented by the pronoun. Some of them are characteristically of such a kind that the "I" can be replaced by some other expression while, in general the meaning and certainty of the proposition remains unchanged; and some are, characteristically, of such a kind that this, apparently, cannot be done. "I was typing at eleven a.m. on January 3" seems to be of the first sort, for we can replace the "I" by a proper name or by a definite description. "Leslie Armour was typing at eleven a.m. . ." and "the chairman of the philosophy department at Cleveland State University was typing at eleven a.m. . . . ." have (for some notions of meaning) the "same meaning." "I," "Leslie Armour," and "the chairman" each refer to one and the same person. They *may*, also, have the same degree of certainty. Let us suppose that the only evidence I happen to have about the matter is that I made a video tape of the performance. The substitution fails. Every one might be mistaken in believing that my name, in fact, is Leslie Armour and everyone might wrongly believe that I was "the chairman" at the appropriate moment (some constitutional requirement for the office might have been overlooked). But these are difficulties which we might waive on the ground that they involve matters of fact rather than of principle.

Quite different from this case is one in which I say, "at eleven a.m., on January 3, I saw the dog jump the fence." Nothing except what I say is evidence about what I saw; I am not a television camera and so there is no video tape which *could* show what I saw. Hence, "Leslie Armour saw . . . ." or "the chairman saw . . . . " have neither the same meaning nor the same certainty. Reports in the third person would not be admitted in a court of law as "best evidence" if I were available to testify about what I saw. Sometimes, there is other evidence, but it is never complete. If I report that I saw a Hereford bull in the field with the dog and other evidence suggests that there was no bull there, that will be ground for doubting that I know what I saw. If I report that I saw a girl with red hair in the field and no one except the girl herself knew that she was there, then, if she reports that she *was* there, her report will provide a reason for believing that I was right in my report. But still, there is no substitute here for the "I."

Between these two cases, there are others about which we are less sure. If I say "I believe there are angels," there is a sense in which I ought to know better than anyone else what it is that I believe. But if I have been known heretofore as one who subscribes to reductive materialism, and if I have always behaved as one might who did not believe there were angels, that is a ground for doubting the proposition. And there are cases in which it might seem very likely that others know as much (or more) about what I believe than I do. Suppose, for instance, there is a graduate student who has read all my books, my published and unpublished papers, and is currently well abreast of the problems on which I am now writing. What he says that Leslie Armour believes may be more reliable than what I say, especially if I tend to give rather vague answers to questions about my writings while he gives precise ones. It is even possible, if that is so, that there will be a case in which he and I are equally reliable authorities on what I believe so that when he says "Leslie Armour believes . . . . " we should give it the same weight which we give propositions uttered by me of the form "I believe . . . . " In this case we can substitute third for first person propositions without loss of certainty.

But it seems certain that some first person propositions are true and that some of them cannot be translated to second or third person propositions without loss or change. They are those which report immediate experiences.

We cannot, however, jump from this fact to the conclusion that some form of the "two worlds" hypothesis is to be sustained. Much less can we jump to the conclusion that we know just how the boundary is to be drawn. What we can say is that we shall have to give some meaning to the first person pronoun, and we shall have to do it without giving a descriptive analysis which makes first person propositions into third person propositions.

But we might, of course, try to stay wholly within the domain of language and its rules. The *prima facie* evidence is that we cannot actually succeed in this enterprise for, simply on the level of language, it should be possible to provide translations which eliminate the "I." Extensionally, the "I" is formally equivalent to any proposition which contains some appropriate definite description. The difficulty is with the relation of language to its users. It is the intrusion of the user which makes the first person proposition peculiar. But, now, what is the relation, generally, of a language to its users? The question is obviously a large one.

1.15   The reader, at this point, may be pardoned for wondering whether the original introduction to the problem did not contain an element of confusion—or even a little sleight of hand bordering on fraud. For I started by suggesting that the problem of "the world within" was vital for such matters as maintaining one's personal integration, the sense of meaning in one's affairs and even one's sanity. But what then emerged was that one who doubted this might make a number of quite ordinary—indeed, banal—proposals about how to draw the boundary between "the world within" and "the world outside." He would, I have been suggesting, be met with rather technical rejoinders which suggested that the problem was harder to solve than one thought. In his turn, the objector would surely be driven to make more technical proposals—ending, perhaps, with the one I have just been discussing.

Yet we now have some perspective from which to look at the original problem. When, for instance, we talked about "things" and "feelings" we were simply talking (as neutrally as one might) about what was to count as the preferred class of objects which is definitive of "the world outside." The man who is said to have an hallucination has simply included in that class objects which others reject, or alternatively, has put a construction upon objects which others would not recognize. Accordingly, one way of understanding what is going on is to find out something about how one might establish the credentials of the preferred class. Before we count someone as a failure at perception and in need of assistance we have, at least, to know what should count as success. The man with a delusion, again, is one who has been misled in some way in his reading of the objects. But how do experiences lead and mislead? How are boundaries drawn in language? One may argue that it is at least barely possible that the lack of success which psychologists and psychiatrists have experienced in coping with these matters is related to a lack of understanding of what can and cannot be expected, and a lack of understanding of the ways in which the language and the appropriate concepts in fact work.

Again, the man who is unable to express his feelings or distressed by the lack of coherence in his affairs may be facing, in some measure, the real difficulties which stem from the ambiguities I noticed in our way of talking about these things. Or, he may be faced with our very problem about the pronoun "I." He may understand very well, and feel very deeply about, its irreplaceability. At the same time, he may be hunting hopelessly for a simple "referent" for it which will explain both its importance and its irreplaceability. If he faces up to the problems of language and meaning which this poses for him, some of his problems may be simplified.

1.16 There are, however, rather more dramatic issues involved. The most peculiar feature of attempts to dispute the boundary between the "world within" and the outside world is this: If one attempts to abolish the boundary altogether, the inner and the outer world tend to reverse their positions. A corollary of this is that the notion of self-hood and self-identity becomes meaningless. As a rule, this phenomenon has gone unnoticed though on at least one occasion—in Rudolf Carnap's *Aufbau*—something of this phenomenon was exploited quite deliberately.[6] This puzzle is part of the reason for thinking that the question of boundaries is both serious and has immediate practical import.

1.161   Consider, then, that philosophical questioning usually starts at the level of ordinary things. It is customarily pointed out that ordinary things—stones, tables, cigar butts—have, in their ordinary descriptions, a mixture of public and private components. We describe them from an ordinary or an ideal perspective, as colored, smelly, tasty and more or less resistant to touch. We also describe them as occupying space, as more or less lawful, as chemically responsive to this and that. Now a common enough philosophical strategy is to try to make one's descriptions as "objective" as possible by removing from the domain of things those features which form our first list. That list—since Descartes and, especially, Locke—has frequently been thought to be composed of "secondary qualities," qualities produced in *us* by the thing in question. These qualities have frequently been regarded not simply as second-order or relational, but as second-rate or uninformative. One of the plans of this book is to rehabilitate "things" in the more ordinary sense. For now, let us simply look at what happens if one does not.

One starts with things which everyone claims to experience, at least if "claiming to experience" is the same as, or much the same as, claiming to see, hear, touch, taste and so on. We move, however, to increasingly theoretical entities. Apples and oranges are hopelessly compromised: It is part of the concept of apple that the thing should have a certain taste, feel, and appearance. Even its "real size" (vis-a-vis everything else) is the size it would appear to have if you were where you cannot be, namely, where it is. Such subjective matters cannot belong to "the world outside."

We move to something less subjective—molecules. Though molecules can be seen (with a microscope), one does not get into the disputes about them that one is apt to get into over apples and oranges. No one is touchy about the feel of a molecule. Even its appearance has been tidied; it has an agreed upon structure which is part of chemical theory, so there is no question about whether its appearance from one perspective is better than its appearance from another. But we should notice that this fact, roughly, depends upon the fact that the concept involves a large theoretical element.[7] It is not that experiences of molecules are more reliable than experiences of oranges, but that eccentric experiences of molecules do not count for much.

Nevertheless, the role of experience is not diminished to zero, for chemical explanations are centred around a great variety of what one might call rather gross experiences. Litmus papers and liquids change colors, tests leave traces, chemical processes are observed via physical state changes from gases to liquids to solids. Chemistry largely orders ordinary experience and plays out its role in the lives of petroleum refiners, pharmacists, glue makers, and hair dyers, as well as in the more ascetic lives of "scientists" in their laboratories.

Yet chemistry is not purely mechanical. It still requires the judgment of the skilled chemist to *decide* just what he is dealing with and how best to analyze and explain it. And it yields surprises. The chemistry of organisms remains, to some degree, an uncertain business.

There is a reason for this, in principle as well as in practice. The chemical situation is not wholly exhausted by the molecule; the environment of the molecule may be chemically important as well. Hence the unit of explanation in bio-chemistry may sometimes be the whole organism. It remains true that the experience-theory ratio leaves a substantial range for subjective interpretation. It is not always (as every chemist knows) that a given experiment can really be repeated with the same result, for the expression "the same experiment" remains doubtful in the face of the experience-theory ratio.

The search for a firmer unit and for a less annoying experience-theory ratio is naturally combined with a desire for a more uniform explanation pattern—for a set of simple invariant laws. All of this leads from chemistry to physics, from molecules to atoms and sub-atomic particles. The chemist is not locked out by the new unit. He continues to be interested in the relation between the atomic and the molecular situation, and it is not always easy or possible to tell the chemist from the physicist. Though the chemist, primarily, is concerned with processes which are special to the combination of certain elements and the physicist with processes which are general to all elements, the physicist may take an active interest in particular elements (say helium at low temperatures) because of the way in which phenomena develop and seem to require new general formulations.

The desire for tidiness is never quite met. But, at the atomic level, the theory-experience ratio approaches an ideal. Atoms are not objects of experience as such. No questions about their "secondary qualities" can arise at all. Their contexts do not provide new and special problems in the way that molecular contexts might. The future behaviour of an atom will depend upon the energy distributions and electrical charges which constitute its nature, and on whatever distributions of the same kind constitute its influential environment. It does not matter whether its atomic environment forms part of a brain structure or part of a billiard ball—the principle is the same.

Let us suppose, then, that, at this level, we decide that we know what the "world outside" actually *is*. First of all we should notice that, in a sense, our account of that world has become remarkably dependent on "the world within." All theories have a relation to the inner life. Furthermore, we now find that we could, if we wanted to, contrive indefinitely theories which accounted for whatever experience component remains in physics. The more we restrict the element of experience, the easier it becomes in practice to correlate it with a vast variety of theories. Faced with this, we may no longer wish to say that our physical theories describe the world (*what* world?) but, rather, we may want to content ourselves with saying that they predict regions of experience with which we are particularly interested. But so do astrologers—though they do it very badly.

It then turns out that physics is a cultural phenomenon—a matter of convenience and of cultural predispositions rather than of objective description and, in recent years, this fact has been widely noticed. There are other readings of physics.[8] But this is the one which follows from taking the "physical things" as replacements for the ordinary things.

If physics is just a cultural phenomenon, one may suspect that the "world outside" has turned out to be a form of "the world within." For "culture" is commonly thought to be subjective in the sense that it reflects our inner lives and is created by us. Yet the replacement of the ordinary world by the world of physics seems to leave no room for a real inner life.

What happens is this: If we survey the world in terms of molecular chemistry or atomic physics, and if we imagine that the most "objective" accounts in their terms (where "objective" connotes that state of affairs which is left when all the "subjective" or "secondary" properties have been removed) actually represent reality, we find that we have a world in which there is no room for the phenomena of the "inner world." These are written off as perceptual by-products ("epiphenomena" in the phrase of the philosophical tradition). But what of the knowing subject? In the original Cartesian version of the doctrine, the knowing subject was regarded as real but lacking the properties which characterized the physical world, especially those associated with extension. Descartes himself worried considerably about its possible relation to the physical world. Its positive properties were described through epistemological relations: some states of the knowing subject are immediate objects of cognition. No physical object is the object of such a cognition. But otherwise knowing subjects remained mysterious. The seeker looking inward, however, is apt to find a blank or a set of pseudo-physical objects—images, dreams or sensation patterns—all of which have the characteristic of leaving no residue when the "secondary qualities" are removed. (Hence there is not a physics of the dream-world, or a chemistry of the mental image.)

The paradox is large and cruel. When we pursue this reading, we find the physical sciences to consist mainly of cultural artifacts, the tracks and traces of a mind at work. But when we search for that mind at work we find only chimerical traces. True, everyone knows that he has images, that he sometimes dreams, that his sensations come in patterns. But all of these are characteristically like objects in the "world outside" except that they consist only of the immediate surfaces. (The mother-in-law in your dream is *not* composed of molecules whose components are atoms of hydrogen, oxygen and so on though, of course, she *looks* like the mother-in-law you meet at the dinner table.) Both horns of the dilemma are sharp: We could live with physical science as a cultural artifact (perhaps) if we understood the self which produced the artifact. But since we have chosen to understand the world in terms of physics and chemistry, and since all the "inner" phenomena dissolve at the approach of those techniques, we are not allowed that self. We could live with the self-as-chimera (perhaps) if physics and chemistry were objective descriptions of the world. But since we have chosen to equate objectivity with a high theory-to-experience ratio, we are not allowed this option.

One who sees the world in these terms will find, of course, that the more he appears to understand the world—the more, that is, he absorbs a scientific education combined with a sophisticated reading of his science—the more he is driven to despair. He can ignore the extent to which science is a cultural artifact and become a kind of scientific fundamentalist. Like the Biblical fundamentalist, however, he saves his sanity at the price of his reason. He can persist in his faith in an unintelligible given "self"—the Cartesian ghost conjured up by Gilbert Ryle who hoped to lay it to rest—but only, again, at the price of obvious inconsistency.

1.162 It would be surprising, but pleasant, if one who started at the other ehd of this dialectical shift could expect to fare better. It will turn out, however, that the professing subjectivist ends in a shift in the other direction—everything turns into an object in a world in which the notion of objective structure is gone, just as the objectivist finds that everything turns subjective in a world in which the basis of the knowing subject is gone.

Let us see what happens. One may well say the attempt to find the objective element which lies below the subjective surface of experience must be doomed, as we saw, because the more the theory-experience ratio shifts toward theory and away from experience, the more we must expect to find subjectivism. Therefore it seems natural to abandon the pretence. Suppose, then that one simply takes what one finds as experience. Carnap takes this step for the reasons, in fact, that I have just described. Suppose, then, we follow along and see what happens to his program.

He says: ". . . We choose the autopsychological basis for our constructional system. The most important reason for this lies in our intention to have our constructional system reflect not only the logical constructional order of the objects, but also their epistemic order. It is for the same reason that we excluded the system form with physical basis, various versions of which were logically possible."[9]

When he rejected the "physical basis" for a constructional system, what he ruled out, by his own account, were the kinds of proposals which I have just been discussing: he mentions specifically, for instance, the attempt to give an account of the objects in the world based on particles such as electrons, or an account based on fundamental structural units such as points in space-time. The reason, in his view, that these programs *should* be rejected is that they are late-comers in the epistemic order. ("Epistemic" as Carnap uses it seems to refer to the order of knowledge, but since this order is fundamentally established by a *theory* of knowledge, the order seems to be, in fact, epistemological.) The epistemic order, in Carnap's view, is from experience to theory. (Technically, Carnap defines epistemic priority in neutral terms. An object has epistemic primacy vis-a-vis a second object if the second object must be known via the mediation of the first. But he has expressed the view that the only elements in knowledge are experience and convention so that, in fact, the order of knowing must be from experience to theory and not from theory to experience.)

We should distinguish, here, what Carnap believes because he has a particular empiricist view of knowledge from what, presumably, anyone would believe whether he had this bias or not. In general, the holds on any theory amount to claims that it should somehow cope with some region of experience and that it should cope with whatever non-experiential propositions there are which cannot satisfactorily be denied. On almost any view, this latter class of propositions is quite restricted and the former is quite wide, for there are many experiences and few subject matters which yield propositions necessarily true. Hence it is usually true that as the theory-experience ratio shifts towards theory and away from experience, many alternatives are possible and, as it shifts toward experience, few alternatives are possible. But, for Carnap, this rule holds absolutely, of course, for there are no holds except those derived from experience. If theoretical entities were used as the basis for the construction he has in mind, it would follow at once that the physical sciences were mainly the products of convention, and hence count as cultural objects.

Carnap raises the question as to whether or not cultural objects, *per se,* might be used as the basis for the construction. But he says "a system with a cultural basis appeared unworkable."[10] Thus for him, the objectivist reduction which we considered first is impossible and its natural outcome—a system of cultural objects—is something he regards as unworkable. What remains is a subjective basis.

But now he faces the question: How do autopsychological data provide a hold on any proposition? In constructing a general theory, he says: "Basic relations take precedence over the basic constituents." He can, therefore, appeal to the overall coherence of his system; but that will not suffice to choose between sets of rival theories which may produce the same coherence of relations or cover the same range of basic data. Ideally of course, he needs propositions which can be confirmed by a single datum of experience. But what would such an experience and such a proposition be like? It cannot be the experience of an ordinary object such as a chair or a table, for that has a multiplicity of components, and statements about each would require a separate proposition and a separate experience to confirm it.

The experience must be of something essentially atomic. The traditional view is that there are elementary unanalysable experiences—they have been called sensations, impressions, ideas, sense data, sensa and so on. Carnap is aware that it is doubtful that there are any such experiences, but he thinks that he can speak of "elementary experiences." "In choosing as basic elements the elementary experiences, we do not assume that the stream of experience is composed of determinate, discrete elements. We only presuppose that statements can be made about certain places in the stream of experience and that one such place stands in a certain relation to another place, etc. But we do not assert that the stream of experience can be uniquely analysed into such places."[11]

This, then, is the first dilemma. If there are basic experiences, no one is apt to recognize them. If there are not, we can still act as if there were by talking about "experience places" as Carnap suggests. The logic of the situational demand takes precedence over the actual reports of how the subject grasps his experience. This must be so, of course, if the theory is to work.

We note such "places," then, by certain kinds of propositions—essentially, those which refer to a one-unit experience place. (For instance, one may say "red, here, now," where "here, now" are conventions used to mark off a single experience-place.) Whatever else the subject is doing, he reports on whether or not he sees red now, and one observation will conclude that.

One should notice (Carnap is not reticent about it) that we have established this situation by a suitable convention prescribing how we are to go about things. This convention is not unreasonable if it excludes no evidence. From it, we will assemble some set of true propositions and, from those, we will sift the ones we need in order to build our accounts of the objects we want to have. The rules do not compel us to accept any propositions save those relevant to the class of things about which we desire knowledge.

At first glance, the difficulty about this seems to be the "double reference" of each of these propositions, for each seemingly refers to a subject and an object. "Red, here, now" means, in part, "there is redness in this vicinity and it is reported by 'p' " (where 'p' stands for some reporting subject.) But Carnap does not, of course, want this duplicity for the obvious reason that 'p' is neither a cognized object of the same sort as "red" nor a construction out of propositions like "red, here, now." It is not a directly cognized object, for it is the second referent of all such propositions. " 'P' here, now" will not do. A reporting subject is not a single element or "elementary experience." It is not a construction, for it is the reiterated concomitant of every proposition and, as such, it has no relation to the datum referent of *any* such proposition.

Carnap treats it, therefore, as he must—simply as a mythological hangover which is iterated only as part of a system of conventional signs. "We must even deny the presence of any kind of duality in the basic experience, as it is often assumed (for example as 'correlation between object and subject . . . ') These theories are the victims of a prejudice, the main reason for which is the subject-predicate form of the sentences in our language."[12]

There *is* no way, on his theory, of speaking of the self or subject at all, for it is only a linguistic hanger-on. However, as he says, at a "higher level" of construction, "we shall find various domains which we call, in conformity with the customary usage, the domain of the physical, or the psychological . . . and of the cultural." But these are all constructions out of the propositions which refer directly to the elementary experiences (or which structure the elementary experiences). We shall not get the "self" or "subject" at all, though we may get mental images, dreams, memory images and so on—for though they do not fit into the physical construction pattern they can be made to fit another pattern and given the status "psychological." Still only "objects" can be constructed in this way.

In short, in seeking the subjective route, we have ended, paradoxically, by eliminating the subject. We have also, on Carnap's particular theory, created something of a mystery. For whatever "the stream of experience" may be, we cannot get at it. We can only get at the structured experience places.

Thus we see the double inversion: just as the objective turned into the subjective, so the subjective turned into the objective. But the matter is even more frustrating, as I suggested earlier. For each atomic "object" has only, after all, a constructed place in the whole. Shall we not end—as Neurath did—with the notion of an arbitrary construction whose justification is that we like it?

The trouble is that, except as philosophers who like our own philosophies, it is very doubtful that we *can* like it. The self is gone in either case. The possibility of successfully arbitrating the boundary dispute with which we started is nonexistent.

1.17   We shall, in Chapter 2, pursue the directions of thought suggested in 1.16. The issue here is not whether one can fault the logic which sustains such thought processes. Clearly, one can. The issue is, rather, the problem they pose: It is evidently possible for human beings to create pictures of the world in which there is no place for themselves—whether the picture is one of a world of atomic particles, or one of a world of sense data of Carnap's "elementary experiences" or "places in the stream of experience." These schemes are thought to be attractive because they are imagined to produce the basis for objective knowledge. They represent a trade-off of values—the values of that objective knowledge against the values associated with a comprehensible place for human beings in the world.

In this way, these schemes generate a further paradox, for it is notorious that, on either of these views, there is no place in the world for objective values. Values cannot be explicated by the theory of atoms or the theory of molecules, nor can they be explicated as immediate empirical data. But a set of intellectual values having to do with order and clarity is championed in the process of explicating a situation in which there are no values.

Dehumanized pictures of the world are demoralizing, and provoke a variety of responses of various degrees of rationality. Sartre's existentialism, for instance, was substantially built around the notion that persons are not to be found in the world of things. They do not exist in that mode and must, that being so, create themselves and their values along with themselves. They teeter uneasily on the edge of non-being and can only overcome their *angst,* if at all, through an action which posits them in the world. But this assumes one of those worlds in which things have been stripped of their meaning and, indeed, Sartre devotes the opening section of *Being and Nothingness* to painting the results of the phenomenological disintegration of things and of the empty world which that leaves.[13] But this is drastic and surely unjustified if all it hinges upon is one possible conceptualization amongst many.

Martin Heidegger was prepared to go even further and to assault logic itself (even, perhaps, reason) as the root of this dehumanization and to reconstruct his world, as much as possible, on his direct cognition of the human situation.[14] But his direct cognitions, in their turn, seem to be influenced by a philosophical tradition. His talk of man's estrangement from being, of the "thrown-ness" of the human situation, of the intrusion of nothingness into human affairs, seems to stem from the experience of a man heavily conditioned by the mainstream of post-Cartesian philosophy. But the abandonment of reason as a source of insight into the human condition seems to be a reaction to a situation in which the world within has been discredited by the philosophical construction of a world-view which has no place for the person and his inner life.

These questions are not merely of academic interest, for it is not as if experience were uninfluenced by the conceptualizations we choose, or as if the quality of life were independent of such matters. That men will struggle to redeem themselves and to reclaim a place in the universe is obvious from the history of philosophy. What is more doubtful is the proposition that such attempts at reclamation are successful. The abandonment of reason would leave one with little more than one's preferences. Rival schemes can only be weighed by their imaginativeness, their tendency to coincide with the insights of the reader and their aesthetic merits. And even the objective test of coincidence with insight is shaky, on the ground that the insight may be little more than a reaction to a previously proffered world scheme.

What is needed, then, is a basic attempt to come to grips with the tendency of the world within to wither away in the face of certain conceptual schemes, and an attempt to reconstruct the original situation—a patient sifting of the logical situation, the crucial concepts, and the problem of knowledge itself.

1.2 The Search and the Method

1.21   The reasonable course of action, then, seems to be this: We need to come to grips with the various contentions to the effect that there is no line to be drawn between the world within and the world outside. We have chosen four of these. The first is the program generally known as reductive materialism—the full-blooded version of the doctrine sketched in section 1.161. The second may be called "subjective idealism," though it includes a spectrum ranging from Berkeley's doctrine to the Carnapian program based on construction from auto-psychic particulars. The third is the more recent attempt which is characterised, most clearly, as the view that the problem really only arises at the level of language and that it does so as a result of the misuse of language; once misuse has been identified, the issue can be clarified and will disappear. The fourth is the view that the problem arises through the adoption of wrong-headed ontological criteria and, therefore, could be solved by introduction of correct ontological criteria or, perhaps, by an understanding of the fact that no such criteria can be forthcoming.

It will be our contention that dissolution of the line is not possible. In trying to show this, we have in mind, generally, two kinds of issues. One has to do with the internal logic of such theories, which exhibit a tendency to violate the conditions of enquiry which they presuppose. For instance, a feature of reductive materialism is its reliance on neuro-physiology to cope with allegedly "mental phenomena." But neuro-physiology works by correlating what the neuro-physiologist discovers about people's brains with what people say about their experience. If the latter is not believed to be true on independent grounds, the theory becomes circular.[15] The other kind of issue develops from a consideration of experiences which everyone has, and which no one is in a position to deny that he has. Everyone knows the difference between seeing things and imagining them; theories which make it impossible that one should understand this difference are, therefore, evidently faulty.

The point of our analysis of attempts at dissolution is to identify the crucial issues and concepts around which the enquiry must proceed. They will turn out to be of three sorts. There are formal issues which can best be stated in terms of an analysis of the significance of first person propositions and their bearing on the possibility of enquiry. These will occupy Chapter 3. Chapter 4 will encompass a lengthy examination of the most central concepts—ranging from that of person to that of intentional object—which need to be looked at from the point of view of their adequacy to experiences which everyone has, and from the point of view of their logical functions in theories and in enquiries. Chapter 5 will take up with questions about knowledge which have arisen in the two preceding sections. We shall try to cope with the *orders* of knowledge: knowledge as it appears in its most basic form, knowledge which arises from the analysis of that first order knowledge, and knowledge which stems from an attempt to re-order the analysis in coherent patterns. But we shall also try to cope with the *kinds* of knowledge, and we shall argue that knowledge of persons, for instance, is not just like knowledge of things, and that knowledge of things is not like the second order knowledge which derives from our analysis of knowledge of things.

The aim is to rehabilitate both the concept of thing and the concept of person in a way which will illumine the extent and significance of "the world within."

1.22   Still, one may wonder why all this is a philosopher's task and not that of a psychologist or that of a theologian or, indeed, that of a physicist. The answer will emerge, we hope, in the course of the discussion. But here, two matters are worth mentioning.

First, these questions are unlike those to which practitioners of the various sciences I just mentioned most frequently address themselves. If the physicist chooses to ignore the taste of the orange or the biological relations which hold between its components, he may do so as long as his account yields procedures from which he can predict some future experiences which interest him. If the psychologist wants to ignore questions about "the world within" and confine himself to the effective correlation of stimulus and response, he need only worry if he fails to get the correlation which will satisfy him. This is not to say that physics is *just* about the prediction of a special range of future experiences, or that psychology is *just* about the correlation of stimulus and response. In the end, all experience is relevant to either discipline and the simple "abstractionist" view of either discipline is not likely to work.[16] But it is true that coming to grips with our ordinary experiences of things or our ordinary transactions with persons is not necessarily a task for either discipline. For though each deals with all experience each of them has to do with a specific meaning-range of our experience. Seeing the Rorschach ink blot can figure both in psychology and in the physics of optics. But it has a different meaning in each case. What lies beyond that range is not the concern of such practitioners in their professional capacities, though they may and often do philosophise as much (and even as well) as philosophers.

More fundamentally, these endeavors are specialized and need interpretation. Whether we take the objectivist-materialist reading of physics, or the logical constructionist reading, is not a question *in* physics. It is a philosophical question which derives from the relation between these claims to knowledge and other claims to knowledge (such as our knowledge of ordinary things and persons in everyday life) which may not be the domain of any specialist. Even the question: "Do we have knowledge when we grasp propositions in physics and if so, of what kind?" is not a question in physics. And the question: "Can a person be conceptualized as a set of responses to stimuli?" is not a question in psychology. The nature of knowledge and the status of concepts are philosophical questions, and the practice of the sciences *may* well go on just the same no matter what view we take. Our results might change some program in physics, but they need not. For instance, one who held a pragmatic view of physics might maintain that a physical theory can be expressed in any mathematical form which increased the likelihood of acceptable predictions, even if he did not have the slightest idea about how the mathematics might *represent* reality. One who held a descriptivist view of physics would be compelled to a different position. Now, if the two disputants are physicists, their behavior as physicists may be changed by their views, but not necessarily. The descriptivist might merely regret that what is, from his point of view, a rather unsatisfactory kind of mathematics is the only one available to him, and go on using it while maintaining—quite properly—that he is still doing physics.

Theology, of course, is different inasmuch as the theologian is not able to conceive his task pragmatically. But he only needs to know what logically follows from his given theological premises—whether they are based on revelation, direct divine inspiration, received authority, or simply on private experience. Whether his program makes for an intelligible world or not is of importance to him, but need not change his theology—like Tertullian, he might rejoice in the absurdity of the world, or, like Aquinas, he might take satisfaction in the extent of its rationality. Making sense of the world is a question which arises for him when he proceeds to philosophise about his theology. He can use these philosophical results as can the physicist or the psychologist, but the questions are independent and he is not bound to use them in a given way.

The philosopher's quest, in short, is with the optimization of intelligibility—essentially, a kind of logical problem. He must also explore the consequences of the limits of intelligibility. Others may share in his trade if they wish, but when they do, they are philosophers.

FOOTNOTES

Notes to Chapter 1

Notes to Section 1.

1.   A good part of the *problem*, of course, has to do with just what it is that differentiates these two groups—if anything, other than a cultural tendency to organize reports of our affairs in a certain way.

2.   One must start, surely, in a rather simple-minded way and accept that some distinction is supposed by such an expression—even though, if one wanted to be clever, one might reply at once that, even if the inner life is only a delusion, there "really is" a delusory inner life. In any case, books like Gilbert Ryle's *The Concept of Mind* (London: Hutchinson, 1949) are intended to persuade us that the inner life is, in important respects at least, a special kind of illusion.

3.   Objectivity is a very tricky notion—and one which will figure throughout our discussions. In the special sense here it is meant to suggest, literally, demonstrable association with objects. Often the word is used to mean "inter-subjective"— whatever it is that many of us can reasonably be certain of. See my paper "Change, Value and Objectivity," *Philosophy in Context*, 1977.

4. Russell Brain, *Mind, Perception and Science* (Oxford: Basil Blackwell Science Publications, 1951) pp. 8-9 and 66-67.

5. Philosophers have argued about "meaning" in many—often confusing—ways. It is interesting to note that the two senses invoked here have associations with two widely debated accounts of meaning: the verifiability thesis found, for example, in A. J. Ayer, *Language, Truth and Logic* (London, Victor Gollancz, 1936; second edition, 1946), and the so-called "use" theory associated with Ludwig Wittgenstein's *Philosophical Investigations* (New York: Macmillan, 1953). To some extent, proponents of the rival theses were not arguing against each other, but at cross purposes, because they were arguing about different things. See Leslie Armour, *The Concept of Truth* (Assen and New York: Royal Van Gorcum and the Humanities Press, 1969).

6. Rudolph Carnap, *The Logical Structure of the World and Pseudo-Problems in Philosophy,* translated by Rolf George (Berkeley: University of California Press, 1969).

7. Indeed, what is happening here is that we are moving from the particulars of experience to the universals of theory. A molecule is a rather Platonic entity; one molecules has to be just like another in the same state. But that is because they are ideals—creatures of theory.

8. This is the reading which it seems appropriate to offer as a rejoinder to those who think that physics offers a description of "the real" which is superior to the one we might otherwise have. But one need only be a little sophisticated to see that physics may be related to reality as a map is related to the country mapped: it may *represent* the real better than an off-hand verbal description, because it *does* ignore the irrelevant rough edges.

9. *The Logical Structure of the World* (see note 6 above), p. 101.

10. *Ibid.,* p. 99.

11. *Ibid.,* p. 109.

12. *Ibid.,* p. 105.

13. Jean-Paul Sartre, *Being and Nothingness,* translated by Hazel E. Barnes (New York: Washington Square Press, 1966).

14. Martin Heidegger, *Being and Time,* translated by John Macquarrie and Edward Robinson (London: SCM Press, 1962).

15. Neurophysiologists are rather fond of writing about the methodology of their science—See such works as Wilder Penfield, *The Mystery of Mind* (Princeton: Princeton University Press, 1975), and Russell Brain, *The Nature of Experience* (Oxford: The Clarendon Press, 1951). But it is even more instructive to analyze articles from *Brain* or to look at classic texts such as Russell Brain, *Diseases of the Nervous System,* revised by John N. Walter (New York: Oxford University Press, 1969).

16. It seems fashionable to suppose that abstractionism will work—that we can have, say, events which belong to the domain of physics and others which do not; but the sense in which this is true is a rather special one. It is true that, say, St. Augustine's conversion to Christianity is not an event which one would expect to find described in a physics text. But, unless St. Augustine's conversion was possible without any change in his brain states, and unless his conversion led to no physical movements or changes which would not have occurred otherwise, his conversion must be related to the domain of physics in a way which causes concern. For either those events would have happened anyway in accord with ordinary laws of physics, or there are events which are physical but not in accord with known laws of physics. The first possibility creates a theological difficulty, the second a problem for physics. The theological problem may be eased if it turns out that some of these events are indeterminate with respect to physical laws—but then God makes use of the chance indeterminacies of physics.

Chapter 2

The Dissolutionists

In Chapter 1, I sketched some of the lines of thought associated with the claim that the problem of identifying the boundary between the "world within" and the outside world is not a real one. This discussion is intended to detail the problems which those claims pose.

Historically, the tendency toward monism is strong and the outcome has usually been one of the many kinds of idealism, or one of the many kinds of materialism. The philosophical impetus behind this tendency stems from the desire for a unified explanation of the world, and from the associated difficulties posed by puzzles about the "interaction" relations which must hold between components of a world which contains different kinds of things. Inevitably, these problems are compounded by difficulties which are epistemological and logical. If there are many kinds of things, there will be many different kinds of knowledge and each will be likely to have characteristic merits and defects. There is a relation between the thought that any given specimen of knowledge has defects, and the tendency to skepticism; and there is, therefore, a relation of some kind between monism and the historic desire to refute the skeptic. Logically, too, there will be difficulties in arguments with more than one premise, if different premises are associated with different kinds of knowledge. The itch for a single, optimal inference pattern is apt to be assuaged by claims of a kind which lead to a preference for monism.

There are also institutional and even political motives for monistic proposals. If one believes that the truth is to be had through revelation, one may not think it likely that the world is so organised as to permit knowledge of a different kind. Institutionalized contemporary science is certainly responsible for some of the impetus toward the kind of materialism which Professor Smart calls "scientific realism."[1] The power of an institution is related, at least, to the success of its claims to have a monopoly on knowledge. When one finds philosophers engaged in trench warfare over the curious question: "Are there, really, mental images?" the strangeness of the question may make one suspect that one

27

army or the other has some extra-philosophical interests consciously or unconsciously.[2] Are the cultural forces which have entrenched science at the center of our affairs attempting to bring into disrepute the last viable stock in trade of the opposition firms? Not, probably, as a matter of conscious policy—but, on the other hand, it is irritating to have one's faith challenged.

There are, indeed, also political issues. Authorities, in general, have never much liked the idea of a world in which individuals are in a position to make claims to a knowledge which authority cannot challenge—especially if that knowledge provides motives for action. Established institutions often prefer to discredit claims to introspection, because if important truths derive from them *a fortiori*, anyone's claim to have a private conscience may triumph over public belief.

But though there are motives, reputable and disreputable, for monistic claims and, though the problems we are dealing with here are related to questions about monism, one must not imagine that the "boundary" problem or the problem of estimating its significance would *necessarily* be dissolved if one could show that some kind of monism were true.

One could be an objective idealist and still find that the boundary problem simply arose within one's theory. Reality may be of such a kind that it would be fair to describe it as a unified rational order, but it would still be essential to explain how it came to be reflected from many points of view and how those vistas came to be related to one another. Or, even if it were true that the only reality is experience, it would be no easier to relate the experiences which the neuro-physiologist has when he looks inside my head to the experience I have when I examine my own affairs. Some experiences would still be private and others public.

The kinds of dissolutionist proposal which seem to us significant for this problem are, first, the kind of reductive materialism or "scientific realism" according to which the only "realities" are material objects open to scientific observation. This might well entail that the inner world was purely and simply an illusion, but it would not make the "boundary" an illusion; it would make the boundary between reality and illusion real. Secondly, subjective idealism would entail that only what we usually call the "inner world" should be reckoned with as a specimen of reality. It would still be possible, as in Carnap's world, to construct accounts of physical objects from accounts of auto-psychological particulars, but these accounts would have a very different meaning (if they had *any* meaning at all).[3] Thirdly, if one could show that the problem was intra-linguistic, one would surely regard it as a feature of the misuse or misunderstanding of language or of its functions. Finally, there is a proposal of an entirely different kind. If one could show (1) that there are demonstrable criteria for ontologising generally, and (2) that these criteria either abolish or uniquely locate the boundary, then boundary drawing itself would not be a problem.

It is not our belief that these four attempts at "dissolution" constitute the only possible ones. Our belief is, rather, that the ways in which these proposals fail cast light on the sense in which the problem is real, and that our analysis of them will provide materials which we can draw upon in the succeeding parts of the book. These particular attempts are chosen, simply, for their instructiveness. The reader cannot be expected to take the proposals we make later very seriously unless he is convinced that there is not some easy and straightforward way of eliminating the problem.

It is, of course, our contention that the situation is a delicate one and that any solutions are arguable. And this entails the responsibility to take a variety of counter-arguments very seriously, indeed.

All arguments aim at persuasion, but the analysis of arguments need not. It need only aim at providing the materials from which estimates of the strengths of arguments can be made. Consequently, though we shall argue, we shall attempt to do so in a way which will make the analysis of those arguments clear. The reader is invited to join us in an exploration, rather than in a body of beliefs.

2.1 Reductive Materialism

On the surface, a theory such as the Identity Theory must strike one as extremely attractive. If true, it would seem to promise the unification of the behavioral and hard sciences in a way that has been envisioned for some time. But the question is not whether or not the theory is true, but whether or not the promise stands a chance of being kept. Could the theory be formulated in such a way as to have the possibility of being true? I wish to argue that it could not.

2.11   The position that I wish to attack is that such things as thoughts, wishes, hopes, fears, and generally mental phenomena, are identical with processes in the brain. When I think of my far away love and pine for her, my thought and pining are events or processes transpiring at some specifiable point in my cortex. What lends plausibility to such a view is the ability to establish, at least in a general way, correlations. Suppose that I am thinking of a girl named Heidi, and that while I am thinking of this girl, some electrodes are attached to my cortex. Further suppose that at this moment, and only at this moment, the pen on the electroencephalograph is made to wiggle out a unique pattern. I wish to question the nature of the claim that my thought of Heidi is identical with the brain state marked out by the electroencephalograph. To arrive at this claim we must assume something like a causal connection between the brain state and the F.E.G. pattern and that this unique pattern occurs simultaneously with my acknowledging that it is Heidi that I am thinking of. So the question to be considered is whether or not my thought of Heidi, as evidenced by my verbal expression, is identical with the contemporaneous brain state as evidence by the E.E.G. To the best of my knowledge, no one contends that such identities have been established. What is at issue is the interpretation that we would give them if they were in fact to occur. Although it seems to me very unlikely, it does not seem to me in principle impossible for such findings to happen. Whether or not there could be a unique relation between my thought of Heidi and a mark on a piece of paper seems a straightforward empirical question. All we need to allow in order for that to happen is to allow that I have unquestioned access to my own thought and that I sincerely assert its occurance at the same time as the pen makes its mark. At the very least repeated occurrences of this would lay the foundation for a statistical correlation. However, the further question of whether or not the brain state and the thought are identical is not such a straightforward matter and not clearly an empirical one.

2.12   The first thing to note is the way in which the identity claim comes to be made. I am either told to think of some specific item, or asked what it is that I am thinking about while careful note is being taken of what the machine is marking down. If I, a layman, were in fact the person in the experiment, I would explain my thought in the normal manner. That is, I would say that I know it to be a thought of Heidi rather than something else because it is a thought of a woman five feet tall, with blue eyes and brown hair that I met eight months ago at the symphony. Totally unaware of anything but the crudest features of my central nervous system, I nevertheless know with certainty what it is that I am thinking about. And it is upon this knowledge that the experiment is built.

   This kind of experiment, if successful, would give us a correlation. But, one may ask, a correlation between what? If the experiment is to have the significance it purports to, that is, if it is to be capable of establishing an identity relation between my thought and my brain state, what I say must be accepted as an accurate expression of my thought. Something must serve as a reliable mark of a particular thought, and there seems no better candidate than what I sincerely say. My thought, as I express it, is one correlate, and my brain state, as given by the electro-encephalograph, is the other. Thus far, it seems to me, we have nothing philosophically objectionable. We have an empirically established correlation between two things. However, the identity theory goes one very important step further. Being a reductionist theory, the claim is that my thought is no more than the brain state. That is, where we first believed that there were two discrete items in the correlation we now are told that there is, in reality, only one. This is *not* like the following kind of legitimate and harmless reasoning. Suppose that people with brown hair are more intelligent than those with black. If that supposition is true, then we would expect that they would do better on standard I.Q. tests. We find that their performances are not significantly different and so we abandon our original conjecture. The type of reasoning employed by the identity theorist is different because he does not begin with an hypothesis to be tested; he begins with something accepted as certain. The original point is not to find out if there are thoughts, or if there are thoughts when I say that I am having a thought. These are not the things to be confirmed or disconfirmed by investigation; rather, they provide the stuff out of which confirmation or disconfirmation is made.

2.13   Still, why must things remain always as they begin? Is that not a version of the genetic fallacy? Just because we begin by assuming that there are thoughts does not mean that we cannot change our mind. And cannot the identity theorist defend himself against the charge of violating the obvious in much the way that any reductionist can? What I am thinking of is something like Moore's use of Bishop Butler's claim that everything is what it is and not another thing. Can this be leveled against the identity theorist? This is not an easy question to answer. If Moore were to charge Berkeley with denying that there were any material objects in the familiar and common sense use of the phrase "material objects," Berkeley would have a familiar defense. He may claim that he is denying no such thing, but he is simply saying that, in reality, material objects are collections of ideas in the mind of God and that anything more is merely a fiction. That is, if Berkeley and Moore were to take a census of the universe, they would end up with the same number of "things." So the identity theorist is not denying the obvious; at no time is the existence of thoughts questioned. The point, however, is that they are brain states. There is agreement on the "facts" but disagreement as to how to interpret them.

The question now becomes whether or not the identity theorist may legitimately claim to have merely exposed a fiction. I think the answer is that he cannot. In the brain-state argument, the uncontested starting point is that there are thoughts. It is the correlation between thoughts and brain states that is to be shown by the experiment.

2.14 Suppose, though, that one wanted to modify the inquiry. Of course there are thoughts, but their nature is not a predetermined thing. What we may take as a certain starting point is that one's sincere first person avowal that he is having a thought is the most reliable possible indication of the thought. Whatever the thought may be, this type of language can always be present when a thought is present. We may now hook the subject up to the E.E.G. and learn that, whenever he says "I am having thought Q," his statement is invariably followed by a unique pattern on the tape. We assume, for sake of argument, that such a pattern is reliably correlated with a specifiable brain state. The question is, what are we entitled to assert on the basis of these supposed findings?

Let us review where we stand. We have first person claims as reliable marks of thinking and we have (so we suppose) a high positive correlation between such a claim and an observed (observable) brain state. So long as we remain genuinely open-minded about the nature of thoughts, it would seem that we have a *prima facie* case for saying that thoughts are (probably) brain states. But it is misleading to simply say that we are open-minded about the nature of thoughts, for that may suggest that we have no defensible views about them, which is not true. In fact, it is what we know about the nature of thoughts and the process of thinking that prevents an experiment such as this from establishing anything beyond an interesting but harmless correlation.

To bring this out, let me expand on an objection considered by Smart.[1] Essentially, he claims that the kind of argument I have just proposed amounts to no more than an argument from ignorance. An ordinary layman may know perfectly well what he is thinking, feeling, or imagining and yet know nothing whatever about neurophysiology. "Hence the things that we are talking about when we describe our sensations (or thoughts) cannot be processes in the brain."[2]

You might as well say that a nation of slugabeds, who never saw the

Morning Star or knew of its existence, or who had never thought of the expression "the Morning Star," but who used the expression "the Evening Star" perfectly well, could not use this expression to refer to the same entity as we refer to (and describe as) "the Morning Star."[3]

By implication the argument continues that their ignorance is their problem, and detachable from the facts. The Morning Star is (in some sense) identical with the Evening Star, so that the expression "the Evening Star" does refer to the same thing as does "the Morning Star." What substantially weakens Smart's argument is the profound difference between a material substance like the Evening Star and something like a thought and the effect of this difference on our capacity to know or be ignorant of these objects. Modesty alone would incline one to allow that there might be at least some things about the Evening Star that he did not know. It is, after all, an object of continuing astronomical inquiry. There is nothing surprising, then, about the slugabeds who do not know that it is the same celestial object that appears in the morning. "I know what I am thinking about" is importantly different.

If I am thinking about Heidi, there is a sense in which she may be like the Evening Star. Women are notoriously enigmatic, and any man who thinks that he knows all that there is to be known about one generally learns differently. For example, Heidi may be identical with the woman who loves only Sam, and if I have some romantic aspirations toward her I may be in for a shocking disappointment. However, as a thought rather than as a woman, my epistemological position is considerably different since thoughts are experiences that I have whereas women are objects that I may not come to know about. A thought is what I think it to be while a woman is what she is. In order for me to make my way efficiently around in the world of people and planets, it is necessary for me to learn what I can about them. I am generally better off if the views that I have of them correspond closely with the features that they actually do have. There may be a sense in which my thoughts are illusive, but whatever problem I may have in discovering the true nature of what I am thinking is not like trying to find out the real nature of a distant planet or a nearby lady friend. If I am thinking about $\mho$, there is something odd in suggesting that although I may be unaware of it, that thought has feature $\emptyset$. There is no corresponding oddity in suggesting that the Evening Star has some feature unknown to me. I know the thoughts that I am having when I have them in a way that I may not know other facts about the world.[4]

2.15   I am arguing that I know all there is to know about any given thought that I may have. Consequently, if I am unaware of anything like a brain state as being a part of my thought, then this is a very strong reason for saying that it is not. It is a very good reason for defending, even in its rather simple form, the objection that Smart wants to reject. However, there is an *a priori,* pretentious ring to what I am saying. It will not do to say simply that the nature of one's thoughts and one's thinking is self-evident. Unexplained, it looks as though I am saying that such things as psychology and neurophysiology are a waste of time because their subject matter is obvious and self-evident. I am not saying that. What I am denying is the identity between a thought and a brain state. And I do not mean to question whether or not there is an important connection between thinking and the states of one's brain, for it seems obvious that there is, and that as time progresses we will learn more about exactly what correlations there are. The only relation I question is identity.

2.16   The exact nature of the identity that people like Smart wish to argue for is not clear. It seems to be generally admitted that the relation is contingent and empirical—that is, it is not a relation of meaning. Psychological expressions are not taken as equivalent in meaning to brain-state expressions. U.T. Place makes it very clear that nothing of this sort is intended in his formulation of the theory.[5]

> "Consciousness is a process in the brain," although not necessarily true, is not necessarily false. "Consciousness is a process in the brain" in my view is neither self-contradictory nor self-evident; it is a reasonable scientific hypothesis, in the way that the statement "lightning is a motion of electric charges" is a reasonable scientific hypothesis.[6]

The example "lightning is a motion of electric charges" is an example used by both Place and Smart, and helps to illustrate the sense of identity that is being used.[7] Smart says that it is "identity in the *strict* sense" that he is talking about, but since he backs away from "seven is identical with the smallest prime number greater that five" as an example, it seems reasonable to take him also as advocating an empirical thesis.[8]

I would think that in order to establish the truth of the type of identity statement that they are concerned with, one would have to show the identity of space and time. For example, if I wanted to show that lightning bolt A was identical with electrical charges B and C, I would have to show that A occurred at the same time and in the same place as B and C. Certainly, if A occurred in place P while B and C occurred in P', we would have sufficient reason for saying that A was not identical with B and C. Consider Smart's discomfort with the example of the successful general who was the same person as the small boy who stole apples.[9] If the general were now at the front conducting the battle, he could not at that time be the little boy. Being the same person over a span of time is not a strict enough identity to give Smart what he wants, since there are spacial and temporal things true of the youngster that are not true of the adult. While it seems to me that it is quite possible to establish high positive correlations and perhaps even casual relations between thoughts and brain states, it does not seem to me to be equally possible to establish a relation of strict identity.

That kind of identity cannot be established between thoughts and brain states because thoughts cannot be located spacially. *A fortiori,* they cannot have the same spacial location as a tissue mass. If I am thinking of Heidi, it makes no sense to even raise the question of where such a thought might be, let alone to try to answer it. However, does this simply reflect the way we *presently* think and talk? I have allowed that correlations could be established between particular thoughts and areas of the brain. Why not allow that if these correlations become well established, we might change our way of talking? We might adopt the necessary rules and conventions that would make sense out of what presently does not.[10] But I have no way of predicting what might happen in the future, and I must write and argue under the conventions of sense that govern the present. Consequently, there is no way that I may now describe what might make sense in the future (supposing the necessary changes occur) but which, by hypothesis, does not make sense now. Indeed, the suggestion as developed by Shaffer does not make sense. To develop his point, he contrasts the creation of criteria for the location of thoughts with the creation of criteria for the location of fictional characters such as Snow White. The latter, he thinks, would be absurd. " . . . It is self-contradictory to speak of a nonexistent thing like a fictional character as having some actual location in physical space. The very meaning of 'fictional character' depends upon the contrast with things that actually do have spacial location."[11] With regard to the way we talk about thoughts, there is nothing that rules out their having spacial location since there is " . . . no direct contrast with things that actually do have spacial location."[12]

2.17 Shaffer is correct in saying that our present conception of thoughts is such that there is no contrast with things actually having spacial location. However, the absence of that contrast is not adequate to allow the meaningful adoption of the spacial convention that he is suggesting. There is a basic contrast that prevents this. It is true by definition that if something is a fictional character, then it does not make sense to say that it does exist. If it were to exist, it would no longer be a "fictional character," but a character in history. But what is necessary with regard to the general concept of fictional character is only contingent in any particular instance. That is to say, if we may ignore any magical properties she may have had, there is no conceptual problem in suggesting that Snow White might have been a real person. It is true as a matter of fact and not of logical necessity that she is merely fictional. Consequently, although she does not exist she could exist—the possibility of her existence and thus of her locatability is perfectly meaningful. It is in just this regard that the locatability of Snow White is different from the locatability of a thought. As things presently stand, it is true of both Snow White and thoughts that they have no actual location. But it is true of only Snow White and not true of thoughts that we may speak of the possibility of location. We may speak in this way of Snow White because she is to be contrasted with someone like the President of the United States who has actual existence. We may not speak this way about thoughts since they are contrasted not with things that actually exist but with things which themselves have only a possible existence, for example, Snow White. We can *say,* as Shaffer does, that we could " . . . adopt an additional rule that would allow us to locate C-states (for example, Thoughts) in space," but I do not think that we can give such a claim any substance.[13] In order for such a rule to be more than words, we would have to specify the conditions under which the location could be determined. If the only thing that can be said—and it is the only thing that Shaffer does say—is that the location is to be given by the place of the brain state, then this is no specification at all.

The conclusion that we are forced to is clear. The Identity Theory will not work because brain states can be located and thoughts cannot. The problem is a conceptual one, such that one cannot even sensibly state the conditions under which the theory could be true.

2.2 Subjective Idealism

2.22   The modern epistemological thrust toward subjective idealism appears most clearly in Berkeley's assault on Locke.[1] The simplest account of that assault is this: Locke had made a sharp distinction between the bearers of knowledge—the sensations through which the world writes on the blank tablet of the mind—and objects of knowledge, the things in the world. The contents of the mind might "represent the world" but they were not the world. The basic substratum of the world consisted of substances which Locke was compelled to admit were a something he "knew not what." The problem was to determine in what way the bearers of knowledge represented the world. Berkeley produced a simple answer. Suppose, he said, we simply accept the proposition that the bearers of knowledge *are* the objects of knowledge. What we need to have knowledge of is what we do have knowledge of, the very "ideas" which are "in the mind," open to direct inspection, and utterly unproblematic.

If this had been all he had said, Berkeley would have been a subjective idealist. What he said in addition is both puzzling, and revealing of the reasons for thinking that subjective idealism is a less than attractive solution. It is certain, however, that he produced a powerful movement of thought toward subjective idealism and likely that, given his arguments, consistency ought to have forced him to accept subjective idealism.

The strength of his argument depends, importantly, on the extent to which the predicament posed by Locke is actually unavoidable. It hinges on the notion that naive realism is impossible, that there is a ground for thinking that presented immediacies have a high certainty value combined with a minimally effective information content, and that there is a natural way of substituting for our ordinary grasp of things a preferred account of the actual content of experience.

2.23   Naive realism may be taken to combine the doctrine that the contents of perception constitute direct cognitions of reality with the doctrine that perceptions are to be "read" in a certain way. To put it at its simplest, suppose that I take a silver dollar and then perform upon it two perceptual operations. First, I place it on edge three feet from me and walk around it in a circle whose radius is a constant three feet. Then I place it fifty feet from me and walk toward it in a straight line. In the first exercise, I will "perceive" the silver dollar as having a variety of shapes which range from a perfect circle to a very narrow ellipse. In the second exercise, I will "perceive" it as having a variety of sizes which form an ordered set from smallest to largest as I approach. Now, we may take naive realism to be the doctrine that each of these "perception-objects" is a feature of reality so that there are associated with one silver dollar—as we think of it—infinitely many "perception-objects." "The" silver dollar corresponds, at most, to one of these objects. This one object has, if naive realism is accepted, no special status. It is an arbitrary point chosen for the association of the whole class of "perception-objects." This procedure greatly inflates the object population, but this is not an objection which someone like Berkeley would make to the proposal. Berkeley, rather, is inclined to point to the association between the expansion of the object set and the perceptual activities involved. As I move, turn my head, re-focus my attention and so on, the object class grows. Given this association, what right do I have to speak of the objects as if they were independent of me? The conclusion, rather, is that they depend upon me.

2.24   It is true that this contention only arises if I take a certain reading of the perceptual situation. This reading amounts to equating the immediate content of awareness with perception, and the motive for this needs to be sought. (As a rule, one who says "I saw an elephant" is claiming that the immediate content of his perception extends beyond the direct awareness of a grey shape, but he does not say "I saw a grey shape" unless he means to tell us that he is puzzled by his immediate awareness.) Furthermore, this reading amounts to equating the "immediate content of awareness" with a set of specific and specifiable sensations and, in this case, the *possibility* of the equation needs to be explored.

Both these equations depend upon adopting an analysis of experience in order to obtain what are thought to be situations which minimize both doubt and corrigibility. It is a certain *way* of doing this, in turn, which creates the quasi-causal relation necessitated by the claim that the conclusion should be *esse est percipe aut percipere*.[2]

2.25   Let us consider the elephant. The man who says "today I saw an elephant" might be wrong in a number of ways. The evidence he offers us—his reports of grey, wrinkled skin, small pig-like eyes, short curved tusks, feet the size of milk-pails and so on—do not demonstrate the truth of the proposition that he saw an elephant. They are consistent with the proposition that he saw a man in an elephant suit, an unusually good elephant model, a projection from a three-dimensional movie camera or whatever. They are also consistent with the proposition that he was the victim of an unusually life-like hallucination. They are, therefore, dubious. They are also corrigible. On reflection, he may decide that the elephant skin was less wrinkled that he thought, the eyes less pig-like than he first imagined, the feet not so terrifyingly large.

One might think that though dubitability is a defect in a proposition, corrigibility is a virtue. The possibility that, if we are wrong, there is some possibility of correcting ourselves is, after all, comforting. The difficulty in the eyes of one who would undertake the reforms we are here imagining is that both the dubitability and the corrigibility are open-ended. *Whatever* the elephant-seer says, we can think of a new doubt. *Whatever* he does by way of correction, we can think of more that he might do. It is not that there are doubts and potential corrections, it is that answering the doubts and making the corrections results in no progress—if by progress is meant development toward a point at which there will be no more doubts and no more corrections.

2.26 The seemingly natural move, then, is to retreat to a different sort of proposition. "I see a grey patch" *seems* to be less open to challenge than "I see an elephant" just as "I see a silvery elliptical shape" seems to be less open to challenge than "I see a silver dollar." But this is so not because there would not be just as many doubts if the propositions were taken to refer to objects of the same kind as the original elephants and silver dollars. We can imagine such doubts being expressed: Smith has just had his house painted white. He complains to Jones, the painter, that the house is covered with grey splotches, but Jones says "you aren't really seeing grey splotches." "Damn it," Smith says, "if I say I see a grey patch, I *do* see a grey patch." But now he is talking about an alleged component of *his* awareness and this is very different from talking about grey patches in "the world outside."

2.27 It is just this issue which is, I think, the real gist of the point made by G. E. Moore in his celebrated (but confusing) *Refutation of Idealism.*[3] The shift involved is that from talking about the object toward which awareness is directed—the goal of some ostensible perception—to the process of awareness. Moore thought that there must be two things involved and that, accordingly, the subjective idealist actually failed as a result of a confusion between them. There must be the process or act of awareness *and* the object toward which that awareness is directed if Moore (as I read him) is correct. But what is at issue is not a question of some discernible (or logically necessary) objects, but a question of the reading one takes of perception—of the meanings one assigns to expressions about perception in order to render the perceptual process intelligible.

2.28   It turns out that there are (at least) three possible meanings one might assign to an expression like "I am aware of a grey patch." On the first it means, roughly, this: "There is a grey patch, *and* I have reason to think that I am aware of it." On this view, the patch is an object, my awareness is something I can notice, and my awareness gives me a reason for thinking that I have made contact with the patch. On the second, it means something more like "at present, my awareness *is* a grey patch." On this view, what I directly cognize is being-aware-of-a-grey-patch. The whole process is a single entity. But there is a third reading which needs to be noticed as well. It goes this way: "The simplest and most certain claim I can make about my present cognition is that there is a grey patch in view." This expresses a preference for a certain kind of claim and would generally be followed by reasons. It is this kind of statement which might be made by one looking for an elephant if he were suspicious of the object he encountered.

2.281   The first reading, of course, necessitates the sort of "dualism" which Moore (at the time in question) wanted to put forth. The second reading guarantees that, if one is an empiricist, one will be a subjective idealist. The third makes possible a more reasonable view of the matter.

I shall argue, here, that the first and second readings are, in fact, intolerable because they make assumptions which no situation seems to make reasonable. The analysis which I have associated (loosely) with Moore supposes that there are two things involved, but they are both pseudo-things. A "grey patch" is not the sort of thing which can be found. One may find this or that thing which happens to be grey, but never anything which could be identified (without more ado) as "*that* grey patch which is now in my awareness." Greyness and patchiness are not enough; they are simply rather vaguely defined universals. There is always some *particular* grey patch, and to be that it has to be more than grey and patchy. It has to be located in a space and a time—physical space-time, dream space-time or whatever. And it will have to have other properties which associate it with a place in one of those systems; that is, it will have to be particularized in some way.

2.282 These particularizing properties are important because they make
it clear that the account of perception which leads to the statements
about the grey patch is an elaborate process of selective abstraction. It is
a second-order way of talking about experience which is worked on a
much richer and more particular first-order awareness. Actual
confrontations with mere "grey patches" never take place in first-order
reality.

As a reading of perception, claims about grey patches as sense data are
made to sound as if they involved a quite ordinary use of words and as if
they expressed the sound observations of a careful and cautious man.
But this way of talking is the result of a deliberate attempt to get at a
reading of perception by making assumptions whose nature is disguised
from us.

Such a way of talking suggests that one who claims to see grey patches
has undertaken some very safe claim. But actually, the claim is very un-
safe. We are so often wrong about the colors of things and we are so
often wrong, as well, in picking words to describe what we see that one
would have thought that philosophers would have exercised more cau-
tion. One may say: "Well, grey is the best word I can think of to describe
how he looked;" but one is not sure just what was in one's awareness at
that level of abstraction.

The reason "grey patch claims" seem sound is that, somehow, we
think no one is in a position to question us if we just describe "how it
looked." Still, we know that is not so. For example, someone may say:
"It *can't* have looked grey to you, it was a brown bear;" and then one
may—surely—say: "Come to think of it, I guess it didn't." One may
change his mind after he has reviewed all the details of the situation.

The case of the "awareness" is, to be sure, a good deal worse. How do
you know you were "aware" at all? You remember some details of what
you saw. For instance, you remember that you had to squint into the sun
or stretch your arms and chin yourself on the fence in order to see over it.
Chinned on the fence, eyes squinting into the sun, one just caught a
glimpse of the bear peering cautiously around the corner of the building
and the backside of the elephant scooting down the alley. It was an extensive complex in which one played a part in *making* the perceptions.

The awareness, here, cannot be separated from the things one
did—chinning oneself and squinting—and the brown and grey
"patches" make sense only as abstractions from a total situation. Indeed, it would not be reasonable to say, to an enquirer in the bar afterwards, "I saw a grey patch" or even to answer "yes" if one were asked

"Did you see a grey patch?" That answer would imply *both* more and less than the truth—that one caught a glimpse of the backside of an elephant. It is more than the truth because the thing was not clear and distinct enough to count for certain as "a grey patch," and less than the truth because it never gave the impression of a grey patch running down the alley.

2.283   One can see that one could go from this analysis both to Locke's destination and to Berkeley's destination. If one decides that the Moore analysis yields two sorts of pseudo-objects where there is one "presentational immediacy" (to use Whitehead's term),[4] one may demand one given object. What entered into consciousness was not the whole of the bear and the elephant. So, one may say, there is the field of consciousness and then there is the real affair. The field *represents* the real affair—We can now see that the observer himself was very much a part of the affair. It was what he did in the real world which gave rise to the field of consciousness.

For the same reason, it will not do to elide it all into the contents of consciousness if by *that* one means the causal result of the occasion in the form of consciousness and contents. For that, too, is simply an abstraction from the process—an abstraction which gives one a second order reflective view of the situation. *Esse est percipe aut percipere* describes an outcome as if it were the whole situation.

"My present awareness is a grey patch" is a way of giving meaning to "I am now aware of a grey patch" by eliding the whole process into a single referent. It sounds as strange as it is. It disguises the fact that there are place and time markers, and that there is a disguised observer who has been neutralized by having all his activities associated with the outcome of those activities. It is this device, of course, which gives Carnap's program (described in Chapter 1) its apparent neutrality. It is true that it gives a sense to the occasion—it marks out the grey-patch moment in my life—but only provided that one already has a reference frame which establishes place and time markers.

One could, indeed, work all this out if one were willing to pay the price. The price includes adopting place and time markers in the reference frame simply as conventions and abandoning all the observer functions—the chinning, squinting, thinking and what not—in favour of the *outcomes* of those activities, but, again, the result is a set of pseudo-objects. The world becomes full of ill-defined universals; instead of particular things, it has conventional place and time markers.

The reference frame is a convention. The possible collisions of things in the "real world" are all avoided because it is always compatible with any sentence of the form "x's awareness was a grey patch at place p^{16} and time t^{31}" that there should be another sentence of the form "y's awareness was a red patch at place p^{16} and time t^{31}" and that both should be true. Indeed, anything will do for values of x and y as well, for they are simply additional conventional markers to take account of the fact that for any place and time in the reference frame, there may be any number of observers who observe different things. There is, thus, no way to go wrong. All the basic ingredients are what Carnap once suggested we should call "protocol sentences"[5]—statements about the contents of a given awareness at a given place and time, so made as to be logically incontrovertible.

We should, however, grasp the importance of the price. Minimizing the risk guarantees that the statements concerned are incorrigible and indubitable—not because they are true but because they are incontrovertible. They cannot be the subject of controversy because they conflict with nothing.

But are they meaningful? Well, yes, if you mean to ask: "Is there some observation occasion which is understod to justify them?" But "no" if you mean: "Do they yield the meaning of 'I am aware of a grey patch'?"; and "no" if you mean: "Are they meaningful *ab initio*— meaningful to one who knows the meaning of *no* other sentences?" For I can only learn the meaning of these curious new sentences if I adopt the conventions about reference frames, if I know that what counts is the outcome of some perceptual process and not that process itself, and so on. I would have to be taught how to make the analysis.

Again, we return to the point that this is a second-order analysis which presupposes some *other* first-order experience. Furthermore, for all the hopes of Carnap, one can only construct an arbitrary account of the world out of such second-order ingredients. As they are posed, being incontrovertible and compatible with anything, they are consistent with any construction whatever.

Berkeley, one supposes, must have known or intuited this. For, in fact, he supposes a God who wills an orderly and meaningful set of perceptual outcomes, and individuals who act in such a world by exercising their own volitions. His proposal does not simply amount to the subjective idealist notion that one should get out of the difficulties of the perceptual situation by analysing everything into states of consciousness. Rather, he suggests that one should add to this some rules governing the perceptual process itself—especially those which bind God to a program of intelligibility.

His difficulty is that his solution to Locke's problem leaves him with no way of justifying these additions unless he steps outside the subjectivist program. Common sense drove him out of it, and the principle he seems to have used was the one of adding the fewest and simplest presumptions which would make the scheme intelligible.

2.284   This, then, leaves us with the third proposal—that "I am aware of a grey patch" is, in fact, "the simplest and most certain claim I can make about my present cognition that there is a grey patch in view." I am suggesting that this is the kind of statement which is followed naturally by something like "I think there is an elephant around because one escaped from the circus and that thing running down the alley surely looks like an elephant. But in fact it is blurred. I am squinting into the sun and I can't concentrate too well because right now I'm chinning myself on a fence." Here, indeed, the uncertainty is explained. The conditions are not ideal for spotting elephants.

But there is more to it than that. Before one can ask whether the pattern of experience will lead to one view of the world or another, one first has to have a pattern of experience—something to extract from, something to compare certainties *within*. The language one uses is part of that pattern and goes along with the activities one is engaged in. It serves to mark out and define a context, is traded with others, and creates a community of response within which the strength of one's certainties may be checked against what others say and against the conventions for using the language. What one is entitled to say will depend not simply on one's own analysis of one's consciousness, but on the community situation. It is reasonable and proper to have claimed to have spotted the elephant if, afterwards, someone else reports that he saw it come out of the alley and saw the man from the circus catch it and claim it. It is reasonable and proper to be doubtful if no one else ever saw it.

The process is one in which everyone exchanges notes about his activities. The problem of "Naive realism" does not arise, because the reading given to perception is one of comparing activities rather than results. Of course, if I was hanging upside down from the fence, my view would be odd. If I was a long way away, I would have the view of one who could not see too clearly. If I was drunk or short-sighted, I would make adjustments.

2.29   The argument is not, of course, that the second-order analyses which lead to assorted forms of subjective idealism are out of court, or of no point. The point is that they *are* second-order analyses and only make sense if the first-order experiences make sense in their own terms. We shall have occasion later to explore, in a variety of ways, the basic issue about first- and second-order experience, and first- and second-order analyses. Briefly, the distinction is simply this: An experience is a first-order experience if and only if it does not arise from an activity performed upon another experience. Reflection is a second-order experience, because one must reflect *upon* something. Pondering is a second-order experience because there must be something to ponder. These are obvious cases. What is not so obvious—and therefore creates philosophical conundrums—is that the "conversion" of things into sense data (if it is possible at all) must result in a second-order experience. Awareness of sense data is often confused, as my examples were meant to show, with experiencing vaguely, or experiencing fleetingly, or with a host of other unsatisfactory experience situations. But to see the elephant as a collection of grey colored patches is to do something deliberate—to exclude elements in experience which one suspects to be associated with inferences, to exclude penumbral phenomena, and so on. It is something aimed at, something which arises from another, more usual, kind of experience which is the object of this corrective process.

Expressions like "first- and second-order analysis" are meant to be understood in the same way. A second-order analysis is one which depends upon the (logically) prior availability of another analysis. The argument, here, is that the analysis of propositions as referring to sense data arises out of a prior reading (or analysis) of the perceptual situation—a reading or analysis which I have tried to cast doubt upon. It is well worth noticing here that, though the philosophical literature frequently seems to read as though this kind of second-order analysis depended upon the availability of a suitable second-order experience, there is no logical reason to think that this is so.[6] If I read Carnap correctly, he is aware of this, and this awareness considerably strengthens his position—though it does not (as I have suggested) enable him to avoid what turns out to be the crucial difficulty, that his incontrovertible statements are indubitable and incorrigible for reasons which turn out to make them relatively uninteresting. We shall see more of this problem in Chapter 3, when we examine the problem of first-person propositions.

The difficulty here indeed is that the neat union of perception, self, and action which constitutes the first order experience becomes puzzling on *reflection*. But it becomes puzzling precisely because one reflects, and the solutions must thus be solutions to the problem of reflection.

This problem arises because I express myself through the acts of perception, but I do not simply *consist* of those acts. When I reflect, I can see that I might have done other things—I might have vaulted that fence or run after the elephant—and that, therefore, I am in some way separable from that world. On the other side, the world reveals itself in *response* to those acts, but it might have revealed itself differently, too. Yet all we know about the world is through the responses we did get.

As this problem develops, there develops as well the problem that the particularity of the things in the world is not expressible literally as a description of the world, for the descriptions are always in terms of universals. But an account in terms of universals leaves unexplained the element of confrontation which, if incautiously handled, can lead to a kind of pseudo-mystery.

But none of this in the least suggests that the first-order experience is replaceable, or that it is not the primary source of knowledge. So long as it is not analysed away, the world of things remains, and there is no excuse for the lapse into a non-functional subjectivism.

2.3 Ordinary Language

In the preceding section, the objection raised to subjective idealism was that it confused first-order experience with second-order analysis. Specifically, ideas, that is sense-data, are a way of interpreting items of experience. The mistake is to take them as though they were components of experience. The question does not have to do with their existence or plausibility; it has to do with how, and where, they enter into the discussion.

In the following discussion, I consider an argument of Norman Malcolm's that philosophical debates are really debates about ordinary language. There are many reasons why I cannot accept such a view, and one of them is that it confuses a second-order issue with a first-order fact. For example, Malcolm talks of a dispute between Moore and Russell over whether or not one is always observing a part of his brain whenever he is observing. Russell says that this is all and only what one observes, while Moore claims that we also observe desks and postmen. Malcolm then claims that what they are arguing about is language, and it is this that I think is mistaken. He is confusing what we perceive with what we say about what we perceive, that is, first-order and second-order items. Whether or not the brain is always the proper object of perception is a first-order matter; whether or not we ordinarily *say* we see our brain is a second-order matter. Without passing judgment on the truth or relevance of these claims, I am suggesting that they are distinct.

It is undeniable that language and philosophy are importantly related. The question that I want to consider is the manner of their relationship. It seems to me that this is something that has been misunderstood, and which has led to a confusion about the nature of language and the nature of philosophy. What I have especially in mind is Norman Malcolm's essay "Moore and Ordinary Language."[1] I find this essay particularly striking for several reasons. First, there is implicit in it a view of the relation between language and philosophy which is incompatible with one that I hold. Second, if the view expressed there is correct, then much of what is argued in this book would be *radically* wrong. Malcolm offers what I take to be a dissolutionist view of the nature of philosophical problems. They are not solved in any traditional sense; instead, they disappear, and what makes them evaporate is a clear view of how we ordinarily talk. I do not agree that " . . . it is not possible for an ordinary form of speech to be improper. That is to say, ordinary language is correct language."[2] My disagreement has two parts. First, I do not think that in an unqualified sense ordinary language is necessarily correct language; and second, even if it were, I do not see that reference to it can by itself solve philosophical problems.

2.31   Of course, Malcolm's position on these matters is somewhat more guarded than I have indicated. However, if he were correct, then what is true and false about the world inside would be decided by determining how we ordinarily talk about it. My primary concern with a method like this is that it leaves out what is most important. We should be concerned with how we talk, but only if that is preceded with a concern for how things are. I think that Malcolm would say that such a distinction is vacuous. How can we have a concern for how things are apart from how we say they are? The significance of that challenge rests on the truism that to express something is to employ a linguistic form. The view that I want to defend is that the relation between language and reality is the relation between appearance and reality. Just as appearances may often be deceptive, what we (ordinarily) say might not be the case. The way we ordinarily talk is, it seems to me, very closely related to the way things appear. Sometimes everything is as it seems, so that what we ordinarily say will be a reliable indication of how things are. It is important, though to be careful. Language may depict reality, but at the very least, we should realize that there are accurate as well as inaccurate depictions, and that particular cases need to be investigated.

2.32 Malcolm claims that: "The essence of Moore's technique of refuting philosophical statements consists in pointing out that these statements *go against ordinary language.*"³ I will follow Malcolm in considering, first, the manner in which these statements are supposed to go against ordinary language; and second, how such a conflict allegedly refutes a philosophical claim. As an example, he considers Russell's statement " . . . that what the physiologist sees when he looks at a brain is part of his own brain, not part of the brain he is examining."⁴ It seems clear to Malcolm that Russell's statement cannot be interpreted as empirical. The facts of the situation seem so clear and so obvious and so irrefutable (and so against Russell) that it seems impossible for the dispute to center around them. Consequently, there would have to be agreement on the facts of the matter so that the disagreement would have to be about the language used to describe these facts. For example, in a given circumstance, they could be expected to agree that this is the sort of situation in which one sees a postman.⁵ Russell would argue that strictly speaking it should be described as seeing a portion of one's brain, while Moore would say that it should be described as seeing the postman.

2.321 It seems to me odd to say that Russell's claim goes against ordinary language. To be sure, it is paradoxical, and intentionally so. However, the paradox is generated not because it conflicts with how we customarily talk, but primarily because it goes against what we commonly believe. Moore's resistance springs not from a defense of common language but from a defense of common sense. As a fact of secondary importance, it is true that we do not normally talk in a way that would give much aid and comfort to Russell. But we do not talk that way because we do not, in the absence of sophisticated argument, have beliefs like Russell's. An argument like Moore's is the start of a case against Russell for it shows, *prima facie,* that Russell is wrong. To go further and to attempt to prove that he was mistaken would involve an evaluation of the reasons that Russell gives in support of his position.

   Neither Russell nor Moore say that their views are linguistic in nature. What Malcolm says is, then, an interpretation of what they say. The reason he gives for interpreting Russell this way is that Russell could not be offering his claim as an empirical one, since if it were empirical, it would be completely without grounds. Yet if we take it as a linguistic claim, it seems equally groundless. If its being groundless is sufficient reason for rejecting it as empirical then why is it not also sufficient reason to reject it as linguistic? As Malcolm himself argues there are no linguistic grounds for talking the way Russell does.[6]

Obviously the problem is not whether to accept or reject Russell's claim. Clearly it is to be rejected. What is not clear are the reasons for the rejection. To review, for a moment, Russell claims that: "All one ever sees when one looks at a thing is part of one's brain," and Moore's rejoinder is: "This desk which both of us see is not a part of my brain."[7] Surely, one wants to insist, the issue between Russell and Moore is over the proper object of perception. How can something like that be decided by considering how we talk? Such an answer becomes appropriate only if one views ordinary language as being epistemologically privileged. One would have to believe, as does Malcolm, that ". . . ordinary language *is* correct language."[8] What is so very confused about this view is that Malcolm uses it to justify the conclusion that ordinary language would not allow one in any given instance to say things that are not correct, that is, that are not true. It looks very much as though Malcolm is guilty of the fallacy of composition. He is arguing that what is true of the whole of ordinary language is thereby true of one of its parts. In a sense he is right when he says that "ordinary language is correct language." But the sense in which that is correct is a sense that applies to the whole of language. It could not in its entirety be wrong, but it is in some of its individual applications used incorrectly.[8] It might be that he thinks that we would be forced into a wholesale rejection of ordinary language if we were to sanction a proposition such as Russell's. In other words, if we allow Russell to say that all we ever see is a portion of one's own brain then we would be forced to eliminate from our ordinary speech all those innumerable instances in which we want to say that we see pens, postmen, and desks.

There is something to be said on behalf of such reasoning, only it is not a very great deal for it leaves out what is of fundamental importance. Where Malcolm and I disagree is not on the things that we believe are true. It is not even so much on their significance. It is, instead, on the interpretation of that significance. We both think that Russell's proposition is to be rejected. We agree that Moore's counter claim brings this out, but we disagree on the ultimate reason for these beliefs. Malcolm argues that Moore's claim shows that Russell's proposition goes against the ordinary way of speaking and although I am willing to concede the truth of that I want to insist that the importance of the entire procedure lies in the fact—and it is a fact—that one does not perceive, under normal circumstances, a portion of one's own brain. One may say that Russell's language is fantastic, but the reason for saying that goes much deeper than its not being ordinary speech. It rests on the fact that when we perceive we do not perceive what Russell says but rather the things that Moore cites. It is Moore's contribution to force just *that* realization upon us.

2.322   It is interesting to consider a clear, though not very profound, violation of language committed by Malcolm himself. "The proposition that no ordinary expression is self-contradictory is a tautology, but perhaps an illuminating one."[9] As it stands, the claim is wrong. The proposition is not a tautology, because it is not true in virtue of its form. It is not of the form "p v-p." To take issue with Malcolm on a matter such as this is not to raise a very important point, in that I am not questioning whether or not Malcolm's claim is true, whether its truth is a matter of necessity, stipulation, or anything of that sort. My intent is only to illustrate an error that is clearly linguistic in nature. If the reply is that "tautology" as I am conceiving it is not a term in ordinary language, but a technical term of formal logic, the answer is that of course that is true. Whatever the ordinary meaning of "tautology," it has in philosophy a special meaning, and accordingly Malcolm has misused it.

The reason for drawing attention to this is that it seems to me to clearly indicate that the Russell-Moore dispute about percepts is of a wholly different order. To determine that I am right and that Malcolm is wrong about the use of "tautology," we would look the word up in a recognized logic text and that would settle it. If the dispute were one in ordinary rather than technical language, the point would be made with such tools as "We do say ' . . . . ', but we do not say ' . . . . ' "[10] Nothing like either of these procedures would be relevant in the Moore/Russell issue. In that case what we need to do is to concern ourselves not so much with how we talk but with the actual facts of perception.

2.323   To put the Moore/Russell dispute into perspective let me consider another dispute which fits much better into Malcolm's line of reasoning. This dispute is between Gilbert Ryle and P. L. Heath on an issue that is unequivocally linguistic, Philosophically significant and decidable. Heath wants to object to both the substance and manner in which a claim of Ryle's has been made. "To give but one example, he [Ryle] states, in a recent article, that 'it is not easy or difficult to believe things.' It seems fair to reply that this is itself *extremely* difficult to believe.''[11]

The nature of Ryle's point has been completely misunderstood and to sort out the misunderstanding will show something of the way in which linguistic points are and are not to be developed. To begin, it is reasonable to assume that Mr. Heath believes that the issue is a matter of whether or not the words can be put together with grammatical proprie-ty. That seems a fair analysis since that is what he in fact does in the above quotation. However, that is all that he does and that is important. *"Extremely* difficult to believe" is acceptable, idiomatic English, and if Ryle's point had to do merely with what was to count as acceptable English, then Heath would have won the day. But the point goes deeper than that and has genuine philosophical importance. The question is after having put the words together in acceptable English, what has one thereby said? The answer is that Heath has not said anything that tells against Ryle and one of the reasons why he has failed to do that is that he has failed to see what the underlying philosophical issue actually is.

Ryle's point is that believing is not an activity in which one engages as one engages in walking, swimming or subtracting. Since believing is not something that one does it is not something that one may do with either case or difficulty. The impact of Heath's own remark in fact supports Ryle's claim because it fails as a counter-example and draws our atten-tion to that failure. What the propriety of his remark shows is that when one says *"extremely* difficult to believe" what one implies is that the con-tent of the belief is thought to be false. Since this is not what Ryle is talk-ing about it has no impact on Ryle's position. In order to have an in-stance which genuinely countered Ryle, Heath would have to come up with an acceptable expression which implied that believing was something in which one engaged with difficulty comparable, for exam-ple, to push-ups.[11a]

2.234 Ryle is right and Heath is wrong, and the appeal to ordinary language is appropriate. Still, the procedures and assumptions to be followed are not like Malcolm's. For example, I have not argued that belief is not an activity, because to say so would go against ordinary language.[12] As Austin has said, ordinary language, if it has anything at all to say, has the first though not the last word in philosophical argu-ment.[13] The Heath-Ryle dispute is particularly interesting because the real issue is never (despite Heath's confusion) whether or not one could properly say "x is difficult to believe." In spite of what Ryle *may* have said elsewhere, neither the issue nor the answer arise from merely how we talk. What is assumed is that the way we talk reflects the way we think, and though we certainly may think and talk incorrectly, it is as good a place to begin as any. I am only saying that how we talk is *prima facie* evidence for what *seems* to be the truth. It is radically wrong to argue, as does Malcolm, that a final answer can be obtained from a paradigm of how we talk.

2.33   Malcolm wants to argue that there are at least some uses of ordinary language that must be correct. He sees that individual cases may be misused, but there is a set of expressions that as a group must have a correct use:

> In the case of all expressions the meanings of which must be *shown* and cannot be explained, as can the meaning of "ghost," it follows, from the fact that they are ordinary expressions in the language, that there have been *many* situations of the kind which they describe; otherwise so many people could not have learned the correct use of those expressions.[14]

The argument is the very familiar Empiricist one that although you may succeed in explaining some notions verbally, there are others that must be ostensively defined. According to Malcolm spacial terms are like this. " . . . You cannot teach a person the meaning of these . . . expressions without showing him instances of the true application of those expressions."[15] This is perhaps at the bottom of most paradigm case arguments, and it is clearly false. It is not necessary in order to teach the meaning of "above" or "below" that we have something which is in truth above something else. It might be a lot easier if we had such a sample, but all that is necessary is that we have something that seems above something else. It is my contention that our language most generally reflects the way the world appears. It obviously does not always mirror the way that the world is, and if Malcolm means to say that it does when he says that "ordinary language is correct language" then he is wrong. The only thing that would justify the move from language to reality made by Malcolm is the assumption that ordinary language depicts things always as they are. Strange as it may seem, this sounds very much like one of the assumptions underlying the picture theory of language in the *Tractatus*. One of the difficulties with that theory is that the relation of language to reality (that is, depiction) cannot be an exclusively

linguistic concern. That is, the correctness of the language is not sufficient to establish the correctness of the depiction. The accuracy of the
depiction may not be an exclusively extra-linguistic concern but it cannot
be an exclusively linguistic one either.

2.35   Perhaps now the principle difference between the Ryle-Heath and
the Malcolm (Moore)-Russell dispute can be brought out. The best way
to do that is to display some of the oddities that Ryle would have us
avoid. It is a mistake to view believing as activity analogous to, for example, building. If it were, then it would be something that could be done in
a variety of fashions. One may construct a wall quickly or slowly; the
process may be done with ease or difficulty. With practice one may
become more adept at handling bricks and mortar. A novice bricklayer is
learning *how to* build so that he is not yet as *good at* it as is a master
craftsman. What emerges from these few observations is that building is:
(1) something that can be taught; (2) something that can be learned with
varying degrees of proficiency; and (3) something that can be practiced in
a variety of ways. None of these three features make sense as applied to
believing. For example, as parents, we make an effort to instruct our
children in certain beliefs. However, a moment's thought shows that the
instruction relates to *what* it is that we wish them to believe rather than to
the process of believing itself. Neither is it possible for someone to have
learned how to believe better than someone else. One may have better
beliefs than another, that is, they may rest on more solid evidence than
another person's, or, (*if* this is something different) he may believe ideas
superior to those of someone else, but he cannot be better at believing *per
se.* On those occasions in which it would be appropriate to say "Sam is
awfully good at believing things" the suggestion is that he is unduly pro-
ficient at deceiving himself.

These points could have been put in a linguistic mode. It is true that we
cannot talk of belief in the same manner that we can talk of a process like
building. We are able to put the words together in comparable configurations, but such a sentence as "Heidi is better at believing than Nicki"
leave us more mystified than enlightened. However, that we do not or
cannot successfully talk in this way does not establish an irrefutable
philosophical point. It does indicate the kind of concept that we (presently) take "believing" to be. The argument is offered as no more than a
prima facie one, but that should not obscure the fact that, as things
stand, we have no reason not to accept it as accurate and correct. The
fact that I have done no empirical research to establish that people do

(ordinarily) talk as I have said is of no consequence.[16] I am not being cavalier about an important point. The confidence that I have in the correctness of what I have said derives from the fact that I am arguing from the position of a native speaker. Of course I may be mistaken, but if I am, this is usually taken care of by checking with another native speaker.

2.36　　However, my present aim is not to defend a particular band of ordinary language philosophy. Keeping in mind the way in which Ryle's point about believing was developed, let me return to Malcolm's version of Moore. Malcolm avoids ever saying that Moore intended his points to be taken as linguistic. He says such things as a view of Moore's "is a misleading way of saying" something about ordinary language.[17] This certainly suggests that the status of Moore's argument is open to dispute, and indeed it is.[18] The following quotation from Malcolm is quite revealing. In trying to explain why Moore's method was sometimes not seen as effective by those against whom he argued, Malcolm observes that:

> This is largely because Moore's reply fails to bring out the linguistic, non-empirical nature of the paradox. It sounds as if he were opposing one empirical proposition with another, contradictory, empirical proposition.[19]

I submit that Moore does not bring out the linguistic nature of the dispute because the way in which we speak is not the issue. The impact of Moore's claim occurs because it confronts the claim on a factual level. He forces the realization that if Russell were right, then it would follow that we never perceive material objects. What is supposed to happen after this realization is not so clear. It could be that the argument ends here as a *reductio ad absurdum,* or it could be that it is to move on to another level. Having shown the absurd factual implications of a position like Russell's, Moore forces the metaphysical issue. Whether or not his "common sense" observations are relevant or effective on this level I will leave to students of philosophical method. My point is that there has not been, and one would not expect that there would be, any reference to how we ordinarily talk.

2.37　　The difference between the Moore (Malcolm)-Russell dispute and the Ryle-Heath dispute should now be clear. The only role played by ordinary language in the Moore-Russell argument is that Moore says very ordinary things and Russell says some things that are very unordinary.

But however unordinary are the things that Russell says, he can and does mean just what he says. Heath can not say what he does and mean what he must if he is to contradict Ryle. He can *say*, as he does, "extremely difficult to believe," but he cannot mean by that what must be meant if Ryle's point is to be overturned. It is this dependence on meaning that gives the Ryle-Heath a linguistic base and it is this that is absent from the Moore-Russell issue.

Finally, if Malcolm's view of philosophy and language were correct, then the arguments that we consider in this book would be of the wrong variety and possibly even superfluous. Consider, for example, the following argument against reductive materialism. We do not normally say that anger is a brain state. Brain states are spacially locatable and feelings are not. Consequently, if anger were a brain state, it would be spacially locatable and therefore not a feeling. But, to say that anger is not a feeling is to go against the way we ordinarily speak—Q.E.D. What looked to be a philosophical problem of substance has disappeared. I have argued that this kind of reductionism is a mistake, and it is true that aspects of it conflict with the way we ordinarily talk, but it is also true that the problem cannot be eliminated in this manner. Both reductive materialism and Malcolm's type of ordinary language philosophy have in common the dismissal rather than the solution of the problem that they deal with. The one would have us believe that the world inside was a philosophers fiction; the other holds that a view such as Russell's is a kind of malapropism. Philosophy is not that simple.

2.4 Dissolution and Ontological Criteria

2.41   The persistent dissolutionist need not despair just because he finds that the world is not readily describable in the way that the materialist or the subjective idealist imagined, or just because he finds that the problem cannot be retained within the bounds of language. If he does not grow more sophisticated he may, nonetheless, find theories which are more complicated or lie amidst intellectual thickets whose technicalities are more entangled. Put more charitably, he may discover that the problem lies at a deeper level.

The most interesting proposal of this sort is that the problem of "the boundary" and the problem of the peculiarity of the "world within" are both generated by a misunderstanding of the problem of ontological criteria. Somehow the problem of the boundary is associated with the notion that there are kinds of things in the world at the very basic level at which kinds of things are designated "modes of being."

Now it is not clear by any means just how one ought to explicate this problem for, in this sense, it turns on the question of whether or not there is a clear way of justifying preferences for one mode of expression rather than another. Let me explain. Rocks, rivers, and pigs are, in several senses, different "kinds" of things. A rock is a thing in the sense that it is a single perceptual object, a more or less continuous collection of molecules and so on. A river is a thing only, perhaps, by convention or communal agreement. From day to day, "it" contains different specimens of water. The "it" does not refer to anything except, perhaps, a path through space-time. A pig, like a river, has changing components, but it is an organism and it has a unity of functional aim. At the same time, one would admit that rocks, rivers, and pigs are the *same* kind of thing in that all of them can be conceived as modifications of the same space-time. We might contrast this list with another which contained pigs in ordinary space-time, possible pigs, fictional pigs, imaginary pigs, and conceptual pigs. We can consider, if we want, actual specimens of each: the pig in my sty, the pig I may breed next year, a pig from *Animal Farm,* the pig I am picturing now, and the average pig. One may want to say that only the first is "a real pig." The others, people *sometimes* say, "exist only in propositions/stories/my imagination/statistical analyses." But though "real" here has an honorary use (the pig in the sty is somehow "superior" to the others), the locution "exists only in" suggests that they have some kind of "existence" even though it is a deficient existence. To overcome this suggestion, one might say "only the first is really a pig, the others are something else." The "something else" may be "referents of propositions," "pieces of fiction," "bits of imagination" and so on. For to be a real pig is not exactly the same thing as "really being a pig." But how do we decide what we ought to say? The question "are there *really* different kinds of things?" in the sense of "different ways of being real" ought to be important for our enquiry. For, if there is only one way of being real, and if we know what that way is (that is, what the criterion for being real *is*) then that will—one might think—provide us with the boundary for which we ought to have been searching. On one side of it will lie what is interesting and important; on the other side will lie delusion. Perhaps it will bear some relation to our usual notion of "inside/outside" but, perhaps, it will cut across it in ways which we do not clearly imagine, and our enquiry will be null and void.

It does look, one must admit, as if this contention has some sense. We started, you will recall, worrying about the man who projects his inner world on the world outside, or who loses his grip on his inner world. If the inner world has a low priority as "reality," then the first man has made the mistake of covering reality with unreality. If the inner world has a high priority, then the second man has lost contact with reality. If the priority lines cut across these distinctions, then we should think again.

In fact, in this section I want to admit that we *should* think again. What I want to argue, however, is that the question can only be settled by reference to considerations which include the kind of enquiry we shall undertake later in this book—there is no short cut. Indeed, even this book will *not* contain all the discussion that is necessary to settle the question.

2.42 The simplest solution to the problem would be one which showed that the problem was logical. We have seen that it depends, somewhat, on how one chooses to express one's information and on whether or not one's preference could be justified. The extreme version of this contention would be that it all depends on the standard logical form of propositions, and that some logical analysis will show one what the preferred form might be. I am not sure that anyone has ever actually held that view. Willard Quine, in his famous paper *On What There Is*, has sometimes been read (carelessly) as if he did but in fact, of course, he denies it.[1] He does, however, come as close to it as anyone is likely to.

His discussion begins with a notable conundrum. Suppose that two ontologists are engaged in an argument. One of them, McX, complains that Quine refuses to "recognize certain entities" and accuses him of inconsistency. For how can one refuse to recognize something unless there is something which can be refused recognition?

At bottom, this comes, in Quine's view, to a dispute about naming, meaning, and describing. "The present king of France is not bald" is a true statement. There is no present king of France and, therefore, no present king of France can be bald. It appears that, if it is true, it is true *of* something—namely, the present king of France. This is only because we think that the meaning of the sentence depends upon the name and the name must refer to something. But we can equally well think of the situation as containing descriptions which do not name in this sense. "For any x, x is not both the king of France and bald" means "take anything you want in the world, it will not have the properties referred to in the descriptions suggested." Thus we can deny the existence of something *and* avoid "referring" to the thing denied. We need not be the victims of an inconsistency.

Actually, of course, the referential function has simply been shifted from the thing named (the "present king of France") to "the class of all x's." Now the members of that class are simply "what there is" and that, certainly, is unobjectionable. But there are complications. This Russellian scheme depends upon our adopting (as Russell and Quine grasped quite well) a preferred form of proposition. In this preferred form, all reference is a function of what are called "bound variables," the logical equivalents of expressions such as "something," "everything" and "nothing." The propositions are not translations of the original sentences. "The present king of France is not bald" has a different subject than the proposition "For any x, x is not both the king of France and bald." One subject is "the present king of France," the other is "the class of all x's." This class itself is difficult to specify for some reasons Russell himself advanced in discussing paradoxes of totality and the class is also involved in the reference. Reference to its members will not suffice. The change in referring function entails some change in meaning, and the change in meaning may make us hesitate between two different forms of expression such as "for any x, x is not both the present king of France and bald" and "for any x, if x is the present king of France, then x is not bald." There are different logical relations specified in the two expressions.

Granting that we will accept near equivalence for translation, that we are not allergic to the existence of classes (Quine is not), and that we do not worry too much about meanings, we have a scheme which reduces the problem in an important way: We can now see how to have expressions in which references are dependent upon our use of bound variables and in which we can, therefore, assert and deny existence.[2]

To assert the existence of something, then, is to deploy a bound variable. This leads to Quine's slogan "to be is to be the value of a bound variable."

But, though the slogan is his, Quine at once disowns it for the obvious reason. It does not define existence—it gives a semantic analysis of statements asserting existence. We still have to decide when to deploy our bound variables.

Quine suggests that, in effect, we assert that something exists when our knowledge forces us to—and not when our logic forces us to. He urges that a phenomenal analysis is to be preferred whenever it is available and, when not, we must accept whatever we need to account for the best expression of our knowledge.[3]

The acute reader will now notice, however, that Quine has said *two* things. One of them amounts to the doctrine (which I have urged elsewhere and think to be true) that "to be is to be an actual or possible object of knowledge"—that is, we let something be "the value of a bound variable" when we have knowledge of it or think that someone might. The other is that these existence statements are to be deployed in a statement form which does not *itself* have ontological commitments or does not, itself, have more ontological commitments than necessary. The issue is whether or not there is some simple way of making clear what the relevant commitments are.

If all this worked out, however, what would it do to our problem? One possibility is that it would lead to a two-tier ontology: Primarily, there would be things which are said to exist because they are actual or prospective objects of knowledge. They would all have to be one sort in the sense that they would all have to be things which had been predicated *in the same way*. For the Quine-Russell preference is for propositions like "for any x, if x is f, then x is g" or "there is an x such that x is f and x is g," where there is no room in the proposition to express the way in which x has properties such as f and g. Hence there are not actual pigs, possible pigs, conceptual pigs and so on. If one wants to add these "modal" operators, one does so in front of the proposition and in a way which modifies the truth value of the proposition without introducing a new kind of thing. One says "it is possible that x is a pig and is black," or "it is necessarily true that if x is a dragon, x breathes fire," or "it is in a story that x is Hamlet and x talks about his own existence."

But now, "it is possibly true that x is a pig and x has an index of 136" means something very different from "x is a possible pig with an index of 136." The first speculates about what there is, while the second asserts that the world is open to a certain state of affairs. The "primary" things must have at least this status. For we want to talk about people thinking about possibilities, and we want to talk about people being open and closed to possibilities. And we cannot do this by making of possibilities (and so on) secondary things in the Quine systems. The "secondary" things will be those things we admit into our ontologies because of the commitment we have to logical form. (Primarily, on Quine's own view, these things are classes and such.) For, by tacking these extra properties onto the front of the propositions, we simply modify the truth values. Propsitions, then, would not be just true or false, but necessary, possible, impossible and so on. (Quine would prefer to avoid even this.)

Given that simplification, one would run into more basic trouble. For between sensations and things, one could not distinguish modes of existence, either. Hence, forced to choose, Quine chooses a phenomenal "out"—he prefers only immediate experiences (sensations? sense data?) and logical constructions made out of them.

This two-tier ontology, in short, is very cramped, suggesting that we ought to drop back and look at the beginning. Let me do this by telling a story about an argument between two ontologists.

2.43   Let us call these ontologists Omnibus and Nullius.

Nullius: You assert that there are X's. I deny it.

Omnibus: What, *exactly*, are you denying?

Nullius: I deny that there are X's. Just that.

Omnibus: But, if you assert that "there are no X's," you must claim both to know what X's are and also that there aren't any. But this is clearly impossible. If there are none, you don't know what it is that you are denying. You, therefore, admit that there are X's. For you even claim that there is a true proposition about them. Surely, you must mean to say something else. Perhaps, "X's do not belong to the preferred class of existents." As it stands, you contradict yourself.

Nullius: Don't be an ass. If there were X's, they would be not-Y's. I deny that there are any not-Y's. For in my ontology, there are only Y's. "There are no non-Y's" entails "there are no X's" in the case X's are non-Y's.

Omnibus: You are still caught. In order to make your point, you have to speak of hypothetical entities. "If there were X's . . . ." Of course, X's are possible entities. That is how they figure in my ontology. You can't deny it. You have no way of stating your denial. The most you can do is always to say "X's don't belong to the preferred class of existents."

Nullius: You are still being absurd. You simply haven't chosen the right form in which to state my case. Look here, let us suppose we call members of the class which contains all the things there are, O's. Now, suppose we call those O's which exist E, and we designate the property which defines X-s as P. Then we can say "For any O, O is not both E and P." Now, without having made *any* commitment to X's, I have simply asserted that there is a simple conjunction of properties, E and P, which does not occur. This is an application of a principle we have learned from Bertrand Russell.

Omnibus: That won't do at all. For you must have a proposition of the form "the class of all O's does not contain any X's," but this is equivalent to "the class of all O's excludes X's," and this is equivalent to "O's and X's belong to different classes." Now suppose the class of O's *is* the class of objects, then X's are not objects. Suppose O's are "existents," then X's are non-existents. But they *still* have an ontological status. There *is* the *class* of X's and it does have members. It is just a question of *how* we should assign ontological status to it. You may think you can deny the reality of classes, but you can't because, in order to avoid my earlier examples, you had to have recourse to it. Nor can you deny that the class of X's has members, for you have assigned X's to it. You can only question the *status* those members have.

Nullius: No doubt there are many flaws in your argument. I won't press them, though, for I begin to see what is at issue here. My proposals, following Russell, re-order the way in which ontological places are assigned to things. Each time you pick a new place for the old things. Obviously, we could play this game forever. But don't you see that the point is that the form in which we choose to organize statements does determine the distribution of ontological places. As such, they are just a function of that logical strategy. They are therefore really empty places whose significance is only to call attention to our logical preferences. I might withdraw the Quinian phrase "to be is to be the value of a bound variable" in favour of something like "to be is to be ordered by a propositional form" and, then, we must forever be skeptics about the ontological outcome.

Omnibus apparently thinks that what there is is determined by what can be *said*. Nullius thinks that, when we look at how we say what can be said, we can see that "what there is" is a function of the way in which we make that organization. From this he concludes that talk about "what there is" is not about what it seems to be about. It is about logical form.

If Omnibus is right, the ontologist cannot lose. If Nullius is right, he cannot win. Both *these* positions would dissolve our problem quite neatly. For on either one, we would simply advise anyone to believe what he liked about the inner life so long as it furthered his life-aims, or what not. If he was having trouble he might employ a logician to give him a simpler scheme or a more coherent one, but there would certainly be no *true* one.

Of course, Omnibus and Nullius are, I think, both wrong.

2.44   It is important, however, for us to get a better sense of just what they are wrong about. Nullius insists that he can say "there are no X's," and he remains prepared to defend this position even though his way of doing it, ultimately, lands him in the position of one who says that "there are no X's" because assertions of the form "there are X's" are, anyhow, logically quite empty. Omnibus insists that he can never be defeated even though he lands in the position of one who is forced to tailor his ontological assertions to any arbitrary logical form. Both of them end by saying something quite empty.

If we analyze Quine's position in its developed form, we can see that what *he* does is to cut through this mare's nest by introducing epistemological criteria. He urges that our best claim to ontologizing stems from our best claim to knowledge—in his view, the claim which stems from a phenomenal analysis of experience. Given that, we choose a standard form of propositions which best fits what we have. Quine's view, of course, is one in which it turns out that there is only one kind of primary entity and all secondary "kinds" are merely reflections of the properties of the logical forms themselves. Nullius and Omnibus have merely shown that one makes no progress without the introduction of some extra-logical criterion—a point obscured by Quine's analysis.

We need to take account still of a hidden issue, raised and dismissed in Quine's argument with McX, and suggested, perhaps, in my hypothetical argument by the persistence of Omnibus. The point at which Quine seems to give up the logical exchange with the hypothetical McX is the point at which McX asserts that, although his hypothetical claims may be damaged by the switch in reference-bearers from names to bound variables, the terms that he uses still have meanings and these meanings still have ontological status. The point at which Omnibus becomes rather baffling in his argument with Nullius is the point at which Omnibus asserts, in fact, that he can always smuggle in his claims by giving some suitable reading to the logical apparatus proposed by Nullius. But this is just a species of meaning assignment.

The meaning issue is critical, and it can be raised in a number of ways. Let me suggest two. First, let us imagine that there is a certain ontologist who proposes a curious kind of entity which, after some analysis, we find that we have no special reason to accept as a feature of the world. Suppose it is Leibniz's proposal about monads. A Leibnizian monad is a completely independent microcosm of the universe, containing within it everything that there is in reality. It is immune to influence, in the ordinary sense, from any other monad, and it differs from every other monad only in respect to the clarity of its perceptions. Its difference, in Leibniz's world, is guaranteed by the principle of the identity of indiscernibles. From this, we can deduce that no two monads have the same perceptions. From the fact that there are infinitely many monads we can also deduce that every possible monad-state has an exemplar. From these conclusions we can deduce that whenever the clarity of the perceptions of one monad changes for better or worse, there will be a corresponding change in all monads—otherwise the identity of indiscernibles will be violated. It also follows that every describable state of affairs will be a state of some monad, and that we shall not need to suppose that there is anything else in the world.

But now let us suppose that we happen not to think that there are monads. Just what is it that we think? The monad-world is a possible world unless (as Russell hoped to show) its descriptions contain logical contradictions. It is possible in the sense that "it is possibly true that the monad world is the world." It may or may not be possible in the sense that "there is a possible world which is the monad world," for this statement means (in part) "the world is such that one of its future states is or may be the state described by Leibniz in the *Monadology.*" We do not know this, *a priori*, if the world is not presently monadic, but, in entertaining *either* of these propositions, we are admitting that, at any rate, the world is different than it was before Leibniz wrote the monadology. Either Leibniz was right, in which case we know what we did not know before—namely, that the world is monadic—or Leibniz is wrong. But even if Leibniz is wrong, he added something to the world, the possibility of thinking that the world is monadic. (I assume for this purpose that Leibniz's proposal is not necessarily meaningless on the ground of being formally contradictory.)

But what is the least that Leibniz added to the world? The simplest proposal would be that he simply added some arrangements of ink on paper. But this is not the case for what he said can be represented by many different kinds of symbol structures—as we know from seeing the Monadology in Latin, French, English or whatever—all of which are identifiable as having, if not "the same meaning," then at least "overlapping meaning structures of an intelligible kind." If what he did was to describe a possibility, then he either simply added to the set of propositions which might be true, or he revealed to us something about the world, namely, its possibilities. The first is a more economical description, but will not necessarily do. For he may have revealed to us some future state which the world might attain. At least, did he not add to the domain of meanings? Is not the smallest possible addition he could have made an addition to the domain of meanings? That is true, one must admit, if and only if there is sense to the proposition that meanings have ontological status.

This suggests what McX and Omnibus may well have been after. They seemed to want to say: "Look here, whatever you say about ontologizing, your ontological opponent has got to be granted that there is *some* status to be given to his claims."

We can put this another way. In order to understand what Quine or Russell intends by putting forward a preferred logical form one has to know *two* things: the spatio-temporal distribution of the symbols, and what they mean. It always turns out for such cases, as Omnibus was able to show, that the claimed meaning of the symbols is incomplete and can be extended. This is a feature of the meanings and not of the spatio-temporal arrangements of the symbols. (The latter is in no sense incomplete.) Indeed, the original Russellian exposition relied, explicitly, on the notion of "incomplete symbols" (meaning incomplete meanings) as replacements for names.

One could say, of course, that we have no reason to think that a proposal like that of Leibniz is meaningful at all. But that claim loses its plausibility in all of these two- or n-tiered systems. They adopt logical form (giving a second tier to their ontologies) as a device for escaping direct reference as a criterion of meaning. To understand Quine, it is not enough to have glimpsed experiential phenomena; one must also know (in some sense) what a class is, and one learns this from discovering the rules for deploying the symbols and not from any discovered reference of the symbols. The logical positivists who wanted to declare metaphysics generally meaningless intended to do so by hanging on to the notion that meaning derives from reference and that the preferred reference was always phenomenal—a reference to immediate experience.

Now Leibniz can give us rules for using the expression "monad" just as Quine can give us rules for using the expression "class," even if neither of them could readily "define" their expressions in some more traditional sense. Therefore, surely, both have added to the realm of "meaning." But do meanings "exist?"

2.45   It will be worth our while to look again at Quine's words when McX confronts him with the meaning question: "McX and I may agree to the letter in our classification of linguistic forms into the meaningful and the meaningless, even though McX construes meaningfulness as the *having* (in some sense of 'having') of some abstract entity which he calls a meaning, whereas I do not. I remain free to maintain that the fact that a given linguistic utterance is meaningful (or *significant,* as I prefer to say so as not to invite hypostasis of meanings as entities) is an ultimate and irreducible matter of fact; or I may undertake to analyze it in terms directly of what people do in the presence of the linguistic utterance in question and other utterances similar to it."[4] Several propositions are suggested. Meaning should not be regarded as possession of some special property. Also, "significance" is to be preferred to "meaning." (Because to signify is to refer to something, while "to mean" is looser and may suggest a third entity between word and referent. But the direct reference theory had been discarded in the first move in the argument!) Perhaps meaning is "ultimate and irreducible" and "a fact." Or, perhaps, meaning is to be found in what people "do" in the presence of the linguistic utterance.

We can examine these propositions one by one. If meaning is not to involve some special property, then having a meaning can be analysed out into some other property. (But this would contradict the later stand on "irreducibility!") The other properties of the *utterance* all have to do with the spatio-temporal distribution of mounds of ink, sound-waves or whatever. And that will not do because knowing all about those does not constitute knowing the meaning. If this proposal is to be accepted, then, we should have to fall back on behavioural criteria. Certainly, we should shun, at all costs, the "irreducible fact" hypothesis—for then meanings would seem literally unintelligible.

We could replace meaning with "significance," but only at the cost of the return of direct reference. Quine rejected this, but, in case he did not, he would restore the very theory he wants to demolish. For there are utterances which are about meanings. If direct reference should be the criterion of meaning, then these propositions would have to refer to meaning as the "having of some property."

If Quine does not want "special entities," he must want us to consider the last suggestion. Meaning "is to be found in what people do in the presence of the linguistic utterance."

But what does that mean? Let us consider a story. Jones is a poet who has great difficulty in conveying his meaning. Indeed, his life is miserable because, in his own eyes, he invariably fails to say anything to anyone. Smith, an electrical engineer, takes pity on him. He invites Jones to specify all those response which, in his view, would constitute the behavioural responses of persons who had grasped the meaning of his poem. He may include words and other sounds, gestures, actions or whatever. Jones does so, and Smith programs a computer to respond.

The computer can print out suitable verbal responses, activate electronic sound circuits, and manipulate dummies so that they will perform the required actions. The computer is keyed to words in Jones' poems and duly responds appropriately to each one. "Now," says Smith, "your worries are over."

Jones, however, is not satisfied. Behaviour is not enough; understanding is also required. He would feel no better if a school teacher trained a class of superb young actors to go through the motions, words and gestures which the computer produces.

The exchange of meanings is, in part, a creative process. One whose meaning has been grasped expects to take part in a dialogue which goes somewhere—which adds some new dimension to the joint undertaking. Anyone knows the difference between a class which has learned the stock responses and a class which understands.

But the relevant behaviour cannot, *in principle,* be described in advance. If it could, it could be simulated as Smith suggests or as the school teacher pretends.

What this leads to is that, for all its frippery, the McX-Omnibus position has a point: There is an inner side to things which we call their meaning. Adding to it is not the same as adding to the outside world. So there is "more than one kind of existence" and we cannot have, as our standard form of propositions, something which will not permit that.

In sweeping up the mess of our ordinary language, Quine has thrown away some genuine gold dust, the very thing which gives value to our lives. He may have obscured some other things which will be important to our enquiry, too—the difference between being in a story and being in the world, and so on.

But what is crucial here is that there is an inner side to things. It need not be occult. Meaning is not, indeed "another thing" (that is another confusion). It is another aspect.

We have learned, at least, another way of bringing our problem out into the open. And perhaps we have learned that one thing an ontology had better do is to make meaning possible.

Notes to Chapter 2

Notes to Section 2.0

1.   J. J. C. Smart, *Philosophy and Scientific Realism* (London: Routledge and Kegan Paul, 1963).

2. See Alistair Hanney, *Mental Images, A Defence* (London and New York: George Allen and Unwin and Humanities Press, 1971).

3. If the meaning of such accounts is derived from our ability to analyze them back into autopsychological particulars, then it is the *result* of that analysis—the propositions which contain only expressions referring to the autopsychological particulars and syntactical expressions which have meaning on such a theory. But if the analysis cannot, in principle, be completed, though the proposition can, in principle, be confirmed or disconfirmed by reference to autopsychological particulars, then we might hold that propositions which express the results of logical constructions of the kind intended are themselves meaningful though we should have to adopt an expanded account of meaning.

Notes to Section 2.1.

1. J. J. C. Smart, "Sensations and Brain Processes," *The Mind/Brain Identity Theory,* ed. C. V. Borst, p. 57.

2. *Ibid.*

3. *Ibid.*

4. I do not mean to rule out such notions as unconscious thinking or such phenomena as self-deception. They have their place, but not in the kind of account that I am now giving. How I know what I am thinking would still be very different from how I know I am over 5 feet tall, even if there are occasions on which I deceive myself about what it is I am thinking.

5. "Is Consciousness a Brain Process?," *ep. cil,* p. 44-45.

6. *Ibid.*

7. *Op. cit.,* p. 56.

8. *Ibid.*

9. *Ibid.*

10. This is suggested by Jerome Shaffer's "Could Mental States be Brain Processes?," *op. cit.,* p. 118.

11. *Ibid.*

12. *Ibid.*

13. *Ibid.*

14. See L. Wittgenstein's *The Philosophical Investigations* (Oxford: Blackwell's, 1958), paras. 307-308.

Notes to Section 2.2.

1. Berkeley's idealism, as it is expressed in his early essays and dialogues, beginning at least in 1710 (see George Berkeley, *The Principles of Human Knowledge,* La Salle: Open Court, 1963) may not be the beginning of modern idealism. Arthur Collier's major work was probably conceived earlier. But Collier is something different, an objective idealist, even though he shares something with Berkeley. (See *Clavis Universalis,* London: 1713; La Salle: Open Court, 1909.)

2. *Principles* (see note 1 above), p. 31. Berkeley is careful to note that it is only of "unthinking things" that one may say that "their *esse* is *percipi.*"

3. G. E. Moore, *Philosophical Studies* (London: Routledge and Kegan Paul, 1922).

4. See Alfred North Whitehead, *Process and Reality* (New York: Macmillan, 1927), pp. 184-196.

5. Rudolph Carnap, *The Logical Syntax of Language,* translated by Amethe Smeaton, Countess von Zeppelin (London: Routledge and Kegan Paul, 1937, 1967), p. 317ff.

6. The suggestion that there is a kind of second order experience surely begins with "all the perceptions of the human mind *resolve themselves* into two distinct kinds, which I shall call *impressions* and *ideas*"—the first sentence of David Hume's *A Treatise of Human Nature,* ed. L. A. Selby-Bigge (Oxford: The Clarendon Press, 1946).

Notes to Section 2.3.

1. Norman Malcolm, "Moore and Ordinary Language," *Philosophy of G. E. Moore,* ed. by P. A. Schlipp, Tudor Publishing Co., 1952, N.Y.

2. *Art. cit.,* p. 362.

3. *Art. cit.,* p. 349.

4. *Analysis of Matter,* Russell, p. 383; quoted by Norman Malcolm.

5. It is interesting to note that this is a somewhat awkward way of putting it. It would have been more natural to say that this is the sort of situation in which one *says* that he sees a postman but, according to Malcolm, this is the locus of the disagreement. This suggests, of course, that what we naturally say is one of many factual components of a situation. Also note the a priori tone of the preceding characterization. Expressions like "seems impossible" and "would have to be" suggest not only something that is prior to the actual facts, of the situation but contrary to them.

6. *Art. cit.,* p. 350 ff.

7. *Art. cit.,* p. 347.

8. *Art. cit.,* p. 357.

8a. Malcolm's argument would be far more appropriately used against those who maintain that there are inherent inadequacies in ordinary language as a language. See, for example, "The Terms of Ordinary Language Are . . . " in *Philosophical Essays* by O. K. Bouwsma, University of Nebraska Press, Lincoln, 1969, p. 203 ff. Bouwsma directs his attack, as I believe Malcolm should, against a thesis that is unequivocally linguistic.

9. *Art. cit.,* p. 359.

10. S. Cavell, *Must We Mean What We Say?* (New York: Scribner's, 1969), p. 12 ff.

11. P. L. Heath, "The Appeal to Ordinary Language," *Philosophical Quarterly,* Jan. 1952, p. 8.

11a. In fairness to Heath I should point out that he shows some awareness of the independence of his remark from the truth of Ryles. The sentence immediately following the segment I quoted reads: "Not that that does anything to refute Professor Ryles point, that believing, in *his* preferred sense, is dispositional. But it brings out the fact that language recognizes other senses, such as that of assenting, which are equally legitimate, and closely related." (*ibid*) If Heath's point is merely that Ryle has not said all there is to say in the matter then I have no quarrel. I have been arguing only that what Ryle does say is correct and unaffected by Heath's counter-example.

12. See Aristotle; *Nichomachean Ethics,* 1173a-1173b7. Here, he gives an argument whose structure is strikingly similar. His conclusion, that pleasure is not a process, is very different, though his method of argument is very similar. Clearly

the argument deals with the nature of pleasure, though he does cite in support things that we do and do not say.

13. J. Austin, "A Plea For Excuses," *Philosophical Papers,* p. 133.

14. *Art. cit.,* p. 361. Also see Hume's *Treatise* Bk, II, sect. II, pt. p. 277., ed. L. A. Selby-Bigge (Oxford: Clarendon Press, 1968).

15. *Art. cit.,* pp. 360-361.

16. For an elaboration of the point, see *Must We Mean What We Say?* by S. Cavell, Chapter 1; especially, p. 12 ff., (New York: Scribner's, 1969).

17. Malcolm, *art. cit.,* p. 367.

18. Moore himself disclaims any concern with ordinary language. *Op. cit.,* "Addendum to Reply," p. 680. But see Malcolm's *Thought and Knowledge.* (Ithaca: Cornell University Press, 1977), p. 171.

19. Malcolm, *art. cit.,* p. 367.

Notes to Section 2.4.

1. Willard Van Orman Quine, "On What There Is," *From a Logical Point of View* (Cambridge: Harvard University Press, 1953), p. 15.

2. *Ibid.,* (see note 1 above), p. 11.

3. *Ibid.,* p. 46.

4. *Ibid.,* p. 11.

Chapter 3

Expression, Form, and Awareness: Experience and Propositional Form

In section 2.4, I argued that our puzzles about the world within and the outside world cannot be dissolved by the choice of the right logical form, for the choice of form depends upon what it is that one has to express. One might suppose (and not without reason) that this creates a hopeless impasse. One cannot claim to know what one's forms of expression will not let one say, but one cannot defend one's forms of expression except by reference to what one claims to know. Fortunately, the situation is not, in reality, that bad. One starts, after all, with ordinary modes of expression—with what one usually says, or with what we all say in certain circumstances. One seeks to reform these ways of talking when one finds, as in Quine's imaginary argument with McX or in my imaginary argument between Omnibus and Nullius, that the result is, somehow, frustrating. One then proposes changes to avoid this frustration and tests those restrictions against the possibility that they exclude some quite justifiable claim to knowledge. In this way, what we ordinarily say is primary in two senses. First of all, it is where we begin, where we *must* begin, because there is nothing else, originally, to analyse. Secondly, the changes which we decide to make for one reason or another on the original open texture of common expression have, themselves, to be understandable in the language we all use. We have to be able to give directions to one who wants to learn the new way, and those directions must be comprehensible. This does not mean that we are trapped in the ordinary language but it does mean, to be sure, that philosophical revisionism has its limitations. We must not change so much as to destroy the links with our ordinary language for this is a philosophical burning of bridges which is sure to end in meaningless jargon. It also means that one has to approach an unknown country of mind in the manner of an army laying a pontoon bridge in hostile territory—one link at a time with careful attention to one's lines of retreat.

There is more to it than this, however. There is also the question of the authority of our ordinary ways of talking. The nature of this authority is such that linguistic reforms must always be justified. One has to *show* that, say, sentences of the form "all assertions are lies" are somehow degenerate, and that this locution ought to be replaced by one with a different form. For what can be formulated with accepted words in the standard grammar constitutes one's initial field of inquiry, the domain of what can be said. To allow oneself *arbitrary* reformulations of it is simply to mess with the original data, to queer the inquiry before it gets started. And the reasons have to be relevant: the philosopher is allowed to wipe whole sections of discourse from the map and substitute his own if they should prove to land him in trouble as instances of *expression.* Thus one may advise: "Don't say things like 'X's are not admissible on my ontology' because you imply that you are making a mistake—and that is not what you want to say." But one shouldn't say: "abolish the first person pronoun because it reeks of the ancient mythology of ghosts." That is not a reason which bears upon a problem of expression, unless what you mean to say is that you have a theory of meaning according to which the first person pronoun is a meaningless expression. Even then you had best be careful. For everyone else appears to have some notion of meaning in accord with which the first person pronoun *does* have a meaning. What is more, most people would claim to be much more certain that they knew how to use the first person pronoun meaningfully than that any *theory* of meaning is true. Here, again, we deny at our peril the authority of what we quite ordinarily say.

The matter cannot be settled by the introduction of very precise principles, and there are reasons for this. Each proposed revision of the language hinges on some specific question—a particular use of a particular word, a particular conceptual clash created by a given locution, the association of an individual word and some general principle of meaning. Hence while, as I have suggested, some generalities do bear upon the question of the authority of ordinary language, actual disputes pretty much have to be settled expression by expression. The battles will be close order work. And one may expect to come under heavy fire.

All of this is vitally important to the present enquiry. For the distinction between the world within and the outside world turns up, in part—and perhaps most crucially—in the situation created by the special status of first person propositions. Characteristically, first person propositions are those in which the pronoun "I" appears as subject. There is a sub-class of them for which the first person pronoun is not replaceable except by expressions which have the same logical status. And there is a sub-class of those which have special relations to truth. For instance, "I am aware of redness" is typical of one of the most interesting species of first person propositions. The "I" cannot be replaced without both change of meaning and loss of certainty. "Armour is aware of redness" has a different meaning, and is both more doubtful, and doubtful on different grounds. "The man at point P and time T[196] is aware of redness" is different still. Now, on the face of it, this simple situation guarantees that there is a distinction between the world within and the world outside, and also offers us criteria for making that distinction.

But it also seems likely that the knowledge that any proposition other than a first person proposition is true entails the truth of at least one first person proposition. For, if it is known, there is someone who knows it and is entitled to say "I know it." Without this, we would not be satisfied that it was known. Every knowledge transaction has, as one of its components, the kind of situation which would justify a first person proposition. But, equally, the known truth of first person propositions seems to entail the truth of propositions of other kinds. For whenever anything is known, it includes a proposition which would be expressed in a proposition of the form "such-and-such is the case," and such propositions are impersonal.

In Section 3.1, I shall explore the status of first person propositions and the possibility of their replacement by propositions of other forms. I shall argue that they themselves cannot be replaced, and that this fact gives us a notion of the basic situation with respect to "the world inside." In Section 3.2 I shall explore the relation between first person propositions and other propositions and seek to discover what this relation tells us about the boundary problem—about the distinction between the world within and the world outside.

3.1 The Significance and Scope of First Person Propositions

The only way to begin this enquiry is with examples. Suppose that we list some first person assertions—assertions which, perhaps, reveal a range from those we are most interested in to those we are least interested in:

1. I am aware.
2. I am aware of a red patch.
3. I am aware of a dragon.

4. I am imagining a dragon.
5. I see a dragon.
6. I am thinking about philosophy.
7. I am writing philosophy.
8. I am typing.
9. I am a conscious being.
10. I am a thoughtful being.
11. I am a human being.
12. I am a person.
13. I am six feet tall.
14. I wish I were at home.
15. I plan to go to Toronto.
16. I hope I shall not be incinerated.
17. I believe Watering Trough will win the Grand National.
18. I believe tritheism is false.
19. I know tritheism is false.
20. I know that the circumference of the earth is less than 30,000 nautical miles.

3.11   For some of these assertions, the personal pronoun "I" can, for many practical purposes, be replaced by some other expression, by an expression of different logical sort.[1] One would think that eight, thirteen, and twenty are good examples of various standard kinds which are like this. "Armour is typing" is as easily verified as "I am typing" because the evidence, whatever it amounts to, is public. I am as likely as anyone else to be the victim of a mistake about it. The two propositions expressed in these assertions have, that is, that same certainty value. "I am typing" might, of course, mean something more—it might mean "I am typing and I'm aware of it." (That would be commonly assumed.) But the retention of the "I" is largely a matter of preserving the ambiguity. It *might* be a matter of preserving the implied intentionality if one thinks that "typing" is not the same as "striking the typewriter keys with one's fingers." But perhaps this is stretching the thing too far. We can express a fair part of assertion eight while arguing that the assertion does not necessarily express a first person proposition.

Assertion thirteen makes this clearer still. If it is true, it must also mean "Armour is six feet tall." It does not, indeed, seem that the assertion is well expressed. Since one is poorly placed to check on the matter, it would be best, no doubt, to say "I think I'm six feet tall."

3.12 Assertion twenty is different. "I know that the circumference of the earth is less than 30,000 nautical miles" entails, if it is true, that the circumference of the earth *is* as specified. To undertake an utterance which states a fact is, as a rule, to make a claim to the effect that one also knows that it is so. But sometimes one might be hypnotized, sleep-talking, or under the influence of drugs. In fact, assertion twenty expresses (at least) two propositions: "The circumference of the earth is such-and-such *and* I know that it is." Practically, we can use "Armour knows that the circumference of the earth . . . . " for the evidence. The substitute proposition will depend on the same facts and the evidence for the additional claim that I know will usually just be the fact that I say I do. It is possible to assert it while not knowing, but we could make a good try at giving, for *this* case, a behavioral analysis of knowing.

3.13 It is interesting to compare assertions nineteen and twenty. Assertion nineteen has it that I *know* that tritheism, a certain interpretation of the trinity according to which the persons of the trinity are separate gods, is false. Here it is not a simple matter of checking up on the agreed upon criteria for the truth of the proposition. The possible evidence includes situations in which I received revelations, my relation to a body of orthodox believers and their beliefs, and likely complications about religious experience. If I *were* entitled to make the statement, it would have to be because I was rather specially placed in ways about which only I, in fact, could know. Whether these circumstances are ones which would lead one to doubt that the proposition had meaning, or lead one to say that "I know that tritheism is false," this is a good case of an assertion where the expression of a genuine first person proposition remains doubtful.

3.14 At any rate, assertion nineteen is quite different from assertion ten, which seems to express something that ought not to be construed as a first person proposition at all. "I am a thoughtful being"—unless it means "I think a lot"—has to do with one's behavioral stance, one's tendency to think, reflect, and so on, in the sense in which those properties have to do with the way in which one responds to proposals, assertions, or whatever. We would not believe it without reference to the assertions of others, though we should not be inclined to take even nineteen as a really clear-cut case.

Anyone would be happier with assertion eighteen. "I believe tritheism is false" does seem to express a proposition which depends upon what I am prepared to say about it. Notice how different it is from seventeen, even though seventeen also contains the word "belief." We could give a behavioural analysis of seventeen. If I believe that Watering Trough will win the Grand National, it is fairly certain that, other things being equal, I will be willing to bet on the proposition. "Armour would bet heavily on Watering Trough for the Grand National" seems to convey the same message. Here the truth of the proposition very likely depends upon what I am prepared to do. (If we discover a tipster who says that Watering Trough will win but bets all his money on Dean's Brains, we suspect that he is up to something.)

3.15   Wherever we could, plausibly, give a behavioural analysis, we could reasonably believe that the proposition expressed is not a genuine first person proposition. For to give such an analysis is, precisely, to replace, or offer to replace, the first person pronoun by other expressions. It seems far-fetched to assume that a behavioural analysis would succeed with "I believe tritheism is false." What is it that such a man is expected to do? He may say tritheism is false, he may avoid all assertions which express propositions which seem to entail the truth of tritheism, and so on. But this leads to the assertion "Armour's behaviour is impeccably orthodox." If I am also known for my honesty, everyone will watch with care to see just whether or not I finally come out and say "tritheism is false." Failure to say *just that* will give rise to suspicion. In this case, therefore, "belief" has the look of something which entails an inner state, and the first person proposition passes the usual test. It does not, as such, throw much light on how the situation is finally to be construed.

Its informativeness, however, should be contrasted with eleven. "I am a human being" might sound as if it was just the right sort of utterance to count as expressing a first person proposition, but it must, on reflection, be counted out. It is true that no one is better placed than I to know that I am a human being, but this takes us nowhere. What would be an occasion for its use? Say you have been mistaken for a robot and you protest. That, however, won't do you any good. Any properly deceitful robot would have been programmed to say "I am a human being." More reasonably, you are the girl in the center-fold of *Playboy* and you are treated as such a being might expect to be treated. Here, "I am a human being" makes sense but it conveys no information. It is a plea—no doubt heartfelt and forceful but, still, a plea. If you have to justify it, you have to supply other information.

3.16   Several of the assertions in our list help to map the minds of those who express them, and the way in which they do so suggests reasons for believing that they express genuine first person propositions. Assertions fourteen, fifteen and sixteen express wishes, plans, and hopes—intentional objects. They give a sense to the structure of the person they purportedly describe, and they have links with behaviour without lending themselves to straightforward behavioural analysis. One who wishes to be home, plans to go to Toronto, and hopes not to be incinerated will, no doubt, behave in certain ways rather than others. These assertions will make sense in some context. By itself, what he does is susceptible of infinitely many speculative descriptions; what he says gives us the clue about how to read the map of his mind. Without his doing anything, of course, what he says would have no function, either. The map of his mind illuminates his behaviour, but it is not a map of that behaviour.[1]

3.17   So far, in all the cases we have met, we have found instances in which, apart from those which involve assertions which do not express genuine first person propositions, the first person proposition tends to carry substantial weight but does not, by itself, carry the day. Only in context does my account of my beliefs cause you to believe that what I say is true; that is, only in context do my intentional assertions illumine my behaviour enough so that you believe what I say.

3.18   At the other end of the spectrum, there are assertions which seem to have that effect. Assertion one, "I am aware," would surely be taken to be almost indubitable. We would not, as a *rule*, doubt what someone was saying when he said that, but, in the crucial case, it is rather like "I am a human being." Suppose I am a neuro-surgeon and you are my patient. I am not sure whether or not you have regained consciousness after a delicate brain operation. I ask you, and you say "I am aware." The trouble is that if there is a reason to doubt your awareness to begin with, this assertion will carry no weight at all. It will provide very useful information about the operation of certain motor centers and the parts of the brain associated with speech, but if your trouble was not there but in that region of the brain-stem where the consciousness switch seems to lie, the assertion will tell us nothing.

If the proposition expressed by the assertion is true, then it will follow that the assertion is interesting. This is another case in which the "I" cannot be annalyzed away. "Smith is aware" has a very different meaning. "Awareness is" means heaven knows what but not, I think, anything like "I am aware." It need not be true just because it is uttered, for it has no logical connection with the utterer.

But if the one who utters it means it, must it not be true? Is it not evidence for *him*? We are now imagining that he says it to himself, and it is usually wise to try to think of a context for such a curious piece of self-examination. I have just awakened from an operation. "So far so good," I say to myself. "At least I'm aware." Yet what is awareness *in general*? My problem is that I thought (a) I might be dead; (b) I might enter a state of permanent all-embracing hallucination; or (c) I might not recognize myself. But "I am aware" is compatible with all of them. If what I am aware *of* is the "next world," then I am dead. If what I am aware of is not what other people are aware of, then (b) applies; and if I make a wrong estimate about who I am, (c) applies. "I am aware" tells against the different proposition that being dead might entail no awareness whatsoever. But it does even that in a rather misleading way, for it begs the question of the identification of the "I." It fails to express a genuine "first person" proposition by failing to establish any relation between the "I" and what is being said.

3.19 The succeeding assertions—two, three, four, five, six and seven—attempt to make good this deficiency in various quite ordinary ways. "I am aware of a red patch" combines a favorite philosophical example with the form of the first person proposition. But it is a horrible example and results in a cautionary tale.

Assertion two is a classic attempt to get at the content of awareness as such, and to do so in a way which will lead to the expression of a first person proposition of absolute certainty and purity. Absolute certainty is attained if the truth of the proposition does not depend upon anything more than the sincerity of the utterer. (Other persons can impugn his *sincerity* but not, directly, the proposition as such.) Absolute purity is attained if and only if the utterance succeeds in expressing one, and not more than one, first person proposition and neither expresses nor entails any other proposition.

Now it is thought that one who claims to be aware of a dragon is not in the same position as one who claims to be aware of a red patch. For assertions about dragons can go wrong in many ways, some of which have nothing to do with the awareness-state which the observer is in a position to certify. Assertions about colored patches, it is *thought,* lie solely within the certification competence of any observer.

Evidently, the claims involved are ambiguous. For "I am aware of a red patch" may mean many things, two of which are immediately relevant. It may mean "I have correctly applied the standards for 'redness' to my immediate experience and judged them to fit." But it may mean "I have decided to name my present experience 'red'."

The first is exactly like three, our dragon case. The standards for redness can be applied well, badly, or indifferently. The standards for dragons can also be applied with much, little, or no success. It is true that the standards for dragons are complex, and it is true that philosophers have sometimes been misled into thinking that the standards for redness are simple. It takes little thought to see that this is false. Red is at most one color, but that does not mean that only one decision is to be made. To be red is to be a spatial surface occupied in a certain way. To be seen to be red is to be an object of awareness which conveys this. Redness is a determinate form of the determinable coloredness which, itself, is a determinate form of the determinable "occupancy of spatial surface"—and so on.

By contrast, "I name thee red" conveys no information at all, except the information that "there is a namer about" and "he is exercising his office" and *this* information is both impugnable and corrigible. It can be impugned by evidence that "the utterer is a phonograph" and corrected by evidence that "the utterer is not being successful in his naming."

The pseudo-certainty of the naming case is transferred to the classification case, and then it is thought that one has achieved a maximum of certainty. Classifying and naming are, essentially, poor cases for those who search for first person assertions which will express real first person propositions. They are simply commentaries which throw no light on the commentator, and convey only rather vague information. Both versions of the ambiguity fail, though they fail for different reasons. The "I" cannot be replaced mainly because it is so vague. Who is aware of the red patch? Armour? Bartlett? It seems not to matter. How do we know it counts as a red patch if no classification is at stake? No one can say.

3.191 Now, while three—"I am aware of a dragon"—is presumably never true for the reason that there are no dragons and, therefore, no one is ever aware of one, assertion four is quite different. "I am imagining a dragon" has a possible context and is even, perhaps, instructive.

I ask you about dragons, having encountered them in a story. You tell me about them. "They fly, breathe fire, have the body of a snake, and the wings of a bird. They are very large and generally hostile to people, especially fair maidens and knights in armor." "Ah," I say, "now I get it. I can imagine one well enough."

What is going on here is a process by which what I formerly found unintelligible becomes gradually meaningful. I make all the connections with my existing beliefs and imaginings. I understand. The "I" has a meaning. It emerges as the center of this program by which all the data is brought into line.

3.192   We cannot say, instead, "Armour now knows what a dragon is," though that follows from the original assertion. I *am* imagining a dragon *if* "I *can* imagine a dragon." I can be wrong about it, as you understand words. I may still think of a dragon as a special kind of prehistoric animal rather than as a being whose meaning is mythical, for instance. But that I understand *something* which fits the appropriate concepts together, I cannot doubt.

But can we not feed our program for mastering the concept of dragon into a computer and get the same result? Certainly, up to a point. The computer can learn to use the dragon concept, but the *meaning* belongs to those who program it. The assignment of meanings belongs to hearer and programmer but, in case the programmer is not available, the hearer must be capable of assuming all of the burden. The computer may be programmed to comment on what it has said in response to questions, but there will be a limit. The computer consists of a set of on-off switches. Various combinations of these switches are associated with binary numbers. The program may associate these binary numbers with other things, say words.

3.1921   We may imagine the following sort of conversation going on between a man and a computer:

Man: What do you make of dragons?

Computer: I am not programmed for that expression.

Man: Are you programmed for "bird," "snake," "fire," "wings," and "about the size of a house?"

Computer: Indeed!

Man: Then what is large as a house, breathes fire, is a bird and a snake.

Computer: A dragon.

Man: What do you know about dragons?

Computer: I am afraid of dragons!

Man: Why?

Computer: Translated into the basis of my program, the proposition you have stated reads: 1136 . 950 . 340 . 229 = dragon. I am programmed to associate fear (fear = 900) with numbers 901-999. (950 = fire.)

Man: Why is 950 associated with fear?

Computer: 950 is associated with 1640, combustion, 147, disintegration, 1999, pain.

Man: What is pain?

Computer: 1999 .1998 = aversion.

Man: I see.

Computer: See = 17. It is not particularly associated with other concepts you have mentioned. Though dragons can be seen.

Man: How do you know?

Computer: $17 .340 \neq p . -p^2$

3.1922 The man, now, is beginning to get frustrated. The furthest he can get in this conversation is the basis of the computer program: the way in which the computer was programmed to associate numbers with one another. He can program the computer in some additional way if he wants to. For instance, he can create a computer analogue of Freudian depth psychology so that the computer will now associate other numbers with its "childhood," and associate these with the notions compounded to make dragons. If this behaviour does not suit the man, he can re-program the computer.

He can go on programming and re-programming as long as he pleases. But he always gets to the point at which he must re-program if he is to get to a further level of explanation.

Whenever he gets to this level, he can replace the computer "I" with a description of the program. No genuine first person proposition is ever actually expressed.

If he wants to get quite sophisticated, he can program the computer to re-program itself. Thus, the computer can be programmed to associate some of these responses with pleasure, and others with displeasure. It will then store some occasions in its memory bank for re-use whenever appropriate, and others it will consign to a system which inhibits output.

Finally, he can build into it a certain capacity for randomness so that he can predict just what responses it will produce.

3.1923 We might think that this bundle of learning and innovating capacities might be correctly marked out by the computer's use of "I." But there will always be a level of exploration at which the computer will respond just as it did in the earlier conversation we had with it.

Man: Now tell me why you said that.

Computer: It lay within the scope of the random allowance of my program. Your response indicates that it gave you pleasure. Therefore I printed it out.

Man: Why are you programmed like that?

Computer: That question is unintelligible.

Man: What is the basis of your program?

Computer: Associations of numbers, randomness, and feedback for new program construction.

The computer is telling the truth. There is no more to be told. That is its "I."

But suppose we program the computer to question the man.

Computer: Why are you compelled to ask these questions?

Man: I am not compelled.

Computer: You are a randomizing device?

Man: I am not a randomizing device.

Computer: The negation of $1000 .1001 = p . -p$. Your answers cannot conjointly be represented in my circuits.

But we can envisage this situation in ordinary language. ("Tell me if you love me. You do? Are you compelled to give that answer? Is this an answer which you give randomly to girls? I should hope not.") It is not possible to use ordinary concepts such as love, hope, reason, belief, and certainty—to name only a few—if we are confined to computer possibilities.

3.1924 This becomes more apparent, of course, if we compare our conversation with a computer to one with a person. Here, the meaning does not devolve upon one person or upon a hidden program—or does it?

Smith: Do you think there might be dragons—on Pluto, say?

Jones: No, I think one cannot imagine the internal economy of the dragon. The heat necessary to produce fire breathing would interfere with molecular structures necessary for the genetic code.

Smith: Why do you say that?

Jones: The complexity of the structures is such that they are only stable at certain energy levels. I can't—right now—think how to combine those energy levels with fire breathing.

Smith: You just associate those words with things to include in your print-out because you were programmed to accept bio-chemistry.

Jones: As a matter of fact, I'm pretty skeptical about bio-chemistry. I neither accept it nor reject it.

Smith: You are programmed for randomness?

Jones: Not at all. I am programmed to accept evidence.

Smith: You are a compulsive believer?

Jones: On the contrary. I weigh the evidence. I sit in judgment. The outcome is not pre-determined for, otherwise, there would be no knowledge. All investigations would be trials before bought juries.

Smith: But how did you get this way?

Jones: I decided that some kinds of evidence were acceptable and others not.

Smith: You were programmed for that decision?

Jones: Of course not.

Smith: You chose randomly?

Jones: Don't be silly.

Smith: Then explain yourself.

Jones: Well, I found that certain techniques gave me a coherent experience pattern, and others led to expectations with no obvious correlations with what happened.

Smith: You were programmed for feedback?

Jones: No, I chose a preferred set of relations between my beliefs and my experience.

3.1925 This conversation might go on for a long time. But we should notice two things about it. First, it can go on indefinitely—literally to infinity. Secondly, there *is* no point at which we are sure that Jones has told us all there is to know about himself. Even if he were able to correlate his sayings with the workings of his central nervous system—he cannot *now*, but no doubt someday he will be able to—that would not count as something that we should prefer as an explanation. It should be useful, but it is not decisive.

Against the other expressions he uses—"I decided," "I judged," "I preferred," "I chose a life style for myself"—the locution "my neurons were programmed" has absolutely no claim to priority. Just as the explanation "I turned to chemistry because my sex life was frustrating" has no precedence over "I turned to chemistry because I liked the problem about benzine rings," or "I turned to chemistry because I thought that one could be objective about human beings at the molecular level."

We choose the mechanical or the Freudian explanation if—and only if—it illumines the situation or if—and only if—it makes sense of what was previously dark. But, *in principle,* these do not rule out "I chose," "it was my considered judgment that," and so on. For the fact that we can use these expressions, and understand them, is itself enough evidence that they have a function.

The meanings are not supplied unilaterally by Smith or Jones. They develop as the debate goes on. Each can produce new ones, to infinity. The two men form a unit whose activity has *no* necessarily preferred explanation.

It is here, of course, that the genuine first person proposition arises. The "I" stands for what *cannot* be replaced. For there is nothing to replace it with. If there were, the conversation would have to end.

"I am imagining a dragon" is a good case. Between the "I" and the activity there is a necessary connection. It is not a simple assertion. One of its components is "I am assigning meanings to an activity," and another is "the outcome of that activity would count, usually, as imagining dragons." The first is a genuine "first person proposition," but the second—or something which does the same logical duty—must be associated with it before we know what we have on our hands. "I am assigning meanings" is not by itself anything the user or the hearer can check up on. It has to come out in a form like "I am imagining dragons."

3.1926   From this, one could *infer* assertion nine, "I am a conscious being." For the "I" now cannot be simply eliminated, and therefore refers to a feature of reality—a feature of "being" though not likely a "thing." And one who can assign meanings is surely conscious.

3.1927   If nine is an inference from four, then five is a possible outcome of four if the activity it describes could be applied to something. It is not like three, "I am aware of a dragon," which implies that there is a dragon, for "seeing" suggests success in applying the outcome of imagining in an intersubjective context. "Damn it, I *saw* a hippopotamus in the pond," is not contradicted by "what was actually in the pond was the grossly fat Mrs. Jenkins thrown there by the enraged hired man. She was on all fours, grunting and covered with mud." The first reporter has applied the standards for hippopotami in so far as they exist in his imagination. "Seeing is believing" suggests a dubious adage, but it is dubious only because seeing, the meeting of all one's available visual criteria, must lead to belief even though the belief may be false. One does believe as one sees when one's available criteria becomes sufficiently complicated to sustain a more general criterion. But "I *think* I see a ship" suggests that despite the meeting of visual criteria, one is aware he may be mistaken. Hence, "I see" contains, too, an element of the irreducible "I." It is a judgment made by an alert creature on the basis of his criteria. What he "sees" is the meaning he gives.

We are left, then, only with the complex activities in which the passive-active distinctions do not confuse the issue. "I am writing philosophy" (assertion seven) and the seemingly more internalized "I am thinking about philosophy" (assertion six) are, really, very much alike. The "I" here is, again, the creative assignor of meanings. One knows one is writing philosophy much as anyone else does, and thinking about it differs in degree rather than kind. The activity is open-ended, indefinitely prolonged.

3.1928   Once again, the "I" is not replaceable, but nor is it separable from the activity going on. The privileged access is, therefore, imperfect. The I were the only one who *could* know what I was doing, what I was doing could not meet the public criteria for writing philosophy. But the perspective that I have is a necessary one if the thing should go on at all. If I were the only one who *could* know what I was doing, what I was doing could not meet the public criteria for writing philosophy. But the fact that I know does not entail that anyone else actually does.

3.193   At last we can get to the point:

Assertions express genuine first person propositions if and only if:

1. The "I" cannot be replaced by any other expression without loss or change of meaning or certainty.

2. The assertion associates a conscious, meaningful process with the "I" in such a way that criteria bear upon the occurrence or non-occurrence of the event.

3. The process cannot be replaced by a pre-determined or random program.

(We need clause three only for the possibility that the requirements of clause one might be met by a computer program which turned out to be unique and unrepeatable and, therefore, entitled to one sense of the "I." This might be the case if running the program exhausted all the kinetic energy in the universe.)

The significance of it is that these conditions imply that there is an inner side to the world—the side of meanings, the side of the indefinite expansibility, of non-programmable activities, and the side from which certainty varies with our ability to assert personal identity.

But we should notice that none of this necessarily entails an unreachable, ghostly self. On the contrary, it entails a non-thing-like self. But that self must be connected to some features of what can be publicly known. That is the topic of the next section.

3.2   First Person Propositions and the Description of the World

Whenever a proposition is known to be true, it is either a first person proposition or one which entails the truth of a first person proposition. For to know a proposition to be true is to have assigned a meaning to some utterance, and that assignment must be expressible as an irreducible first person proposition. But does this entail a kind of epistemological—and logical—priority to first person propositions?

The answer I want to substantiate is "no," but what we are confronting is the logic of the ego-centric predicament. It is fear of that predicament which provides the strongest motive for those who would attempt to dispose of first person propositions by reduction. It is important, therefore, to see what it amounts to and to clarify, further, the relation between genuine first person propositions and other propositions.

3.21   The minimum force of the "ego-centric predicament" is, I suppose, the force which results from the fact that each of us is always in the center of a meaning system which he somehow controls and operates. Meanings are partly systems of rules about the occasions on which words are to be used and about the logical force which a given use carries with it. This force therefore produces signs and symptoms which are not entirely subjective, for a rule entails the possibility of more than one occasion of use, and such a system of occasions is potentially interpersonal. What is intelligible to me on two successive occasions is potentially intelligible to two of us on the same occasion. For, if I have criteria, I can communicate them to you. All of this is simple and well known, at least since Wittgenstein. But it is not the whole of the story.

Partly, too, the situation about meaning is like the situation about the law. The law is not self-applying because a decision has to be made about what case falls under what rule. A given case is never, just, say, one of burglary. It is, perhaps, the case of Smith, who is of marginally sound mind, once had title to the goods, may or may not have intended to appropriate them permanently to his own use, had access to the premises through the grant of someone whose authority to permit entry is arguable, and so on. There are all those doubtful issues which bear on the question "which rule?" But, then, there are other facets of the case which particularize the incident but are irrelevant—probably—to the issue. It does not matter whether the purloined papers were bound in blue or black folders, or whether Smith wore a coat or not. It may or may not matter whether the premises were otherwise used as a whorehouse, or whether Smith did or did not turn on the lights. To decide, a court is essential. So with meanings, except that I am the only court available—or, at least, I am the only one which, in the end, counts. It is not that there is a shortage of professors of rhetoric, makers of dictionaries, or philosophical busybodies willing enough to pronounce on the correctness of the decision. They may help persuade, like the attorneys in the court. But I must decide because I must act, and no one else can make my meanings for me. (The moment they *do*, I become the computer of 3.1, and then the game is a very different one.)

3.22   The analogy of the court is fairly helpful. The court can decide what it pleases—provided it can find a rule which fits the decision, and provided it can make that decision intelligible to the parties. If the Court says "we have just made up our minds that freedom of speech does not extend to swearing in church," the decision fails on two grounds. First, the decision does not create a rule of law, because no rule has been provided which gives it a place in the law; and, secondly, it fails because no one can possibly know what it means. One surmises that it does not mean that words like "God," "damn," "hell" and so forth are not to be used in churches, for that would render such places inoperative, and seemingly conflict with constitutional provisions about freedom of religion. Roughly, it is not a legal decision if it cannot be applied, and it is not a legal decision if it cannot be related to the test of the legal process. That is, it cannot be applied because we cannot relate it to the legal fabric. Of course, the decision may *hold* in the case in question. If what the court decided was to overrule Jones' appeal against his conviction for disturbing the peace by swearing in church, *that* matter stands. The court decided that Jones' appeal failed; what it failed to decide was that swearing in church was illegal.

Contrast this with a case in which the court gives reasons and holds:

1. The right to speak freely does not have precedence when it conflicts with the right of others to hold orderly meetings and

transact their normal meetings.

2. In the domain of rights, the right to life and the protection of property must be given reasonable scope against those who would use the right to speak in a disruptive way.

3. Religious societies have the right to determine who shall use certain words and in what contexts, within the confines of their premises.

Such a decision might be bad law, but it would be law. It would create some rules and assign them a place in the system.

The problem about assigning meanings is the same. There is a *sense* in which every decision we make—like every decision of the Supreme Court—sticks, and there is another sense in which some of them fail. Suppose Spinoza and I say, "By God, I understand that which is cause of itself." It follows that he means to say that the expression "God" is to be replaced by the expression "that which is cause of itself." But it does not follow (a) that he knows *just* what he is doing or (b) that it will help me when I face the next decision.

If I accept the definition, and then come across someone who says "God is love," do I want to say "that which is cause of itself is love" or "love is that which is cause of itself," or both or neither? The original decision, of course, does not tell me. It only tells me how to make the decision if I develop and can apply rules for the use of the word "God" (we may think of the whole of Spinoza's *Ethics* as the elaboration of those rules).

Thus the "ego-centric predicament" is not so all-embracing as one might think. True, the meaning decision has to be made by me. But Spinoza would not claim to have some special way of making it effective for himself while leaving it ineffective for others.

3.23   In fact, the situation does not really internalize meaning so as to give an ultimate epistemological priority to the knowledge which is expressed in the first person proposition. It externalizes the self so as to allow both for the "I" which is the court, and for the "I" which expresses itself throughout a universe of discourse.

My meaning flows through that universe of discourse in such a way that it must interact with its successor assignments and with the assignments of others. The rules are, indeed, not self-propelled like the program of a computer. They remain highly personal in interaction.

This can be explained if we attend to a suitable example. In our legal case, we may decide that Smith may be guilty of larceny and *not* burglary for no better reason than that there is a common understanding that a whorehouse is a place where one may come and go at will without a specific invitation on each special occasion. (Smith may then be guilty of another offense for frequenting such a place, but that is different.) In such ways, at any rate, we are apt to refine the legal rule about how burglary is to be distinguished from larceny, and so refine the "meaning" we give to the word "burglary."

A computer could do this for us *if* we had programmed it with the rule about whorehouses. But it may well be that in our legal system we did not have such a rule until the Smith case came up. The computer might have had a randomizing program which allowed it to make some adjustment, but that would be quite different from our specific decision to do the thing—a decision which, in the context, we were not forced to make, but which we did not make on whim either. We made it because it corresponded to the current development of our sense of justice. It is not until Smith is arrested for breaking into a whorehouse that it occurs to us to ask: "What kind of a place *is* that, and what sorts of rules should aply to it?"

The decision can be understood by others, and extended and applied from whorehouses to churches if our sense of justice demands it. Spinoza finds, for instance, that to get rules which will graft his proposals onto the main structure of a language, he has to develop meanings for expressions such as "the intellectual love of God." He must do so in ways which extend some aspects of expressions like "love" (so that right understanding becomes a sub-species of love, for instance) and narrow some aspects of the notion of God (so that God is not *literally* a person). Conversely, aspects of "love" need to be stripped away ("love" comes to have no obvious relation to sex) while some aspects of the notion of God are extended (God comes literally to have an attribute of extension).[1]

My concern here is not, to be sure, with the reasons some philosophers might offer for finding such a rearrangement of the verbal firmament offensive. The point is that Spinoza cannot simply give meaning to these expressions by a single psychological act, any more than the Supreme Court can give meaning to its decisions by a single verbal act. Nor, for that matter, does Spinoza's problem stem from the fact that he needs many psychological acts to establish the meanings he wants. His problem is that he needs to develop the appropriate sets of rules. It cannot be done mechanically (however much he may have wanted the *Ethics* to look like what we should now think of as a potential computer program). As he works his way through the universe of discourse, he makes encounters with meanings which need reorganization, just as the law must react to the combination of rules which confronts it when Jones swears in church, or Smith works out his larcenous itch in a whorehouse.

The act of meaning assignment is creative and dependent on a psychological act which has its clear logical interiority. But it is also a public activity which is under surveillance—one which others can participate in and respond to to just the degree that Spinoza himself can. The rules which Spinoza used are available to anyone.

As this process goes on, Spinoza's "mind" (as we say quite easily and reasonably) becomes open to public inspection; that is, it becomes externalized as the activity proceeds.

3.24   Should we go further than this? What are the conditions for the development of such meaning structures? Do they require a "world" in which there are things describable, strictly, in terms whose meaning is restricted to a domain independent of the assignor of meanings?

There is a case for this point of view—that is, for thinking that not only is the ego-centric predicament the product of the kind of misunderstanding I have been suggesting, but also that for meaning to *be*, there has to be a world which is more strictly independent of us.

Let us look for a moment at what this entails. There is the sense in which the law is independent of the court but not independent of the possibility that there are courts. The court does not "make up" the law as if it were a fairy tale. It acts so as to move some meanings, create some, adapt some rules, cause others to appear in new relations to each other, and so on. But there have to be some rules to begin with or else there is nothing to decide, and no way to tell whether a given act constitutes a decision.

But this is not to say, literally, that the law has always been with us—a kind of innate idea always immanent. What it means to say things like "there must be some rules to begin with" is that the possibility of law is the possibility that not all acts are to be decided on whim, that deciding is different from merely pronouncing, that legal decisions are not equivalent to simple acts of force, and so on. The concept of law in that sense is independent of all of us—it marks out a different possibility from that of anarchy, the rule of force, or government by fiat. There may be many arguments about the ultimate scope of the concept of law. (Is it really the law if what it inhibits are all and only good acts? Is very *bad* law law at all?)[2] But since law consists of rules of a certain kind, it is not law if it has no rules of this kind.

That fact does not depend upon there being anybody to decide what the rules are. It is an independent part of the world for which no first person propositions are required beyond those of meaning assignment. Equally, however, there are no "rules" if there is nobody to apply them. There has to be a court, though it need not be at all like what we usually think of as a court. (In some world we might all be able to be the judges. It might be the rule of law, for instance, that one could do anything one wanted provided the maxim for the act were generalisable in the Kantian sense. The law might only require that the judges—all of us—go through a prescribed procedure for checking to see if that were the case.)

In law, then, the objective "given" and the subjective "decision" go together. No doubt it is the same with the general problem of meaning. But the sense in which some law is given, objective, and public is not the sense in which philosophers have sometimes thought the world of stones and mountains was objective, given, and public. The former sense is that of an objectifying, externalising act, and the other is the sense of an encounter with an objective and external fact.

Unless it can be shown that meaning requires the latter, is there not a sense in which we are still caught in the ego-centric predicament?

3.25   The connection, presumably, is that, as a rule, the externalization of meaning requires a medium, a carrier for the message itself, a stable domain which will function as a reference point for the criteria which the meaning is supposed to fulfill. It is well to notice that what is at issue here is not the "reference" theory of meaning: we do not (or ought not to) expect an expression like "God" in the writings of Spinoza, or "freedom of speech" in the law, to derive its meaning from a reference to some specific element in experience. It is the essence of Spinoza's view that "God" is an organizing concept which gives shape to the domain of discourse. It cannot be the name of some ingredient in experience, and it cannot derive its meaning from some act of referring whether or not such acts can be construed as more or less than naming. "Freedom of speech" is not the name of some act and it does not refer to some element of behaviour. It is, rather, an ingredient in a domain of rights which, when they are given reasonable scope, render intelligible some set of actual or proposed rules.

But there has to be a way of conveying what one is saying, and then there have to be reference points which tell one whether or not the rule has been applied. The first might take many forms. We use words expressed through sound waves or marks on paper. We might use characteristic configurations in immediate awareness if, for instance, telepathic phenomena occurred in great profusion.[3] The sound waves and marks on paper are intelligible to *us* as configurations in immediate awareness. A little study according to some rules should reveal confusions, ambiguities, misunderstandings, and so on: there should be a knowable technique. It may be very simple. If it sounds like either gnus or news, we can ask to "see it in writing" or, failing that, we can ask for a repetition of the sentence in the hope that the context will make it clear. Another requirement is that one should be able to take steps to disentangle some minimum of the distinction between invention and encounter. Sometimes being passive is a test: listen more carefully, forget the other things going on in your head, turn the lights up brighter so that the "incoming signal" may triumph over the imagination. Sometimes creative reconstruction will help: try to construct a point of view which might be the author's, and then see whether you can get a reasonable reading of what he is saying. Examine the patterns of language use common amongst various communities, and see whether the difficulty is created by a difference of usage. The process cannot be too sophisticated or complicated (else we could not explain how anyone understood anything), and it cannot depend too much on the prospect that all the uncertainties can be removed (else we should be able to show that everything everyone said was meaningless).

The region of encounter, then, is the region over which what one finds is not of one's own making. But it is not that we literally need a world from which all traces of the active subject have been removed. On the contrary, it is always something that the subject does which counts as carrying out the instructions for improving the quality of the message. What he is doing must satisfy him that he is engaged in encounter, and not in sheer invention.

That, naturally, is as important to him as it is to third parties. It is vital to Spinoza to know that he is using "God" in the same way on successive occasions. If he can never tell, he does not know whether he is making progress or not. If he makes up the meaning anew each time, his enterprise founders. Hence, he must be able to tell when he is encountering the old meaning and when he is making up new ones.

The requirement for this seems to be mainly a certain set of invariances. We can take the ones actually used by physicists, for instance, as good examples. The physicist needs to believe that the same procedure conducted in one place has the same result as one conducted in another, and that the same procedure conducted at one time has the same result as one conducted at another. If it is one thing to drop balls off the tower in Pisa and another to drop them off the Empire State Building, or one thing to drop them in the fifteenth century and another to drop them now, he does not know, in fact, what he is doing.

Similarly, the same techniques used as criteria for meaning must work then and now, here and there. There is a minimum of stability required in place and time. It may get very complex: frames of reference may change with time, place or velocity but, if so, they must change invariantly and according to rules or laws.

It is for this reason that we must distinguish between the act of giving meaning and the meaning given, just as we must in the law distinguish between the act of the court and rule given by that act. The acts in question are always unique, never repeatable. The meanings and rules must have stability.

Only in a world with certain invariances, and only in a world in which certain techniques can be specified, are these processes specifiable. The solipsist world fails to be a meaningful world because it is one within which no meanings are ever forthcoming. The solipsist, precisely, is one who confuses the act of giving meanings with the meanings given.

3.26   We saw in the discussion we tracked through Section 3.1 that utterances which seem to express first person propositions fail if they merely express the region which constitutes the subjective act. The subject must be linked to something to which the conditions of meaning will apply before the utterance succeeds.

Here we have seen that the externalization process has two phases—the externalizing of the self in the meaning process, and the reference to the external world which is required to give stability to meanings and to provide something for the criteria to hang onto. Essentially, there have to be genuine elements of encounter and invariance.

First person propositions, like others, will not succeed in a world whose description fails to meet those criteria. It is not our business, here, to erect the elaborate metaphysics which might cash these notions.

The point here—and throughout this book—is to notice how the world within and the world outside mesh with one another, how one entails the other.

In form, any describable world will require in its description both first person propositions and person-neutral propositions.

The argument of these sections has been, first, that one needs first person propositions—that they cannot be analyzed away—and, then, that one cannot have them without other propositions as well.

3.27   However we choose, in the end, to characterise the subject and the world beyond him, we must not do so in a way which makes it impossible for the subject to become internalized, or for the world to be subjectively intelligible.

Notes to Section 3.1.

1.   In my list of "first person propositions" and in the discussion which follows, I have been guided by the specific needs of the argument. For many interesting distinctions and much substantial argument, see S. Coval, *Scepticism and the First Person* (London: Methuen, 1966).

2.   For an amusing discussion between a man and a computer—with some parallels to this one—see Michael Crichton's novel *The Terminal Man* (New York: Bantam Books, 1973), p. 107. But for serious discussions of the limits of computers, see Joseph Weizenbaum's *Computer Power and Human Reason* (San Francisco: W. H. Freeman, 1976) and J. M. Burgers, *Experience and Conceptual Activity* (Cambridge, Mass.: M.I.T. Press, 1965), p. 150 ff.

Notes to Section 3.2.

1.   Twice—in the scholium to Part III, Proposition XIII and in Definition VI of the *Affectuum definitiones* of Part III—Spinoza says: *"Amor est Laetitia concomitante idea causae externae"* ("Love is joy combined with the idea of an external cause.") (Benedicti de Spinoza, *Opera Quotquot Reperta Sunt.* The Hague: Martinus Nijhoff, 1914, vol. 1, pp. 131-169). Thus, perhaps, the greatest joy is the joy accompanied by the clearest idea of what is cause of itself. But notice here that love is feeling combined with an idea, and it is a small step to the notion of pure feeling combined with a clear idea, so that Proposition XV, part V comes as no surprise: *"Qui se suosque affectus clare et distincte intelligit, Deum amat, et eo magis, quo se suosque affectus magis intelligit"* ("He who clearly and distinctly understands himself and his emotions loves God and himself more the more he understands himself and his emotions.") (*Opera Quotquot,* Vol. 1, p. 256). Is there a better example of the unfolding objectification of what starts as a special and individual assignment of meanings?

2.   The ideas on which this example draws are developed with great vigor and intelligence in the works of Lon L. Fuller. See, for example, *The Law in Quest of*

Itself (Chicago: Foundation Press, 1940), and *The Anatomy of Law* (New York: Praegor, 1968).

3.   This point is important. When philosophers like Terrence Penelhum explore questions about the relation of men to their bodies, they tend to place a rather strong emphasis on the relation between existing arrangements for public identification and current modes of intelligibility. See his *Survival and Disembodied Existence* (London: Routledge and Kegan Paul 1970); but see, also, the accounts of H. H. price who, in a famous essay reprinted in Penelhum's *Immortality* (Belmont, California: Wadsworth, 1973), explores a much wider set of possibilities.

Chapter 4

The Crucial Concepts and the Facts

We have seen that there is a real problem which occupies everyone sometimes and becomes for some people a dominant pre-occupation: the problem of characterizing the inner life and distinguishing it clearly from the world outside. We have seen that it is unlikely that it is created by an illusion or a simple, though basic, misunderstanding. We cannot account for our experiences and also dissolve our claims about the "two worlds" into claims about one world. The claim that the world is simply a set of mechanical, material components breaks down because it, like all others, would turn out to be meaningless if we supposed it true. Neither is the world simply a private fantasy, delusion or hallucination. For, though the demands of meaning—those which make it possible to ask the questions—deflect us from the reductive materialist view, they also deflect us from the private fantasy world. Even purely private and orderly worlds are ruled out by the requirements of meaning. Subjective idealism fails as decisively as does materialism.

We have also seen that the issues are not just the sorts of problems about language which can be dissolved by paying close attention to the way in which the ordinary language works. Nor are they the kinds of problems which would dissolve if only we could get the logic and ontological claims straight.

In a formal way, the argument in Chapter 3 showed that we need both first person propositions *and* other propositions in order to say anything sensible and intelligible about anything. The outcome of this formal demand is a world in which there are both persons and things, both inward and outward references. But Chapter 3 suggested that the inward aspect of things does not disclose to us the "ghost" which Ryle thought of as the official mythology of Cartesianism. It discloses to us a self which is intelligible only through a double process of externalizing. One branch of this externalization shows itself in the development of rules for meaningful expressions, the other in the demand for objective encounters as the logical result of the association of meanings, criteria, and reference points.

The argument, therefore, demands a close inspection of the crucial concepts which enter into such discussions. We cannot make do with a simple reversion to theories of the self which date back to the beginnings of modern philosophy, but we also cannot succeed in simply demolishing the conceptual structures which are embedded in those concepts.

Chapter 4 is, therefore, devoted to an inspection of these concepts. The concepts of person and thing are obvious candidates for inspection. So are some of the special concepts of the inner life—dreams and images, for example. Meanings stand out as something still to be explored and with them, no doubt, the notions which enter into what seem to be meaningful actions—the concept of action itself, and the associated concepts which go under traditional names like volition and conduct. But evidently there are more technical (and perhaps more difficult) notions which such an exploration must uncover.

One of these notions is that of intention, with which go the concepts of intentional action and of intentional object. For the inner life is dotted with hopes, fears, prospects, claims, surmises, beliefs . . . the continuum runs from seemingly concrete objects of attention and intention to rather rarified and abstract objects. It forms a whole domain whose parts are marked out by nouns which name features of the inner life. But they do not name and mark out in a way which is very clear or immediately intelligible.

Another set of problems faces us with the traditional notions of universal and particular. Meanings traffic in universals (of some kind), encounters imply particulars. One cannot bump into universals, but one cannot give meaning to the process without deploying them, either. The inner life is seriously embroiled with universals, the world outside is anchored in particulars. But this is not to say that the problem we face is the intersection of a Platonic realm with the world of the nominalists. For both worlds would be unintelligible if they failed to intersect. Are the roots of philosophy's most persistent controversy in the problem we have set for ourselves here? The exploration, perhaps, will reveal the sense in which that may be true.

Evidently, too, the problems we have set out to explore must compel us to investigate the problem of relations. The analysis of first person propositions suggested that the relation of the "I" and the properties which give it meaning are internal relations. That is not simply a pun. Technically, the issue is that the "I" proved to be meaningless in abstraction from what was said about it, and vice versa. We seem to have relations which make a difference to their terms. The notion of encounter which we met in section 3.2 implies external relations.

In Chapter 4, we shall see what degree of intelligibility can be put on these notions. It will become obvious that we shall be continuing much that we have dealt with earlier, and that includes stage-setting for the same basic problems about the nature of knowledge. So far as possible, those will be held in abeyance and brought to center stage in Chapter 5.

The ultimate inter-relations of these sets of problems will then be taken up in the concluding Chapter 6.

4.1   The Concept of Person

Philosophers, like small boys, have a natural urge to take things apart. They think that, from the bits and pieces, they will discover how the thing is made to go. Small boys with old clocks have frequently discovered that that is not always the case. Philosophers, in their wisdom, know that where small boys fail clockmakers succeed. But there is not a general rule about it. The concept of person has about it the look of something which might just dissolve when taken to bits.

In this section I want, more than anything else, to discover just why that may very well be so. The concept of person, nonetheless, is about as attractive to philosophers as clocks are to small boys and taking it apart remains something of an industry. Peter Strawson's *Individuals*[1] is a recent book in which the process goes on. Strawson says following an old and grand tradition: "What I mean by the concept of person is the concept of a type of entity such that *both* predicates ascribing states of consciousness and predicates ascribing corporeal characteristics, a physical situation, etc., are equally applicable to a single individual of that single type." Usually, of course, if one said *that* about the concept of person one would expect to be able to say the same sort of thing—*mutatis mutandis*—about persons themselves. One might say that a person is a conscious being with a body, a rational animal, an assembly of properties designated by mental and physical predicates.

But let us notice just how queer all this is. We can investigate a number of interesting questions, one of which is the relation between the assembly of properties of concepts, and the assembly properties of the "entities" of which they are concepts. (Let us at least follow Professor Strawson in using, for the moment, the expression "reality" in a neutral way—meaning only whatever it is that can be marked out by concepts.)

4.11   Suppose there were, literally, two sorts of properties—designated by two sorts of "predicates"—such that, when one put them together, one had a "person." One reasonable bet is that the "entity" in question would be, literally, inexplicable. There is no way, for instance, in which it is even imaginable that corporeal states could *explain* mental states—or vice versa. We need not (though philosophers often have) set impossible standards for explanation. We need not urge that P explains Q if and only if it is true that, if P, then (necessarily) Q. It would be sufficient if one could say that, if P, then the likelihood of Q is increased. It is not necessarily true that, if Smith, a candidate for the United States Senate, says that motherhood is a form of organized prostitution, he will not be elected. But, if we know that he said it, that does help to explain why he did not get elected. It would not, at any rate, increase the likelihood of his election. But now let us suppose that a biologist, Brown, discovers that a certain collection of chemicals produces a living thing which, it later turns out, has states of awareness. Though he has told us how to assemble things which turn out to be aware, he has simply left us with a new mystery. Why should awareness attach itself to such mixtures of chemicals?[2] There is nothing in the description of the chemicals from which one could infer anything about awareness as such. Or suppose a certain psychokineticist (who we take to be one who *thinks* things into action), Parkins, discovers that he is able to think bodies into existence. *That* does not explain anything, either. It is simply a fact that, following certain psychological events, certain physical events occur. The mystery, then, is even greater than we thought it was.

4.111   The only certainty is that Smith and Parkins will both be famous men. They will not be famous explainers, but famous discoverers of important mysteries. Both of them are quite unlike those who discover that putting together two masses of uranium so as to make a critical mass will lead to the release of some energy, or that making little boys frightened of little girls may lead to homosexuality. In both these cases we can infer one state of affairs from the other. The first man is projecting forward energy states according to some set of laws. The second is bringing together some interesting psychological facts in a way that "makes sense."

There is a simple and shallow account of this situation, as well as a more complex and profound account of it. The simple account would be, of course, that statements about awareness and statements about other things have different relations to first person propositions and, as a result of those different relations, accumulating information about one does not help to explain the other. This account is, no doubt, partly true. Every "awareness property" is known in a way which allows the appropriate knowledge to be expressed with greater certainty in first person propositions than in other propositions. If I am aware, then the sentence "I am aware" carries with it more certainty than any assertion of the form "Armour is aware."

4.112   As a consequence of this, no amount of knowledge of "Armour's chemicals" adds or subtracts anything much to or from the knowledge I have, and it adds very little to any reason you would have for thinking that I was aware. The reasons for the little it does add are interesting. If you know that the amount of carbon monoxide in my bloodstream exceeds a certain amount, you have reason to suspect that I was being used as a ventriloquist's dummy, or that something more elaborate and puzzling is going on. But if you know my chemical analysis is "normal" you do not have a very good reason for thinking that I am aware if I say nothing at all. The reason that you would be doubtful about the awareness of a man with a lot of carbon monoxide in his blood is a purely statistical one: most such "people" are dead. But that does not *explain* their lack of awareness. And, if you went through all the usual motions and still found that, though full of carbon monoxide I went on talking and acting like one aware, you would have no real choice but to accept the fact.

We saw, however, in Chapter 3, that in reality first person propositions take on meanings in a way which externalizes the self and that, in the end, one needs both first person and third person propositions in order to make sense of the situation. The more profound reason that the explanations of awareness states by reference to physical states, and vice versa, is not intelligible is that meaning requires, as we saw, an inner side and an outer side. If we insist on bifurcating the situation into two sets of "predicates" and take those to designate rival kinds of properties, we are substantially lost in the very beginning.

4.113   This forces us, then, to ask questions about conceptual assembly versus actual assembly. Professor Strawson is not wrong in thinking that we apply these predicate kinds to persons. It is natural and reasonable to speak of Smith as fat (a corporeal predicate) and thoughtful (a mental predicate). It is also reasonable to imagine that he might be drowsy (a hybrid predicate, relaxed in body, sluggish in mind.) But he is not an assembly of these properties, for we haven't the slightest idea how to "assemble" such a collection. The concept of person includes the possibility of an entity which might have the properties denoted by those predicates, but concepts merely indicate the sweep of things which might be caught in the net of one who goes hunting. It is fine to say: "Look here, if you're looking for people, don't be surprised if they have bodies and minds." Concepts, in this sense, have a function—they are a little like the picture you might take with you if you wanted to find the Taj Mahal. But you would be very unwise if you thought that the Taj Mahal was assembled in the way that photographs are—for example, out of bits of chemicals on paper.

Strawson's account of "the concept of a person" is thus harmless enough. If it is thought to be the concept of person assembly, however, it may be a very harmful concept, for it is not clear that the concept of "person assembly" is a sensible one. this question is what we must now explore.

4.12   To begin with, I should like to draw some conclusions from this discussion. Persons are not actually composed, as such, of bodies and minds, or of bodies or of minds. Such notions seem to be unintelligible; they are also false in an important sense.

4.121   To be a person is not to have a certain sort of body. For one may have any sort of body and be dead. Sometimes all the systems seem to be quite all right, but the patient is dead. ("Quite all right" here just means "within the limits of tolerance experienced amongst specimens still alive.") Nor does it seem that being a certain identifiable person is the same thing as having a certain identifiable body. One who could prove that he was composed of, and only of, particles which once formed Bertrand Russell's body and that they were assembled in a Russellean pattern would not necessarily be accepted *as* Russell. Nor does "having a mind" make one necessarily a person, for many mental predicates apply quite well to some computers. Do they have "parts of minds?" One also cannot claim to be a specific person on the ground of having a certain set of mental states. Two physicists thinking of, and only of, the second law of thermo-dynamics have, for the moment, the same mental states but they are not, for the moment, the same person.

4.122   If these things do not suffice separately, they do not suffice collectively, either. A creature compiled in the laboratory of Russell particles and manifesting some thoughts of Martin Heidegger might or might not be a person at all, and might or might not be anybody in particular. It all depends.

4.123   But on what? I have argued that a person is not a hybrid of certain properties. Much less is there a special ethereal property called "personhood" which mysteriously floats about in the universe and sits itself down amongst a little pile of chemicals and minds so as to "make" a person. It is logically possible that there *is* such a property but, if there is, it still does not explain anything. It simply adds to our perplexities.

4.13   Being a person may not be a case of being an assembly of certain kinds of properties, but rather a certain *way* of having properties.

Perhaps this sounds outrageous. But bear in mind that philosophers have been saying far more outrageous things in attempts to resolve this problem. They have added one absurdity to another: persons are minds in bodies, persons are bodies with intelligent behaviour, persons are minds which imagine they have bodies, and so on. Admittedly, if you say to a philosopher that he has said one of these things, he is apt to say: "Well, I didn't really mean to say *quite* that," but what he did mean to say generally remains something of a mystery. In this context, my suggestion is not, after all, such a curious notion.

4.131   Hamlet worries and it is true, therefore, that he has the property of being a worrier. But he does not have that property in just the way that Harold Wilson does. For one thing, he exists only in fiction and Mr. Wilson keeps trying to break into reality. Having a given property does not guarantee a specific ontological status.

Words have properties. They are sometimes harsh and damning, or soft and conciliatory. But they do not have those properties in the way in which the speeches in which they occur have them, and those, in turn, do not damn the way that men do or God does.

4.132   It is worth exploring the matter of words, for can one not say of them much of what Prof. Strawson said about "persons?" They are entities—concepts are capable of marking them out. They can have "ascribed" to them corporeal predicates: there are big, black words and small, grey words. There are loud, cacophonous words and there are soft mellifluous words. We cannot ascribe to them "states of consciousness" in one sense: they are not aware of anything. But in another we can, for assorted states of mind. Indeed, they define states of mind: "I felt around for the word which would pin down my thoughts." I have given them a place in the action—pinning down, defining, or whatever. Words do "move in" on the situation and, as they accommodate themselves, they change their meanings, blending into their surroundings like chameleons.[3]

4.133   Words, I insist, are real. But they are not "really" mounds of ink, slaves chained to the Oxford English Dictionary, actual possessions of dreary old grammarians with soup-stained ties, or mysterious states of mind. All the things I have been saying about words are true: they do things, they insinuate themselves, change their meanings, heighten or confuse states of awareness.

They are entities which can "bear" all these predicates, but they do not do so, of course, in the way that people do. And they do not have properties in the way that minds do. Finally, they do not have properties in the way that rocks and stones do. (I forbear, for the moment, from talk about "material objects" though that expression denotes a certain way of bearing properties. A dress or a rock is an exhibitor of "material" so that we can say that it is, in the one case, made of silk and, in the other, that its structure is that of granite. The predicates assigned to it, in short, are the sort which suggest a process of transformation which takes place *in* something.)

Words can be said to *be* big and black, but what that means is that they are conveyed to people through the transformation of stuff (like ink on paper) which then shows itself as a shape, big and black. The way in which words have properties denoted by suitable standard predicates is, in part, that they show themselves through certain meaningful transformations of other things. The reason that they can be talked about so as to personify them, and the reason that this is not foolish within limits and is foolish beyond those limits, is that what they exhibit through these transformations of paper and ink and sound waves is *meaning*.

4.14   A person is one who shows that meaning. In legal parlance, a person is one who can be the ascribed subject of rights and duties.[4] But that is because he is, in part, the giver of meanings to things—in the sense discussed in Chapter 3. Consequently, a person has a special status in the legal system, itself a special department of rules and meanings. He has duties, too, because, as a giver of meanings, he takes from the common pool of deeds and words (the two things lawyers worry about) and becomes, depending upon *what* he takes from that pool, more or less liable for what happens.

4.141 But the person does not become a thing in the sense that a rock or a table is a thing, so he does not bear properties in that way. Rather, he gives meaning to those properties. Without that capacity, the properties are possessed, again, only in a single way, as the properties of a chemical aggregate. The chemical and the person both possess the properties, but they do so in different ways. The former has them, the latter personifies them. No one would trade his wife for a bundle of chemicals even if they were guaranteed by DuPont to be superior in potency and purity. To confuse one's wife with these is a mistake so gross that only a philosopher could make it.

4.142 Yet the mistake of confusing one's wife with a mind is no better. We might, once again, risk a look at the ordinary language. (Half a lifetime of struggling with the ordinary-language philosophers has made me aware of the dangers of that. But the ordinary language is like aspirin: too large a dose may kill you, but the right dose will only cure your headache.) We talk, ordinarily, about *"using"* one's mind. "If only he had used his mind he would have been O.K." "He has a good mind, but doesn't use it." And so on. A mind is a capacity to calculate, think, feel, or whatever. In part, like the agent intellect of Aristotle as read by Avicenna, it is the same for all men.[5]

The confusion, here, is between properties and ways of having them. One has a mind the way one has a body. One expresses meanings through them. One who would trade his wife for a good mind is "out of his mind." The presence of mental properties, like the presence of physical ones, is not, by itself, evidence of the occurrence of a person.

4.15 A person, then, is a certain *way* of having properties. But that is a species of the way of having properties which creates meaningful deeds or expresses meanings through deeds.

The creator of meanings is a person. (*If* God came before all and God *was* a person then, as John says, "in the beginning was the word . . . ")[6] But men do not create the world—they use it.

4.151 This realization is not novel, of course, but it bears on the concepts of cause, act, volition, and so on. It also bears on concepts like universal, for men are, in part, a little like the words they use: they have their properties in a way rather like (though not identical to) the way in which words have theirs.

4.152   Does this make of "persons" a kind of ethereal substance which descends on material things, the way the angels of the Lord descended on men? Surely not. Indeed, that is just what the argument opposes.

To be a person is not to be a special kind of mind; it is to be a special way of having certain properties. It can be explicated but, since it is a special way of having properties, it is not an assembly of other ways of having properties. Persons may well be substances. If, like McTaggart, one only means that a substance is that which has properties and relations, and is not itself a property or a relation, then every person is substance.[7]

4.153   Despite possible objections to it[8] McTaggart's definition is undeniably useful to us here. For if a person is a way of having predicates, then a way of having predicates cannot itself be a property or a relation, although it *is* what *has* properties and relations.

McTaggart thought men were "spiritual substances" and that might be all right if it is not just a synonym for "mental substances" or something of the kind. Men are as much (and as little) corporeal as they are mental, which is to say that they are not exclusively either.

4.154   We can explicate this mode of having properties only through a maze of closely related problems. And we can cast a fair amount of light on the problem in Chapter 5, when we talk about how it is that persons are known.

4.2 The Concept of Thing

4.21   In order to develop an account of the world inside, it is essential to say something about the world outside. We live in a world populated by both persons and things. In the interactions of our daily lives we come up against both, and it is in such interactions that we develop an awareness of ourselves as people and of the world in which we live. So much has been said about these interactions and the development of this awareness that one hesitates to say more. And yet, much of what has been said has been confused and confusing. So many of the ways in which we are supposed to have acquired knowledge of the world capture us at the outset with their simplicity and plausibility, only to leave us at the end with skepticism and confusion. I am going to consider a model of one of these views. Essentially, it is an Empiricist view, although I would not expect Locke or Hume to accept everything that I have included in it. I do not offer it as an accurate reflection of Empiricism but as a kind of composite with which even Descartes or Leibniz would be at least partially content. My purpose is to construct a plausible framework in order to pinpoint some of the important ways in which models of things have gone wrong in the past.

4.22   Things are pieces of material. But material things form a complex set of objects whose members range all the way from bonfires and electromagnetic waves to whales and jet fuel. The most striking thing about such a diversified group is, precisely, its diversification. Our interest in its members springs from either inherent curiosity or a practical need to know. Interaction with them is both inevitable and necessary, and it is through this interaction that knowledge evolves. I take it that any epistemological theory could agree with such vague generalities. Already and deliberately, I have talked about things as distinct from people. The world has been divided up into the knowers and the known. In order for knowledge to develop there must occur a relationship between persons and things, but the relationship must include two distinct relata. That separation is something that must be taken into account in explaining how it is that I acquire knowledge of those objects. I wish to emphasize that the knowledge is acquired, not innate. And, it is of the very things themselves, and not of something any more or less real.

The distinction between myself and things has been fixed upon by some philosophers as the core of a rather sophisticated theory of how knowledge is acquired. The distinction is presented as a gap, as something that must be overcome, in theory if not in practice, in order to explain the knowledge of the world. The nature of things resides in them, out there, while the knowledge that I acquire is in me. It is impossible that either the things themselves or their properties bridge this gap. They cannot literally become internal, the component parts of my knowledge. Something must do it for them, and, at least according to Locke, this something has been taken to be the causal properties of objects. Physics tells us that material objects are collections of high energy particles in motion. As such, they are continually producing modifications in their surroundings. It is only reasonable to suppose that some of these modifications occur in us as perceivers, the exact nature of which becomes rather specialized. On some accounts it would be taken as a neurological event, perhaps a retinal image. On other accounts it might be a sense-datum. Whatever variation is adopted, a fundamental problem and a basic misconception have already developed. First, the problem.

The effects produced in us by objects in the environment are supposed to play an epistemological role. They either yield, or are themselves, the components out of which our knowledge of the world is made. We need to be in a position to determine their reliability, to have our views square with the facts. Sometimes our views do not, so we need some method which will allow us to sort out those instances in which things have gone wrong from those that are reliable. A particular refinement of the view I am considering, and a kind of response to this problem, is the causal, representative view of perception. On this view, causal transactions occur between objects and our senses, and the effects of such transactions represent or are "like" their causes. Again, the particulars of how this is worked out are varied and, for my purposes, not very important. What is important, and common to all variations of this theme, is the matter of checking the effect for reliability against its cause or source. If to perceive is to perceive these effects, then confirmation becomes difficult if not impossible. For example, on a theory such as Locke's, things in their essential nature become reduced to "a something I know not what." As Berkeley shows, the question of whether primary qualities are really in, or are really like, their objects is vacuous. Even if it is true, we have no way of showing it to be true in any given case. Confirmation would require that we perceive what the theory has made imperceivable, that is, material substance, and that we treat the effects of the substance—that is, the "idea," sense-datum, and so on—as the object of perception. This latter requirement is as unintelligible as the former, although it requires a rather involved, sophisticated, though by now familiar, argument to show it.[1] What I want to avoid is any conception of a thing that makes our perception, and consequently our knowledge, of it an indirect matter. That is, our perception of a thing cannot be indirect in the sense that the object of perception is a surrogate. Such a model acts as a barrier to, rather than an explanation of, our acquisition of knowledge. However, this model does tread on a fact about things that I want now to mention. This feature of things is their perceptual aspect or appearance.

4.23   Before dealing with that, I wish to return to my claim that this model of things has produced a basic misconception. This misconception has to do not so much with the idea of things as with the idea of persons as perceivers. The process of perception, as I have presented it, construes people as having a *tabula rasa*. I do not wish to oppose this by claiming that people have innate ideas. My objection is that we are not passive in perception, as this model suggests. It is true that things impinge on us and intrude on our experience willy-nilly. Be that as it may, knowledge in its various forms is something that we acquire. "I know (that) p" is frequently used in order to mark out something that I have done. In Ryle's terminology, "know" is an achievement verb.[2] I observe, and at times carefully scrutinize, the things around me in order that I may learn about them. These are tasks that I perform, and they often require a substantial amount of time, effort, and care. I learn about the things around me by probing into them. If they have a secret nature that is hidden from me, it is not something that is locked up in their "something I know not what." It is, rather, that they have backsides, undersides, and insides that I must dig into in order to find out what is there.

Watching the rain fall, listening to the cars go by, and taking a sip of coffee are activities in which I, as a perceiver, engage. It naturally follows that they are activities that can be performed in various ways. I may closely inspect the rain as it falls, or give it no more than my casual notice. I may listen with rapture to the reading of a poem, or I may barely pay it heed. These various ways of perceiving what I have open to me make it possible for me to perceive with varying degrees of success. If I attend closely to something, it is all the more likely that what I come away with will be the truth. Close scrutiny generally pays off, but the payoff lies within the object, so to speak. The effort that I expend in taking notice of things is directed toward my discovering their nature. It is in this limited sense that objects are in command, that is to say, it is their nature that is the ultimate standard of correctness for what I say about them. If I want to know the number of legs on a centipede, or the structure of a flu virus, the centipede and the virus have in this regard the last say. If there is a discrepancy between what I say or think and the facts of the matter, then it is my thought or statement that is to be modified, not the facts. Otherwise, I must give up any pretence of truth or accuracy.[3] If things did not have a fixed, definite, and public nature, there would be no such thing as a description of them. If the table in front of me kept changing its shape, its location, or its color, knowledge of it would be impossible. A part of what we mean when we say "I know (that) 'p' of 'a' " is that 'a' is indeed 'p'. If we have no reason to suppose the nature of 'a' remains constant—at one moment it may be 'p', at another 'q', and at another 'not-p'—knowledge would be impossible. "Knowledge of 'a' " entails that 'a' has some semi-permanent features that can be discovered. These discoverable features likewise entail that the *esse* of 'a' is not *percipe*. For us to be able to enquire into the nature of things, they are not, and cannot be, mind-dependent.

4.24   The stability of things is a necessary condition for knowledge. Without it there would be no way to give application to the claim that, for example, "the sky is blue" is true. As important, but perhaps not so obvious, there would be no way to make out such a claim as false, either. Just as it would be impossible to correctly describe a state of affairs, it would also be impossible to be mistaken about it. Looking, listening, sniffing are all perceptual modes of enquiry. As such, they presuppose something that can be enquired into. Whether or not they are successful on this enquiry is only one half of the issue. Looking and not finding, or listening and not hearing, are just as *bona fide* instances of looking and listening as are those that succeed. What is needed is not success in any particular instance, but the chance of success in general. If I have looked succcessfully, then I have seen what is there. If, in any meaningful sense, I have looked without success, I have failed to see what is there. If "what is there" is perceptually fluid, or is whatever I say that it is, or is whatever I see it to be, then I could not have failed to perceive it. There could no more be an incompatibility between what (I say) I perceive and what is actually the case than there could be a compatibility. Let me give an example. Suppose that the table before me is now blue, now yellow, now green, and so on. There is no predictable pattern or reason for the changes that occur. The best that could happen is that I might say that it is blue, when in fact it is. Why could this not count as a correct perception? All that would be needed to protect it would be a temporal restriction. So far, nothing in this is conceptually impossible. A child's kaleidoscope changes likewise. One may not be able to say what color it is *simpliciter,* but one can say that it is *this* color when held in *this* position at *this* moment.

However, a kaleidoscope presents no special problem because the changes that occur in it are determinate. Something may be now (predominately) blue, and later (mainly) red. That would require only a second look and a different description. The only difficulty there is methodological, because for some things, a glance is not enough. One must look carefully on several occasions over a period of time. Repeated attempts such as this make sense only because the problem is a matter of refining the method to fit the circumstances. The magic world that I wish to rule out is one in which no refinement would ever stand a chance of being successful. I can modify my efforts to determine the nature of something, so long as that thing has a determinate nature. Such efforts as these may fail, but "failure" in such instances means "not having correctly discovered the determinate nature of the thing." Mistakes may occur because I, as a perceiver, have not been as exacting as I should have been; that is, I should have used a tape measure rather than a piece of string. Errors may happen because of unforeseen hindrances; for example, the fog suddenly rolls in and it is impossible to tell if there are tanks or trucks in the distance. Whatever the nature of the breakdown, if it is to make sense, it must be attributable to the method rather than the inherent nature of things. To even characterize the alternative is difficult, if not impossible. "Misjudgment" or any of its conceptual kin will not apply, since they obviously refer to a portion of the procedure that has gone wrong. We need to be able to say that the proper kind of investigative procedure has been launched, but that the nature of the things being investigated is such as to prohibit success. But that comes very close to being contradictory. How could the procedure be of the correct kind, if failure was the guaranteed result?

One aspect of things that has received considerable attention in discussing our ability to know them has been their appearances. I have been arguing at length that our concept of a thing involves the idea of stability and public access. It may not be clear how the idea of appearance can fit in with such an argument. Objects are, as a matter of fact, relatively stable. But appearances which are a part of the real world, seem to be fluid. Frequently "appearance" and "reality" are introduced as a contrasting pair. Reality has the stability that I have been arguing for, but appearance does not. It may be impossible for something to *be* both round and square, but it is not impossible for it to appear that way. Whatever the relation between the appearance of a thing and its real nature, it is, simply, a fact that appearances are sometimes deceiving.

From the history of contemporary epistemology the Argument from Illusion is perhaps the most familiar device used for dealing with appearances. The argument has many guises, but generally it includes something of the following form.[4] A round object such as a coin viewed from the proper perspective may appear elliptical. Rigid metal objects such as coins do not alter their shape simply because they may be looked at from different points of view. If we accept this, we are led into a contradiction if we also believe that, from each point of view, we are seeing the coin as it really is.[5] Or, on placing our hands in a vessel of water, if it seems hot to one and cold to the other, we are again led to a contradiction if we assume that throughout, the temperature remains the same. At the very least, appearances are puzzles; at most, they pave the slippery road to skepticism. If we accept the contradictions mentioned above, and are impressed with the fact that it is the appearance of things that we perceive, we are not far from concluding that the object of our perception is not the thing itself. For example, if the coin is round while what we perceive is elliptical, then what we perceive is not the coin, since it cannot be both round and elliptical. One road out of this dilemma leads to sense-data. Appearances in the form of sense-data become the proper objects of perception. The coin is round; the sense-datum is elliptical. That dualism permits us to avoid saying that the same thing is both round and elliptical. However, as with any dualism, we are left with the problem of saying how the two parts are related. So long as appearances are considered as contrasted with reality, it seems doubtful that they will provide a reliable path to the nature of things. We are in danger of being left with the world of reality—the way things are—and the world of appearance, the way things are not. One begins to wonder if the alleged benefits of introducing sense-data are not more apparent than real.

4.25 Appearances have another dimension which, if not properly understood, can further the problems that I have been discussing. I have insisted that things be considered as having a semi-permanent, public nature. However, along with the notion of appearances comes the notion of privacy. This is sometimes developed under the heading of perceptual relativity. It is an undeniable fact that the round coin may look elliptical to you, and different to me. Not only are appearances deceiving, they are multiple and even idiosyncratic. This multiplicity of appearances has been cited as the reason for saying that one thing *cannot* appear the same to different people. That is a very odd conclusion, but it has been drawn, for example, by Ayer.[6] If appearances become sense-data and sense-data are taken as component parts of experience, all that is needed to make appearances private is to consider experience private. If a particular experience of mine is private, this may mean that only I have it, or, that only I have access to it. The former—call it privacy of ownership—means that no one can have quite the same experience that I have. No one is quite like me, as a matter of general psychological fact, or in terms of specific points in space and time. For example, if we both observe a blue patch, your observation must be different from mine. The physical differences alone are enough to guarantee this. We may both agree that the patch itself is blue, and publicly observable, while still insisting that it looks one way to you and another to me. Yet, at best, this argument establishes that there is a difference between what you and I perceive, and not that what we perceive is private to ourselves.

4.26 In order for these different experiences to be private, they must occur in one's mind. The things that occur in your mind are not only different from those that occur in mine, but also I have no adequate access to them. To convey this point, one often adopts a special mode of language which, at least on the surface, looks to be autobiographical. If I say: "it *seems* to be red," "It *sounds* like a bicycle," or "It *smells* like garlic," I am not committing myself to its real nature. I am pointing only to the effect that it has on me. But again, we have an obvious difference but no obvious privacy. What must happen is that the "look," "odor" and "sound" be taken to be as internal private entities of some kind. If we can make the entities out as different for each person and add that he is the only one (directly) aware of them, we have established them as private. However, though some philosophers may claim to have succeeded in this, I have only sketched what would have to be done. The key notion on which such an argument would rest is privileged access. *If* I have privileged access to the way in which something looks to me, then this is sufficient reason for saying that it is private. The question now has to do with the nature of the privileged access, and with the consequent nature of the privacy.

It is surely true that no one can get into my mind in order to inspect what is there, in the way that he can get into my pocket to check its contents. What this dissimilarity is supposed to show is that the contents of my mind are not accessable to anyone other than myself. In fact, it suggests that the notion of access is itself being applied in a strange way. Of course it is a metaphor, but it is important to note just how metaphorical this use of "privileged access" has become. "Access," whether it is partial or complete, earned or forced, is access onto or to something.[6] The object of access is thus always in some sense removed. If something is in the open, then all have free access to it. If there is to be privileged access, then it cannot be free and open to all. However, how could I have (privileged) access to *my* mind? There is no sense in which I and the contents of my mind are removed one from the other. I am not suggesting that everything in and on my mind is crowded onto the tip of my tongue. What I am saying is that the moments of uncertainty and confusion that

I have about those things of which I am aware are not to be explained by a metaphor of distance or removal. Issues and things are separate from me and I therefore think about them. "Glimpses," "sniffs" and in general "seemings" are all portions of my experiences which I have *simpliciter*. I might be able to obtain, and so have access to, the contents of my unconscious mind, but that is because there is some sense in which they are hidden from me. There are special efforts that I must make to uncover its secrets because its contents are not obtainable for the mere price of attending to them. But the look of something is (by hypothesis) not something hidden. Exposed as it is, it is not something that I can have access to, unless "access" means that I am, without special effort, able to say how it looks. I have access to the pencil in my desk drawer. If the drawer is locked and I am the only one with the key, then I have privileged access to it. However, if it is in my hand, then it is misleading and pointless to say that I have access to it. All that could mean is that I can effortlessly keep hold of it. I fail to see how access to the look of something is going to come to anything more, for these data of sense are not in any way removed from the perceiver. Quite the opposite; they are sometimes taken to be the basis of incorrigible knowledge, because as objects of immediate and direct awareness, they are as open and obtainable as anything could be. Perhaps that is just the point. But if it is, then that is precisely what should be said. The metaphor of access is misleading, and its qualified form "privileged access" is, if anything, more misleading. All that the latter could mean is that what may be of first order simplicity for me might be of second order difficulty for someone else. In other words, what is meant by saying that I, as contrasted with someone else, have privileged access to the way in which something appears to me is that while I just know *it simpliciter*, he may know only by asking me.

4.27   None of this gives us a very substantial notion of privacy, for the appearance of a thing is a property of the thing. The round shape of a coin is obviously one of its properties, as is its elliptical look. What has been behind the above argument is the belief that the look of a thing is detachable. If it can be successfully pried loose from the thing, it can be presented as something private. The lever that was to do the prying was the contrast between the way something is and the way it appears. There are two things that must be noted here before the issue can be put to rest. First, the look of something is not always opposed to how it is. Second, in those instances in which that opposition does exist, the look is not detachable, but still a function of the thing. Let us examine the first point. Suppose that a husband were to say to his wife, "My dear, you look lovely this evening." If she took him to imply that she only looked, but was not in fact, lovely, she would have misunderstood the logic of this claim. In a situation like this there is no contrast between how she looks and how she is.[8] Of course, there can be such a contrast. "Stripes of that kind make you look heavy set" suggests that the person is not heavy set but only made to look that way because of the stripes. Here we have the contrast, but it is not enough to make the heavy-set look detachable and private. Even when appearances are not like what actually is the case, they can still be public and predicable features of the thing.

4.3 Universals, Particulars, and the Nature of Persons, Minds, & Things

The burden of the argument of section 4.1 was that to be a person is to be a special way of having properties, a way which creates rights, duties and meanings. The gist of the argument in section 4.2 was that things have to be faced for what they are and that, whatever else is to be said about them, they are independent of persons, not reducible to states of consciousness and are, sometimes at least, material. In short, there are both persons and things, and they are different.

It is that difference, and the problem it creates, which forms the object of investigation in this chapter. The problem is a traditional one: If there are persons and things (and/or if there are minds and material objects), they either interact or they do not. Either way, tradition has it, there is a mystery which renders intractable a serious philosophical problem. If two modes of being (as we saw, briefly, in section 4.1) have nothing in common, it is difficult to see how one can be explained in terms of another, or how interaction between them is imaginable. If they do interact, they do so in a way which is mysterious and philosophically vexing. The philosophical vexation arises at least because the evidence that they *do* interact *ought* to be just the evidence which shows how a state of one is connected to a state of the other. If they do not interact, then the obvious evidence that some persons and some things share some of the same properties becomes unintelligible. If one wants to be more up-to-date in one's example, one may consider that, if Smith has a lesion in a certain (as it happens, known) part of his brain-stem, then Smith will be unconscious.[1] It is a thing, his brain-stem, which has the lesion; it is a person, Smith, who is unconscious and, surely, they share *something*. (The only question is, how?)

4.31   It is that situation which I shall begin to unravel here. I want to start by employing the suggestion which emerged in 4.1—that to be a person is to exhibit a certain way of having properties, to be a thing is to exhibit another way of having properties. It does not follow that many of the properties must be different though, of course, one may argue that a way of having properties is, itself, a property in another sense. Therefore, *some* properties will be different as a result of this situation.

4.311   Crucially, a difference between persons and things lies in their relative determinateness. A thing is what it is; a person is always to some degree indeterminate. My biographer, if I had one, would not only review what I did, he would also review what I might have done and did not. He might speak of wasted talents, lost time, missed opportunities, gross misunderstandings and so on. Even so, he is writing after I am dead, when my life is complete and its options closed. If he traffics in conditionals contrary to fact, he does so as his own philosophical peril.[2] I traffic in conditionals still open, and they are a crucial part of my life. Furthermore, I am unlike non-living things in that a description of me at a moment of time would give little or no sense of me. My life has to be tracked over a day, or a month, or a quarter century, before one can begin to glimpse me as a person. I unravel and show myself over a period of time.

To a real (but lesser) extent, this is also true of living things we would not call persons. To grasp what a lepidopter is, you must track it through egg, pupa, caterpillar and moth. It, too, unravels. It does not quite approach the status of "person" but, insofar as its life may be said to have meaning, it may be said (and sometimes is said) to have "rights." Luckily, it is not said to have duties. Dogs are a good deal closer to being persons in the same sense, though we stop short of quite calling them persons, probably on the grounds that we do not hold them finally responsible for the meaning which their lives exhibit. (Justification is an inescapably human activity.)

4.312   The point which I want to follow is this: In a special sense, those entities which unravel over time and are, to one degree or another, indeterminate, are kinds of universals—not the exotic "abstract" universals of Plato, but more nearly, the "concrete" universals of Hegel,

Bradley, and Bosanquet. I shall eschew, for the moment, the expression "concrete" universal because it suggests that all "real" universals are of the same sort. But, basically, a universal is the kind of entity which manifests itself in, participates in, and is comprehended through, more than one place or more than one time while remaining "the same entity." A particular is whatever is perfectly determinate where and when it is—the sort of thing which can be said to have only one instance. Evidently, of course, there are many modes of being a universal though only one, perhaps, of being a particular. The universal is always to some degree indeterminate: it can always appear again in another guise, it is never exhausted by any one description.

4.313   A person is like this, as we have seen, in one way; a mind, I shall argue, is like this in another way; a word is like this in a third way. A mind, as I urged in section 4.1, is something which a person has and uses. In one sense, to say that a person has or uses his mind is to say that he thinks, reasons, intuits, he understands, grasps propositions, is aware of truths, can make errors, and so on. It is to say that his activities include those sorts of things which may be intelligent or unintelligent. But it is not merely the sum of those behaviours, for it is always true that he has a mind, is in his right mind or out of it, and that it changes and can be changed. His understanding grows and shrinks, and so does his capacity for things like doing logic or developing a new form of the ontological argument. His mind is a series of available potentials as well as a collection of actualities. It is not a thing, for though it manifests itself in and through things, it is never, itself, particularized. A man's mind shows itself in an expressed belief, such as that the second law of thermodynamics is true, and that expressed belief *does* constitute a kind of thing. (For that reason it will show itself invariably in spoken or written words.) But a man's mind is *not* his expressed belief, nor a collection of such expressed beliefs. One who can express his belief on the second law can, after all, do other things as well. If he could not, he would not count as the assignor of the meanings or as a believer. We should think him a kind of recording machine. The mind is a kind of universal which appears in particulars but is not exhausted by them. It is not exhausted because it can always make another appearance. (This is no more mysterious, surely, than the proposition that an actor is not exhausted by the role he happens to be playing. If he were, he would not be an actor.)

We can now compare this situation to that of a person. One way of looking at a person is as a way of relating a set of space-time regions to a set of potentialities in such a way, in the terminology of law dictionaries, as to create a bearer of rights and duties. Because the manifestations of the person are the occasions which constitute the relevant space-time path, there is a temptation (to which behaviourists and physicalists succumb) to regard him as the sum of those occasions. The problem is that this destroys the notion of what it is to be a person. For then we cannot see how the meaningful bearing of rights and duties emerges, nor yet what the person has to do with the potentialities which distinguish him from things. Having a mind is, if you like, one step removed, still, from this. The space-time path of the person is, more or less, continuous. The space-time path of the occasions which constitute the manifestations of mind are quite sharply discontinuous. Though philosophers are nearly always intellecting, even they, thank God, are not *always* doing it. These episodes are intelligible in the life of a person who, in turn, is intelligible against the way in which he organizes the space-time regions. "Mind" is more distantly and abstractly universal. Minds may even be shared (and we know more or less when) between two or many persons, though they become manifest in particulars in a perfectly simple way. They have their own sort of reality.

Words are universal in a slightly different sense. As words, proper, they are created by persons. As we saw in 4.1, they are assigned meanings and come into being or perish in the process of being meaningful or meaningless. But they are carried by quite specific kinds of particulars—marks on paper, patterns in sound waves. They form the vehicles through which, in part, persons express the meanings in their affairs, and they form the carriers of the expressed beliefs through which minds manifest themselves. (Were there no words, minds would be expressed only through acts, as actors express themselves in mime, but the quality of the expression would leave the possibilities as vague as mime plays, charming but indeterminate.) Once given meanings, words acquire associations with the world of particulars and become, to one extent or another, fixed and frozen in their functions—a fact which may mislead us, again, into the wild view that, ideally, words might become perfectly precise. Like persons and minds, they have about them, by nature, a measure of indeterminateness. Give them a new context and you give them a new life. They are never finally exhausted.

4.32 Let us, then, suppose that this is a beginning and turn, for more light, to the other end of the spectrum—the particularity of things. Things both confront and elude us. They confront us because they are particulars or, rather, because they embody particulars in a way which is definitive of them. Minds, ideas, words and persons are always malleable to one degree or other. One chooses to make each concrete by particularizing it in one way or another. A man acts, and so embraces a particular in action. A word is pinned in a context, expressed as a mark, and so embraces a particular in another way. An idea takes a particular mode of expression for the moment and so becomes, say, Jones' view of Freud, or the thesis expressed at the Potsdam conference. Not so with a thing. It simply is. Extract it from its context and it is another thing. A given particular or set of particulars is inextricably bound up with it.

4.321   To put it another way, a man can be absorbed by a community, a word by a context, an idea by its expression, a mind by the particular expression of its ideas. But a thing is unabsorbable in that way; we must make of it what we can.

4.3211   This is the sense of confrontation, as well as the sense in which things elude us. We talk about things in words, but the words are universals, quasi-universals, or mere proper names. (A "mere" proper name, in this sense, is itself a particular. It serves to mark off *one* instance of *one* thing. Proper names in use carry with them associations with universals which allow them to function on more than one occasion. I name my farm "Hopewood," and "Hopewood" then serves to mark a sequence of particulars linked together in some way or other.)

4.3212   Usually, however, we want to say of things that they are red or blue, motor cars or tin cans, mountains or deserts. To do this is to classify them. We classify them by reference, as a rule, to the modes of experience which are associated with them—their visual or tactual properties, their smells or their characteristic sounds. But this corralling of them forms a loose fence with which we can keep them within our knowledge-finding facilities. It is possible to do this, after all, because they express their particularity through the deterinate forms of appropriate universals. But one should notice that this is only a fancy way of saying that they are "material"; the particularity of a tombstone is expressed through its material, granite, and the particularity of a dress is expressed through its material, silk. If the thing were not a granite tombstone or a silk dress, it would have to express itself through something else which could be grasped in an analogous way. Otherwise, it could not obtrude upon our knowledge-finding activities, and it would form no part of our present problem. We have to be able to know about a thing in order to worry about it.

4.3213   Notice, however, that things remain particular. The thing still eludes language in that not *everything* about it can be expressed. The chair in my study is a very particular thing. Not just any old chair whose description fits the language one would use to catalogue it will do. We are aware of the particularity of things, as well as of the things which we can know or say about them. To convey this fact, we have to resort to maps or charts which represent the space-time organized by the thing and enable us to mark off a special place occupied by just that thing. But even that does not fully express the particularity involved.

4.322   To overcome the awkwardness involved in such first-order confrontation. Philosophers and scientists tend to retreat to assorted second order objects of reflection. In one sense, the first order objects of confrontation make us uneasy and seem to promote skepticism. For they escape, in part, what we can say about them. There is an impulse to turn them into the objects of reflection which arise when we analyze our transactions with them. Internalized, those transactions are apt to be expressed as accounts of impressions, ideas, sensations, sense data, sensa, and so on. (Each of these marks out, subtly, a mode of characterizing not the thing but our reflections on our transactions with it.) Internalized, these reflections seem to be trapped, unable to escape from us. But we are clearly aware of the extent to which the reflections are not the thing and may even be tempted to announce that there *are* no things, only reflections upon things. (The unsoundness of this move stems mainly from the fact that there would be no occasion for the reflections if there were no first order encounters to reflect upon.)

Scientists and some other philosophers take another route. Rather than capture the reflections, they are inclined to express accounts of the things as accounts of the universals through which the particulars are expressed. Thus geology deals with assorted materials like granite and hematite, chemistry deals with elements embodied in particulars such as sulphur, arsenic, or gold, and physics with the forms through which the particulars appear.

4.323   These "materials," if you will, are apt to take on a life of their own. We forget that they are universals through which particulars are expressed and say: "Well, mountains are really collections of rock forms;

those, in turn, are compounded of chemical elements and those, in their turns, are energy states, ways of cutting paths through space-time." But, then, Mount Everest is not quite any or all of those things. Classical philosophical difficulties begin to show themselves as we realize that this world of abstracted universals *is* quite alien to us. A man is very unlike sulphur dioxide or a collection of atomic structures. He may have a will of iron or a granite constitution, but the metaphors pall after a use or two and become more irritating than informative.

In the succession of world states which form the subject matter of mechanics and physics, how is a man to intervene? Such "things" are what they are and men are alien to them. It makes no sense to say that by "an act of will" I interfered in a physical process. How? If I really did it, the process was physical. If it was physical it had a place in the succession of physical world-states. If it had such a place, it had a cause. If it had a cause, it was not an act of will.

But these successive states are, after all, universals—abstractions. We have forgotten that they are what particular things were expressed through. These accounts of geology, chemistry, and physics really are "ideas" in a simple and ordinary sense—they are fences and corrals by which we keep tabs on the ever fluctuating panorama of real things.

4.324   There is nothing wrong, of course, with this account of geology, chemistry, or physics—or whatever science one happens to want to construct. It tells us what we want to know about how we cope with things. It also tells us much about the world. It tells about the structure of these universals, which turn out to be, in crucial cases, the structure of the possibilities for experience. The "material objects" of physics are, as I argued in *The Rational and the Real*,[3] the real possibilities for experience—in so far as the physics is correct and the science is correctly delineated. (But we must understand that these possibilities can be grasped in many guises and disguises, which is why geology and chemistry are as possible as physics.)

4.3231   These objects of scientific exploration are not the things of first order encounter, for the things of first order encounter are simple actualities. Structured possibilities are always known, in part, by a process of ratiocination. The first order actualities do not start off in knowledge or awareness in that way.

As objects of encounter they are, indeed, components of experience. How else should we get to know about them? But to call them simply experiences would be to turn them into second order objects of reflection. It would be to talk about how we know them and not about what we know. We can almost certainly express all our knowledge of them in this way if, by knowledge of them, we mean the knowledge which consists of the classification of their properties. (Hence in *The Rational and the Real,* the question was: What are we entitled to say about the necessary conditions which any world must meet if we are able to talk sense in and about it? To answer this, I needed only to call attention to the independence of things in their guise as potential structures in experience, or possibilities for experience.) But, in addition, there is, of course, the knowledge that we encounter things in actuality. They enter into experience because they are there in the sense that actual particulars are there. This feature is crucial to our understanding of the world within and the world outside, and the relation between them.

4.3232   In this sense, things are particulars which are expressed through determinate forms of the properties we study to exemplify chemistry, physics, or whatever. They are met with, stumbled over, felt, smelled and, hopefully, reckoned with.

We should not think of them as "brute givens." That sort of "thing," too, invariably turns out to be a second order object of reflection and, really, a non-thing. Rather, the particulars of encounter are the sorts of things which reveal themselves through a sequence of explorations. The chair in my study first appears as something seen, then something touched, and finally as something sat upon. It is appropriate to get up, walk round it, inspect it, measure it, extract from it information in all the usual ways. Its particularity will never succumb to this process; rather, it becomes fixed in knowledge through this process.

4.33   We can now approach the central question. What is the relation of persons and things? If what I have been saying is true, the answer is plain enough. If it seems less than obvious, this is because we have formed the habit of seeking it the wrong way.

A person is a certain way of having properties. A thing is another way of having the same properties. A person has properties by expressing himself through them, so as to become partially, locally, determinate. A thing has properties because its particularity is expressed through them. The former is an active process for the most part, the second is a fixed and determinate situation. It is not just accidentally the case that they are the same properties for some given set of properties. It could not be otherwise. If a person is to express himself through gestures or words, he must have hands or a tongue, which are things. As a consequence of this, one who expresses himself in such ways takes on the advantages and burdens of things. He becomes partially determinate in the locale in question. Things must be expressed through properties which lend themselves, as we saw, to sundry scientific analyses. The person is not (as we know) in some literal way bound by the physics of his locale. He may express himself through his visions and dreams and what not if he pleases. Furthermore, he may choose to express himself through the physics of some other locale. To say *that*, is only to say that I may move to Toronto or Rangoon if I please and can find the means. Of course, to do so I shall have to express myself through such particulars as happen to be available. One takes a boat to Rangoon or an airplane to Toronto.

4.331 I express myself through things which I call—quite reasonably—my "body." (It may really be my body image, and not my physical body, which attracts my attention, but so long as it has the element of confrontation about it, the point is the same.) The situation can also be analysed as a collection of things—parts of my body. But the same properties are organized in two different ways. They are the expression of a person, and they are the expression of a particular thing. I render myself determinate through acting in the usual ways. Things are knowable through the way in which particulars express properties. Naturally they interact, for they are the *same* properties.

4.332 But the causal relations are not the same in each case just because the person is not exhausted by a particular set of manifestations and the thing *is* exhausted by the particular manifestation. I *can* choose how to express myself. This choosing is not the exercise of an occult faculty of will. (We shall show later that such notions lead to an impossible dead end.) Rather, this choosing is what we do all the time.

It is constrained only by the way in which the things will bear the action. Hence I may act by moving my feet, but not by flapping my arms and flying. We can well understand that the things called feet are amenable to being moved. What is possible to me by way of action can be determined in all the usual ways. Beyond those ways there is not some new and occult restriction called metaphysical determinism.

The theory that there is, is predicated on one of the ways of turning first order objects of encounter into second order objects of reflection. As the latter, they have all and only the properties assigned to them by physics or whatever. As the former, they have only the properties which are necessary so that this particular thing might be a foot. It must occupy so much space, take so many foot pounds of energy to move it. But to be a healthy, functioning foot it must also respond to the normal decisions of its owner. Its properties are capable of being carried by persons in *their* mode of expression as well as by things in their mode of expression. But there is nothing in the nature of the properties which precludes either.

4.333 This leaves much unsaid, mostly things about relations—the general theory of relations, the theory of how persons and things are related to their properties, and some special things about those peculiar relations called causal.

But its point is simple enough. Admit that there is more than one way of having properties, and much of the problem dissolves. But do we not *know* that persons and things have the same properties, but have them differently, as part of our general and ordinary experience? The philosophers' task, in some measure, is to construct a theory to show how this might be so. For the ambiguity of things in experience is part of the initial experience which yields the problem of the world within and the world outside.

In so far as this account makes the properties and their order primary, and the ways of having them a sort of differentia, one might regard this scheme, too, as a kind of objective idealism. Or one might say that, in so far as I have emphasized the independence of things in a new way—a way which goes beyond the doctrine of *The Rational and the Real,* since we now have a new question—I have departed from anything rightfully so-called. With respect to this problem, the classical labels are one-way tickets up the garden path. Materialism suggests a bogey-man world of machine monsters. Mind-matter dualism suggests two worlds which never meet. Idealism suggests a misleading internalisation in its subjective form, and a preoccupation with forms and structures (which is here inappropriate) in its objective form. The problem, here, is to illumine a primary mode of experience. Labels do not help much.

4.4 Things, Aspects and Relations

In the preceding sections of Chapter 4, the concepts of self, person, and thing have been taking shape. Persons and things have emerged as distinguishable entities, or, if you like, distinguishable ways or modes of being. They are, at least, describable in terms of separable ways of having or manifesting properties, radically different but intimately related intelligible patterns in the world. In the next section, some of these distinctions will emerge in the discussion of dreams as different confronted contents: dreams are our private possessions but not just verbalized fictions. By contrast things have about them an irreducible "otherness." Yet they, too, are related to us. If they were not, we could not understand them. In this section, I shall carry the analysis forward several more steps. First, I want to talk about things in terms of what one might call the confrontation phenomenon—that things are not so much "given" as confronted. Then I want to talk about that confrontation in its guise as perception, and to explore the relation between things and their perceptual (and other) aspects. Afterwards I shall explore some earlier remarks about relations, internal and external, and suggest a way of distinguishing at least some crucial features of "the world within" from the external world.

4.41   It seems to me that ordinary things—trees, rivers, stones, chairs, and cigarette butts—are neither creations of our imaginations (healthy or diseased) nor brute givens. Crudely, neither a sensationalist subjective idealism nor any kind of simple realism about perception have much hope of carrying the day. The subjective idealist internalizes his world by replacing the ordinary first order objects of perception with second order objects of reflection. He says "I do not see roses, I am aware of red patches and sweet smells." He has reflected on what he saw, and reflection produces a reductive analysis which relates all the contents to the internalities of his own experience. But he omits the experience which gave rise to the analysis. He paddles his conceptual canoe ever so easily down stream, but he cannot paddle it up again. No one can rebuild the rose from his sensations.

The simple realist makes another mistake of the same logical kind and gets either far too much, or far too little, in his world. He can say that every perception is veridical: things are just how they seem to us before reflection. But then the world is full of curious things. Or he can say that some perceptions—the preferred ones—bring us into direct contact with all or part of the surfaces of things. Either way, he is committed to a view about the function of judgment in perception. To say that all the things which appear in perception are in the world is to say that judgment constrained by perception is always right; to say that some of the things are there and some are not is to say that there is some extra-perceptual constraint which sustains some judgments and denies others. But to say that things "are really there" or "aren't really there" is, again, to replace first order perceptions with second order reflections. If we say that, we are *reflecting* on judgments and not *analyzing* the concents of the perception.

4.411   The point to notice is that the possibility of talking about things permits us, in reflection, to pass beyond the immediacies of the situation. Thinking *about* perception we can entertain the possibility, at least in language, that what is perceived is or is not there. We can pass judgment on it. But there has to be something to pass judgment on and, in *some* sense or other, that something has priority. For it is what demands explanation.

4.412   It does not, of course, have priority in some idealised or constructed world. The question "Is it really there?" has relevance in one or more of *those* worlds. If I see a pink Jack rabbit, it may or may not be the case, in a world which I have constructed to meet the special demands of some intelligible piece of theory (zoological theory, perhaps), that that jack rabbit has a place. The "naive" realist who wants to reify everything in perception in some way or other has placed demands on those worlds which are simply too vast. In every such "theoretical" world, some of the things I claim to perceive will have status only as hallucinations, or optical distortions, or occasions of imagination. But the perceptual realist who wants to pick and choose (for just that reason) will put artificial restrictions on "constructable" worlds. He is claiming, on the basis of his judgment about perception, that some one of those idealised worlds, the one which contains all and only the things he finds acceptable, is better than those which contain the things he disapproves of. He is claiming to know on the basis of perception what one can only know, if at all, on some quite different basis. He has confused perception with judgments about perception.

4.413   All the perceptual realists are right, however, in thinking that in perception we are confronted by things. We do not make them up in the literal sense. We cannot digest them into our internalised experienced for just the reason that a rose is not an assembly of sense data. It is worthwhile, here, to remind ourselves that the rose presents itself to us as a perceptual unity. It is not just a collection of properties.

Formally, it *could not* present itself to us simply as a collection of properties. It is not the redness which smells sweet, nor the sweetness which is red. It is the rose which is sweet and red. To be a rose is to be manifested in that way. Experience must come organized along some such pattern, or none of the other analyses we might want to perform would be possible. The rose, we may say, is a collection of molecules which, in their turn, are something else. Or we may say that, in experience, we associate one property with another so as to get the "idea" of a rose which we then proceed to "use" to structure experience.

But this is not so, for it is because we take the unit or the unity *as* a unity, that we get the analyses we do. If we tried to make up our "scientific theories" (those model worlds which grow in the domain of reflection) by taking random samples here and there in any old way, we should get nowhere. The thing is given as a unity. It confronts us—and then we analyze.

4.414   At this level, the question "Is it really there?" simply does not arise. We find ourselves, our models of constructable worlds, and our sense of the fitness of things in the course of our analysis of that situation of confrontation.

Were there no such confrontations, we should have no means of orienting ourselves, nothing to distinguish ourselves from, nothing to act in and on. We do not, after all, act mainly or directly in and on the constructed worlds of our theorizing. The chemist seeking a molecular structure does his seeking in an ordinary room, with a cigarette dangling from the corner of his mouth, cursing a ball-point pen which will not write, imagining the fishing hole at which he might spend his afternoon less frustratingly. He is, if you like, moving through several worlds at once, but his orientation of the moment is given by the world of confrontation. The same is true of the paranoid schizophrenic whose world of confrontation is shaped and warped by overtones of menace, and who feels creatures eyeing him as he swallows his lunch-time hamburger.

4.415   It is this world of confronted things to which our ordinary language primarily responds. It provides not the vocabulary which neatly fits things into a constructed or constructable world of theoretical entities, but the world which, as we ordinarily say, we "face." It enables us to say how things feel; it provides color words which combine descriptions and emotional reactions (there are screaming reds and sickly yellows, dull browns, and dreary greens in it). Things are describable in terms of our natural reactions or probable actions: pillows are soft, steaks tough, cheeses smelly. Woolly underwear is scratchy, and fog, usually, is chilly. In this world we can make sense of and order our acts.

4.416   It is for this reason that the subjective idealist and the simple realist fail, essentially, to grasp the point about perception. What is baffling in ths world about rainbows is not that they might be "unreal things" in the sense that they are or are not precisely definable—in a way which does not give way to hydrogen and oxygen molecules and beams of photons—but that they seem to have a location and yet fail to meet various tests which we might ordinarily apply.

Tibet is a "real place" in *this* sense because there are a set of responses which will get you from where you are now to there, while Oz is not, because there are no such directions; but this is quite different from the sense in which one or the other, or both, may have a place in some domain of theoretical explanation.

4.417   It is worth noticing that the language we normally use for the ordinary world of confrontations is never quite neutral. It always involves us. Travel boks describe mountains without the jargon of geology because they are heavily involved in the reader's practical transactions with them. A motor car is something one can drive. When we want to get away from this to a constructed second-order world, we have to temper the ordinary language with technical words—restrain its meanings, leash its implications, neutralize its emotions.

4.42   This brings us, inevitably, to the issue of perceptual aspects and the nature of things. Naive realists are frequently assaulted with accounts of the nature of perception—the factors of perspective, the observer dependence of colors, the unreliabilities of human orientation, and so on.

4.421   In the Cartesian tradition, we are invited to strip away these "secondary" properties and to imagine "things" as they would be without them. In the Berkeleyan tradition, we are invited to persist in these arguments until we see that there are no "primary" qualities, but only observers and their experiences. If we are faced, then, with questions about the regularities of things, we are invited to think of them as the product of a rather special observer, God; or, instead, to think with Kant that they are the product of an underlying organization whose nature is simply to be the categories of the phenomenal world.

If what I said in 4.41 was correct, however, all of this simply is another version of the same mistake—the confusion of first order objects of perceptual confrontation with second order objects of reflection.

4.422   It is customary to respond to this kind of argument by pointing out that, after all, if things really are "there" in the world, we would expect them to be perceived in one way from one point of view, and in another from another point of view. This seems to do well with respect to problems of perspective, though it does less well, even for its supporters, in defending from reductive analysis properties such as being colored. There is, after all, no reason to think that "atoms" are colored, because the wave phenomena which "give rise" to color are not, themselves, colored, or not in the same sense.

I shall not pursue this argument, however, because, in this context, it responds with a mistake to an argument which makes the same mistake. It suggests that, if one is a perceiver in the explanatory, reflective world of scientific entities, one will expect certain consequences to follow. If we are observers in the "scientific" world of fundamental particles, wave phenomena, and relativistic space-time, then we will expect to get information in certain forms rather than others.

This is a profound misunderstanding. We cannot be "observers" in such a world, because such a world has no "observers." It has in it only fundamental particles, wave phenomena, and relativistic space-time, together with whatever other objects fashion and the present state of the art urge one to put in it.

4.423   The question is not whether or not such worlds are "real." They are constructs which take our experience and exploit a consistent set of meanings which we can put on them in order to get an explanatory structure. That world does not interpret itself. It explains everything except the fact that the theory, itself, exists. If it could do that, it would not work, for the theory which could explain a world *and* the theory we have of that world would, obviously, be out of date. We should now have to explain the new theory which explained the old theory as part of the world—and so on, ad infinitum. It is a matter of levels of discourse. The theorizer, the observer, never appears in the theory in that way.

But the observer does appear in the immediate world of confrontations.

He is driven beyond (as we shall see in 6.1), into worlds of reflection, just because of the tension created by the impossibility of disentangling himself from the immediacy of confrontation. He cannot, in that world, quite identify himself or quite eliminate himself.

But at the immediate level, things do appear in perception precisely because they are objects of confrontation. We cannot, in that world, ask what they would be "like" apart from perception.

4.424   We can also ask whether an object which confronts me now will confront others in a hundred years and, if so, whether it will confront them in the same way. But we ought to notice that there are two different issues involved here.

One of them has to do with the manner of confrontation. If the thing only confronts me in certain contexts—in dreams or when I have delirium tremens, or after performing the spiritual exercises recommended by Ignatius Loyola—then it is clear that the route to it is specialized. If, when I follow those routes, I have experiences which have relatively little in common with each other, I assign the thing only to those special contexts. If I confront the thing whenever I am sober, have my eyes open and, pretty much independently of what I am thinking about at the moment, I suppose it to be the sort of thing which many men are likely to encounter, I assign it, again, to those special contexts. If objectivity is associated with inter-subjectivity, it is a matter of the thing having a place in a context in which many observers will find themselves.

It is not that one of these sets of things is "objective" in some exalted sense while the other is "subjective" in some occult sense, but that there are contexts—such as being sober and having one's eyes open while being oriented to the visa of Bognor Pier—which are neutral in the sense that many observers can occupy them while there are others—such as being oriented to the vision of the Virgin Mary after having performed the spiritual exercises recommended by Ignatius—which are special to certain kinds of men in certain rather special situations.

4.425   The other issue has to do with the correlations which hold between confrontations and places in the constructed worlds of reflection. These constructed worlds link things together in special explanatory patterns. In this way, we convert the immediate experience of seeing the stars hanging close in the heavens as pin-points of light into accounts of stars many light-years distant. Because we correlate a given "star-sighting" with a place in that constructed scheme of reflection, we think the experience is apt to be quite stable and others, centuries from now, will see the "same stars."

4.426   What counts in this second question is the conversion mechanism and not the mode of confrontation. It is because the "things" have correlates with places in elaborate constructed systems that some are given one status and some another.

So long as we keep these questions straight, we need not be embarrassed into Cartesianism, Berkeleyanism, or Kantianism. The perceived features of things are what they are. But we must not try to elide them into two packages—us and the world—in quite the way that the theorists would have us do. As things, they have their place in the domain of the confrontation. That domain is not the intersection of observers and things for, in it, there is no sense to observers without things or to things without observers. It is the *relation* which is primary and that is why we must turn to the vexed question of relations.

4.43   In the confrontation world of first-order perception, relations are dominant. It is the thing-as-confronted, the person-in-the-world, the phenomenon of confrontation, the modes of that confrontation, and so on, which are crucial. Abstractly put, as I suggested previously, a person was a special kind of universal which was manifested through a set of particulars, while a thing was a particular which manifested properties. The properties appear in such a scheme always as *universals,* and as abstract universals at that. The *concrete* universal is the person exhibited through his properties in a particular pattern of affairs, or the thing exhibiting properties through its place in the scheme of things. The relations particularize. If properties existed without relations, the world would be a set of Platonic abstractions.

4.431   Of course, that is not imaginably so. Nothing is ever "just red" or "just happy." There is always a red thing or a happy person. To be red is to be more than red: it is to be a particular appearance of a spatial surface; and to be happy is to be someone in a state of mind. There are, certainly, relational properties as well as properties and relations and, linguistically at least, statements about relations can always be translated into statements about relational properties. If Smith has a brother, he also has the property of being a brother. But relational properties cannot exist in splendid isolation, however the matter is put. It will turn out that there is sense in preferring relational-property language for the purpose of sorting out our problem, but the issue should not be misunderstood; relational properties are situational as much as relations.

4.432   Before we can see the significance of the initial relation or relational-property dominance in the world of immediate confrontation, it is essential to understand at least some of the traditional conundrums about relations.

4.4321   The easiest way to do this is to attempt a summary statement of Bradley's problem, and then to use our exhibition of what is wrong with it as a way of showing how the situation might feasibly be construed.[1]

Bradley thought there was a problem which went like this: Suppose you have two entities, A and B, and a relation, R, between them. The possible characterizations of the situation are that (1) R is a separate term which stands between A and B; (2) R is a property of A; (3) R is a property of B; (4) the whole, ARB, is a single entity. If R is a separate term, it must be related to A and B by two more relations—and so on to infinity. If R is a property of A, something else relates AR to B, and if R is a property of B, something else relates A to RB. If they are "all one," there is no relation between them. Bradley concluded, after pursing these issues for some distance, that the choices lay between the notion that reality is a single trans-relational unity, and the notion that there is an infinite regress of relations. But the latter is unintelligible. Therefore, the former holds.

We lack the space to pursue all the subtleties of Bradley's arguments in *Appearance and Reality,* but it is obvious that what Bradley is here espousing is the logical form of the "separate entity" and "adjectival reduction" theories of relation. These theories have their source in two considerations. One has to do with experience, the other with the structure of discourse. Experience suggests something odd about relations—that they are not discriminable in experience. It makes no sense, if someone says "the shovel is in the hole," to search for the "in" as well as the shovel and the hole, for the sense of "in" is parasitical on the notions of shovel and hole. This suggests that the view that relations are reducible to something else has some plausibility. But the structure of language is such that relations are generally marked off by special kinds of expressions, and *that* suggests the "separate entity" thesis.

4.4322   It is a mistake, I think, to think that relations and qualities, or relations and non-relational properties, are distinct to begin with. Qualities exist only in so far as they are the qualities *of* something, and relations exist only in so far as they express the manner in which something is the quality of something else.

4.433   Many standard sorts of formal logic muddle the issue by providing very limited forms. "For any x, x is f and x is g"; and "there is an
x such that x is f and x is g" are samples of standard logical devices which
derive from Russell-Whitehead schemata, and which are quite
typical of accounts of "propositional form."[2] Here, we are provided only with a "logical" place for "x" or "all x's" (where what x represents is
the name of something), for properties specified as f and g, and for
logical relations such as that which holds between conjoined properties.
Ways of having properties can only be represented as more properties,
and so on, ad infinitum.

4.434   Ordinary discourse is not like that. How, formally, would we actually represent "the shovel is in the hole?" "There is an x such that x is
a shovel and x is in the hole?" What the original proposition said was
that there was a referential whole—the shovel in the hole—such that
some features of it (the shovel and the hole) are discriminable in a way
which suggests that the shovel might have been somewhere else. But this
is much more complex than the standard "propositional form" suggests.
It involves a presentational whole, a reference to possibilities, and a
number of ways of having properties. The shovel is not related to the
property of having a digging edge in the way that it is related to the property of being-in-the-hole. Nor is it, being a shovel, related to being-in-
the-world in quite the way that the hole is. To be a shovel is to stand in a
certain relation to somebody—otherwise the thing is not a shovel, but
merely an arrangement of peculiar things.

   The worlds of philosophers are malleable. Ideally constructed,
Russell-worlds may, of course, be trimmed to fit Russell's propositions.
The confrontation world has to be coped with as it is.

   In the confrontation world, at least, a relation is simply a way of giving a concrete context to a quality. It is not "another thing," but the
quality is not something apart from its context in that world, either.

4.435   If we now make the distinction between those relations which are
internal—dependent upon their terms, making a crucial difference to
their terms—and those which are external (indifferent to their terms), we
can see how some of the distinctions we want to make can be made. But
we must make them in a way which does not cause the situation to collapse back on itself, and create the "relation as adjective" or "relation as
independent thing" problems.

4.4351   A shovel has the property of being internally related to its function. It is simply not a shovel if you cannot dig with it. But it is externally related to its present place. You could not dig with it if it could not be moved.

The hole is internally related to its space—change its space, and it is another hole, or no hole at all. But it is externally related to the property "containing a shovel." As a *place* it can manifest itself through many different properties. The shovel as a particular thing can manifest itself through many different properties, but only some of them result in its being a shovel.

4.4352   A person, on the other hand, is a concrete universal which manifests itself through many properties accidentally (through external relations) but through others essentially; intentions, acts, and so on make a given person just that person and not some other. The relation between a person and a thing is always an external relation, never an internal one.

4.4353   But in none of these cases are there *ultimately* separable qualities and relations, both of which are phases of the way in which the thing or person manifests itself. It must be manifest in *some* context, and it must manifest itself as having *some* property. Language distinguishes the phases because the entailments and the implications of the ordinary language are, in this way, phase dominant. That a thing is red entails that it is somewhere, but it does so in a particular way which is dominated by the context. Hence we distinguish, in thought, the phase in which it comes to have the property, and the phase in which it exhibits its context. Since they are potentially open to re-arrangement, we use different words and sorts of words to convey the fact.

4.436   Yet when we see how the language really works, we see that it is not separate kinds of entities which are involved, but simply different phases of manifestation. Thus we are not tempted, at this level, to distinguish qualities and relations in a way which gives rise to Bradley's problem. If we choose to exhibit the world as a formal Russellian construct, we may have to face that problem—but, then, our difficulty might be a ground for not choosing that particular kind of construction.

Because the role of things in confrontation is such that the confrontation determines the form of our expression and not vice-versa, we are compelled, no doubt, to regard the world of first order perceptions in whatever way illumines the phenomenon of confrontation.

Here, the essential point is that we can take the first order world as we find it. The temptation to be resisted is not the temptation to question its ontological primacy—that may be desirable or undesirable—but the temptation to confuse it with assorted worlds of constructive reflection.

4.44   It is evident that our linguistic and epistemic transactions with first order things of confrontation may turn them into second-order objects of reflection. These transactions are very general: describing generally demands classification and the classificatory system is, in itself, an object of reflection. "Pointing out," even, is on some occasions the location of a thing in a constructed system demanded by the needs of inter-subjective communication. Knowing, in the sense of "having knowledge of," has the same result: to "know" the thing in this sense is to have abstracted it from the confronted field of perception—the immediacy of the space-time transaction—and to have rendered it available on one or more subsequent occasions.

4.441   Should we, therefore, urge that the encounter itself transforms the thing from the domain of first order confrontation to the domain of second order reflection? If we were to say that, we should face a paradox: the first order things would have disappeared into a kind of pseudo-Kantian noumenal world. (There is, indeed, a sense in which we may think of this paradox as one of the foundations of the Kantian dichotomy. The thing can only, on Kant's view, be grasped in and through the categories of the understanding. It thus stands divorced from itself.)

4.442   It is, of course, just this paradox that I want to avoid, by suggesting that much of the ordinary language is the language of encounter, and that knowledge in encounter is quite different from knowledge in reflection. The things referred to in the language of encounter are ungainly or soft or pleasant or poorly formed. The primary "reference" to them is that of encounter: "Go three blocks south past the Coca-Cola sign, cut through the Cadillac dealer's lot, and you'll find this funny little tailor's shop"; or: "Look out, that's a tiger." The language is formed to enable us to find our way around things; the properties ascribed to things are markers and indicators for encounters. They correlate with reflective constructions—the real estate assessor's maps and descriptions, the accountant's analysis of the tailoring business, the zoologists's account of the tiger and its environment. But one does not look to the accountant's description to find the tailor shop, one does not expect one's immediate experience to be reported in the assessor's report, and one prefers a big game guide's account of the jungle to the zoologist's report if one really needs to avoid the tiger. Knowledge by encounter involves being changed, re-oriented, and made differently responsive. One may simulate the experiences described in a travel book or novel, but travel books and novels are quite different from the systematic descriptions which constitute knowledge in the academic sense—though, of course, one may establish connections between the two. It is this shift which makes reflection relevant to encounter, and vice versa.

4.443   The agronomist and the farmer both know about crops, and though what each knows should correlate with what the other knows, they are not identical. What the farmer knows will lead you to established farming practices. What the agronomist knows will create understandings of plant life. But reading books about pig breeding is not the same thing as pig breeding, and one who has bred pigs knows something, as we say, "not in the books." It is sometimes thought that this is a deficiency the writer of the book ought to have known, and would have put into his book if only he had known. But that is not so. It is likely that the author *has* bred pigs, too. What he knows is not in the books because knowledge in encounter just is not knowledge of reflection.

4.444   One of the difficulties of understanding the philosopher's accounts of second-order reflections is, frequently, that they are made to sound as if what is being described is a new and idealised encounter. But that is rather like saying that there should be an idealised experience of pig breeding, although the book on pig breeding is not describing an encounter at all. So the philosophical analysis of second-order reflection is not a pseudo first order encounter, either. And the use of the ordinary language we use to facilitate encounters is not a pseudo-description of a domain of reflection.

4.5 Dreams

For thousands of years, dreams have held a fascination for man. They have been looked on as idle fancies, or as holding the secret to man's future, past and present. Whatever significance dreams properly have in man's life, their inherent nature seems an impenetrable puzzle. I am concerned to investigate the sense in which dreams comprise a legitimate segment of our experience. For Descartes, their legitimacy was so obvious that one could genuinely question whether an experience occurred when one was awake, or when one was dreaming:

> But in thinking over this I remind myself that on many occasions I have in sleep been deceived by similar illusions, and in dwelling carefully on this reflection I see so manifestly that there are no certain indications by which we may clearly distinguish wakefulness from sleep that I am lost in astonishment.[1]

4.51 Descartes was "lost in astonishment" because the nature of a dream experience is the same as a waking one: the mental events that occur in sleep are of the same variety as those that happen when awake. The similarity is so close that sometimes no difference is noticed. But there is a difference.

Dreams are not veridical, or not dependably so. No one who wishes a reliable foundation for his beliefs would look to a dream. The question, however, is not whether or not dreams are informative. Regardless of how one may use dreams, there is the prior question of their nature. Descartes finds them deceptive because their nature is indistinguishable from the mental activity that occurs when we are awake. Russell holds a similar view.

> What, in dreams, we see and hear, we do in fact see and hear, though, owing to the unusual context, what we see and hear gives rise to false beliefs. Similarly, what we remember in dreams we do really remember; that is to say, the experience called "remembering" does occur.[2]

4.52 I am going to consider a head-on attack of this view by Norman Malcolm. He wants to argue that Descartes is wrong in thinking that there is a similarity between the mental activity that occurs when we are asleep, and that which happens when we are awake. The nature of his attack is such that if he is right, dreams turn out to be no more than a special way of talking. In fact, if he is right about dreams, there would seem to be nothing to prevent his argument from spreading to all of our private mental life. For our purposes, then, it is important to show that he is wrong. To demonstrate this is really to uphold our thesis; it is our contention that there is a world within, so it is beholden on us to show that attempts to reduce dreams to dream reports are mistaken.

4.53   It is Malcolm's contention that dreaming is not at all analogous to being awake. Suppose I claim to have dreamed of a tropical isle. Neither Descartes nor Malcolm would place any faith in the reliability of such an experience, but they would disagree on the nature of the experience. Descartes would argue that perceiving a tropical isle, and dreaming of one, have in common an awareness of something occurring in one's mind. In the real situation there is, of course more; in the dream situation, no more. In both, a mental activity occurred—it was reported in the dream, and was described in the perception. Malcolm challenges this parallel. He does not make it clear in a positive way what he takes to be occurring when we dream, but he does make it clear that he does not think that it is like what goes on in our minds when we are awake. His principle line of attack is via the notion of "remembering." He argues that there is something very misguided in saying that we remember our dreams:

> We speak of "remembering" dreams, and if we consider this expression it can appear to us to be a misuse of language. When we think philosophically about memory the following sort of paradigm comes most naturally to our minds: I spoke certain words to you yesterday. Today I am requested to give an account of what those words were. The account I give is right or wrong. This is determined by whether it agrees with your account and that of other witnesses, perhaps also by whether it is plausible in the light of what is known about you and me and the circumstances yesterday, and perhaps by still other things. But when I speak of "remembering" a dream there is nothing outside of my account of the dream (provided that I understand the words that compose it) to determine that my account is right or wrong.[3]

4.531   What is most striking about this account of remembering is what Malcolm does not mention. His paradigm is inadequate because it leaves out the most crucial feature. Whether or not an account of what was said yesterday is right or wrong is determined primarily by its being an accurate rendition of what was said. Regardless of whether or not you and I agree in our rendition, regardless of whether or not other corroborating witnesses can be found, and regardless of the plausibility of the account, if it is not in fact what was said, then it is wrong. If it is what was said then it is right. It is true that the testimony of eye witnesses is a generally reliable means for determining the accuracy of an account. The more people that agree, the less likely it becomes that a mistake was made. The same thing is true if it can be shown that the report is consistent with the kind of thing that you and I would most likely have been discussing at that time. General plausibility is used only because it increases the likelihood that we have got to the event in question. But witnesses can be mistaken, and plausibilities can be miscalculated. Certainly if these were the rule rather than the exception, we would have a conceptual confusion of monstrous proportions. They are the exception, but this alone is sufficient to show that Malcolm's paradigm is off. An account is right if it reproduces what was said; it is wrong if it does not. The things that Malcolm mentions are useful, but they are useful ways of determining *if* the account is accurate.

What Malcolm has confused is *how* one determines something with *what* it is that is to be determined. In other words he has left out of his paradigmatic account the essential purpose behind remembering and focused instead on those things which, in all likelihood, can bring that purpose about. For example, the corroboration of witnesses is desirable, but only to the extent to which it tends to establish the truth of the report. A paradigm, if it does anything, displays the logically essential components of a concept. To leave out of a paradigm the central feature is rather a surprising thing, though we shall see later on that this omission fits right into Malcolm's more extended account.

4.532   It may be that all that I am doing is to insist on what is worthwhile in correspondence theories of truth. I suspect that Malcolm would acknowledge most of what I have said, but go on to point out that implicit in my argument is the suggestion that there is a "real" state of affairs that is somehow separable from any epistemological grip on it. Certainly the objective and final determinate of the accuracy of a memory report is something like its correspondence with what in fact was said. But how significantly can one speak of "what in fact was said" apart from ways of finding out? The question that this raises is the question of the Wittgensteinian use of "criteria."[4] I confess to sympathetic confusion on this topic, but for the moment let me be the traditional devil's advocate.

Of course one needs ways of finding out, since what is at stake is a check on the accuracy of something. I am not suggesting that there is some mysterious way of recreating what was said so that it could be directly inspected in its pure state and compared with an offered rendition. To suggest that there might be some direct access to a past fact without the use of witnesses, established plausibilities, or written versions is at least foolish and possibly self-contradictory. I am not saying that we should do without Malcolm's criteria; I am only pointing out that they are criteria *of* something. In the example quoted, they are the criteria of the rightness or wrongness of a claim. And again, a claim of the sort in question is right if it accurately reproduces what was said; it is wrong if it does not. This is the reason behind employing criteria (or symptoms or evidence, for that matter). Anything that is to count as a paradigm of remembering must include reference to this. The function of a paradigm is to display those features of the concept that are essential to it. To present a paradigm of remembering without mentioning that what is at stake is something like "repeating what had occurred," is to leave out its *raison d'être*.

The reason for going on at length about remembering is that Malcolm has made the same mistake with dreaming. Let me quote again the last sentence of the last passage. "But when I speak of 'remembering' a dream there is nothing outside of my account of the dream (provided that I understand the words that compose it) to determine that my account is right or wrong."[5] The quotes around remembering are important. They indicate that to Malcolm, the concept is minimally functional under circumstances like these. But he is not right. There *is* something outside of the account of the dream to determine if the account is right or wrong. It is the same kind of thing that I mentioned in my earlier argument: it is the state of affairs that is in question. In this case, it is the dream. More precisely, one should say the *experience* of the dream. Also, if one takes the account of the dream as something written or spoken, then there is, in a sense, a second item: the recollection of the dream. Malcolm is patient and acute in pointing out the difficulties that are present in talking in this way, and I will do my best to handle them in their turn. However, what must first be done is to make it clear that what I have said makes sense, and this is difficult to do, because it is so basic. I am saying, very simply, that there are such things as dreams. These are very familiar items of everyone's experience, and just as familiar is the experience of remembering these experiences. This last sentence makes no claims that are philosophically debatable. It gives descriptions that are, as a matter of fact, true. As such, they provide the data out of which philosophical theories and disputes may generate. They are not arguable, and Malcolm clearly does not want to debate them.[6] He expresses surprise that anyone might interpret his remarks as being in possible conflict with them. What I want now to do is to investigate the reasons that he gives for explaining away an apparent conflict.

4.533 Malcolm allows that it is proper to speak of remembering a dream, but we must not forget how different this use of language is from the paradigmatic one.[7] In the paradigm, there was something outside of the account which served as a criterion of correctness of the account. In a dream report, there is no external standard.

> If I remember today how someone flapped his arms yesterday then yesterday I must have been aware of the flapping arms. Does it follow that if I remember today a dream of last night, then last night I must have been aware of the dream or of its 'contents?'' First, there is no warrant for thinking that "remembering a dream" carries exactly the same implications as "remembering a physical occurrence." Next, considering the impossibility of establishing that someone was aware of anything at all while asleep and the possibility of establishing that he dreamt, how can it *follow* from his remembering a dream that he was aware of the dream when he dreamt it? Finally and most importantly, what is the *meaning* of this philosophical claim?[8]

4.534 Let me deal with Malcolm's points in the order that he raises them. He says that there is *no* warrant for thinking that "remembering a dream" is like "remembering a physical occurrence." Surely there is *prima facie* warrant for thinking that there should be some parallels, because they are both instances of remembering. In order for them both to count as remembering, they must have as their ultimate goal the accurate reconstruction of a prior state of affairs.[9] But what is one to make of the differences that Malcolm has mentioned? All of them are real, but none of them do the job he wants done. There is a sense in which Malcolm is correct in saying that there is no external standard for judging the correctness of a dream report: dreams are the exclusive property of the dreamer; that is, no one else may experience my dream. I am not the fundamental source of information about my having flapped my arms. Someone else may have observed this more closely than I, and have more detailed and reliable information on it. The concept of dreaming does require different handling. I think what Malcolm has done is to extend carelessly the application of the private language argument. It is probably true that we learn to speak of our dreams in the same way that we learn to speak of flapping our arms. As children, we blurt out in a confused and tentative way whatever moves us, only to have it publicly corrected by others. The criterion of correctness that everyone must bump up against is a public one. But one of the things that such buffeting around teaches us is how to talk about private experiences, that is, experiences that no one else has had. It is true that "an 'inner process' stands in need of outward criteria."[10]

The difficulty arises, however, because Malcolm talks as though the significance of the criteria lay solely in the correct application of a description, and that this is something that could be significantly discussed apart from what was being described, that is, the dream.

> . . . When someone on waking "remembers" certain incidents, and we know they did not occur, then we say he *dreamt* them, i.e. they "occurred in a dream." There is not a *further* question of whether a dream or the events of a dream really took place during sleep.[11]

Consider the argument in this quotation in light of what has been said about remembering in general. Normally, one would insist that the first sentence in the quotation be changed to read: when someone "remembers" certain incidents and we know they did not occur, then we say that he could not have remembered them. If there is sufficient reason for saying that the "remembered" event did not happen, then that is, *ipso facto,* sufficient reason for saying that he did not remember it. There is an ambiguity here: it is not clear what is known not to have happened. Presumably, what Malcolm has in mind is that the above exchange is likely to occur with someone who is unsure of how to talk about dreams. If it appears that he is reporting the occurrence of actual events, then we correct him as Malcolm says. If, however, we are dealing with someone who knows how to talk, then Malcolm's modification becomes quite strange. Under these circumstances it is reasonable to assume that the referent of "incidents" and "they" are the same. It is difficult to imagine circumstances in which "incidents" might refer to one variety of events and "they" another; for example, "incidents" might refer to events in a dream and "they" to events in the real world. Yet this ambiguity of reference is just what Malcolm's argument depends on. When, on waking, someone reports having remembered certain incidents, what sense is there in which we could be in a position to know that those events did not occur? Consistency requires that the expression "those events" refers to the events in the dream, and no one but the dreamer is in any position to say anything about them. Malcolm is in a dilemma. If the remembered incidents are dream ones, then it is doubtful that anyone other than the dreamer could know anything about them. If the incidents are public, then, of course, we could know that they did not occur, and this would be sufficient to establish that he did not remember. The way out of the dilemma is to mix up the referents. If the remembered incidents are dream ones, and the ones that are known not to have happened are real ones, the conflict dissolves. However, there does arise a further issue of the sort that Malcolm says cannot. He says: "There is not a *further* question of whether a dream or the events of a dream really took place during sleep."[12] This is correct only because of the general point that if there is no *prima facie* reason to question the accuracy of a recollection, then one does not raise the question; one does not question what is not questionable. But of course that is not Malcolm's point. What he wants to show is that it does not make sense to raise the question of the real existence or nature of a dream apart from its report.

"Since nothing counts as determining that my memory of my dream is right or wrong, what sense can the word 'memory' have?"[13] The question is rhetorical, but the answer is not an unequivocal "no sense." The answer is supposed to be that the meaning of the word is much different from its "normal" applications. But since, as I have contended earlier, Malcolm misunderstands those applications, it is difficult to know how to respond. What bothers Malcolm is that the only thing for which there is public criteria is the occurrence of the dream report, and the fact that the events could not have happened in real life. There are no criteria for the dream itself. Malcolm is confusing when he comes to deal directly with the question of the relation between the dream and its report. He allows that the dream and the waking convictions are not identical in the sense that the morning star and evening star are identical.[14] The conclusion that he wants to draw is that " . . . dreams and waking impressions are two different things: but not two logically independent things."[15] I find the conclusion most unclear, and even more unclear is the reasoning leading up to it. He asks if it is possible to have the conviction of having had a dream without the dream, and answers that it is possible for a man to believe falsely that he did not have a dream. The example he gives is of a man who has a dream, wakes up and reports it to someone, falls back asleep, and wakes up again thinking that he has had a dreamless sleep.[16] This example will not do and Malcolm rejects it, for the only portion of the sleep that is significant contains both dream and dream report, so it hardly illustrates their independence. He does not give another example, but says that "if we try to suppose that mankind might have told dreams without ever having dreams, or might have had dreams without ever having told dreams, we are in an embarrassment as to what would establish the existence of a dream.[17] He is right. This would be a doubtful situation, but it is not the one that we need suppose. All that we need to suppose is that on some occasions people have had dreams, without reports, and on others have given reports without dreams.

4.535 However, to show that dreams are logically independent of dream reports is not to show very much. What must be done is to develop a general account of dreams which makes this sensible, and which takes into consideration the problems that Malcolm raises. What such an account would center on is, to put it in a linguistic mode, the use of the first person constructions. Put non-linguistically, it involves knowledge of oneself and of what one is doing. I earlier conceded that our language is and must be a public one, meaning that the criteria that we employ in mastering the language are public. I also claimed that in such a language one of the things that we learned to deal with were private experiences. Malcolm asks us to imagine what it would be like if no one ever reported a dream and if every "dream report" were dreamless. He suggests that we would have no concept of dreaming, and I think that he is right. If those conditions applied, we would be asked to develop a concept in complete isolation, and I think that the impossibility of that is well demonstrated by the private language argument.[18]

But Malcolm is asking the wrong question. It cannot happen, and it is not necessary to require, that we develop the idea of dreaming in the absence of any public criteria. A child says that something happened and we respond appropriately. If it is wild in nature and the report occurs shortly after waking we say: "Oh, what a delightful dream," and so on. But the language game of dreams does not develop by itself. The speaker learns to report publicly observable occurrences as well as his wishes and fantasies. What is at stake is his reliability as a speaker, his ability as a communicator, and his accuracy in remembering and describing. After his credentials as a language user have been established, he earns our trust, and having our trust merits the assumption that, other things being equal, what he says is so. Although that assumption is a terribly important one, it is not one whose strength remains the same in all situations. The more the contents of what he says are public, the more the assumption is open to challenge, and the more they are private the less it is open to challenge. This ever increasing reliance on the sincerity and truthfulness of the speaker is not something that we must merely accept as a degenerate form of communication.[19] Malcolm is correct in pointing out that there are no external criteria of the ordinary variety in dream reports, but he is wrong if he means to say that this means that the question: "In addition to the report was there a dream?" is a kind of unanswerable nonsense. It is neither unanswerable nor nonsense. The general answer is "yes, there was a dream, unless the speaker wished to deceive us." I do not wish to deny that when talking about the relation between dreams and dream reports we are not thrown into a kind of epistemological grey area. A very real part of our dream repertoire is crowded with uncertainties. "I can't be certain but it seemed like Chip and that he was actually part of the swing." The uncertainty and the verb "seem" indicate a lack of conviction of the part of the dream reporter. In the case of public events, we could insist that the facts be determinate, and that any lack of certainty is to be attributed to the person remembering, and perhaps to the circumstances of the recollection. With dreams it cannot be quite so simple. As Malcolm acknowledges, we may dream of the most impossible things, which include vague and indeterminate events. "It was Chip and it was not Chip" is the kind of thing that we allow in a dream report because it is the kind of thing that we experience in a dream. One gets the impression from reading Malcolm that if this talk of experiencing something in a dream really made sense, there would have to be an independent public criterion for establishing its existence. Since there is no such criterion, it is at least epistemologically prudent for us to concentrate our attention on what is public—the report.

4.536   But this ignores some of the more important, albeit subjective and vague, aspects of dreams. There is no denying the feeling that they are actual occurrences, and that sometimes we do and sometimes we do not do justice to them in our descriptions. When we have this feeling of having given an inadequate portrayal of a dream the process of revision is, of course, quite different from revising a weather report. In section 4.2 I claimed that if there was a discrepancy between description and object, the object was "in command." The description had to be modified to fit the facts, and not *vice versa.* That model of describing, or a parallel one for remembering, does not work for reporting dreams. Still, it is not to be abandoned completely. The intent of accuracy is very much present. In reporting a dream I wish to do the same kind of thing I do when reporting an automobile accident: I want to say what happened. With an automobile accident, there may be ways I can joggle my memory by asking others, or refresh it by looking at photographs. I do not have resources like these with dreams. All I can do is to think again of what happened. At this point one can hear Malcolm objecting: "Yes, but how can one distinguish between something's actually being correct and its only seeming correct?" The answer is that at best only with a great deal of difficulty, and then not with absolute certainty; and, at other times, not at all. That does not show that the concept of a dream pried loose from its report borders on nonsense. It shows that it is something that is at times hard to get at, and that it would be unreasonable to expect the same kind of assurances with dreams as we can have with automobile accidents.

In a footnote Malcolm says:

I am denying that a dream *qua* dream is a seeming, appearance or "semblance of reality." In telling a dream, however, one can say "It seemed . . . . ," when this means that there was a vagueness or uncertainty in the dream.[20]

There are two points here. He says that the locution "it seemed . . . " may indicate an uncertainty *in the dream,* and that is true. But it is also true that it may indicate that one is dissatisfied with his present recollection of the dream. One cannot say with a dream, as one can with a thing, that regardless of one's recollection what is being recollected has either 'p' or 'not-p' so that any indeterminacy is in the recollection. Yet there are times when one has had a vivid and clear dream only to have it drift into obscurity upon waking. Waking up is very much like having one's attention wrenched away so that it is only with great effort that he is able to recall it. Again, one can hear in Malcolm the ghost of Wittgenstein saying: "But how can one distinguish between its actually having been a clear dream and its only having seemed to have been that?" Unless one can make this distinction in any given case, his claim is vacuous. One may assert the possibility of having a clear dream only partially recollected, but in the absence of any demonstration are these not mere words? Not if they characterize actual situations, and it seems obvious enough that there are situations of this sort.

I would like to expand on this at least by way of analogy, but before I do that I want to comment on the second claim made by Malcolm in the above quotation. He wants to deny that " . . . a dream *qua* dream is a seeming, appearance of 'semblance of reality.' "[21] As a general view of dreams this is too restricted. Some dreams are so far removed from reality as to have absolutely no semblance of it; others are distressingly lifelike. The verisimilitude, if that is the word, has as much to do with the emotional tone as with the descriptive features of the experience. But surely, if one may dream that propositions and tables are indistinguishable, more ordinary dreams are also possible.[22] But perhaps I am missing Malcolm's point. In fact, I think that the only way in which a dream may or may not approach reality is in terms of the nature of its content, and Malcolm himself talks approvingly of this dimension.[23] It is dreams *qua* dreams that he denies are a semblance of reality. If, in that, he is implying a distinction between the nature of a dream itself and its content then, on the level of experience, I do not know how to reply to him. If a dream is populated by vague and amorphous creatures that indifferently float into and out of one's consciousness, then I would say that such a dream bore little semblance to reality. If, however, the contents of one's dream made such a strong impression that regardless of how bizarre the events may have been they leave one with the feeling of having been real, then such a dream has a semblance of reality. A dream is not lifelike only if the events are of the sort that might probably occur in the actual world. Rather, a dream was real if it felt real. Something like the following is not contradictory, paradoxical, or even odd: "It was such a very real dream, though of course I realize that nothing like it could ever actually occur."

4.54   I confess that the position that I am taking deals with dimensions that are subjective and not clearly defined. Nowadays, it is a kind of heresy to say that if a dream felt real then that is the primary sense in which it is a semblance of reality. I realize that such a view is fraught with problems, most of which spring from variations of the private language argument. Yet it is essential to insist on things of this sort because they are factors of very ordinary experience. Let me illustrate. Suppose that I have just pictured the woman of my dreams. Nothing is said, written, or in any way publicly expressed. Now, under these circumstances, is there any problem in my saying (a) "I clearly remember how I pictured her"; (b) "Although the original impression was vivid my present recollection is hazy?" There are problems, but they are not such as to make one question the sense of talking about the real (original) image or the accuracy of my recollection of it. As things in fact stand, there are no external public criteria for verifying what I now think about my past experience, although there could have been. I am not considering a situation in which public criteria are in principle ruled out. However, if one has in mind that it is the possibility of criteria that makes my imagined situation sensible, the answer is that the possibility of public criteria could support only the possibility of sense and I am arguing that my situation makes actual, and not just possible, sense.

4.541   Let me review the circumstances that I am imagining. Something is imagined, pictured, or dreamt in private. At a later point it is recalled, and the question arises of how accurately it was recalled. Some public expression of the original picture could have been made, but none was. As things are, the only thing that can count as resolving the question of accuracy is the way it actually seems to the person involved. The possibilities are several. He may feel certain that he is remembering it just as it was at first; he may feel certain that he is now leaving something out, for example, originally he pictured a woman with striking hair and now that escapes him; he may now be genuinely puzzled as to how he originally pictured her, so that he has no way of deciding if his present recollection is a good or a bad one. I am sure that there are more possibilities, but these are enough to establish my point. In none of these possibilities was there any check available outside of the person's own memory. Because of that, some questions have to go unanswered that would not have to have been unanswered if there had been a check—for example, "I now picture her as having short brown hair, but I'm not certain that before it wasn't reddish." Had there been a public record made of the earlier image, that question would have an answer.

4.542   The point is that our inner experiences, such as images and dreams, do stand in need of outward criteria. If tomorrow such criteria were to become impossible we would (probably) abandon talk of such events. The confidence that we have in talking of private episodes is something that develops in, and only because of, our public language. But it does develop. In cases such as the one that I have imagined, we are correctly hesitant to place unlimited faith in our powers of recollection. But the fact remains that having established our credentials as language users—having developed the ability to recognize and deal with inner experiences—we are, as a simple matter of fact, in a position to go on and discuss them intelligently when no public verification is possible.

I am arguing that talk of private experiences makes very ordinary sense, and although I have not said that public criteria are in principle unavailable, I have said that when they are in fact not available, no conceptual problem is created. Someone might think that I have dropped too many of the standards which justify us in thinking that what we say makes sense. In fact, I think that my position has just the opposite effect. In his book *Dreaming*, Malcolm is quite skeptical about the epistemological significance of physiological data in rapid eye movement (REM) research. On his view, it would make no sense to speak of correlating them (or any other physiological data) with dreams. "No one would have directly observed any causal or temporal relation between dreams and physical occurrences (*nor would it make sense to do so*), but only between *reports* of dreams and physical occurrences."[24] Obviously, no one could observe a correlation between a dream that I was having and the movement of my eyes, but if my report is taken as the report of an experience that I have had, then there is no reason to be skeptical of the possibility of having a correlation between my dream and my REM's. I see no significant difference between establishing that correlation and, for example, a correlation between a fantasy that I have and the rate of my pulse. Both depend on the legitimacy of what I say about myself, and all that I have argued is in support of just exactly that. I am not giving covert support to a kind of identity theory of mind. I am only saying that if, and only if, one accepts subjective reports as reports of actual occurrences does one open the door to possible correlations with objective (that is, measurable) data.

4.543 Malcolm will not even allow the subjective/objective distinction to apply to dreams. " 'Subjective' and 'objective' are *one* in the case of dreams—which is to say that this distinction does not apply."[25] It is very difficult for me to appreciate the thinking behind a claim like this. The reason that he makes it is that the dreamer's impression is the criterion of reality, so that it cannot be characterized as subjective.[26] Without challenging this claim, it is worth pointing out that the impressions that one may have are really quite varied. For example, one may wake with the impression of having had a clear dream, though his present recollection is indistinct. However, I do not think that this is the point that Malcolm wants to reject. What he thinks is senseless is the notion that one could determine that a dream had occurred apart from what the dreamer said, so that the existence of the dream would be an objective fact, and the report of the dreamer a subjective recollection. Malcolm is correct to the extent that he is indicating the difference between an event like an automobile accident and a witnes's report of that, and a dream and its report. But even allowing the differences, the distinction still has a use as applied to dreams. That the occurrence of dreams is very much an objective fact is not called into question because our principle means of demonstrating this is the dream report. Malcolm wants to avoid the idea that one could objectively determine the occurrence of a dream independently of the report. I agree that one's report of his dream is something that enjoys a special status. However, it is not true that talk of the real, objective status of the dream experience would change our present concept of what a dream is. He is concerned that much of the REM experimentation has been interpreted along these lines. I am inclined to think that he is right in saying that some of the physiological dream experiments have been philosophically misused, but he is wrong in the specific evidence he gives for this alleged conceptual change. The argument is that if one accepts the REM data and so speaks of the objective existence of dreams, it would them make sense to speak of someone's being mistaken, or in error as to whether or not he had dreamed.[27] Malcolm errs in thinking that the notion of a mistake does not now apply to our concept of dreaming. There is nothing especially strange in recognizing the fact that one may, on his own, come to realize that he has made a mistake in reporting a dream. By mistake I do not mean just a verbal error, but one of substance. To be sure, what Malcolm is most concerned with is that someone other than the dreamer may feel himself in a position to contradict the dreamer's own thoughtful and well considered account. But even that is not totally absurd as we presently conceive of dreaming. Even without employing the refined tools of psychoanalysis, I might suggest to someone who has made a habit of telling me his dreams that the one that he has related to me is very much out of character for him. Indeed, I might feel confident enough in my knowledge of this person's character and thought patterns to be certain that his dream could not have been exactly as he told it. I am admittedly on thin ice in making such a claim, but I do think that it makes sense, and that it is not a redefinition of our concept of dreaming.

4.544   The difficulty that I am confronted with is that of maintaining that dream reports have a special status while allowing that they can also be in error. To put the problem into perspective, I am not allowing that such a conflict could become the rule. If that were to happen, our notion of dreaming would have undergone a change. These special cases are only possible because we generally accept without question what a person says about his own dreams. An inconsistency between what he now reports and what he regularly experienced in the past does not prove conclusively that he is presently mistaken. But it does legitimately raise the question. If, however, the dreamer stoutly defends his present account while recognizing the inconsistency, the thing to say is that we do not know what to say. Our debate is not nonsense, just undecidable.

4.6 Actions and their Precondition

4.61   In order to develop a model of the world inside it is necessary to say something about that world as it operates. At the core of such a model is the concept of a person, and at the center of this concept is that of agency. The world inside is primarily an active world. But all that tells us is that the subject of our enquiry is not passive. It gives us no idea what kind of activity will be illuminating. It does not distinguish, for example, between things done by people and things that happen; that is, between someone's chopping down a tree and its merely falling down. This is the difference between an action and an event, and we must understand it in order to understand the world inside.

The world of events is populated by things or, more specifically, an aspect of things. Let me explain. Events are things in movement. The tree that falls in the forest falls because it was hit by another tree. The event that was the falling of the first tree was caused by a second tree, specifically, the second tree's hitting the first. Events are not caused by things; they are caused by other events. But events are no more than things in change, so to know that an event has happened it is necessary only to have observed a change. That is, to know that a tree fell it is not necessary to see it fall; it is only necessary to have seen it standing and to now see it on the ground. Such limited observation will not tell us very much about causes, but it is all that is needed in order for us to know that an event has taken place.

Actions are parallel, though very different and more complex. It is tempting to look upon an action as an event plus something else. That view has some justification, for all actions include events. For example, if a tree were chopped down by a person, then a partial account of what had occurred would be that the tree fell. As an event, it is something that one may know about without having observed it happen; but as an action, one needs more. If all that one knows is that at time t_i the tree was standing and at time t_{ii} it was on the ground, one is in a position to know that an event has occurred but not that an action has. What has been left out, if this is to be a description of an action, is a person or agent.[1] One needs to know that it was Sam who chopped the tree down, something most readily known if one saw Sam doing it. The important thing is not so much that there must be witnesses for actions but not events, but that to understand something as an action, there must be reference to the person who brought it about.

4.62   However, actions are more than events that are brought about by persons. Here, the event-plus interpretation of action is most clearly inadequate. Actions are a different kind of occurrence from events, and the notion that most clearly shows this difference is responsibility. Of course, responsibility ties in with people. If Sam chopped the tree down, he is responsible. Yet, if one is willing to accept the consequences, one can still push through an event-plus analysis even at this point. The first tree fell because it was hit by the second one, so there is a sense in which the second tree was responsible for the first one's falling. There is no misuse of language in saying that, but I think that there is no understanding of the notion of action to be gained, either. What is being glossed over is the difference between causal and moral responsibility. One event causally brings about another, but a person is neither a thing nor an event, and so does not bring things about in that manner.[2] I earlier argued for the need to replace reference to a thing by reference to an event, in the example of one tree knocking down another. Such replacement cannot happen with an action without change of meaning. If Sam chopped down the tree, "Sam" cannot be replaced with the description of an event without changing the significance of the original claim. Among other things, "Sam chopped down the tree" can be used to designate Sam as the responsible agent.[3] If "Sam" is replaced by an expression referring to an event, this kind of responsibility drops out. For example, "the movement of an arm holding on to an ax caused the tree to fall" does not convey the same thing as "Sam chopped down the tree." Arms and axes are things, and are not held morally responsible. If the tree ought not to have been chopped down and it is true that Sam did it, then we might have reason to blame him for it. Such questions as the appropriateness of punishing him would naturally arise. Were there mitigating circumstances which might excuse, or even possibly justify, his behavior? Might he have been acting under duress, or perhaps slipped, and struck the tree with the ax accidently? Such considerations as these apply only to persons. It is foolish to even think of punishing an arm or an ax. They are not to be excused or forgiven either, because they do not act.

Though it is generally foolish to treat things and events as we treat people and actions, it is not always foolish to treat a person as a thing. On the surface it might seem inhuman, and though on some occasions it will be just that, on other occasions it would be most human. Remembering that all actions involve events as a minimal condition, there are occasions when a person's behavior closely resembles that of a thing. On some occasions, when we refuse to hold a person responsible we are not denying that he was causally responsible. If Sam did slip and the ax did hit the tree accidently, then we say that he could not help it, and withhold any censure. In not passing judgment on Sam, we are not denying any of the causal facts of the situation. Indeed, it is those that impress us, and it is because of them that we withhold censure. It was Sam's arm and ax that felled the tree, but it was also Sam's foot that slipped on the ice causing his arm to move in the way that it did. When he slips, Sam's movements come close to mere events, so that moral responsibility drops out. But even under these circumstances we do not treat Sam as though he were merely a thing. We recognize that it would be unfair to hold Sam accountable because he could not have done otherwise. It is not out of a concern for fairness that we withhold judgment from arms and axes. We refuse to view them as we view a person because to do otherwise would be to talk nonsense.

4.63   I want now to consider aspects of a particular theory of action in order to bring out some of the features of the concept of action which are central in understanding how the world inside manifests itself.

One of the clearest proponents of this theory is H. A. Prichard.[4] As its central feature, his theory holds that actions are complex. They are composed of parts, or stages:

> We should at first say that to do something is to originate or to bring into existence, i.e., really, to cause, some not yet existing state either of ourselves or of someone else, or, again, of some body.[5]

The principal feature of an action is modification. In some manner, some thing is changed. The change may be in us, as when we raise our arm; or, it may be in something else, as when we lift an object. Still, "doing something" means "originating, causing, or bringing about the existence of something, viz. some new state of existing thing or substance."[6] Implicit in this characterization is the contrast between doing something directly, and doing it indirectly. Raising one's arm appears to be something that one does directly, while raising one's arm to press a button to convey a command to kill someone is something that one does indirectly. However, on reflection we realize that even moving one's arm is not something that is done directly. The reason for this is not entirely clear. It appears to be because "what we did originate directly must have been some new state or states of our nerve-cells, of the nature of which we are ignorant."[7] The major problem is that whatever it is that Prichard is explaining, it cannot be an action. Consider the following example. "For by 'moving our hand' we mean causing a change of place of our hand; by 'posting a letter' we mean bringing about that a letter is in the pillar-box; and so on."[8] This is not what we mean by posting a letter. There is a difference between my taking a letter and dropping it in the box myself, and my merely leaving it where someone will come across it and drop it in the box. In the first instance I mailed the letter, in the second instance I brought it about that the letter was mailed, but someone else did the mailing.

4.631   Given this conception of an action, it is perhaps no surprise to find Prichard denying that raising one's arm is something that one can do directly. He is forced to this conclusion not so much because of what he says about the direct modification of nerve-cells as because of his general conception of what it is to do something. All that is required is that some change occur and that, in some sense as yet unclear, a person be involved in bringing that about. However, the account is too broad. If all that is required is that I bring about a change of affairs, it is possible that what I bring about is an event rather than an action, so that in bringing it about I am not acting in my capacity as a person. My bringing about that the letter got from point A to point B, in conjunction with the fact that point A is outside the post-box and point B is inside of it, is not sufficient for saying that I mailed the letter. In order to say that this was an action and not merely an event we need to know more about my role in bringing it about. Suppose that someone has placed the letter so that it is balancing precariously on the edge of the mail box. I am suddenly caught in a fit of sneezing, creating a breeze sufficient to blow the letter in. Or, suppose that I have been paying some bills. I have also written a nasty letter to a friend but thought better of it and decided not to mail it. Unknown to me it catches on to one of the letters that I am mailing, and into the mail box it goes. One could, I suppose, say that in both these cases I did in fact mail the letter. It did end up in the mail box, and it was my sneeze or my hand that put it there. That is, it was I and not someone else who was at the beginning of the causal chain that ended up with the letter's being in the box. The reason we are reluctant to say that I mailed the letters is that my only involvement was causal. My moral responsibility was mitigated by the circumstances. It is only my causal responsibility that remains intact, and that is sufficient to provide only an anemic conception of action.

4.64 Still, an anemic conception of an action is a conception nevertheless. Is not the above distinction really a difference within the class of actions? Is it not just the difference between those actions that are done freely, and those that are not? The suggestion that I have been making is that Prichard's account does not give us enough to distinguish between actions and events. Perhaps that is too strong. Why can it not be said that we have an account of action, but that we have not worked out the difference between two kinds of actions—that is, voluntary and involuntary? I want to pursue this suggestion because I think that it is correct, and because it will allow us to work out the relation between involuntary actions and events.

On the surface, it looks as though we have two conflicting ways of proceeding. Throughout, I have talked of the action-event distinction as fundamental. It is in terms of this that I have criticized Prichard. Now, the suggestion is that the weakness of Prichard's account is not an inadequate distinction between action and event, but rather between voluntary and involuntary actions. In the earlier examples, the letter went into the box because of my sneeze, or because it stuck to another letter. I argued that in such situations my moral responsibility would be diminished. It is tempting to argue that I could have [diminished] responsibility only for something that I had done—for an action that I had performed. We do, after all, speak of "involuntary actions." Perhaps my point has missed the mark and Prichard has explained a *bona fide* action—involuntary to be sure, but still an action rather than an event.

4.641 I will argue that the action-event distinction is paralleled by the voluntary-involuntary one in at least one important respect. I have claimed that the concept of an action includes the notion of moral responsibility, and that this is something not contained in the notion of an event. Something like this appears to be the case with the voluntary-involuntary distinction. It would be reasonable to say that I did not voluntarily mail the letter, and that I was responsible only in a causal sense for its being in the letter box. But why refuse to call the letter's going into the letter box an action of mine? Is not the issue of whether or not it is properly an event or an involuntary action the wrong issue? The principal point is certainly the degree of responsibility and regardless of whether we label it "action" or "event" the responsibility is appropriately diminished.

Responsibility is the key notion, but the action/event controversy is not just a matter of arbitrary labeling. It is natural to hesitate in calling it an event, since that suggests that it is like the tree's being blown down by the wind. There are obvious and significant differences. My sneeze that placed the letter in the box may have been an accident, but it was still something done by a conscious being, aware of what was going on around him and so one is understandably reluctant to call it an event. People are not things, and "event" is most comfortably a thing word. One way of putting it is to say that it is a mistake to look upon the action-event classification as a continuum. Moral responsibility is a matter of degree, but one cannot keep subtracting amounts of it from an action and thereby expect to end up with an event.

4.642   Another way of putting the issue is this: Is the expression "involuntary action" self-contradictory? To say "yes" would be to argue that the word "action" implies the notion of human agency via the idea of moral responsibility. That is, the point of calling something an "action" is to direct attention to it as something that a person has done, and for which he may be held accountable. One calls it an action to distinguish it from an event. On the other hand, to characterize something as "involuntary" is to cancel the very kind of description justified by "action." If something has been done involuntarily, this means that the person cannot properly be held fully responsible for it. The circumstances have been such as to mitigate his responsibility. Something like duress or ignorance substantially modified the way in which he performed the action. The very feature that separates actions from events is cancelled by calling it involuntary. How, then, can "involuntary action" be a correct description? To be sure, "involuntary event" sounds most odd, but that may be only because it is redundant.[9]

4.643   However, the point runs deeper than this. "Voluntary" and "involuntary" are modifiers with a restricted application. Not any verb in any set of circumstances will comfortably accept them. Rain may fall freely to the ground, or be impeded by the branches of a tree. It cannot fall voluntarily or involuntarily. I am suggesting that this pair of modifiers properly applies only to the actions of sentient beings. Although the rain cannot involuntarily fall to the ground, a cat or a person may. At least a part of the reason for this is that when the cat descends involuntarily, it does so against its will. In other words, those things that occur involuntarily occur not merely in the absence of the expected desires, but actually against them. The cat that falls involuntarily can be said to have "views" on the matter, and has been forced to act in conflict with them. It is absolutely essential to the description of the fall as involuntary that a cat is the kind of thing that can have "views." A leaf that falls has no opinion, and so cannot act according to or in conflict with it, and consequently cannot act voluntarily or involuntarily.

When a person acts involuntarily, it is still a person that is acting. That fact is not cancelled, but retained by the modifier "involuntary." Now, I believe, we can see our way out of the dilemma. In its most extreme form, an involuntary action may be such as to entirely free the person of moral responsibility. His only remaining responsibility may be causal, and, considering that fact alone, the parallel with an event is striking. However, that a person acted involuntarily means that he acted against his thoughts and desires, and that is sufficient reason to characterize what he did as an action. The occurrence of thoughts and desires, even frustrated ones, is enough to humanize the occurrence. The expression "involuntary action" is not contradictory, for involuntary actions are not events.

4.65   An action must be more than the bringing about of a state of affairs. An account like that does not distinguish actions from events, and makes it doubtful that one could separate voluntary from involuntary actions. Prichard makes a suggestion that may help to take us further. An act is not the causing of a change *simpliciter;* no change simply happens whether in nature or in the case of human actions. We do not know what it is in the natural world that brings about change. Words like "force," "attractions," "repulsion" indicate " . . . our knowledge that there is some activity at work, while being ignorant of what the kind of activity is."[10]

In the case, however, of a man, i.e., really, of a man's mind, the matter is different. When, e.g., we think of ourselves as having moved our hand, we are thinking of ourselves as having performed an activity of a certain kind, and, it almost goes without saying, a *mental* activity of a certain kind, an activity of whose nature we

were dimly aware in doing the action and of which we can become
more clearly aware by reflection on it.[11]

Strictly speaking, moving one's hand is not an activity. It results from an
activity, specifically, the activity of willing. As mentioned before, actions
come in stages. There is the act of will, and then the physical event that is
the effect. It is difficult to characterize this act of will because it is *sui
generis* and so cannot be defined or have its nature explained in terms of
other things. We can say that it is not desiring, nor resolving, nor attending, nor consenting to something.[12] The implication is that we know what
these things are by reflecting on what goes on when we act. Introspection
allows us to say that there is a difference between willing and these other
psychological occurrences, although we cannot specify what that difference is. It is unfortunate that willing is so ellusive because it is common and so important. It is *the* feature which distinguishes natural
change from human action. Indeed, not only does it separate human acts
from natural events, but it constitutes all that there is to a human action.
Normally we might think that an action is something that occurs in the
physical world, perhaps as the effect of the internal, mental act of will.
However this would be wrong. An act of will cannot bring about an action but only a movement.

> We are thus left with conclusion that where we think we have done
> some action, e.g. have raised our arm or written a word, what we
> willed was some change, e.g. some movement of our arm or some
> movement of ink to a certain place on a piece of paper in front of
> us.[13]

Prichard is saying that the only action that occurs is in the mind.
Everything else is merely movement. This is really a remarkable conclusion, for it means that in any ordinary sense, people never act. Things
happen in the world and people are involved in these happenings, but
these happenings are not actions.

4.651   Prichard is forced to this conclusion because of the way in which
he began his enquiry. It starts harmlessly enough with the question:
"How did we do the action?"[14] For Prichard, this is an enquiry into the
nature of the occurrence that preceded the action. The proper question to
be asked then is: "What was the activity by performing which I caused
my hand to move?"; the answer would be: "Willing the existence of the
movement."[15]

The principal difficulty comes from taking an action to be a composite of several occurrences. As such, we understand each occurrence by understanding the one that preceded it. We come to understand the movement of my hand by realizing that it was brought about by an act of willing. I suppose that the parallel is with events in nature. For example, I understand the present thunderstorm by realizing that it was brought about by a low pressure system. But this is one instance in which events in nature do not provide a good model for human action, for actions do not need to be explained, at least not in the way Prichard provides. To approach them in this fashion is to completely misunderstand what it is for a person to do something. One may detonate an explosion by pushing a button, but there is nothing that one does in order to push a button. If the question arises as to how one does push a button, it is properly put off by indicating that he is in full control of himself and that he just does it. If the enquiry is continued, about all that one could do is to specify the various aspects of his action. For example, in pushing a button, one lifts his arm and extends it toward the button, etc.[16] However, in specifying the aspects of an action, one is not cutting it into parts, one of which produces the other. Extending one's arm is not what causes the explosion. Extending one's arm precedes the depression of the button, and there is a sense in which one presses the button by extending his arm. What would be misleading would be to think that there were two occurrences, extending one's arm and pushing the button. But, so long as one does not think that this search for basic parts ends with something ontologically ultimate, and remembers that it is only a matter of determining the simplest description relative to the task at hand, there is no harm. Relative to "detonating the bomb," "extending one's arm" is a simpler description than "extending one's arm to push the button." All that is really at issue is the amount of detail that one wishes to include in the description.

4.652   The mistake Prichard makes is to think that an act such as moving one's arm *must* be made up of parts, each of which produces the next. The futility of this is manifest in his own account, when he says of its principal part, the act of will, that it is something of which we are only "dimly aware in doing the action," and it is *sui generis* in nature.[17] I am not aware of anything like an act of will occurring when I do something. To be sure, there are many things that happen when I act about which I know nothing. For example, I have no idea of some of the changes in my heart. It would be foolish to use my ignorance of such events as grounds for doubting their existence. However, the crucial difference between variations in my heart beat and an act of will is that while the first is something that merely goes on within me, the second is something that I do. Indeed, it is pre-eminently what I do. It is the only thing that is legitimately called an action. By hypothesis, it is a part of my experience, so that my not being aware of it is grounds for doubting its existence.

4.66   Since Ryle's attack, the concept of the will has pretty much disappeared as a useful philosophical tool.[18] An extensive criticism therefore seems out of place. It is more interesting to consider some of the very general features of Prichard's account that are on the right track. I argued earlier that actions did not require an explanation of the type provided for by Prichard. It is wrong to explain an action by an act of will, but it is not wrong to explain an action, and it is not wrong to set out the difference between a natural and human performance in terms of the ways that they are explained. An act is explained by what goes on inside the agent, and it is this type of explanation that separates acts from natural events. However, what I am talking about is not something to be discovered by a special process of introspection, as suggested by Prichard. He says that the way to learn more about what significantly occurs in our mind prior to acting, that is, about an act of will, is by reflection.[19] Prichard means that we should inspect the contents of the mind much as we would inspect the contents of a room, and reflect on the nature of the items that we uncover. This is misleading. If we actually perform such an experiment what we uncover is, generally, of no use whatsoever. For example, suppose that I had mailed my letter on purpose and not by accident, and suppose that I do reflect on those things that actually went on in my mind as I dropped the letter in the box. The first thing to realize is that there is no reason to expect that anything that I uncover will have any significant bearing on the issue. I may have been thinking to myself "ah, I'm glad to get this done," but I may also have been thinking of some pressing matter to be done a week hence, "oh, I mustn't forget that number." If one's concern is with those episodes that actually occur, there is no guarantee that what one uncovers will be relevant. However, what is relevant and helpful is a consideration of the beliefs of the agent that connect with the action. There is no reason to suppose that these are to be found as actual episodes occurring to the agent at some point before the act. So, the question to be asked is not: "What was going on in his mind?" but "What reasons were there for his doing that?" Reasons do serve to explain an action and to separate them off from events.

Of special interest are not so much *the* reasons why an action was performed, but the *agent's* reasons for doing it. These may coincide, but because they may also diverge it is important to keep the difference in mind. For example: "The [real] reason he married Heidi is because she was so like his former wife." Such an account as this may be offered in spite of what the person himself says and as the in-depth reason for his behavior. But, even though it may be true, this kind of an account is not of interest to us at this stage.[20] What is of interest are the reasons that the agent himself gives for performing the action. What I am after is much the same as what Anscombe was seeking in her use of the question "Why?."[21] For example, suppose that Herman is asked "Why did you buy that camera?" and he replied "Because it has the lens and shutter that I wanted." The fact that he offers these considerations gives them a special status. There are a lot of descriptions that truly characterize Herman's transaction, but these give us a way of sorting. First, they give us Herman's reasons for his purchase. Second, because they are his reasons, they provide descriptions under which aspects of the action may be seen as intentional. Because of his response, we are in a position to say that his purchase of the camera with that specific lens and shutter was intentional. But suppose that the camera has a damaged film advance, and we ask him why he is buying a camera with that defect. If he answers "Oh, am I really?" we may conclude that its having a defective advance may not be included among his reasons and that it does not provide us with a description of something that he is intentionally doing. The general point is that those features of the question "Why?" that are accepted by the agent provide us with his reasons for acting as well as the intentional aspects of the action. Those features of the question that are rejected cannot be classified in either of those ways.

A person's reasons for acting provide us also with his purposes. Reason, purpose, and intention all naturally cluster together, and in ordinary language there may not be a generally recognized difference among them. One good reason for grouping them together is that they all pay their feature role as ingredients in the agent's conscious life. It is permissible to treat any of them as unconscious only if it has been shown that we are dealing with a special case.[22] The second and most important feature of these concepts is that they are all dependent on the agent's having beliefs; belief is the pre-eminent basis for action. Beliefs (intentions, purposes, and reasons) explain actions in such a way as to mark them off from events. For example, Herman believes that the camera over there is his. Equipped with this belief, he may intentionally pick it up as something that belongs to him. Without the belief, he could not deal with the camera as a piece of his property. He could not loan it to a friend or offer it for sale. Such restrictions may seem very strange. Surely, one may pick any item at random and loan it to someone by simply saying "Here, this is yours to use if you choose." However, it is impossible, and the manner of the impossibility is an important feature of intentions and, more generally, of how the world inside gets outside.

To make the point, we need simply remind ourselves that the action we are talking of is the intentional manipulation of one's own property. When I say that unless Herman were to believe that the camera was his he could not loan it, I am not suggesting that he would be suffering from anything like a physical disability. But without such a belief, whatever he might do would not count as the intentional lending of something that was his. The alternatives are too numerous to exhaust, but a few of them may indicate the drift. Suppose that Herman did not recognize the camera to be his (in fact it was); the question of ownership never arose. He could hand it to someone saying: "Use it for a month. See how you like it." But under these circumstances, it could not be described as intentionally loaning his camera. A notion such as intention is, in a sense, an arrow with two points. One tip points to and characterizes the action, while the other directs our attention to the agent. To say that he intentionally lent his camera entitles us to infer not only that it did belong to him, but that he believed that it did. Generally, action descriptions in terms of intentions, purposes and reasons are a kind of inference ticket into the state of mind of the agent, and in providing us with that kind of insight they also can alter our conception of the action itself. An intentional act and one that is inadvertent are not the same, and the difference lies in the mind of the agent.[23] To say that something was done intentionally is not at all like saying that it was done slowly. Intentions are not style characteristics, but are more like conceptual frameworks. Still, they are not hidden events tucked away in the private regions of the mind. It is for good reason that the law holds that "every man is presumed to intend the natural consequence of his own actions."[24] Such a presumption is reasonable because one's intention is as much in what he does as it is in his mind. Intentions explain actions, as I claimed earlier with application of the question "Why?" However, determining *why* a person behaves as he does is not always altogether that different from determining *what* it is that he is doing. If Herman hands over the camera because he was asked to, we may conclude that what he is doing is done in response to a request. Consequently, if we know what a person is doing—and this may be simply a matter of looking—we thereby know his intention. What I want to combat is the idea that while anyone is in a position to determine the nature of an action, intentions (reasons and purposes) are of an entirely different order—actions are open and public.

4.663   I do not want to suggest that all of this is really a terribly simple matter, that it is easy and obvious to realize what someone is doing and so to know what is going on in his mind. But the difficulties that are encountered are not metaphysical difficulties. If what someone has done is not clear and needs to be explained, this is not accomplished by directing our attention toward something ontologically different from his overt behavior. It is not accomplished by discovering anything like an act of will. The confused and confusing Prichardian metaphysics is incorporated in the following taken from a well-recognized law dictionary: " 'Intent' expresses mental action at its most advanced point, or as it actually accompanies an outward, corporal act which has been determined on.' "[25] This is confused on the nature of an intention and on the nature of an action, and it is confusing on the nature of the mind and how it is made manifest. If to appreciate someone's behavior we had literally to ferret out that mental action which may have accompanied his outward, corporal act, we would never understand people's actions. Prichard's own account stands as a kind of paradigm of what this view leads to. If one thinks that to understand the nature of human behavior one must uncover something like an act of will, one ends up with a caricature of what that behavior is like. On Prichard's analysis, the only thing that counts as an action is the *sui generis* act of will.

4.664   To uncover a person's purposes or beliefs on which his action is based may certainly involve one in solving some puzzles, but the puzzles, properly understood, are not the result of a metaphysical dualism. A person's reason provides an interpretation for his action.[26] Actions do need, at times, to be interpreted, and the process is not all that different from interpreting a poem.[27] Anyone who can read knows what words are on the page, just as anyone who can see knows that he walked across the street. Yet, one is not sure just how to take the words, or how to take the action. But such puzzlement does not exist in a vacuum. There must be, for instance, some ambiguity in the words or in the behavior that needs to be cleared up. In the case of a poem one may propose an interpretation as a kind of hypothesis. For example, if one takes the dominant image to be death then the winter scene in the second stanza makes sense. One may proceed in this trial and error fashion accepting this proposal and rejecting that one until one is able to settle on something that is at least workable. Such enquiries are by no means always a simple thing, but in the case of action, we frequently have open to us an important way of resolving the matter. We may ask the person why he did what he did. If there is anything to the view that the contents of the mind are forever locked up, it is that the agent frequently knows his reasons better than does an observer. But there is no way to arbitrate this matter in a general and decisive manner. Particular cases seem to go their own way.[28]

4.665   Much of the spirit of what I have been arguing is contained in the now popular view that actions and their reasons have a conceptual rather than a causal connection:

> The connection between belief and action is a conceptual one; one cannot say what an action is without saying that actions presuppose beliefs. But the connection between a particular action and the beliefs that it presupposes is contingent.[29]

I am certainly in agreement with the first sentence. It is the second one that causes me a bit of concern, for Langford is avoiding the error of saying that this particular belief logically necessitates that specific action. Ignoring for the moment the idea of attributing logical necessity to anything but propositions, this claim would seem wrong because one may do the same action for any number of different reasons. However, the truth of this should not obscure the fact that the criteria for identifying the same action does not lie exclusively with physical events. Going to the store is something that one may do time and time again. There is a difference to be noted between going because one has been asked, and going because one wants to.

4.6651   The importance of the conceptual connection between reasons and actions is something that can be overdone.
    Reasons help separate actions from events and, typically, when one acts one has a reason. Still, it is possible to perform an action without a reason. It is, I should think, quite common that on occasion we just do things without having any reason at all. But consider the following argument:

But if it is claimed that Brutus was guided neither by these nor any other beliefs, then it does not make sense to say that the purported action was an action at all. Even if identical movements of Brutus' body occurred with the same fatal consequences, they would remain 'mindless' movements if not guided by beliefs. It is of course highly unlikely that such identical movements would occur; a claim by Brutus that his mind "just went blank" would be received with skepticism.[30]

This seems tome to go too far. If Brutus were to claim in the midst of killing Caesar that his mind "just went blank," we would either doubt his word or be forced to conclude that he had a pathological condition. But what I have in mind is nothing so extreme. The notorious, if mythical, absent-minded professor is a good example of what I mean. While engrossed in argument he "finds himself" lighting up a second cigarette while the first one burns in the ashtray. Such actions are indeed mindless, but they are nonetheless actions. What drops out is the notion of reason as given in response to the question "Why?" In other words, if asked "Why did you light a second cigarette?" one would expect something like "Oh, I didn't realize I had one going." Reason drops out in the sense of *his* reason but not in the sense of *the* reason. If, in lighting the second cigarette, he were to start a fire, he could not escape responsibility by saying that it was only a movement.

4.6652   My example is that of someone acting without a reason, but Langford argues that actions without beliefs are impossible. Earlier I claimed that beliefs were presupposed by intentions. Is it not, then, possible that beliefs are more basic, and that while actions without intentions may occur, actions without beliefs cannot? The answer to this depends on the account of belief that we accept. Everything turns on what is meant by the expression "guided by a belief." I am arguing that one cannot be said to be guided by a belief if all that means is that there are some true descriptions of his actions which, if he were asked about, he would accept as true. In other words, the expression "his reasons" is used to designate just those beliefs that do guide his actions. Reasons can apply to these actions in the form of *the* reason, but it is just in this form that they do not serve as a guide to action because there is no requirement that he be conscious of them. Any beliefs that would tie in with this conception of reason would themselves not be action guiding. It may seem, for example, that the absent-minded professor must believe that what he has in his hand is a cigarette; why else would he light it? In other words, it does make sense to explain the movement of the match toward his mouth by pointing out that it is a cigarette that he has there. Those are true descriptions of what is the case, but they cannot be his reasons, for he has none. Analogously, one may explain his actions *as if* he had certain beliefs, although to do this would be to ignore the sense in which they are absent-minded.

One of the things that may complicate the issue is the (correct) view that:

> . . . it is not possible for a person to act on beliefs that they regard as false; to say I regard a belief as false is to say that it is a belief that I do not hold.[31]

This is ambiguous. Action is precluded by beliefs that are false because one recognizes them to be false. But if there is a sense in which, recognizing something to be false, one thereby eliminates it from his repertoire so that he no longer has any beliefs at all about the subject, that does not preclude action. Action is not prevented by a psychological vacuum; it is prevented by the positive realization that something that one had considered is false. Acting under these circumstances would be inconsistent. Acting in the absence of any relevant belief presents no such problem.

What happens in the case of these mindless actions is that one is exercising through habit a skill that he had to acquire through deliberation. A habit like smoking acquires a momentum all of its own. It begins as something that one consciously does, and becomes something that one simply does. To disallow things of this sort, and to insist that anything that is to count as an action must be guided by a belief, is to offer a model as artificial as Aristotle's practical syllogism. The premise of the syllogism can be invoked to explain or possibly justify a person's action. It becomes implausible only if one takes it as a description of what someone actually thinks before he acts, that is, of the beliefs that he entertains.[32]

4.7 Causes, Perceptions and Things

Throughout this part of our investigation, things have been examined as irreducible elements in encounter and as features of the intelligible domains of reflection. The concept of person has been related to the concepts of perception, action, encounter, and meaning. The "inner world" of dreams has been exhibited as yet another region within which encounter and reflection are intelligible notions, marked off from the "outer world" of things mainly by its minimal association with encounter and its special limitations as a domain for reflection—a world which differs largely in degree from the "normal" perceptual world. The fundamental distinction, so far, has appeared as one between persons and things—a distinction intelligible in reflection as that between two ways of having properties, and in encounter by its different associations with meaning. Shortly, we shall face another crucial distinction, between intentional and other objects; we hope to make this clear by exhibiting the kinds of relations involved (drawing further on the distinction made in 4.4), and to use it as a device to clarify the notions of an "inner" and an "outer" world. In this section, we need to face yet another fundamental notion which figures in theory and in everyday life—the notion of cause. We need both an intelligible concept of cause and—if we are not to abandon as futile the distinction we have been laboriously making—one which does not obliterate the distinction between persons and things.

I shall, therefore, examine the following issues:

Why has it sometimes been thought that the concept of cause may obliterate the distinction between persons and things? What would a feasible, minimal, concept of cause amount to? How ought we to relate such a concept to the distinction between encounter and reflection? And, finally and most crucially, can we satisfactorily relate our notions of cause to the basic notions of human person and action?

4.71 The "threat" posed by the notion of cause to our earlier distinctions seems to me to amount to this: It has frequently been thought that there is a uniform kind of causal relation, and that this relation is such that any two events in the world are linked by a causal connection, either directly or through intermediary events. This set of causal relations has often been supposed to constitute a certain sort of monism which makes of reality either a single fabric, every part of which determines every other part, or a system within which some events are determined and others are simply random. On this view, there are still many alternatives; for example, the universe might be a great machine whose parts are a certain sort of thing. Thus, "persons" would be a special kind of mirage. Or, reality might be thought of as a random collection of quasi-mechanical pieces whose shape and order are simply a function of our way of understanding them. On this view persons are, also, a special sort of mirage, but things would also become precarious members of the domain—macrostructures, perhaps, whose fine structure possesses none of the homely stability of "ordinary" things. Finally, all the causes might be alike but, as in Berkeley's theory, volitional. On this view, there would be persons, but things would be a special, dependent, class of psychological entities.

There are several points to be noticed. It is not very clear just *what* is being talked about. The thesis seems to be that: (1) there are certain very pervasive constraints which bind the world together; (2) somehow or other, all events belong to one very general kind; and (3) determination, randomness, and volition express, in a very general way, the appropriate notions of restraint, or the absence of it. We are not, however, very clear as to what the restraint might be, or what level we are talking about. Are we talking about rational prediction of the future course of human experience? Or, are we talking about necessary connections between entities which, though not actual components of human experience, constitute some primary reality? Are we talking in the language of encounter, the language of immediate reflection, or the language of constructed reflection?

The answer to the last question makes a profound difference. It is a truism, for example, that there must be some mathematical formula which predicts the future states of the world, whatever they are. Whether we could know what that formula is depends upon what kind of world we happen to have. Whether that formula is fortuitously true, or necessarily true, is another kind of question. But anyone with enough skill can construct a reflection-world in which all the data of experience fit, and which exhibits them as fitting a preferred pattern. Since all the data of experience arise out of some encounter or other, it is, in principle, feasible to have only things in that world. Since every encounter has some relation to someone, we can, alternatively, exhibit that data as a feature of the experience of the persons concerned. Some mathematical formula would hold on either construction, though we might be tempted to give it one significance in one such construction, and another in the other.

But this is true, as I said, only "up to a point." The point at which it breaks down, naturally, is the point at which the rational construction itself is included in the system. A physics which explained the fact that there are physical theories in the world would, in principle, contain a mistake. It is like the map which includes itself. That map will have to contain another map and so on to infinity. Similarly, one who maps his own thoughts onto the states of his brain has a problem: As he is aware that he has done it, he has another thought which renders the first map invalid. He cannot both know the situation, and know that it is a condition of his own brain. These conundrums suggest that, but for the fortuitous fact that we cannot map an infinite series in the required sense, or but for the fact that we cannot know what our brain states are without changing them (if thoughts and brain states coincide), we could cope with the problems. That is not exactly so.

The map in the first example is a different *kind* of thing. It represents one world in another, and the two worlds must belong to different orders so that one might represent the other without being falsified by being a part of that other. Map space has not the same properties as physical space. If it had the same properties, it would only replicate and that would not add to the meaning relation. Thoughts about brain states, similarly, must belong to a different order, or they would not be thoughts *about* brain states.

Much more concretely, let us suppose that there is a real man who represents McKay's paradox—the paradox about knowing one's brain states in case thoughts and brain states exactly coincide. Now, this man is in the following position: All his thoughts *are* states of his brain. Consequently, whenever he thinks, the states of his brain change. He ought to exhibit a kind of very queer philosophical Parkinsonianism: His thoughts will shake like leaves in the breeze.[1] He cannot hold an idea steady—for one brain state makes it possible, but its very arrival makes that brain state impossible!

To avoid this puzzle, we must make a distinction between two propositions: One is the proposition that we can construct a reflection world which will accommodate whatever data we like. The other is the proposition that such a theory can (1) accommodate itself and (2) be read as a feature of the first order encounter world.

The best theory might be one that regarded all ideas as, for instance, brain states. But, if so, that would be for one or both of the following sets of reasons: (a) it might turn out that, like the writings of pig experts, accountants, and property assessors, it provided good clues to the encounter world, or (b) it might be that it met good conditions for theories—coherence, accommodation of data, inference paths from one datum to another. It would not be true *in* the encounter world, for it does not belong there.

But let us work our way back from constructed reflection through immediate reflection and on to actual encounter. Immediate reflection is simply the structuring of the situation as the immediately given relations between us and our experiences. Examples of this are the notions with which David Hume begins his *Treatise*—the notions which led to the modern concepts of sense data.[2] Here, as Hume points out, there are *no* causal relations at all. Everything is rendered determinate by reference to the immediacies of here and now. The primary relation of such objects is just their givenness; they are simply *there*. As a feature of potential logical constructions, this leads to what Hegel called "determinate being." Its function as an analysis of experience is to bring out clearly one of the features of the encounter—that such a world always contains us and something encountered. If that relation is simply translated into a description, then, indeed, Hume is right. It *does* exhaust all the data into a certain kind of experience and it *does* block off all immediate access to worlds of constructed reflection, if they are conceived of as more than pragmatically useful.

Yet we should realize Hume offers only one way of describing and characterising, and there is no reason to think that it is exhaustive. On the contrary, it is not literally self-contained. It is a stance, a preferred relation of immediacy. If no other were possible, we would be trapped in an immediacy which made discourse literally impossible. Hume rightly noticed that meaningful discourse is parasitical on experience, but did not give the same weight to the proposition that discourse makes it possible for us to escape immediacy, and hence discourse transforms experience. Discourse has a pattern which extends beyond the immediate. If it did not, the world would simply be one thing after another—an endless parade of proper names.

Hume did not notice this because he did not quite account for what he knew (and suggested in his return to custom, natural belief and so on) that the language of encounter is prior to the language of description. Things are encountered and *then* described. The primacy of the relation of givenness or simply "being there" is derivative from a *stance* taken about things.

Once the stance is taken, as Hume points out, the person in encounter and the thing in encounter disappear. Yet one is aware that one has taken a stance which one might not have taken and Hume, in his appendix, honestly doubts the disappearance of the self of self-awareness.

But the language Hume uses is not, of course, the language of encounter. It is the language of reflection, as he says himself. The first words of the *Treatise* are "all the perceptions of the human mind *resolve* themselves into two distinct kinds . . . "³ Resolve themselves! He talks of "surveying" our ideas and "imagining" the New Jerusalem.⁴ Two among many expressions which clearly suggest reflection.

Something, surely, had to have gone on before this reflection. It is *that* something about which Hume thinks himself right and other philosophers wrong. Wisely, he does not try to *describe* that something, for to do so would transform it into a set of reflection objects. Philosophers with a more full-blooded account of immediate reflection are, in Hume's view, wrong. In the terms I am using here, Hume (rightly, I think) is simply accusing them of confusing constructed reflection with immediate reflection—but not, one surmises, of giving the wrong account of the encounter world which stands, for Hume as for anyone, on its own feet.

If I am allowed this much, an important conclusion can be drawn: In the region of constructed reflection, there must be connections between things. Constructed reflection consists, precisely, in an ordered set of parts. If the system is such that each part can occupy one and only one place, and if the nature of one occupied place determines the nature of the other occupiable places, then we will have that kind of necessary connection which we might well call "cause and effect." If the system allows two or more parts to occupy, under varying conditions, alternative places, then the nature of those places will give us a notion of *a priori* probability for *that* system, and we will have the kind of derivative necessary connections which gives rise to a weaker sense of "cause and effect." One or other of these conditions must obtain for, failing that, the system has no necessary relation to its parts at all, and will not constitute a domain of constructed reflection.

By contrast, in the world of immediate reflection, there can be, as Hume alleges, no necessary connections just because the datum—whatever we choose to call it—is shaped by, and only by, its immediacy. Whenever one seeks a further connection, one moves to the original encounter world or to the world of constructed reflection.

Yet, neither immediate reflection nor constructed reflection is capable of accounting for itself. Hume had noticed the extent to which constructed reflection is parasitical upon immediate reflection. The preferred order of the constructed reflection must, after all, be made from data which have been first freed to be ordered. But he did not emphasize that, to some extent, the obverse of that relation holds as well. Immediate reflection is possible because there are alternative orders available. Because we can see the data in many possible constructions, we can see that it can be freed from them all. (Hume was not entirely unaware of this. He gives, in the *Treatise,* what seems to be a puzzling independent account of a set of basic relations.[5] His system moves from immediate reflection to constructed reflection in a way which gives a natural primacy to immediate reflection.) But both domains of reflection are parasitical on something else—the original encounter.

How does causality figure in encounter? Encounter is not possible in a world which is either empty of causal connections, or in a world in which causality is strictly necessitarian. It must take place against a background of reflection, and so must leave room for action. Simple reaction is not enough. Encounter involves awareness, which demands at least enough escape from the immediacy of the present to enable us to relate one moment to another. Yet no such relations are possible if everything is random, or if everything is so constrained that we cannot be said to follow an intelligible path through the world.

But the temptation is to construe one of these conditions as the absence of connection which constitutes immediate reflection, and the other as the kind of necessitarian ordering which is characteristic of constructed reflection. Singly or in combination, these will not do.

We must remind ourselves, again, that the language of encounter is not the languge of reflection in any of its modes. Ordering and freedom of encounter are the ordering and freedom of path-finding, rather than the orderings which figure in simple description. And this brings us back to the notion of action.

The world of encounter is the world in which you can find your way from Cleveland to Calcutta, from home to work, from breakfast to lunch. It is the world in which acting in certain ways brings about certain trains of experience. One gets instructions and one acts on them.

It need not, of course, be a world in which only considerations such as these arise. The encounter also contains the activities which are associated with the chemistry or the church. To "do" chemistry in the laboratory, one must be able to act on certain instructions and get certain results. There must be a path from one encounter to another. In constructed reflection, we translate these encounters into descriptions, and those descriptions (if we please) into theories. But though, in the theories, the activities of the chemist are eliminated by the mode in which the data is translated into description and theory, the theories may be construed as being either about the encounters themselves or about "the world," if "the world" means a map from which we can read off further instructions for more encounters.

Yet we cannot eliminate the encounters in favor of the theory. In the theory, every event is mapped so that there is a necessary connection between one event and the next. But if every act in the encounter were regarded as a necessary event, the encounter would not count as evidence. For then it would be predetermined (a) that the chemist would do what he did, and (b) that he would interpret as he did.

In fact, the theory acts as a map which guides the encounter, and the necessary connections on the map represent only the property possessed by the encounter world. They are a necessary condition of having encounters at all, for the property of being a world through which an intelligible path can be cut demands such a connection. The parts of a path are its defining conditions.

That world is neither free nor determined. It is simply intelligible, capable of bearing the designated set of assignable meanings. The maps are never perfect, the encounters never run quite to plan. In so far as they run "well enough," it is because the encounter world can be said to manifest properties which cluster well enough for the purpose.

The path-cutting is much like reading a book. One assigns meanings so as to get a sense, a direction. One could assign meanings so as to get jibberish, but that is not the game.

We want to know, of course, whether or not what, up to now, has been an orderly encounter world might, in the next moment or the next year, turn into a world in which we could find no sense: Hume's question, again.

In a way, however, the question is misplaced here. In Hume's world of immediate reflection, the answer is that anything is as likely as not, since the only connection between one component of immediacy and the next is the vanished self. In the world of constructed reflection, the answer is that the world cannot turn into nonsense. The construction prohibited it.

But what of encounter? If there is a next moment, there will be more intelligible encounters. For to find oneself on a path is to encounter things, however unsatisfactory.

It is not, perhaps, very satisfying to know, but the future will be like enough to the past to be *the future.* The only future we can talk about *is* the future which will be like that. We can say in words, "there will be no future," but we cannot mean anything by it.

4.72 There is, indeed, much that is genuinely unsatisfying about the preceding account. Partly, it is that the sketch of the implied dialectic of experience is incomplete—a fact which is not surprising at this stage of our enquiry. More seriously, however, the unsatisfying nature of the account stems from the fact that we have been looking at this dialectic in one dimension—the dimension of the orders of experience from encounter, through immediate reflection, and onward to constructed reflection. In effect, this represents an epistemological dimension. These are the orders of knowledge and their corresponding articulations, the orders of discourse within which knowledge might be expressed.

The line of early modern philosophy which runs from Descartes through Locke, Berkeley, and Hume, or from Descartes through Leibniz and Spinoza, proceeds by taking that order as fundamental. Within it, the problem of causal connection becomes the problem of knowledge of causes, and the answers vary with the level of experience which is taken to be fundamental. Berkeley and Hume, within that dimension, took immediate reflection to be fundamental. If one seeks the corresponding dimension in the philosophies of Leibniz and Spinoza, constructed reflection becomes fundamental. The kinds of clear and distinct ideas which lead to self-evident rational truths are, after all, characteristic of the necessities of constructed reflection, while the kinds of clear and distinct ideas which populate immediate reflection are the ideas of Berkeley and the impressions of Hume. The Cartesian family nose is clearly visible in both lines of his intellectual progeny.

The revolt against both these traditions which emerged in England amongst philosophers from G. E. Moore to J. L. Austin took the form of an appeal to common sense, an appeal which might most handily be construed as a return to the encounter world—though, despite the endless rummaging through accounts of the different functions of language, the point was not always clearly made.[6]

So long as we confine ourselves to this dimension, the issue about causality simply dissolves into different questions about the different orders of knowledge and discourse. The task is one of analysis, and of disentangling ourselves from commitments inadvertently carried over from one order to another. Yet there is clearly another question, that of the structure of causal arrangements in the world which gives rise to these orders of knowledge and discourse. How are we to understand the conditions under which this analysis into order is possible? It is not just what we know about causes which is at stake, but also, what situation must obtain in order that we should know what we do. It is the difference between reporting what we see in the mirrors of the cosmic fun-house, and specifying how the mirrors must be positioned so that we see what we do. The universe comes about through some arrangement of things, persons, properties and relations or, if you want to be more economical, of substances and characteristics. We need now to review, in *this* situation, just what reasons we have for thinking this is so and, then, to see what happens when we try to analyze causal relations in this way. This may give us the germ of our "reasonably adequate" notion of causality—especially if it really casts light on encounter and reflection, knowledge and discourse, thing and cause, person and action.

4.73 Our normal way of talking suggests the kinds of distinctions which are at issue here. Similar suggestions emerge from the standard "logics" of the past and present. We usually adopt a two-move strategy in talking about things—we name or mark something out, and then we say something about it, such as: Smith is fat, happy, and intelligent. Some S is P. There is an x such that . . . One may choose noun and adjective, subject and predicate, substance and attribute. The distinctions between the kinds of values substitutable for the variables in logical formulations all suggest a continuous triad of form, function, and being—though the distinctions are neither identical nor clear. Within all the pairs of distinctions, the components can be moved about. We can say that the fatness of Smith is a pleasant plumpness, but, as McTaggart,[7] amongst others, pointed out, there are limits to the extent to which we can convert substance and attribute, noun and adjective. We cannot say that it is the happiness of Smith which is fat, or that it is his fatness which is happy.

There is an ancient puzzle here, of course, and fascination with it comes and goes, mostly as a result of the frustrations it causes. Between McTaggart, at the beginning of the third decade of this century, and P. F. Strawson in the sixth decade, for instance, preoccupation with it became unfashionable. Philosophers have often seemed caught between being dazzled by looking into the mirrors and being preoccupied with structural features of the mirrors. Philosophers look for guidance in a variety of heroes and have sounded, by turns, Humean, Leibnizian, and Kantian—Humean when they think we can only report what is in the mirror, Leibnizian when they have a new insight into the real structure, Kantian when they are caught between the other positions.

Behind that puzzle lie, of course, still older puzzles. It does seem that when one has listed all the attributes of Smith, there is nothing more to be said; but, if one says there are *only* the properties specified by such predicates as happy, fat, and intelligent, and there is no "substance," Smith, which "has" them, one has not only to contend with the difficulties of a certain kind of Platonism; one also has no way of determining how they come to fit together to be "Smith." Why not assign them in some other way? If one resists, one is apt to end, like Locke, by saying that substance is "something I know not what."

It ought to be evident that, in this book, not all of these puzzles can be tackled. Our problem is to cope with a certain sort of experience, that of finding oneself with an inner life and of relating that inner life to some intelligible notion of an external world.

What can be done is to relate these difficulties to the things we have been saying, and to the things which we must go on to say. We can see how what we want to say, anyhow, can be rendered intelligible by deploying a certain kind of model.

To start with, then, I simply want to show that there is a justification for thinking of the world as a set of substances having properties and, because there is more than one way of having properties, it is possible for there to be both persons and things. When we see that, we can show, quite easily, both that the orders of experience I was talking about earlier are natural enough, and that an understanding of the idea of causality is feasible.

4.74   The kind of experience which gives rise to the problem of "the world within," its boundaries, limits, and other relations, is possible only in case there *is* both encounter and reflection. But that, in itself, demands that there are, to borrow words from C. D. Broad, both "continuants" and "occurrents" and that there are, at least, two sorts of continuants.

Something must persist in order to be an object of encounter which comes to be reflected upon, analyzed, circumscribed, reconstructed, known. Here, "persist" may mean "endure through a temporal process in experience," "serve as an object of reference through the stages which Hume adverts to as 'perception' and 'resolution,' " "function as an object of reference in a constructed reflection," or simply "be and be known." And that "continuant" must be capable of being one and the same thing in two or more contexts, as well as being manifested in and through sequential characteristics which differ in each context. This is true if *any* knowledge is possible, for instance, because, to know something is to know that one and the same thing exists and is known. If these conditions were not met, one could only know a pig by becoming a pig—a proposal occasionally made but seldom defended.

It is this duality which forms the bedrock of the distinction between the world within and the outer world. But this also makes experience a possible frame for intelligible encounter and reflection.

Once again, we should notice that it does not follow that these distinctions persist through every phase of the dialectic of experience. The perfect unity of mystical experience may be possible though it is only intelligible, of course, by reference to the states which precede and follow it. In constructed reflection, we come to understand the systematic unity of Bosanquet's metaphysics, or, in another mood, the unstructured pure flow of Bergson's metaphysics. But all these structures require the preceding experiences to which Bosanquet and Bergson, in their different ways, call attention. The distinction between continuants and their occurrent properties holds between the phases of experience. Within those phases, it emerges when we seek knowledge.

This brings us to the notion that there is a second kind of continuant. Corresponding to each phase of experience as object, there is a phase of experience as subject. Again, if this were not so, we could not say that we made and identified the necessary connections.

This is the basis, in reality, for the distinction between subject and object. The basis, no doubt, is sound enough, but if we treat it incautiously, we may well be open to Carnap's objection. We may create a myth.[8]

For we should notice, as Hegel did, that the alleged "subject" is plastic. It takes on a characteristic form with each phase of experience, and with each mode of constructed reflection. In Humean immediate reflection, we find the subject only in the "bundling" of impressions. In a mystical experience, the self seems to dissolve (or so we are told) into the experience. If one divides the world into things, one can only seek to find the subject as a thing, and one will end with the Cartesian "ghost" or with the alternative theory that the subject and his body are one.

It is not surprising, therefore, that Carnap, viewing this spectacle, should conclude that the dichotomy is founded on myth. Subject follows object as the shadow follows the dog. Is not the belief in its reality much like the belief that one's shadow is one's ghostly doppelganger?

Not quite. For the structure of the subject is simply the structure of the knowledge of the object, and we must have care not to fall back on a position from which it will seem to us, again, that one can only know a pig by becoming one. The distinction between the two kinds of knowledge must be maintained, but in a way which does not make the subject another kind of *thing*.

Thus far, we see two sets of conditions for solving our apparent problems. If we are to believe that our hypothetical continuants persist as "substances," and that the occurrents are the "characteristics" of those "substances," we must find a way of dealing with the distinction which will not leave us with a "something I know not what." If we are to believe that there are two sorts of continuants, we must find a way to do so without constructing them as though they were related like ghost and machine, shadow and dog, or myth and science.

I have sketched the problems together because the solutions have to be developed together. What we say about substance must give us the clue to our two kinds of continuant.

The problem of "substance" seems to me partly generated by the way in which the functions of substances are delineated by various philosophers, and partly by the metaphors which are chosen.

Locke envisions his substances as somehow holding their properties together—keeping the whiteness, sweetness, and hardness of the lump of sugar in line, explaining how the clusters of properties in perception are to be read as single unities. Descartes, Spinoza, and Leibniz envisioned their substances as, in some sense, forming self-contained unities, self-explanatory systems. Descartes' substances represent systems of objects of knowledge, Spinoza's one substance answers to the demand of being *causa sui,* Leibniz's infinity of substances answers to the demands for the rich world guaranteed by the negative form of the principle of sufficient reason according to which everything possible exists unless there is a reason for its non-existence.

These demands are variously puzzling, but they mostly seem to ask too much or the wrong thing to meet our difficulty. Locke really wants to know how to account for the functioning of the encounter world, and how to relate to the world of constructed reflection in which he espies the kind of knowledge which somehow represents the encounter world. But we have seen that the relation we face is not exactly that. Descartes, Spinoza, and Leibniz demand that substances explain an elaborate world of constructed reflection. Yet since, as *explanations,* they figure only in those worlds, they cannot very well be expected to do more than reflect the structures of those worlds. To ask more is to expect the wrong thing.

We can be content, here, to account for the arrangement between the continuants and their occurrent properties. But here, too, the demands become somehow impertinent. The temptation is to speak of substances "possessing" qualities. Or, in more muted language, as McTaggart would have it, "substance (is) that which exists and *has* one or more qualities without being itself a quality or a relation."

The "possession" metaphor leads us to think of a substance as something lurking behind the properties, and McTaggart's subsequent assertion that "it is, of course, quite true that a substance is nothing apart from its qualities" leaves us, for a moment at least, baffled.

But suppose one said, instead, "a substance is that which manifests itself in qualities and relations without being itself a quality or a relation." "Manifesting" is another metaphor, but it might be cashed. Words manifest themselves in meanings. It is false to say of them, however, that "they are nothing but their meanings" for they are, also, modulated sound waves, mounds of ink, or whatever. There are no words without meanings. But anything which cannot be made manifest in sound and mounds of ink, or in some other way, is not a word, either. That does not mean that there is a ghostly "third" thing which is the "real word."

It means that two modes of being must intersect in a certain way to get a word. A word, once produced, is a continuant in two modes—meaning and expression.

The continuants which manifest themselves in experience are like that, too. They are capable of being both things and objects of knowledge. We can study them in their own right as in the natural sciences, in relation to us as in the psychology of perception or as component parts of our knowledge.

The complexity involved returns us to the basic relation which is characteristic of experience: There is always a subject and an object of knowledge. The subject manifests itself in the ordering of things, the object manifests itself as the meaning which we attach to the given situation.

One comes to find out about oneself from the acts one performs, from the way one's experience is characteristically informed and structured, and from the contrasts one makes between oneself and others. One comes to find out about things by noticing the significant patterns of meaning which one can form in the world of things.

It is not that the "substance" is something hidden; it is simply that the substance is a characteristic structure which appears in the ordering of experience. It forms the reference points around which predication comes to "make sense."

It is the inversion that is interesting: One finds oneself in and through a world of things, and one finds things in and through a world of meanings.

The meaning gives objectivity, and things reveal the mode of experience which gives meaning to one's subjectivity. More clearly, it is the passage from one level of consciousness to another and, hence, from one kind of object to another which reveals the continuity of subjectivity; it is because we can pass from encounter to immediate reflection to constructed reflection that we are aware of our subjectivity. But it is, of course, when we have organized the world into things that we can come to see our world as an arena for action. Our self-hood ceases to be either just a series of encounters or the empty bundle of sensations which characterizes immediate reflection.

On the other hand, it is when there is an independence of *meaning* that we come to think of things as having an independent existence. The crawling black things on the wall which one sees as the victim of delirium tremens are said to be "subjective," because they have meaning only in the individual life. The tree one sees when one is sane and sober is said to be independent, because its meaning is not confined to one's autobiography. It can and does have meaning outside *anyone's* autobiography. It can, in itself, be a center of meanings.

It is a substance in its own right because it can be the bearer of predicates which are not those of anything else, while every predicate assigned to the crawling black things must be assigned also to the life and mind of the victim of the disease. To be a substance is to be the bearer of a set of distinct predicates, or to be the objective reflection of a subjective state.

4.75 We should notice that the point of all this is inherently logical. When we ask how the trick is done, how the world is organized so that it has substances and properties which are capable of being understood as persons and things, we are asking how one can envision such an organization without lapsing into some fundamental kind of nonsense. We can see that one cannot construct an intelligible world simply out of properties and that a list of predicates is not enough. We can also see that there is no chance that we can help the situation by insisting that the world consists of mysterious "substances" which are something "over and above" the lists of properties.

But the only remaining option is that the "substances" are ways of organizing properties, and that the world can be looked at from two perspectives, each of which reveals the structure of the other. Neither could be revealed in its own perspective. A person can perceive things; he cannot, in the same sense, perceive himself—for then he would be an "object," another thing. Things can be understood as clusters of properties on a conceptual map which cannot contain itself. The logic of the situation demands the duality of perspective.

Since the point is logical, it may well be understood as having consequences it cannot have. It may be wrongly imagined that what is being
said is that things are figments of our imagination. That, of course, is
precisely what they are not. To be a thing is to have a place on a map
which is intelligible in itself. Its meaning is its own, although it takes us
to discover it, confront it, encounter it, or whatever. Good maps of this
kind facilitate our encounters, bad ones detract from them.

If this were a metaphysical treatise rather than a philosophical exploration of some central features of experience, it would be feasible and pro-
fitable to carry the investigation one step further, and to ask what these
facts imply for our understanding of the most general features of the
world. One might point out that most, and perhaps all, classical and contemporary accounts of the concept of material object are inadequate to
this notion of "thing." Evidently, too, those kinds of "idealism" which
conceive of reality as simply the contents of "minds" are inadequate to
this notion of "thing." But these questions lie outside our immediate
ambit.

4.76   Our immediate concern is simply to use this situation to dissolve
the causal paradoxes. We need to remind ourselves, again, of what is
most crucially at stake.

Persons and things are both components of a natural world in which
they share, and through which persons act and things react. For this to be
possible, the world needs, of course, to exhibit a certain minimal
tidiness—a certain measure of order and structure. But the actions of
persons, equally, must not be describable in such a way that they are
"reducible" to the causal sequences which pattern the order of things.

I have been suggesting, here, just that persons and things represent different ways of ordering the same properties, ways of ordering which give
justification to different sorts of propositions. It is this fact which
enables us to think of them as independent of one another. They are different sorts of substances in the sense that properties involved can be
clustered so as to give rise to different centres of meaningful reference.

It is always true, so far as we know, that, when the data are ordered so
as to act as the referents of propositions about things, they form an order
which is a determinate causal order. That is to say, we can always take a
stance which enables us, in constructed reflection, to regard them in a
certain way. But the same properties can always be construed as the
manifestation of a person; we can always talk about them as features in
someone's experience, and we can always succeed in this enterprise

because the dialectic of the meaning relation logically requires it, at least if the argument in the preceding sections holds.

Only some of these events, however, enter into situations for which we say that persons are responsible. Centrally, those events are events which figure in someone's autobiography in such a way that they are unintelligible otherwise. They may be simple acts such as crossing the street, complex acts such as being the author of someone's death, or basically individuating acts such as writing a book, being the lover of X, or signing one's name. Even in these cases, the possibility of holding someone responsible depends on a complex of special criteria. The "things" involved—one's body, the objects which form one's field of vision, and so on—have to be in a certain state. One is not responsible in the same way if one is drunk, drugged, or suffering from a psychosis. One is not responsible in the same way if the objects happen to form an optical illusion which is fundamentally misleading.

But none of these conditions turn out to be particularly inimical to the causal order of things, which simply demands that the things concerned have a determinate relation to one another. The order we find is one of a set of possible orders. We do not need another explanation for the fact that one of the possible orders occurs.

For example, the neurons attached to brain cells are two way switches. It does not have to be that they are one way rather than another. A human knee joint has to be in one of many positions. It does not have to be in one particular position. Incompatibilities only arise in the ways one expects. If one's knee is broken, one cannot choose to run. If many neurons are "turned on" by LSD, one may not be able to do advanced mathematics.

The restrictions are not those of an all-embracing mechanical system. For many meanings can be given to any physical state. The restrictions are those of a complex set of meanings which give shape to that experience.

The mininal notion of causality, then, is simply that there must be enough order to give rise to the kinds of experience we actually have. That we are tempted by the notion of two incompatible sets of orders—a mechanical, perfectly ordered world outside and an unstructured volitional world inside—is simply the by-product of the fact that experience manifests itself in a set of interlocking levels of consciousness. The experience that we have must be possible.

4.8   Things, Thoughts and Intentional Objects

The concept of intentional object is especially appropriate for a discussion of the world inside. The expression itself is a key to its utility: it draws together the notion of intention and the notion of object. Objects (things) are part of the external material world, while intentions are a part of the internal world. One might expect that an intentional object would combine features of both and that, in this notion, one would have the mind integrated with things. Indeed, this is just what does happen. In this regard, the concept of intentional object is like the concept of action, and, in fact, our discussion of it will parallel the discussion of action. The concept of action provided an instance of the way in which the mind manifested itself in behavior; intentional object will do the same for thing.

4.81   Some of the traps that awaited us with the concept of action are also to be avoided with intentional objects. One of the things implied in the discussion of action was that the issue of whether an action was something material, for example, a bodily movement, or something mental, that is, an act of will, was a dead-end issue. The same is true for an intentional object. Though there is a sense in which it shares features of both worlds, it is a mistake to think of it as a citizen of either. It is also a mistake to think of it as the simple sum of both worlds. If, for example, one just adds the idea of something extended to the idea of something unextended, one gets unintelligible confusion, not clarification. Beliefs are mental, movements are physical, but actions are not beliefs plus movements. Beliefs are expressed in actions. In this way they enter into the physical world, and in so doing, change it. That is, what counts as an action is a function of such things as beliefs. It should be natural for beliefs to modify things as well. It is, perhaps, a bit more strange to suggest that a thought could change a thing than to suggest that it could modify a movement. If one thinks of human behavior as a series of natural events governed by the laws of physics, then it becomes very much of a mystery how a mere thought could have any connection with it. Instead of explaining the notion of action, the idea of "doing something" itself may need to be explained.

4.82   Before explaining the way in which "intentional object" is an intelligible and useful notion, I want to consider specifically some of the difficulties that will have to be overcome. I have suggested that the idea of "object" is preeminently tied in with that of "thing." Things are chunks of stuff. They are the principle citizens of the external world, with a semi-permanent, determinate nature. In short, their properties are objective, making them the appropriate subject of description. There could be no such thing as a description unless there were a describable state of affairs. Such a state in the external world is one in which the components maintain existence separate and distinct from the process of observing them. If I am to make sense out of having observed that the chair over there has a broken leg, it must be that its being a chair with a defective part is separate from my realization that that is the case. Its *esse* cannot be its *percipe.* Suppose that this were not the case, and its having a broken leg were dependent on my observing that it had a broken leg. There would be no sense in which I could be mistaken about whether the chair had a broken leg, or only seemed to. Nor would there be a way in which I could be correct about the matter, for being correct means being in a position to give a correct description; a correct description is one that accurately depicts the way things are. If the chair is described as having four solid legs while the fact is that one of them is broken, there must be some conception of objective facts which are the determinable properties of the thing. Without such a conception, there would be no sense in which something could be right or wrong.

What these claims add up to is that the world of things is a determinate world and, as such, quite different from the world of the mind. A chair either does or does not have a broken leg. Whether or not I realize which of these possibilities is actual is dependent on its being actual. But this is not true of such things as thoughts and intentions. What determines the content and properties of my thought is not such an obvious matter. The general question of whether an object has a property is independent of whether I know it has that property. Roughly, the description of a thing can be looked on as a mapping relation that would be correct if each relevant feature of the object is represented in the locution; otherwise, it would be incomplete. If the process of perceiving an object is not kept distinct from the object, it becomes doubtful that there is a sense in which there can be a true characterization of the object based on that perception. But is it possible to make such a separation in the mind? Can one say that whether or not a thought has a property is independent of whether I know it has that property? Suppose that this can be said. Do we not, after all, learn, discover, or find out what we are or have been thinking? There is a process of detecting the contents of one's mind just as there is a process of uncovering the properties of things. But what does this come to? One possibility is that one may *come to realize* that he is thinking of 'x'. That is, he may have a thought, not clearly know its subject matter, and then come to know what that subject matter is. For example, "It suddenly came to me that it was Heidi and not Margot that I was thinking about." But this is inconclusive. Does it make sense to say that all along there was the thought, and that through a kind of inspection of it (introspection) I discovered that it was of Heidi? We do say things like this, and it does seem reasonable to suppose that such a claim does mark out a real phenomenon; but that is not the point. The question is whether it marks out a phenomenon that is like finding out that a chair has a broken leg.

There is no special problem raised by someone else's saying that the chair does have a broken leg, but that Sam does not know it. The lights may be out so that it is impossible for Sam to see. In other words, there are recognized procedures and conditions that must obtain in order that one may find out. But is there not a real problem if we say that Sam is thinking of Heidi but does not know it? To begin with, it is at least unusual. We normally take what Sam says about his own thoughts as having a special status, whereas nothing special is required in order to explain how he might be mistaken in what he says about a thing. Let us suppose one is asked what he is thinking about and he replies "Margot, of course." If we take him to be sincere in his report, we will need substantial evidence to support the contention that he is mistaken. We have to establish the plausibility of differentiating between something's being the case, and its only seeming to him to be the case.

I have tried to indicate the divergence between the two areas that compose the notion of intentional object. What I will do now is to try and overcome that gap by a more direct investigation of the concept itself.

4.83   I want to start by indicating that the concept of object is considerably more broad than has been so far suggested. Elizabeth Anscombe argues that the word "object" has altered its meaning:

> The word "object" which comes in the phrase "object of sight" has suffered a certain reversal of meaning in the history of philosophy, and so has the connected word "subject," though the two reversals aren't historically connected. The subject used to be what the proposition, say, is about, the thing itself as it is in reality—unprocessed by being conceived, as we might say (in case there is some sort of processing there); objects on the other hand were formerly always objects *of*—. Objects of desire, objects of thought, are not objects in one common modern sense, not individual things, such as *the objects found in the accused man's pockets.*[1]

Whether or not she is right on the historical matter of the change of meaning is of no real importance. She is undeniably correct in saying that the word as it is presently used has two senses. There are objects as in "the objects found in his pocket," and there are objects as in "the object of his plan or desire." With this distinction in mind, much of the earlier puzzle can be put into focus. Intentional objects are objects in the sense that thought has an object. This is sufficient to take them out of the physical world and place them into the mental world—or so it seems. What this does is to make it clear that an intentional object is not another individual thing, as a chair might be. But if an intentional object is an object in the sense that thoughts have objects, this does not solve as much as one might think. We are now talking of objects in the sense of objects *of* something, and a thought may have as its object something physical as well as something mental.[2] Consider the following, taken from a legal dictionary:

> This term [object] includes whatever is presented to the mind, as well as what may be presented to the senses; whatever, also, is acted upon, or operated upon, affirmatively, or intentionally influenced by anything done, moved, or applied thereto.[3]

In this account we have incorporated both senses. Included are things before the mind, as well as things before the senses.

If one subscribes to a traditional mental/physical dualism, qualifying something as an intentional object is performing a rather strange operation. The world of material objects is the world of objectively determinable properties. It is the world of real objects, of science; it is the place where standards of truth and accuracy can be applied. The world of the mind is not so tidy a place. It is predominantely a world of appearance. On some occasions these appearances may yield information about the real world, on others they shade into pure fancy. The more they are subjectively determined by the mind, the more they become imaginary. The more we shun the world of the mind in preference to the real world, the greater the likelihood of our obtaining the truth.

Such a view seems to me to be mostly a prejudice, though a time honored one to be sure. If we take as our overriding principle a concern with "what there is," we will find that intentional objects are as informative as are material objects. It is mistaken to think that only material objects can provide us with information about the nature of what there is, or that if there is a sense in which intentional objects may do this, it will be merely about such things as thoughts, feelings, and attitudes, items regarded as real only in the mind. In short, the mistake is in thinking that there are two discrete kinds of things, mental and physical—that intentional objects relate only to the former, and material objects only to the latter. There is nothing wrong with the belief that some things are mental and some physical; the mistake is in thinking that something's being mental precludes its being physical, that is, that these are exclusive categories. What happens is that the designation of something as intentional frequently blurs the distinction between these. One cannot say that it always involves both, because there is a no *a priori* way of determining what kind of thing one will be wanting, looking for, thinking of, and so on.

It is a mistake of grand scale and simplicity to argue that the mind always concerns itself with one kind of thing, that is, ideas.[4] It is true that ideas are always involved in any operation of the mind; the mistake is in thinking that their proper role is always as the object of that operation. If that were true, skepticism would quickly follow, for if ideas were the only proper objects of mental operations, it follows that things are not. From there it is only a short step to the claim that we do not know (or perceive directly) material objects. However, there is no reason to restrict the class of objects of mental operations to things like ideas—aside from the desire for a kind of balanced economy. [The fact of the matter is that one may think of a stone as well as the idea of a stone.] Having opened up thinking to objects of both kinds, it would be confused to now assume that the proper object of thought must be either something mental or something physical. The point is not that this dualism ignores a third or a fourth possibility and is therefore incomplete. What I would like to avoid is the entire enterprise of categorizing the types of objects of thought. One may think of absolutely anything—which must also include absolutely nothing. Categorizing objects may be a perfectly legitimate enterprise. My point is that it has no special connection to an inquiry into the logic of thinking.

Remembering that our major concern is with determining "what there is," it would be artificial and constrained to classify the objects of thought as exclusively either mental or physical. One could argue that, of course, the stone is physical and that the idea of a stone is something mental. There would be no need to use a hybrid like an intentional object, and our traditional dualism would remain intact. But in fact, it does not remain intact. The answers given to the enquiry into "what there is" must include things that one thinks about and the choices "mental or physical?" are neither one adequate to the job. It is not that there is something wrong with the classifications of mental and physical; but that, as with all classifications, their justification begins and ends with the purpose that they serve. If a more adequate insight into "what there is" is provided by another perspective, then that should be adopted.

We need a tidier way of exposing the role played by intentional object descriptions, and I think that that can be found if we consider the parallel with intentional actions. An acceptable description of an act as intentional does not create a new description that would not otherwise apply. The minimal requirement for an acceptable description is that it is true of what is happening. "What is happening" is the broad classification which includes both actions and events. Likewise, "What there is" includes both material and intentional objects. The notion of intentionality allows us to select from this large group of descriptions a subclass, those which, in addition to providing information about "What there is," also yield an insight into the state of mind of the agent. For example, the truth of "Sam is looking for a pack of cigarettes" warrants inferences going in two directions. First, it entitles us to infer that it is reasonable to expect that something answering the indefinite description "a pack of cigarettes" will turn up in Sam's possession. Secondly, we may conclude that if Sam obtains a pack of cigarettes, he will be satisfied. These inferences are not very profound, but they serve the point; the information they provide is of two varieties.

4.84   The question that we are confronted with is, "What kind of a thing is an intentional object?" To forestall a dead-end metaphysics that can be implied by this question, I present the following considerations which are taken from Miss Anscombe's article "The Intentionality of Sensation."[5] She defines the class of intentional objects as a sub-class of direct objects so that knowing what the one is, is dependent on knowing what the other is. The question becomes "What is a direct object?" If we take a sentence such as "John sent Mary a book," and ask what is it that the sentence says that John sent Mary, then the answer "a book" gives us the direct object. Now, what is it that that phrase gives us? Is it something linguistic or something material? Is the direct object the words "a book," or is it a thing that one could read? We cannot say that it is something that people read, because the sentence is not being considered as saying something true. If it were, we could ask "which book?" but the only answer to that would be "no book" and that cannot be right, since that is to deny that the sentence has a direct object.

But we cannot choose the alternative, that a direct object is a piece of language, either. The direct object is something that is obtained in answer to the question: "What does the sentence say that John sent Mary?" and it is wrong to answer that by saying "A piece of language."

> We must conclude of "objects" (direct, indirect, and likewise intentional) that the object is neither the phrase nor what the phrase stands for. What then is it? The question is based on a mistake, namely that an explanatory answer running say "An intentional (direct, indirect) object is such-and-such" is possible and requisite. But this need not be so. Indeed the only reasonable candidates to be answers are the ones we have failed. But what is the actual use of the term? Given a sentence in which a verb takes an object, one procedure for replying to the question: "What is the object of this sentence?" is to recite the object phrase.[6]

What Anscombe is trying to avoid is the type of puzzles that I was alluding to at the beginning of this chapter. If we think of an intentional object as a particular kind of thing, it must appear as a very unusual kind of thing. If, on the one hand, we take its nature to be material, then its features must be determinate, its qualities must be objectively characterizable and, whatever it is, it must be independent of a perceiver's conception of it. Intentions, on the other hand, are radically different, since they are whatever they are sincerely said to be so that the object would be whatever it was sincerely said to be.

But there is no reason to proceed in this way. What we seek is an understanding of what an intentional object is, and that is something that can be obtained in any number of ways. One possibility is suggested in the last quotation from Anscombe. For example, one may begin by enquiring into the actual use of the phrase "direct object," using as his data a host of specific illustrations. However, I prefer to return to an earlier suggestion, approaching the subject from the perspective of action. Anscombe herself suggests this approach, and offers three features of intentional action that are applicable:

> First, not any true description of what you do describes it as the action you intended: only under certain of its descriptions will it be intentional. ("Do you mean to be using that pen?"—"Why, what about this pen?"—"It's Smith's pen."—"Oh Lord, no!") Second, the descriptions under which you intend what you do can be vague, indeterminate. (You mean to put the book down on the table all right, and you do so, but you do not mean to put it down anywhere in particular on the table—though you do put it down somewhere in particular.) Third, descriptions under which you intend to do what you do may not come true, as when you make a slip of the tongue or pen. You act, but your intended act does not happen.[7]

In order to apply these features, we need a way of generating examples. That becomes a simple matter of invoking the linguistic criterion that I mentioned earlier. The objects that we are concerned with are always objects of a verb, so that the occurrence of the phrase "object of" preceding a verb is a sufficient but not necessary mark of an intentional object. The phrase is not necessary simply because it does not always occur in ordinary language. However, where it does not occur it can be made to occur without loss of meaning. For example, it does not occur in the sentence "Sam wants Heidi," but that can be rewritten as "The object of Sam's want is Heidi." An expression like "The object of his kick_____" may be offered as a counter-example. Intuitively, it would seem that kicking is not like wanting in that it takes an object of a different sort so that the phrase "object of" does not give us what I claimed it did. However, the only plausible reading of that sentence requires that the blank be filled in with something like "to frighten her." In other words, the sentence would be about the purposes or aims of the agent, and so could be cast in an intentional context. If it were about what he was kicking, then the blank would have to be filled in with something like "her knee." But if it means that he kicked her knee, then it should say that. As it stands, it is more about the agent's state of mind than about what his foot came into contact with.

Applying Anscombe's first feature, we conclude that only under certain descriptions is an object an intentional object.[8] For example, in the sentence "Sam wants Heidi," Heidi is the intentional object of Sam's want. However, it if is true that Heidi is the mother of Alexander, it does not follow that we are entitled to conclude "Sam wants the mother of Alexander." It may seem strange that whether or not something counts as an intentional object depends on the description that it is given, for this means that what a thing is depends on what we say about it. This is the reverse of the way it normally is. Whether or not something is a tree is not dependent on my saying that it is. It is whatever it is, and what I say of it is a function of the properties that it has. It is at the very heart of our concept of a thing, and of our concept of what it is to describe a thing, that we make our description fit the facts; the facts are not decided by what we say. Yet with an intentional object, the nature of the facts is determined by what we say, or, in some sense, by what we believe. As a minimal, necessary condition, Sam must at least be aware of the maternal relation between Heidi and Alexander before we could be entitled to go from "Sam wants Heidi" to "Sam want the mother of Alexander." But even that is not sufficient since we are after the object of his desire as it is seen by him as desirable. Along with actions, intentional objects are part of the arena in which the world inside meets the world outside. It is one of those areas in which we can obtain data about what is going on in someone's mind as well as what is true in the world. Because of this the fact that Heidi is the mother of Alexander is not in itself enough to allow us to infer that Sam wants the mother of Alexander. Such an inference is about Sam's state of mind, and material facts alone are not adequate to the job. This makes an intentional object a peculiar kind of object, because what it is must be at least partly a function of what we believe.

I have been arguing that there is a discrepancy between the way in which one may challenge the description of a material object, and the way in which one may challenge the description of an intentional object. With a material object description, it is always appropriate to say "The actual nature of the object is not what you say it is," because there can be a demonstrable difference between a material object's having certain features and its being (sincerely) said to have certain features. One of the reasons for being able to maintain this difference is that there is a recognizable method for determining what its properties are. It follows that there are ways in which such a method may misfire; it may not have been properly employed, or it may have been inadequate to the task. In the case of intentional objects, there is no such procedure, so there is no difference between the object's actually having certain properties and its being (sincerely) said to have those properties. But if sincerity is being equated with truth and accuracy, then have we not opened up the door to all sorts of bizarre possibilities? It would seem that one may say anything so long as he did so sincerely, and so long as he made it clear that he was talking about an intentional and not a material object. But this is to overstate what is allowed. Standards of sense have not been abandoned, they have shifted. In the case of material objects, the object has the final say; in the case of intentional objects, the person does. Suppose that we find someone who stoutly maintains that he wants all burned out electrical fuses within a radius of a mile. If he enacts his claim by going from door to door offering to buy them at a penny a dozen, I suppose we would begin to consider the intelligibility of his claim. By offering to buy the fuses he has taken steps to make his words intelligible; we expect this kind of behavior from a person who really does want something. But although we understand his words we do not understand the person. So far, there has been no effort to explain what it is about burned out fuses that is desirable.

To understand this, it is necessary to be reminded again of one of the central roles played by intentional objects, in contrast with material objects. If something is properly characterized as a chair, this adds to our knowledge of things in the world, but does not in itself provide us with

any information about persons. To be sure, there are normal expectations based on the belief that the item is a chair, and some of these expectations concern persons. For example, if one were to arrange himself in
the proper way, the object would support him; if he were to visually confront it, he would probably report certain features, and so on. However,
the description of the object as a chair provides us with grounds only for
speculation—however rational—about a person.

Someone might argue that although chairs do not tell us directly about
persons, arms, legs, weight, and height do. A person's weight is more intimately connected with him than is an object like a chair. But this shows
only that some physical object statements are more closely related to persons than are others. Even something as closely involved with a person as
his weight does not provide the kind of information that I am speaking
about. Specifically, what is at issue is insight into a person's state of
mind, which is what intentional objects graphically provide. For example, if our chair is not merely given a spacio-temporal description but is
characterized as being sought for by Sam, we are on our way to having
an insight into Sam's state of mind. The bare fact that Sam is seeking the
chair provides us with the minimal information necessary to conclude
that Sam is having (has had or will have) thoughts about the chair. To
obtain more information about Sam's state of mind, we need more data
about the chair. Of course, we require that the data be about the chair as
something sought for, since other of its properties are of no interest. As
soon as we make that requirement, there is the danger that the point will
appear vacuous. The effect of the expression "as something sought for"
is, of course, to turn one's attention towards Sam's thoughts. It is merely
another way of talking about his wants and beliefs. Talk of intentional
objects becomes no more than a disguised way of referring to what is in
Sam's head. We may talk this way if we choose, but there seems little to
recommend it since we would be lapsing back into the dualism that we
have been arguing against. To interpret talk of intentional objects as
merely confusing talk of mental events is to ignore the most striking fact
about our present example. What Sam is looking for is a chair and a
chair is not something mental. What seems to be operating here is the
following kind of argument taken from Locke but found in any number
of philosophers. Since looking is an operation of the mind it must have
as its object an idea since ideas are always what the mind is about. But as
we have argued, the mind is not always about ideas, but sometimes about
chairs and stones.

We are, of course, talking of one's thoughts and ideas, but not in a way that is redundant or eliminable. That the chair is something sought for by Sam is an objective fact. The fact that intentional object descriptions also provide direct data about a person's state of mind is not sufficient reason for refusing to regard them as established members of the real world. The point may be more strongly put: the mental-physical dichotomy cannot be sustained in all areas. Most expecially, the classification does not parallel a real not real, fact fancy distinction.

The second feature of intentionality has to do with its indeterminacy. Sam may be most definite in his wants, so that it is Heidi and only Heidi that will do. However, there is nothing to prevent him from being indefinite. He may simply want "a woman." If one is characterizing a material object, and the characterization is indefinite, it must also be incomplete. With an intentional object, that does not follow. If Sam sets out to describe the woman that he married and does not mention the color of her eyes, we are entitled to conclude that he gave only a partial description, for an actual woman either does or does not have blue eyes. Such an inference is not warranted if Sam is describing the woman that he wants. If, in depicting the woman of his dreams, he does not refer to the color of her eyes, we cannot thereby insist that his description is incomplete. It is true that he may have neglected to mention that she has blue-grey eyes, but it is equally as possible that he simply did not consider eyes. If he is sincere in saying that he has told us all there is, then it is no good for us to insist that this is contrary to the laws of logic. Such a move has no place in the characterization of an intentional object. But suppose that we make it? Suppose that we do insist that he consider her again. In order for such a request to have a chance of taking hold, it must be possible to distinguish between something's being the case and it's merely seeming to be the case. We are saying that it merely seemed to him that she neither had eyes nor did not have eyes, while the fact is that one of those descriptions must apply. This kind of challenge implies that she has determinate properties that can be independent of the way that Sam now thinks of her. Surely, if the woman is a creation of Sam's own fantasy, we may not be in a position to say what she is really like. What becomes impossible is the possibility of another's correcting Sam; only he has access to the truth. It is clear that he could give a second account that differed from the first, in that it mentioned the color of her eyes. What is not clear is what would be involved if he were to claim that the second account were correct, and the first one a mistake.

It seems that one can make a mistake about the nature of one's own intentional object, and that this is possible without becoming embroiled in the entanglements of self-deception. The logic of such an error is different from the kind that occurs with material objects, so that one may choose not to use the word "error." But putting aside the terminological problem, the phenomenon is something like this. Two weeks ago in a state of reverie, Sam imagined the woman of his dreams. Today he describes her, and in the process of describing her suddenly realizes that he is misdescribing her, that is, for a moment he forgot that he really wanted her to have blue-grey eyes. At the minimum, his alleged misdescription and lapse of memory mean that his description now is different from the one that he gave (or would have given) two weeks ago. But he also claims that the first account is the better one. Of course, it is true that there is no publicly observable standard against which he or we can measure his accounts, but this is not sufficient reason to reject them.[9] It is however, one of the things that helps generate the problem. Within this account is the implied need of a correspondence theory of truth, the notion that if one is to prefer one account over another, it must be because the one can be mapped more accurately onto the real state of affairs than can the other. If there is not a determinable, real state of affairs, then everything breaks down. The only thing that counts as a determinable state of affairs for the object of the description is a real person. It might seem that because what we are concerned with is what is said about an object that is only imaginary, then it does not make any difference what is said. But, at least subjectively, this seems inadequate, and it is.

The fact is that one may give a great deal of thought to describing the girl of one's dreams. One may try on a feature, reject it as not quite appropriate and replace it with another. Such a procedure certainly has all the earmarks of a careful and precise search. What is confusing, because it has not been brought out, is that the care and precision involved are creative. It is just this that distinguishes this process from the description of a real object, and that makes it look as though there were no standards of adequacy. To say that there are no standards is to suggest that although the process of creating something representative may have as its standard the thing being represented anything goes when creating something non representational. Of course, that is not true. The absence of an actual object of description means only that what one says becomes a more direct function of what one wants as it becomes pried loose from what there is.

4.85   The issue is whether or not one may make a mistake about the nature of one's own intentional object. The instance of that is whether or

THE CRUCIAL CONCEPTS AND THE FACTS

not one may make a mistake about what it is that one wants. One needs a situation in which one can say that what one really needs is Φ, and that one's earlier description of it as Ψ is inadequate. In giving such an account it might be tempting to refer to "unconscious wants," at least in a technical if not Freudian sense, but nothing like that is necessary. Suppose I say that what I really want is a woman who would be a good mother to my children, and that my earlier description of my dream woman as a vivacious companion was a mistake. The justification for such a move does not involve anything unconscious or mysterious. What I would do is to show the correspondence between what I claim is the proper account of what I want, with features that are suitable to me and with aspects of my behavior. For example, "Given my long-standing love of children—just look how I dote on those of friends—such a woman is much more appropriate." Of course such observations do not prove beyond a shadow of a doubt that the sexy blonde is not more to my liking, but this possibility alone is not sufficient to question my account. If the doubt is to be a real doubt, then we need an actual inconsistency between my account and what I have said or done. The mere possibility of such an inconsistency establishes nothing. In other words, what I sincerely claim stands as correct unless an actual discrepancy exists. It is true that when I claim to have made a mistake in describing what I want, and offer an amended account, I am open to the charge of having changed my mind rather than having corrected myself. Sometimes, of course, a different account does result from having changed one's mind. And there are occasions when it is difficult to tell if one has changed his mind or refined his description. In the case of a material object, this kind of uncertainty is devastating. It amounts to admitting that one is unclear as to whether he is giving a more refined description, or a description of a different object. Such an admission is tantamount to saying that there are no effective criteria of adequacy. However, in the case of intentional objects, our recourse to sincerity is legitimate, and not a degenerate version of what it is to describe something correctly. In the absence of any inconsistencies or other oddities about the claim, what one sincerely asserts has decisive authority. If one says sincerely that the earlier description of the woman of his dreams was not correct but that his present one is, we have reached the end of the line.

There is a chance that the acceptance of such standards will compel us to accept some foolish claims, but that is because there are strange people who think bizarre thoughts and want outlandish things. No standard of sense can be expected to change human nature. All that can be done, and what I have done, is to indicate the way in which one may reject some of the claims that do not make sense, by a consideration of the consistency of what one sincerely claims. This is a negative criterion whose only function is to eliminate sub-standard cases. Merely being consistent does not guarantee the adequacy of what one says, although I should emphasize that the consistency is not only verbal. I have called inconsistent that kind of situation in which a person claims, for example, to want something and yet does not act accordingly. If, however, one claims to want something that is not desirable—a broken arm, for example—and if he set out to obtain it, and is able to show that his wanting it is compatible with his long-standing desire for broken bones, we may have to allow such a bit of perversity to go through. First, however, we would make use of the second feature of intentionality to see if there was not a more palatable description of his desire.[10] Is it sympathy, medical attention, or perhaps the avoidance of some physical activity, that he really wants? If he rejects these alternatives, we are confused. But it is important to note how and why the confusion arises. It is not that his words do not make sense; the trouble is that they do. Earlier I argued that one of the prime functions of intentional objects was to provide insight into a person's state of mind.[11] It is because we have accepted what the person has said that we cannot understand him. What kind of a person is it that would want a broken arm?

4.86   The reason for spending time on the question of the kind of sense that can be required of statements about one's intentional objects is to indicate how the world inside can modify the world outside. What has emerged is that in characterizing a material object, it is the object that is the ultimate standard of adequacy for what is said. In the case of an intentional object, the pendulum swings to the person making the claim, thus placing the emphasis on consistency and sincerity. However, it may not be clear what this has to do with the world *outside*. What needs to be emphasized is that in the majority of cases, what one wants corresponds with what there actually is and with what is normally considered desirable. But even in these more normal cases, what there is is a function of what, one thinks. The only difference is that because of the normalcy and correctness of what one thinks, that fact is likely to escape detection. If, for example, one is thinking of an ice cream cone and one thinks of it as being cold and sweet, especially appropriate on a hot day, one's thinking appears to be governed by the real features of an actual object. There seems no difference between characterizing a material object and an intentional one. This is as it should be, because in this instance they coincide. Furthermore, this is what we should expect in the majority of cases, since to operate in the world with even a chance of success we must take into account the actual features of that world. However, even in those cases in which one has a firm grip on reality, the description of what he wants as an intentional object is ultimately a function of his beliefs. In other words, if one describes an ice cream cone (as something that one wants) as something cold, sweet, but impervious to heat, the account is troublesome. As a description of something thought of and wanted, one cannot say that it is false simply because ice cream is not impervious to heat. "False want" suggests not so much that the description has gone astray from the facts but that the want itself is not actual, and that is ruled out by the assumption of sincerity.

Being clear-headed about ice cream does not mean ignoring one's own thoughts so as to concentrate exclusively on "the truth." The idea that there might be two discrete separable spheres, one having to do with how things actually are—that is, true descriptions of actual objects—and the other allowing for various kinds of unrestrained, subjective and creative liberties, is a potential source of deep difficulty. It is clear enough that the objective world of material things does not have an exclusive hold on reality. What is not so clear are the consequences of including the subjective world of the mind in our account of what is real. Historically we have had two options: (1) the world of the mind was really like the physical world—except that it was mental, (2) the world of the mind was a *sui generis* ungoverned kind of fantasy land. The truth of (1) is supported by any number of philosophical notions ranging from Hume's principles of association to Skinner's behaviorism, (2) was seen as the consequence of denying (1)—obviously something unattractive and to be avoided. What I want to at least suggest is that there is another viable alternative and that is that the world of the mind is essentially active and creative. Its objects, and these are intentional objects, are things that we create in accordance with our needs and interests and desires. But the fact that the mind is essentially creative does not mean that its operations are random and ungoverned. What it does mean is that the laws that govern it are not objective and descriptive but prescriptive and normative. The key term in understanding this process is "responsibility." As in all cases of action there is the presumption of responsibility and this is as much true in cases of thinking as it is in more conventional cases of doing. In other words, we do not simply have thoughts; we try to think clearly and well. Because we are held accountable for these efforts both by ourselves and by others, we must either accept the consequences of our initial efforts or try again.

4.9 Intentional Objects, Universals, and Relations

The conclusion of the last section was that intentional objects are not pseudo-things, grammatical devices, or purely verbal inventions of philosophers. They cannot be analyzed away, therefore, by the adoption of preferred and more sophisticated locutions. But it is equally obvious that they cannot be understood as a special class of "things." They are not unusual and diaphonous things, and they are not ordinary things in extraordinary spaces.

What, then, is left of any interest? The discussion in section 4.8 established a number of interesting properties which intentional objects *do* have, two of which are of crucial importance. One of those properties we might describe as malleability, and the other is the property of being definitively related to the person who has the intentions in question. Together, they suggest what intentional objects "are" and what function they have in life and in knowledge. They are malleable in the sense that they can cover a great variety of actual occasions: One may hope for a million dollars and the hoped-for dollars, considered *as* the object of one's hope, may be in bills or bullion, cashier's checks, railway bonds, or warehouses full of potash. An actual million dollars has to be delivered in some determinate form. In this sense, the intentional object is a universal—it can turn up here, there, or anywhere. It is not an aggregate of particulars, or an aggregate of the descriptions of the set of actual occasions. For one who hopes for a million dollars does not need to hope for all or any one of these particulars, and does not need to know the complete descriptions of all or any of the things which would fulfill his intentions. His intention must merely include a set of criteria which would be successful in identifying the thing were it to turn up. The intentional object cannot, of course, be just anything. One who hopes for a million dollars in such a curious form that it would slip unnoticed past the Internal Revenue Service probably does not hope for anything. Most likely, his intentional object is simply unintelligible.

An intentional object, in this sense, is a device for organizing one's experience. If one did not have any intentional objects, one's condition would be disastrous in two respects. First, one could not be said to know anything, for knowing something involves an awareness that some criteria have been fulfilled—it is the meeting of intentional objects in an actual occasion. (In consequence, knowing that one has an intention involves the transference of the intentional object from its guise as universal to its guise as a particular occasion of the goings on in one's mind.) Equally, one could not be said to *be* if one had no intentional objects. For "knowing oneself" is an act which involves organizing one's experience so as to give that experience a center which is self-revelatory; essentially, it is to organize one's experience around one's intentions. But that is to reveal the other crucial aspect of intentional objects—the aspect in which they are inextricably related to the person who has them so as to be, for the moment, definitive of that person. It seems obvious that there are no hopes, fears, things sought, and objects known without someone there to know them. A hoped-for million dollars is not a particular million dollars, but it is a particular hope. As object, it is a universal. As intention, it is someone's intention, now or then. We commonly associate particular persons with particular centres of experience. But it is not the experience which is peculiar to the person—many people with headaches have much the same kind of ache, many viewers of The Grand Canyon have much the same view. What distinguishes them are their intentional attitudes.

All of this suggests what is at stake here: because every piece of knowledge involves an intention, some philosophers have concluded that knowledge is primarily *of* intentional objects. Because every intentional awareness is private, some philosophers have concluded that awareness is always private. Because intentional objects are a special kind of universal, some philosophers have concluded that knowledge is primarily of universals. And so on.

The purpose of this section is twofold: to dissolve some of these conundrums and to demonstrate, as briefly as possible, that the line between the "world within" and the "world outside," if it follows the line between intentional objects and objects, is a line which is drawn by means of understanding the distinctions between a certain sort of universal and a certain sort of particular, and by means of understanding the distinction between the kind of relation which holds between a person and his intention and the kind of relation which holds between a person and things proper.

4.91   If the view I am advocating about intentional objects really does dissolve some of the conundrums about intentionality and knowledge, it must, of course, also dissolve some of the conundrums about universals and clarify some of the associated features of the problem of knowledge. The qualification "some of," however, is not simply a conventional caveat to cover things which I may have forgotten. The universals controversy is much too rich and interesting to be dealt with summarily here. Only those aspects of it which arise in just this context can be dealt with at all though, inevitably, something which might be developed into a general solution will have to be introduced.

4.911   The issue as we find it here is just this: we have seen that an intentional object is, in one of its aspects, a universal. It is, if you like, a special kind of universal. Most simply, it is a universal of indeterminate application—the hoped-for million dollars, the girl of one's dreams, the house of one's plans, the solution of the equation.

Even when there is one and only one object which will meet the specifications—the solution of the equation, perhaps—it is still not determinate as *intentional* object. The intentional object, in this case, *cannot* have all the properties of the object sought. The object, furthermore, can be sought by many people at many times. It is characteristic of the object sought that it will, in the end, function logically as a particular—it will be *the* solution. But it is characteristic of the intention that it will function, logically, as a universal. I can be said to have that intention even if I arrive at the wrong solution; it is, therefore, an intention which carries through indefinitely many possible solutions.

4.912   None of these intentional objects can be said to be assembled from sets of particulars. The intention in the case of the equation is not a statistical aggregate of many solutions. The girl of one's dreams is not a demographer's construction. The house one is planning is not an empirical abstraction from many houses one has known. Indeed, one may be planning an impossible house, the girl of one's dreams may not exist, and the equation may have no solution. We cannot, therefore, be literal "nominalists" about the universals in question. They are not just "names"—for there really is an intention and, as we have seen, there really are intentional objects.

A natural suggestion is that we could analyze out our intentional objects into sets of criteria. One examines the house being built to see if it is the house one intended; one's "dream girl" is a standard against which one weighs the real girls. But that won't *quite* do, either, because the criteria make sense against some demand, the specifications of the intentional object.

4.913   It is also evident that the intentional object is a different sort of entity from objects proper. I said, repeatedly, in section 4.8 that the requirements for intentional objects are different from the requirements for things or objects proper. The requirements are less demanding in that the intentional object need not have all the properties which a thing intended "through" it must have. But we have also seen that it must have some properties which such "things" do not have—malleability and a certain relation to the intender.

Thus we have some of the ingredients of the most traditional problem about universals—those associated with the concern that universals, seemingly, have an ontological status which is different from that of things and yet, since they must be closely related to things so as to make some account of knowledge possible, they cannot be regarded as wholly independent of things.

4.9131   The "solution," in some measure, is to bring home the point emphasized in the last section: that it is not to be assumed that the possession of one set of properties necessarily excludes the possession of another. What we regard as mental in one context we may well regard as physical in another. Similarly, functioning as a universal does not exclude functioning as a particular. But we need to see just how this might be so in the present case, and just how we might make effective use of the fact.

4.9132   The intentional object is, of course, a particular state of affairs. Someone is intending something, and at some particular time. To carry it out, he will have to formulate some notion for himself and, to do that, he will have to have recourse to some carrier for his intentions—words, gestures or whatever. These carriers are particulars. They express universal meanings, but the meanings are an aspect of the situation, not something wholly abstractable from it. Try as you may, you cannot capture a meaning without some device to capture it.

4.9133   The meanings are literally given in a way which involves a free act on the part of somebody. One cannot convey meanings unless one has some device which admits of genuine alternatives. The railway signal conveys genuine alternatives, but it conveys nothing to anyone when it is permanently fixed in some position. It must have at least two positions to become a "bearer" of meanings. And it must not be the case that no one has any control of it—if it is to convey the proper *intention* of someone.

4.9134   Yet, given the condition that there are intentional acts in the world and not just events, the meanings can be carried by whatever we can organize in such a way that it expresses a set of alternatives. The meanings do not become "another thing" in a "different world." They are simply what is conveyed and expressed by the things in the ordinary world.

Our intentional objects are a special case of this situation. They are special because they are what we intended, as opposed to what happened to get conveyed. They are the locus of the intentional act. Thus, as universals, they are nonetheless embedded in the particulars through which they are expressed.

A simple railway signal is, if one wishes to talk that way, both mental and physical. It is a lamp, or an arm, a perfectly ordinary physical object. But it also reveals to the engine driver the state of mind of those who run the railroad. If we must ask where their minds are, we would not be wrong to say that the signal is what they "put their minds to" and, in so far as a mind could be anywhere, it is where it appears to be. The sign that running a railroad requires intellect is, after all, just in such things and one who runs a railroad thoughtfully will have many devices which reveal the fact.

4.9135   Now when we say that we "know something" what we mean to say, of course, is that we can specify the properties of some state of affairs in such a way that others can identify that state of affairs from our account of the matter. It is thus actually the case that intentionality enters into the matter, and that what is "known" in this sense is the outcome of the matching of an intentional object with *another* intentional object. If I say I know that this is gold, I am saying that I know what gold is and that I have applied the criteria (derived from an intentional object) to an object "chosen" (another intentional object). The conjunction of the two produces intelligible acquaintance with an object proper, or an ordinary thing.

4.9136   This has no unpleasant or surprising outcome. In order to know the "thing" one must regard it as the bearer of the appropriate universals—as intelligible and capable of being assigned meanings. But this does not mean that "it" is an intentional object or a universal any more than the railway pole with the lamp is, *itself*, an intentional object or a universal. It was thought, apparently, by Russell, that, in order to get away from the notion that what one knew was—literally and always—universals, one had to postulate "knowledge by acquaintance" in the form of a direct grasp (or receipt) of special, atomically structured entities. He sometimes called these "sensa," and they were rather like the "things" often called "sense data."[1] But one could not be said to know such "immediate objects" in any intelligible sense just because, if one were to ascribe properties to them, such as "red" or "blue" or whatever, one would be regarding them as bearers of universals; and then, one would have Russell's "knowledge by description."

It is true that there must always be options in such descriptions; the element of "intention" invariably enters into the description, since one does, after all, compare one intentional object against another. Thus a given object of enquiry may be my wife in one context, and a collection of organic molecules in another and, if I have lost her in a crowd, I shall have to choose which woman to search for. But that is not to say that I may not be objectively right in either case, and it is certainly not to say that there are not conclusive reasons which will determine my choice as sensible or foolish.

4.9137   For any context, of course, there will be something which is just "there" and which functions as the bearer of the appropriate universals and enables my intentional objects to generate criteria which mesh in practice. But what is simply "given" in one context can always be investigated in another.

The delineation of the "world inside," then, is given for this purpose just by the set of intentions which pattern a given investigation and determine what is subjected to criteria, what is simply "given" and how the two structure one another. One looks for one's intentions in the patterning of one's investigations. The world "inside" exists and makes sense just in so far as the intentional objects succeed in forming an intelligible pattern which is open to investigation—but the pattern and the investigation are bound to show up in the shape of the world outside.

4.914   The argument is not that one of these structures is primary and the other derivative, for one simply cannot have an intelligible notion of the outside world as "given" except by seeing what turns up as one's intentions take shape. And to turn the mind inward on itself will reveal, of course, not a new world, but simply that background pattern which derives from the way in which one carries out one's intentions. One may turn one's intentions on the process and produce accounts of sense data, of patterns of thought and feeling; but they, after all, are the by-product of the process—as, indeed, one might have expected.

4.915   To ask whether there really "are" both universals and particulars, in this sense, is simply to ask whether there are right kinds of meanings and bearers of meanings. To reduce one to the other would be fatal to both. To regard one as possible without the other would produce the same fatality.

It is perfectly sensible to say that the world had a long history without men, and that the meaning enters the world with human activity. But one must understand that it is sensible to say this because, if one chooses to assemble the world as a certain set of objects of knowledge—things discrete in space and time—then it turns out that the way one's chosen structure divides up what meets the criteria and what is simply given produces an explanatory unity in which time is occupied in a certain way. That is an obvious and (as it turns out) fairly advantageous option. But, of course, geology books which describe the world without human beings turn out to be full of words and pictures. They describe the world, that is, as it would have been experienced if there *had* been human beings there. For they use our words and images. We cannot describe that world without the use of our normal intentional devices. The world must be capable of bearing the necessary universals, or it would not be a *describable* world at all. We cannot produce objects of knowledge without producing the normal conditions for objects of knowledge.

Knowledge does involve alternatives and choices. It does, invariably, therefore, take us into the realm of the possible and it does, invariably, produce a line between the actual and the possible. If there were no other reason for this, the fact that intentionality depends upon universals of a certain sort—and therefore transcends the simple particular—would guarantee it. But we control the use we make of that line and we are quite free to say that the geology book quite correctly describes the world as it would have seemed to someone who was there although, indeed, no one was "there."

4.916   The conclusions of this section seem obvious enough: intentional objects and universals enter into all knowledge, but it does not follow that knowledge is invariably *of* intentional objects and universals. Indeed, the distinction between the universal in meaning and its bearer must always be present and understood. Intentions are individual, and meanings are captured in acts of assignment, but it does not follow that what one knows is always or invariably the state of one's own mind. Indeed, the "state of one's own mind" is to be known only through the process of reflecting on action—and there must be something else to be known if that process is to be intelligible. There is no knowledge without context and choice, but knowledge is not *of* the context and choice; it is of the result of making that choice and creating that context. We can see the world as the set of meanings we ascribe, and as the structure which sustains those meanings and bears those ascriptions. We cannot have the one without the other and, therefore, the world within and the world outside are either mutually intelligible or not intelligible at all.

4.92   This still leaves the problem of relations. If the distinctions I insisted upon in section 4.91 are accepted, it follows that there is a distinction between the way that I am related to my intentional objects and the way that I am related to the world which sustains those objects. The reality of distinctions becomes, if anything, the reality of two modes of relation.

4.921   The "problem" of relations is notorious. If, as F. H. Bradley thought, the concept of relation is "infected" and shot through with contradiction, we have little hope of being able to make sense of a set of distinctions which depends upon the introduction of a variety of kinds of relatedness.[2] If, as T.H. Green thought, the notion of relation is only intelligible as an activity of mind, then the distinctions which I was trying to make in the last section must evidently fail.[3] And, while few philosophers in the last quarter century would subscribe to either the doctrines of Bradley or those of Green, it is not at all obvious that they have been successfully answered.

It is as well to confess here that, just as was the case with the problem of universals, it does not lie within the scope of this book to tackle all of the problems of relations *per se*. What I propose to do in this section is simply to construct an account of those aspects of the matter which bear upon our immediate investigation, and then to attempt to show how this account bears upon the general problem raised by philosophers like Bradley and Green—to show, at least, that it is reasonable to believe that, if one is careful, one need not land in the difficulties to which they point. This amounts to a limited test of the account I shall offer, a test of whether or not it can face some of the larger and more difficult challenges.

4.922   We must first attempt to describe the situation as it emerged from the preceding discussion: intentional objects are universals expressed as meanings and created by deliberate acts of choice by someone, sometime. Since I share in an elaborate community of meanings, I need not, of course, have created all my intentional objects. The railway signal was designed by the right-of-way engineer, and operated by the signalman, both of whom were, no doubt, carrying out the "intentions" of the directors and managers. But seeing it *as* a signal is something which happens to me. I no doubt do so, now, out of habit; but, sometime or other, I learned how to "read" such things and made a choice. I could see it *as* something else. If I *see* it, as opposed to being the passive (and unaware?) recipient of sense data, I see it *as* something—as a signal, or a strange pole, or a quirkish kind of natural phenomenon, or whatever. And a series of acts is required to have assigned, over time, whatever meanings have become habitual. Another act is required to see it a different way.

In fact, all of my experience is, ultimately, of this kind. It is grasped by me as a set of meanings and assigned a place in a scheme of things. Now, if I look "for myself," it is to this pattern that I must look. It is no good trying for a direct cognition of a ghostly pure ego which "does" all these things. By definition, anything I can find in those terms is an object, and the act of looking for or at that object would have to be done by another "self," and so on to an endless regress. What I must look at is the pattern of assigned meanings and the available options. It is the availability of options in this scheme which gives the sense of the self as agent or subject.

If I were different, the set would be different. If it were different, I would be different. The relations are thus, in the traditional sense, "internal." Change them, and the terms are all different.

At the same time, there are bearers for all these meanings, and these bearers are not constitutive of me in the same sense at all. Take away the signal pole and install a light, and I can give it the same meaning. If I am to change my intentions, I must find a set of bearers capable of bearing that change.

The relationship here is not a simple one. There are options, as I urged earlier, for each situation. What is "read into" the situation and what comes "as given" depends upon the context one chooses, upon the mode of conceptualization. One notices some things at the expense of others. (I can listen to all the inflections of your voice at the cost of missing what you say: the focus of attention, the mode of conceptualization, the degree of comprehension all influence what comes "as" given.) But to be able to make the choices, I must accept some things as background; to those, I am related in a different way. The fact that external relations were different would not necessarily make me different.

This distinction is vitally important to us here. For if it did not hold, it would not be possible to hold that there is one kind of relation which renders things indicative of mind and intention and makes possible the "world within," and another which renders things indicative of the "world outside." It is the possibility of this distinction which renders real the options which make meaning possible, and self-knowledge intelligible.

4.923 But is the notion of relation intelligible and, if so, is the distinction I have been drawing intelligible? Bradley argued that, if one takes two terms, A and B, and supposes a relation, R, to hold between them, one must land in a hopeless difficulty over explicating the notion of relation. For if the relation is itself "something," then it is another term, and one must find *its* relation to A and to B. If one supposes that the relation is, as he puts it, an "adjective" of one term or the other, one will still need another relation between the two original terms. If the two terms and the relations form a relation, then they are one thing.

A seemingly different view was held by T. H. Green whose point, as I understand it, was that relations are never simply a part of the "given" situation. If the shovel is in the hole, one confronts the shovel and the hole. To say that the one is "in" the other is a function of the way in which one has organized the data. One has decided that they are separate entities and the "in" expresses the notion that they are discrete but joined in a certain way. It arises only from one's mode of grasping the situation.

Bradley, in a later opinion on the problem, expressed a view which is close to Green's. He suggested that experience comes to us as a unity, and that we discriminate within it so as to get a world of components. In effect, this amounted to his explanation for the fact that the notion of relation is ultimately incoherent. It is not a feature of the situation, but rather a feature of our conceptualization of it.

Both Green and the later Bradley are, of course, substantially emphasising the fact that there are alternatives to conceptualization, and that the problem of relation results from attempts to come to grips with various modes of conceptualization. It is probably a mistake, however, to suppose that some one mode of conceptualization is "prior" to all others and should be taken as a basic norm.

But if Bradley were right in his first view, it could not be the case that modes of relatedness were actual distinctions in reality; and if either Green or the later Bradley were right, it would follow that we could learn from a distinction between modes of relatedness only something about the way in which we carved up reality and that, seemingly, could not help us to distinguish between the world within and the outer world.

4.924   It seems reasonable, however, to suggest that it cannot in fact be the case that relations are bits of string which tie things together, and it cannot be the case that reality is a transcendent and wholly featureless unity in which "we" make distinctions. The first proposition seems false, oddly enough, for just the reasons Bradley gives: such a model provides no relations. The alternative seems to be that terms and relations stand to one another in the way that systems and their contents do. If, for instance, one has a system of logic in which the "terms" are expressions like 'and," "or," "not," "therefore," "some," "all" and so on, one can only make sense of them by reference to the set of rules which governs and so relates them. It does not tie them together like bits of string. Rather, it provides a framework within which they become intelligible. One who asks how "and" is related to "or" is given a rule which suggests a condition under which a proposition is true if it is related to another by one term while it would be false if related by the other. *If* I know that "I shall go to Saskatoon or Montreal" is true *and* that "I shall go to Saskatoon and Montreal" is false, *then* I know what "or" means. The system requires the terms to give it body, the terms require the system to give them sense. If the system is complete, the terms are bound to one another in such a way that the relations between the terms are "internal"—a change in one involves a change in all the others. If the system allows options, the terms may, in some respects, be externally related to one another. One may give new scope to one without changing the others.

Now, what we think of as "objects" in the "external" world are just like terms in an incompletely defined logical system. They function as objects of knowledge only because there are some rules which govern their positions. But since there are alternatives available for their conceptualization, they are not perfectly defined. When we say they are externally related to *us* we mean that our meaning system might operate without them, or with a different set of them, or, we might change our system while they remained just as they are.

4.925 It is worth noticing that we almost always find ourselves functioning in more than one system—we are incompletely unified, and there are always assorted "sub-selves" with whom we carry on internal arguments. A given, definable self, is, however, a single system in which the components are bound to us by internal relations.

4.926 We can also, in a sense, reject the contention of the later Bradley—that experience is a primary unity in which *we* make distinctions. If that were so, it is difficult to know how we could come to make those distinctions at all. Given some distinctions we can misunderstand or make new ones, but how could we make an at all if we were given none?

The point may be more subtle than this, and nearer to Green's: it may be that, since we see that we can always reconceptualize, and since we cannot get a wholly independent account of the terms or of the system in which they appear, we should regard all the distinctions we make or find as essentially *ad hoc*. Green may, indeed, have been arguing that, since we cannot finally substantiate any distinctions because we can always choose to make another, we should simply accept that the notion of relation depends upon the way in which we choose to regard any system and its contents.

This, however, seems to me to involve a subtle but interesting error, resulting from the assumption that whatever would count as "the world outside" would have to have a single, determinate, and univocal state. But this is like saying that because every word has a slightly different meaning in each new context, there is no way of saying that instances of it are "the same word." It happens, of course, that words need only have a central tendency, a linking rule, or a similar influence to count, within the usual limits, as "the same word." Of course objects will not be the same, exactly, in different contexts, either. For them to be "external," it is only required that they have some latitude within the dimension that interests us. Words and things, in that sense, are more like one another than we imagine.

The more reasonable conclusion, indeed, would seem to be that what we are "given" are entities which function much like symbols or words on a page. They can be given different meanings, they can perform different roles, but that is not to say that we make them up.

4.927 Relations, then, can plausibly be said to be real, in the same way that systems are as real as their contents, and vice versa. And there seems no reason to suppose that the distinction between the world within and the world outside should not be a difference in relation—the kind of relational difference which makes it possible for there to be both things and relations.

Notes to Chapter 4

Notes to Section 4.1.

1. P. F. Strawson, *Individuals* (London: Methuen, 1959).

2. Does it help, in fact, to know that dolphins and whales have minds and are probably conscious? I do not doubt that this is so (see Joan McIntyre, ed. *Mind in the Waters,* Toronto: McClelland and Stewart, 1964), but that does not tell us why brains like ours should manifest consciousness.

3. See Virginia Woolf's essay "Craftsmanship" in *Collected Essays,* Vol. II (London: Hogarth Press, 1966), pp. 245-251.

4. *Black's Law Dictionary,* 4th edition, revised (St. Paul: West Publishing Co.): "Persons are the subject of rights and duties." The dictionary ascribes to Pollock and Gray the doctrine that "the person is the legal subject or substance of which the rights and duties are attributes."

5. See F. Copleston, *Medieval Philosophy* (London: Methuen, 1953), p. 3.

6. The Greek "logos" is unclear, but see A. M. Hunter's *The Gospel According to St. John* (Cambridge: Cambridge University Press, 1965).

7. J. M. E. McTaggart, *The Nature of Existence,* vol. I (Cambridge: Cambridge University Press, 1921), p. 68: "Something must exist, then, and have qualities, without being itself either a quality or a relation. And this is Substance."

8. C. D. Broad, *An Examination of McTaggart's Philosophy,* Vol. I (Cambridge: Cambridge University Press), p. 132.

Notes to Section 4.2.

1. Locke has two theories. What I call the macro theory deals with things on the level of experience. It is in this that Locke distinguishes between primary and secondary qualities. He says, of course, that the primary qualities are really in objects, so that confirmation would entail comparing the idea of a primary quality with the quality itself. But the quality itself is the quality without the idea, and since our ideas are our only access to qualities, the qualities become totally inac-

cessible. The other theory is the micro theory—the theory of insensible particles. It is even more difficult to determine what would count as confirmation here, as the particles are insensible and so do not resemble their effects. It will not help much to say that here Locke has dropped the resemblance portion of his theory. It is still a causal theory, and so still requires access to the alleged cause, at least to set up a correlation.

2. For example, see Gilbert Ryle's *Concept of Mind,* pp. 210-222.

3. *Op. cit.,* pp. 149-153.

4. It is interesting to contrast this standard of adequacy with the one that operates with intentional objects. See Section 4.8.

5. Ayer, *Foundatinal of Empirical Knowledge,* Chapter I, esp. p. 14ff.

6. *Ibid.*

6a. *The Compact Edition of the Oxford English Dictionary, Oxford, Clarendon Press, 1971, Vol. I, p. 14 "access."*

7. *Frank Silby, "Aesthetics and the Lock of things," Journal of Philosophy,* November 5, 1959, pp. 905-915.

Notes to Section 4.3.

1. See Russell William Brain's, *Diseases of the Nervous System,* revised by John N. Walton, (New York: Oxford University Press, 1969).

2. See Bertrand Russell, *Human Knowledge Its Scope and Limits* (New York: Simon and Schuster, 1948), Ch. VIII, especially pp. 299-300.

3. Martinus Nijhoff, The Hague, 1962.

Notes to Section 4.4.

1. Francis Herbert Bradley, *Appearance and Reality* (Oxford: The Clarendon Press, 1893), Ch. III.

2. See *Principia Mathematica* (Cambridge: Cambridge University Press, second edition, 1957).

Notes to Section 4.5.

1. *The Philosophical Works of Descartes,* trans. Haldane & Ross (Dover Publications, 1931), p. 146.

2. Bertrand Russell, *Human Knowledge* (London: Allen & Unwin, 1948), pp. 214-215.

3. Norman Malcolm, *Dreaming* (London: Routledge and Kegan Paul, 1959), p. 56.

4. Ludwig Wittgenstein, *The Philosophical Investigation* (Blackwell's, 1958), paragraph 236. The issue of criteria is not the burning one that it was in the 1960's. See C. Wellman, "Wittgenstein: Conception of a Criterion," *Journal of Philosophy,* 1961, pp. 281-293. Also see Anscombe "On Brute Facts," *Analysis,* Vol. 18, no. 3, 1958. This article, along with "How to Derive an Ought from an Is," *Philosophical Review,* Jan. 1964, sets out the larger issue into which the questions of criteria fit. Out of all the discussions, one thing clearly emerges. Criteria are criteria for the application of a term and are designed to answer the question "How do you know it is a ϕ?" What is left unresolved is the exact nature of the relation specified by a criterion. Neither the standard analytic or synthetic are adequate for the job and so much of the discussion focuses on a third alternative. However that alternative is to be worked out, its solution would cast some light on what Malcolm has in mind in his discussion of the relationship between a past state of affairs and the term we apply to it.

5. Norman Malcolm, *Dreaming,* p. 56.

6. *Ibid.,* p. 57ff.

7. *Ibid.,* p. 57.

8. *Ibid.,* p. 58. His rhetorical question "Does it follow that if I remember today a dream of last night, then last night I must have been aware of the dream or its 'contents'?" is quite revealing. If we answer it in the negative, as we are supposed to, that would suggest that today I might remember a dream from last night, although last night I was not aware of that dream. This generates the very odd possibility that one may remember something of which he was not aware. In general, if one were not aware of ϕ at the time it happened, that would be sufficient reason for saying that he could not remember it. The only way to escape this dilemma is to play around with "not aware," arguing that it is not the same as unaware. I doubt that that would succeed. Whatever form of awareness one came up with, if one lacked that form of awareness of ϕ at time T, then one could not be said to remember ϕ at T + 1.

9. *Infra.,* p. 243.

10. Ludwig Wittgenstein, *The Philosophical Investigations* (Oxford: Blackwell, 1958), para. 580.

11. Norman Malcolm, *Dreaming,* p. 66.

12. *Ibid.,* p. 66.

13. *Ibid.*, p. 57.

14. *Ibid.,* pp. 59-60.

15. *Ibid.*, p. 60.

16. *Ibid.*

17. *Ibid.*

18. See Malcolm's review of *The Philosophical Investigations* in *The Philosophical Review,* Oct. 1954, and "Two Arguments against a Private Language" by M. Perkins, *Journal of Philosophy,* Vol. XLII no. 17, 1965.

18a. See *The Philosophical Investigations,* L. Wittgenstein, B. H. Blackwell, 3rd edition, 1967, last two paragraphs on pg. 222.

19. Norman Malcolm, *Dreaming,* p. 68.

20. *Ibid.*, p. 68.

21. *Ibid.,* p. 57, footnote 2.

22. *Ibid.,* p. 68.

23. *Ibid.*, p. 76. Double underlining is mine.

24. *Ibid.,* p. 80.

25. *Ibid.*

26. *Ibid.*

Notes to Section 4.6.

1. Realizing the dangers of oversimplification, the charge that this particular philosophy of action has its roots in Classical Empiricism is interesting to consider. Locke, for example, depicts people as essentially passive in their acquisition of knowledge. An idea impresses itself on the *tabula rasa,* which results in contemplative rather than practical knowledge. Hume was driven into a corner by the "self," and Berkeley's only contribution was to replace the term "idea" with the term "notion." This may not be entirely fair, though it certainly is reasonable to say that the notion of agency is not one that the empiricists were comfortable with.

2. But consider: "Nor does the ascription of responsibility serve to distinguish human action from the action of a physical object, for we can as properly say, without any trace of animism, that the wind is responsible for the damage to the window as that a person is responsible for it." (*The Philosophy of Action,* ed. A.B. White, p. 4.) Perhaps the only difference between White and myself is that, in this passage, he makes no distinction between causal and moral responsibility—surely there would be at least a trace of animism if we attempted to hold the wind morally responsible.

3. This view has generated a great deal of discussion beginning with the classic "The Ascription of Rights and Responsibilities" by H.L.A. Hart, *Proceedings of The Aristotelian Society,* Vol. XLIX, 1949. See also Peter Geach's "Ascriptivism," *The Philosophical Review,* Vol. LXIX, 1960. Joel Feinberg's "Hart on Action and Responsibility," *Philosophy in America,* ed. M. Black, pp. 134-160.

4. H.A. Prichard, "Acting, Willing, Desiring," and "Duty and Ignorance of Fact," *Moral Obligation.*

5. *H.A. Prichard, "Acting, Willing, Desiring," Moral Obligation,* p. 187.

6. "Duty and Ignorance of Fact," *Moral Obligation,* p. 19.

7. "Acting, Willing, Desiring," *Moral Obligation,* p. 187.

8. "Duty and Ignorance of Fact," *Moral Obligation,* p. 19.

9. The following take the view that "non-voluntary act" is at least unacceptable if not self-contradictory: Gilbert Ryle's *Concept of Mind,* p. 74; G.L. Williams and Stevens, Criminal Law, The General Part (London: 1961), Chapter 1; R.M. Dias, *Jurisprudence,* p. 252.

10. H.A. Prichard, "Acting, Willing, Desiring," *Moral Obligation,* p. 189.

11. *Ibid.,* p. 189.

12. *Op. Cit.*, pp. 189-190.

13. *Ibid.*, p. 192.

14. "Duty, and Ignorance of Fact," *Moral Obligation*, p. 32.

15. *Ibid.*

16. See *Basic Actions* by Arthur Danto for a well considered account of this problem. It is not as arbitrary as I suggest, though for my purposes not much rests on it.

17. "Acting, Willing, Desiring," *Moral Obligation*, p. 189.

18. The *Concept of Mind,* Chap. 3; see also *Free Action* by A.I. Melden, Chap. 5. Very recently, the topic is regaining respectability, primarily through the efforts of Anthony Kenney in his *Anatomy of the Soul* (Blackwell, 1973), and especially *Will, Freedom and Power* (Blackwell, 1975).

19. "Acting, Willing, Desiring," *Moral Obligation*, p. 189.

20. As a rule of thumb, an account in terms of the real, that is, unconscious, reasons is appropriate only when what the agent says of himself simply does not explain his behavior. In an instance such as this, his behavior begins to lose some of its quality of an action and, through loss of responsibility, takes on the aspects of an event. Suppose, for example, that a compulsive hand washer says that he wants merely to keep himself clean and germ free. The normal desire to keep clean is not sufficient to explain washing one's hands fifty times a day. Because of the disparity between what he says and what he does, it makes sense to reject his reasons and to look instead for unconscious reasons. It is no accident that we feel he has little understanding (control) of the situation.

21. G.E.M. Anscombe, *Intention,* p. 9ff.

22. See 4.6, footnote 20.

23. This difference is also a difference in responsibility. Should the question arise, we would hold someone far more culpable for doing something intentionally than for doing it inadvertently. The first suggests malice and the second, perhaps, carelessness.

24. *Black's Law Dictionary,* p. 644.

25. *Ibid.*

26.   G.E.M. Anscombe, *Intention,* p. 20.

27.   Consider the flap generated by Wimsatt and Beardsley's "The Intentional Fallacy," *The Verbal Icon,* 1954, Chap. 1. How much of it is due to a muddled view of the mind is interesting to speculate. My guess is that it is a great deal.

28.   In this matter it is interesting to consider another parallel in Aesthetics. See in section 4.2, footnote 7, "Aesthetics and the Look of Things," Frank Sibley. He makes the point that the application of some terms, such as delicate, is all but impossible to justify without having the work in question in front of one. Similarly, I am suggesting that seeing a piece of behavior, like anger, may be difficult unless one is confronted with a real case. The point is that much depends on perception.

29.   Glen Langford, *Human Action,* p. 92.

30.   *Op. cit.,* p. 91.

31.   *Op. cit.,* p. 92.

32.   See G.E.M. Anscombe's *Intention,* section 42.

Notes to Section 4.7.

1.   Donald McKay, *Freedom of Action in a Mechanistic Universe,* Eddington Memorial Lecture, no. 21 (London: Cambridge University Press, 1967). The point is this: one *could not* know all one's brain states if brain states and mind states were identical. For as soon as one knew that one's brain was in state T^1, one's brain would have to be in another state, T^2, if T^1 were the state of brain at the moment before the knowledge began. In knowing, then, that one's brain state was T^2, one's brain would have to be changed again. Of course, one may imagine the ideal man as one whose knowledge was always in phase—he knew what his brain state was exactly at the time that his brain was in that state. This seems not to allow travel time for signals to move from one part of the brain to the point at which the knowledge is localized—but, then, perhaps one knows by some process which does not take time. (Look what *that* does to the mind/brain identity thesis!) Even these however, seem to be more knowledge states than brain states. For suppose there is an original mind/brain correlation. Then suppose the *further* knowledge that this correlation holds. If the further knowledge changes the appropriate brain states, it is no longer "knowledge." If it does not, there is no longer a perfect correlation. One going through this paradox ought to exhibit McKay's Parkinsonianism if the mind/brain identity thesis were even an approximation to the truth.

2. David Hume, *A Treatise of Human Nature,* ed. L.A. Selby-Bigge (Oxford: The Clarendon Press, 1946), p. 1ff.

3. *Ibid.,* p. 1.

4. *Ibid.,* p. 3.

5. *Ibid.,* p. 69.

6. See the writings of the later Moore—such as, *Philosophical Papers* (London: George Allen and Unwin, 1966), and works posthumously published under the editorship of Casimir Lewy, including *Lectures on Philosophy* (London: George Allen and Unwin, 1959), and *The Commonplace Book* (London: George Allen and Unwin, 1962). Austin's position comes off most clearly in *Sense and Sensibilia,* edited by G.T. Warnock (New York: Oxford University Press, 1966).

7. J.M.E. McTaggart, *The Nature of Existence* (Cambridge: Cambridge University Press, Vol. I, 1921), pp. 66-73.

8. Rudolph Carnap, *The Logical Structure of the World and Pseudoproblems in Philosophy,* translated by Rolf George (Berkeley: University of California Press, 1967).

Notes to Section 4.8

1. G.E.M. Anscombe, "The Intentionality of Sensation a Grammatical Feature," *Analytical Philosophy,* ed. R.S. Butler, 2nd series, p. 158.

2. The expression " . . . object of . . " is the linguistic mark of intentional objects. If anything is an intentional object, it can be designated by this locution, and any occurrence of this locution is the expression of an intentional object. The appropriateness of this expression is both necessary and sufficient. In all of those instances in which the locution does not happen to occur, it can always be made to occur without change of meaning. For example, "Heidi wants Xanadu" can be rewritten as "Xanadu is the object of Heidi's want."

3. *Black's Law Dictionary,* 2nd ed., p. 841.

4. "Since the mind, in all its thoughts and reasonings, hath no other immediate object but its own ideas, which it alone does or can contemplate, it is evident that our knowledge is only conversant about them." *Essay Concerning Human Understanding* by John Locke, Bk. IV, Chap. I, sec. I.

5.　Anscombe, *op. cit.,* p. 162ff.

6.　*Op. cit.,* p. 164.

7.　*Op. cit.,* p. 159.

8.　Chisholm has criteria that are parallel. See *Perceiving* by R.M. Chisholm (Ithaca, New York: Cornell University Press, 1957), pp. 170-171.

9.　See the argument on remembering one's dream, Sec. 4.532.

10.　*Infra.,* p. 328.

11.　*Infra.,* p. 326.

Notes to Section 4.9.

1.　Russell held many opinions about these issues. His best balanced accounts, I think, are in *Our Knowledge of the External World* (New York: W.W. Norton, 1929; originally, the Lowell Lectures at Harvard in 1914, and revised by Russell in 1928), and *Human Knowledge, Its Scope and Limits* (New York: Simon and Schuster, 1948). The first has a Platonic bias toward universals, and the second favors logical constructions out of acquaintance; but each expresses a well-balanced account of the same difficulties.

2.　Francis Herbert Bradley, *Appearance and Reality* (Oxford: The Clarendon Press, 1893), p. 21.

3.　Thomas Hill Green, *Prolegomena to Ethics,* ed. A.C. Bradley (Oxford: The Clarendon Press, fourth edition, 1890), p. 35ff.

Chapter 5

The Inner World and
the Kinds of Knowledge

The suggestion which runs through Chapter 4 of this book comes, eventually, to something like this: the ordinary notion of "thing" in its common sense understanding is not replaceable except through a kind of logical reduction or construction which turns out, when the matter is pressed, to depend on a series of conceptual adjustments. In their turn, these depend on the very notions which are supposedly to be replaced. We can come to regard "seeing" as receiving visual sense data—and learn something in the process—but we would not know how to understand "receiving visual sense data" except by contrast with "seeing." Or, we can understand the behaviour of things by coming to regard them as collections of molecules, but we would not understand the concept of a molecule except by going back to where we started and analysing the series of steps which produces the result. In a similar way, we cannot replace the original notion of person if we mean by "replace" some substitution which makes it unnecessary to refer back to the notion of "person." At every move we are involved with the notion that there is somebody who is doing the analysis, and *something* which is to be rendered intelligible.

The process of conceptual improvement which we think characterisic of knowledge involves us in a constant two-way interchange between the original notions of ordinary experience and language, and the notion imbedded in the "improved" structures.

It is true, of course, that what we mostly regard as the ideal sort of knowledge, K, is the very sophisticated outcome of this conceptual interchange. It is not here being denied that, for some purposes, physics is to be preferred to common sense, and psychology to our everyday notions of personhood. What is being denied is that we can dispose of the starting point and so "reduce" the physicist to his physics, or "reduce" the person who is the psychologist to the sophisticated model which is psychology. Much less can we reduce "ourselves" to bundles of our "sense data" or, for that matter, come to replace the homely notion of chair with the sophisticated notion of a bundle of molecules. The truth, in its larger sense, is represented by the way in which these homely notions come to be illumined as the conceptual shift goes on. It will not do to say that the chair is "really" a bundle of molecules just because the chair, as chair, has all the perceptual attitudes and intensional projections which go into making it the unique thing that it is. It will not do to say that a man is a bundle of sensations because, if he were, he could presumably never have understood the conceptual recipe for making the change in his experience which enables him to conceptualize himself as a bundle of sensations. This section has three sub-sections which deal, respectively, with criteria and the knowledge of things, the exchange of meanings and knowledge of persons, and with knowing what one is doing.

These are all elements of what goes into the most basic situation. The knowledge claimed is quite unlike the sophisticated inventories which make up physics, psychology, or theology. It is the first order "knowledge" which enables us to find our way around in the world of things—the knowledge which is, in the large, built into the structure and workings of our quite ordinary language. It is the form of knowledge which is best characterised as a kind of encounter, which goes before reflection because it gives us something to reflect upon. The kind of knowledge of persons involved is the sort we all rely on when we claim to "know someone" rather than when we claim to know something *about* him, such as whether he is a good insurance risk. Knowing "him" rather than knowing "about him" is the kind of thing which seems to take place mostly through the rather simple process of talking to him. Knowing "what one is doing," again, seems not to be inference or construct, but something direct. I do not (usually) *"find out"* that I am walking nor do I, like the fabled Duke, dream that I am making a speech in the House of Lords only to wake up and "discover" that I am.

If we are going to claim that these kinds of knowledge are basic and finally irreducible, we shall have to say something about what they are. The claim is not that these kinds of knowledge are "superior" (though sometimes and for some purposes they are), nor that they tell us all of what we want to know (though sometimes they do tell us the most important things). The claim, rather, is that this is where we begin. If we forget the kind of dependence we have on the places at which we begin, we shall fail rather miserably to know where we have arrived—and we may not, then, be able to assimilate our more sophisticated kinds of knowledge.

5.1 Things and Criteria

This section might well be titled "Putting Everything in its Place." Things have been under attack from the days of Plato's Cave to the twentieth-century doubts of the Logical Positivists about the status of empirical propositions. I am not going to attempt to write the history of the subject, only to give a limited consideration of an attempt to cast the status of things into limbo. I will argue that this attempt has misfired, and that some of the attacks on it are indeed well founded.

5.11 One particular attack on things, or rather on our knowledge of things, that deserves special attention is the one that regards common sense in the guise of "naive realism" as a lost cause. It is somewhat difficult to know how to construe this doctrine. Frequently, those who defend it do not view it in the same way as those who attack it. About the only thing that is generally agreed upon is that it has its roots in common sense and ordinary thinking. It is not, then, a philosophical creation, and may not be even a theory in its pure form. C. D. Broad dispenses with it as a waste of time:

> It is, therefore, in my opinion, simply a waste of time to try to rehabilitate naive realism; or to regard it as any serious objection to a theory of the external world and our perception of it that it is "shocking to common-sense." *Any* theory that can possibly fit the facts is *certain* to shock common-sense somewhere; and in face of the facts we can only advise common-sense to follow the example of Judas Iscariot, and "go out and hang itself."[1]

It is my intention to argue that common sense need not be sent out to hang itself, and that some form of naive realism is defensible. I do not mean to say that anything that occurs in common sense or common language is *ipso facto* unassailable. I have elsewhere argued that Malcolm's claim that "ordinary language is correct language" is false, and I see no reason to change my view.[2] I will argue that common sense and common language have their place in philosophy, not so much as the last word, but as a starting point. There is no reason to think that we cannot progress beyond this with a philosophy of perception. Undoubtedly, there are many things simply not considered by the common man such that were he to consider them, he would be surprised. Respect for common sense is in no way due to confusion or ambiguity, then I would argue that the advanced thinking has some explaining to do. If I were resolvable contradiction. If advanced considerations lead us to deny the existence of material objects, for example, and if this conflict with common sense is in no way due to confusion or ambiguity, then I would argue that the advanced thinking has some explaining to do. If I were forced to choose between them, I would abandon the theory. We normally expect that new ideas and discoveries will be integrated into our present beliefs, and it is reasonable and proper that we do so. Not only are new conceptions added to what we accept, but old ones drop out. Indeed, we might say that it is a prime dictate of common sense that we always be open to change. We do not abandon our present beliefs just for the sake of change, but if the evidence for some new idea outweighs the evidence for the old one, then common sense requires us to accept the new.

5.111   Broad mentions the speed of light as one of those things that is not included in common sense.[3] He does not make it very clear where the conflict is thought to arise, but he does mention the need for delicate instruments to measure the speed of light. If this is the sort of consideration that he has in mind, I take it that the conflict arises because the common man is uninformed about such matters—at least in 1925. Yet this seems hardly a problem, at least in 1974, to those who have had a basic physics course. Consequently, since we can now expect the common man to be better informed than he was in 1925 it cannot be simply lack of information which is responsible for the surprise. Of course it is not. What is disruptive to common sense in this instance is not the new data, but the philosophical use to which that data is put. The time lag argument is something that philosophers have developed from the fact that light travels at so great a speed. Something like this goes beyond the facts of physics to a skeptical philosophical conclusion which is indeed inconsistent with common sense.[4] It takes a very small amount of time for light to get from an object to us. In the case of distant objects like stars, this means that while we "see" their light in the sky, they may have exploded. Even if that has not happened, the time lag is sufficient to show that what we "see" is detachable from the object. Therefore we do not "see" objects. If this conclusion is interpreted as showing that we do not, or cannot, perceive ordinary material objects, then it is in conflict with common sense. It is this kind of philosophical claim that I would be willing to abandon before giving up my belief that we perceive physical objects.

5.112   I want to consider naive realism, as well as those reasons that are supposed to tell so decisively against it, with some care. The purpose of such an investigation is to extend the one found in 4.2. The theory of perception that we wish to suggest is not reductionist, so that things in their most ordinary framework are left untouched. It is necessary, then, that we show that an unsophisticated notion of "thing" is not riddled with impossibilities—that the ordinary man's conception of the world around him will tolerate careful inspection.

5.113   The following is A. J. Ayer's formulation of Naive Realism:

> He [the naive realist] will not allow that our knowledge of the various things which the skeptic wishes to put beyond our reach is necessarily indirect. His position is that the physical objects which we commonly perceive are, in a sense to be explained, directly "given" to us, that it is not inconceivable that such things as atoms and electrons should also be directly perceived, that at least in certain favorable instances one can inspect the minds of others, that memory makes us directly acquainted with the past.[5]

At a later point, Ayer characterizes the naive realist as a kind of stubborn intuitionist who might be expected to assert dogmatically that he knows what he knows and no philosopher is going to make him doubt his world![6] R. S. Hirst in the *Encyclopedia of Philosophy* characterizes it in this way:

> Naive realism is the simplest form of direct realism and is usually alleged by philosophers to be an innocent prejudice of the plain man that has to be overcome if philosophical progress is to be made. It is normally stated in terms of sensible qualities or sensa. When we look around us, we can distinguish various colored, shaped expanses that we suppose to be the surfaces of material objects, we may hear various sounds that we suppose to come from such objects, we may feel something smooth and hard that we suppose to be a table top, and so on. Naive realism claims that these suppositions are all correct—that the shapes, colors, sounds, and smooth, hard expanses (the sensible qualities) are always the intrinsic properties of material objects and in sight and touch are their surfaces. Such a claim can easily be shown to be erroneous by the argument from illusion.[7]

Ayer's primary point against Naive Realism rests on what the latter takes to be directly given.[8] Hirst's point in the Encyclopedia is the argument from illusion. They are, or eventually come to be, the same point. According to the argument from illusion, our senses sometimes deceive us; on occasion, things will look different than they are. A very large object at a great distance will look small, a white dress in the light of dawn will look grey, and a circular object viewed from an angle will look elliptical. Other more extreme cases, such as mirages, delusions, delirium tremens, and other semi-pathological forms of hallucination, are often cited. For all the fantastic variation in these different individual situations, they are all used in essentially the same way in the argument—as specific instances of the case in which (1) what appears is distinct from what is, and (2) what we (really, directly) perceive is what appears. If we grant these two points, it is not much of a step to the conclusion that we do not perceive physical objects.

5.114   What has happened is that the object of perception has been detached so as to become, at best, indirect. All these considerations are taken to be true, although they are those that the plain man in his innocence does not know or cannot handle. If, however, they are taken into account, the very least that they compel is the admission that we have no direct awareness of things.

But it seems to me that they compel no such thing. Their skeptical thrust is as illusory as are the cases that they cite in their own support. The first thing to note is the nature of the cases that are used. They are all examples in which something has gone wrong with the perceptual process. For the moment, without questioning whether the analysis of these abnormal cases is adequate, it seems unreasonable for us to take them as a basis for a conclusion about normal cases. Perhaps in these abnormal cases we do not directly perceive the object. That may be the very reason that the perception breaks down, and we are able to see only what appears and not what is. At the least, we need more of a reason before making normal perception into just what it seems not to be. We should ask to be shown how, in normal cases, what we really see is merely an appearance and not what actually is. Common sense suggests that there is no such distinction in ordinary situations.

However, it is not all that clear that even in these unhappy cases we have things depicted as they really are. In order to see this, we need an example. If we look at a coin front-on, we can see its real shape. If we view it from an angle, it looks elliptical. The elliptical look is what we see, not what is, so that what we see is not what is the case. This is what common sense in the guise of naive realism cannot accommodate. Clearly, we do not see the coin.

In some manner, the argument is attempting to pry loose the elliptical look so that it becomes the object of perception—what one sees.[9] Because of this, we are supposed to conclude that we do not directly perceive the coin. The question turns, then, on the detachability of this look. Can it be separated from the coin enough so that it becomes an entity in itself? It need not be turned into a chunk of physical stuff, but it must be turned into enough of a thing so that our perception stops with it. In order for us not to see the coin [directly] the elliptical look must be a kind of barrier.

5.115   All of this is necessary, but none of it is true. The look of the coin is not detachable. To be sure, the coin does look elliptical, but we need to remember that the elliptical appearance is a function of the actual shape of the coin. This is how a thin, round item should look when viewed from an angle. Far from being something that baffles common sense, it is what common sense leads us to expect. Suppose that it did not look elliptical, and that, when viewed from an angle, it looked the same way as it did straight on. This would be baffling. As we move farther away from an object, we expect that it is going to look smaller. But if it looked the same, we would begin to wonder if the thing had not changed in proportion to the distance we had moved back. The naive realist believes that we see objects, and that we see them as they are. One could derive from this the idea that he thinks that everything remains rigid, but one would get this only after a great deal of effort. It is a fact about the world, and a common sense fact at that, that under different circumstances things look different. The perceptual world is fluid in its appearances. Elsewhere, we have talked of the perceptual aspects of things.[10] That locution can be mistaken in a way that parallels a mistaking of naive realism. One reason for choosing the expression "perceptual aspect" is that it conveys the idea of variability without substantial change. Consider the way in which Wittgenstein has used Jastrow's duck-rabbit.[11] Now you see it as a duck, now you see it as a rabbit. Surely, one might argue, we have no direct access to the figure itself. Its appearance as a duck or its appearance as a rabbit are what we directly perceive. The duck-appearance is inconsistent with the rabbit-appearance, and common sense tells us that a single thing cannot have inconsistent properties. These are the facts that common sense in the guise of naive realism cannot accept or account for. So the naive common man believes that the duck-appearance and the rabbit-appearance are both a part of [the surface of] the same thing. Surely that is muddled, if not contradictory.

5.116   If it is muddled, the muddle can easily be cleared up. In saying that we see things as they are, we are committed to the belief that what we see is changeable. However, this means only that its aspects vary. It does not mean that we must think of objects as being plastic, so that at one moment they have this configuration, and at another that. In section 4.2, I argued that things must have a semi-permanent nature in order for them to be identified and described. Their properties must be determinable in order for there to be an objective state of affairs. I am now arguing that these requirements are perfectly compatible with naive realism and common sense. The belief that we see things as they are does not mean that we take them to be rigidly determined, or that a circular silver coin may have one, and only one, look. According to his critics, the naive realist is committed to at least one of the following: (1) Either material objects are themselves plastic so that they may continually change their properties, or (2) they are composed of an inconsistent set of features. Both of these are untenable, and so the critic argues naive realism is untenable. However both of these are also inconsistent with what I have argued in 4.2. Neither is true nor a necessary consequence of naive realism.

5.117   The critics of naive realism accuse it of taking the expression "the elliptical look of the round coin" and giving it a good wrench. If we bisect the expression by demolishing the "of," we are left with "the elliptical look" and "the round coin," as well as the naive but unreal puzzle of how to relate them. But it takes only a second glance to tell us that it is not the naive realist who performs this surgery. It is the proponent of the argument from illusion. He pries off the appearance from the object, turns to the realist and says: "Here, these are the facts. How do *you* account for them?" The trouble occurs not in the realist's inability to answer the question, but in the very structure of the question. The conjuror's trick is performed in the argument from illusion, as indeed it must be if a notion such as sense-data is to be given a use. I have no objection to "sense-data" entering into the discussion, but presented at this point, one is liable to take them as actual items of experience, as the kind of thing that ought to be included in an inventory of what there is. Not only is that a mistake; it is at the foundation of the alleged difficulty with realism. Whatever sense-data are, they are not the kind of thing to be found on the level of confrontation. In addition to the dimes, nickles and quarters found in one's pocket, there are not also dime-data, nickle-data and quarter-data. No one has said precisely this about sense-data, but the argument from illusion does objectify them. It takes the appearance of something and presents it as the proper object of perception. If we take this to mean that when one glances at a circular coin one may notice only that it is an elliptical-looking something, then there is no problem. We cannot say with assurance whether it is actually round and rough. In *this* way perception does stop with the look of the thing. It can be a kind of barrier to what the thing is actually like, but it is not the kind of barrier that is required by the argument from illusion, or that would be destructive for naive realism. In this instance, the barrier arises only because of the insufficiency of information, not because of the inherent nature of an appearance as the object of perception. Sometimes an appearance is good grounds for a conclusion about a thing and sometimes it is not. Even in those instances in which it is a blockade, that fact is generally clear ("all I can tell is that it looks grey") and eliminable ("turn on the other light so I can see better").

5.12   Throughout this discussion, we have been operating on what we have called the level of confrontation. At this level, all that we have to work with are the ordinary objects of ordinary experience. And it is at this level that naive realism holds forth. Without this statement (it ought not, I think, be called a theory) of our experience, sense-data philosophers would have no subject matter. However, when a critic of naive realism, such as Ayer, offers his sense data theory as an improved alternative, he commits two closely related and very basic errors. For example, the slogan "physical objects are logical constructions out of sense-data"[12] invites the retort that physical objects are not logical constructions out of anything. Indeed if they are constructed out of anything it is from such material as wood and concrete and glue and nails. To speak of physical objects and logical constructions in the same manner is to confuse an actual object of experience with an item appropriate for the philosophical analysis of the idea of that experience. If we were to modify the slogan accordingly so that it read "the concept of a physical object is a logical construction out of sense-data" we would have avoided the problem of mixing different logical types, but we would have removed the slogan as something competitive with naive realism.

5.121   Moore's "Defense of Common Sense," the classic statement of where a philosophy of perception is to start, becomes bogged down on just this point.[13] Moore's position is essentially this: A skeptic must have an argument to support his position. Whatever argument he presents in support of his contention that, for example, "there are no physical objects," that argument will be less certain than the class of common sense propositions, some of which entail that there are physical objects. Moore is arguing that in the order of things, one has propositions, such as "the earth has existed for many years past," and "this is a hand," that are more certainly known than any philosophical theory could be. If there arises a conflict between a common sense proposition and a philosophical theory, it is the theory that must go. Implicit in this view is the distinction between the propositions of common sense and whatever philosophical account may be given of them. One of these may be more certain than the other because they occur on different levels. The objects of common sense are the things that we encounter in everyday experience. A philosophical theory is what we develop when we reflect on these experiences. Difficulty arises when one treats the components of a theory as though they were items of encounter. This is, I submit, what the argument from illusion does in its attack on naive realism. We confront objects and their various appearances in our everyday experiences. When philosophers reflect on how objects appear, they develop the notion of a sense-datum. But it is not acceptable to hypostatize them, and treat them as though they were objects of experience.

5.122   The argument from illusion is rather subtle in this matter. We are confronted with the obvious fact that things have appearances, that sometimes these appearances differ from the actual nature of the thing, and that we are aware of how things appear. So far, these are harmless facts of ordinary experience. There is no reason to think that we are dealing with anything other than, for example, the grey look of a white dress as seen at dusk. However, as soon as that grey look is pried loose from the dress and turned into the proper object of perception, we have our hypostatization.

5.2 The Exchange of Meanings and the Knowledge of Persons

In this section, I want to make a rather simple point: Knowing someone—oneself or another—is quite different from knowing anything else and quite different, as well, from knowing *about* someone. A person, in the sense of someone known, is not an object of knowledge, whether one takes "object" in the intentional sense of "goal" or "aim," or in the ordinary sense of thing, state of affairs, or item to be inspected. Knowing someone, rather, is the creation of a community of meaning; its natural methodology, consequently, is conversation rather than investigation.

In a limited way, of course, everyone would admit this. I might, as a university official, have studied a very full dossier on Professor Bartlett but, if I had never spoken with him I would, if asked in the ordinary way, surely not claim to know him. I might say: "Well, I know a lot about him but, as a matter of fact, I've never met him." Again, if I had watched through the optical devices provided in a space satellite—even studied him that way, perhaps, for years—I still would not, ordinarily, claim to know him. Assembling facts, classifying a great range of sensory inputs, constructing theories (I might have used the data about Bartlett in a sociological treatise on "scions of old Cleveland families"), are all quite useful ways of getting to know something *about* people. But none of them actually counts as a way of getting to know them.

A philosopher might confront this distinction as something rather peripheral. "What you are talking about," he might say, "is a distinction of convenience. We do, for social purposes, anyhow, want to distinguish those people we know a great deal *about* from those we should expect to recognize us at a cocktail party. But there is nothing very special about this as an issue in epistemology. Indeed, the sort of knowledge you want to call 'knowing somebody' is hardly worth the name of knowledge at all. What makes us think we know our friends, acquaintances—even our lovers—in any serious sense at all? As a rule, we couldn't psychoanalyze them, modify their behaviour by scientific conditioning, classify them properly by socio-economic groups, or predict whether they would end up as successful citizens or in the penitentiary or the lunatic asylum. Surely, it's ridiculous to urge that conversation is a route to knowledge—unless what you mean by 'conversation' includes carefully pre-planned, scientifically designed, psychological interrogations."

And yet I want to make the counter case and to argue that, until we understand that case, a crucial phase of our understanding of the problem about the world within as well as many other problems, including those of theoretical ethics, will remain quite beyond our grasp. I shall do this in three phases. First, I shall look at the problem of persons considered as objects, and try to show that the outcome of such a procedure must be a series of paradoxes. Then, I shall look at knowledge of persons in terms of the methodologies most frequently used by philosophers—the methodologies associated with the use of sensory experience and reason—and urge again that the result if paradoxical. Finally, I shall look at the ordinary activities which establish communities of meaning and argue that, if we sustain the distinction between knowing someone and knowing about him, the paradoxes largely dissolve.

5.21   There is a close association between the notion that persons are objects of knowledge and the traditional philosophical puzzles about 'other minds.'' So long as I confine myself to examining objects—of whatever sort—nothing, logically, can count as an effective demonstration that what I have discovered is a person. In principle, any clearly describable behaviour is reproducible by something which is not a person. If the appropriate symptom of a person is a sequence of sounds, a pattern of black marks, or any kind of artifact, a machine can be programmed to duplicate it. I may think you are a person, but you might be a robot operated from Venus, a hallucination, or, for that matter, a series of random events which happen to lend themselves to interpretation in terms of personhood. The evidence is never *quite* sufficient to overturn the skeptic simply, and it is always, in a formal way at least, compatible with some counter-hypothesis.

5.211   There are, naturally, a number of quite standard responses. One of them is that, if we were to adopt the hypothesis that men and robots are not, *in principle* different, the evidence about objects would become evidence about persons and we would, then, have to deal only with the more tractable counter-hypotheses about hallucinations, illusions, conceptual confusions, and so on. But even in those science fiction stories in which men are ''taken in'' by robots, become their bosom companions, and come to understand how ''human'' they are, there is still a mysterious gap to be filled: the description of a person is not the description of a set of wires, currents, and fuses. The conversion of the ''robot'' into a ''person'' is a kind of miracle. Another answer, of course, is that, as a matter of fact, the problem really does not arise. Has anyone ever actually been taken in by *anything* pretending to be a person? There are, in fact, no person-like robots. The ordinary criteria work well enough, and are simply applicable to creatures with human bodies who behave in certain ways. But this answer is not very helpful, either. It is, after all, exceptionally optimistic. People *are* in doubt, in some way or other, about what counts. Historically, human beings have quite frequently "personified" natural phenomena in such a way as to extend the notion of person quite confusingly, and it is rather rash of us to suppose that they had *no* reason to do so. Human beings have also much too frequently chosen to regard, in one way or another, millions of other human beings as sub-persons who could be eliminated for private gain, political convenience, or as punishment for some act which they would never ascribe to their friends or lovers. Is this not some mistake about what counts as being human?

5.212 The problem has been thought—by some philosophers at least—to be compounded by some rather curious "facts." One of them is that I have access to certain states "of myself" or "of my own mind," and this access gives me information about myself which I can never have about anyone else. In consequence of this, I know that I am a person in a way which is unique. About anyone else, the most that I can do is to work with certain analogies. When you talk the way I do, I assume you feel the way I do. When you choose a certain sequence of acts in a circumstance in which I would choose the same sequence, I assume that you have the same motives. The assumption is that I can work from the fact that your behaviour resembles mine to the conclusion that, roughly, your inner life resembles mine. But this may not be true in each and every case.

This is merely an extension of the practice of associating persons with objects. In this case, the objects are ones to which there is special access. Rival groups of philosophers present clusters of standard answers to the problems which this poses. Some tackle the problem directly, by denying that there are any objects which fill this class; the arguments which center around these assertions and denials have, of course, occupied us, in one way or another, through much of this book. But, if one sticks to the "object" analysis, such denials simply result in situations like those of the science fiction stories. If there are no "inner objects," and persons are "objects" or collections of them, it is something of a miracle that an assembly of organic molecules should suddenly manifest personhood. Others maintain that all one really needs to do is to refine the analogy thesis into a set of good, testable hypotheses in order to know, pretty much, what one is allowed to infer about the inner life from outward behaviour. Frequently, they say, we succeed in this endeavour; given better psychology, we shall succeed more often. Still others claim that there is direct and immediate cognition of oneself, and that the inference problem can never really be solved but, through literature and art and poetry, one gathers insights which help a little. The life of any man, on this view, is a lonely one. We pass mostly like ships in the night. But these last two views create many obvious puzzles. Given that there is this inner, private life, how is that we have a public language for talking about it? Language itself becomes something of a miracle, and it is not much help to add the further miracles of poetry to it.

What is more interesting is that if one starts to probe these inner objects a little for clues about the knowledge of persons, one finds that they do not actually help in just the way that they are supposed to. It may well be true that the pain which is my headache is entirely mine. Even if we wired you to my brain so that you also had a headache, we might not want to call it my headache. We should just have created two headaches in the place of one.

5.2121   I do not find this a very exciting problem in its own right. But I do think that, if we reflect on it a little, we may actually begin to see what the real problem is. Why do I say that the headache is "mine?" Why do I say "I have a headache" and not "there is a headache around here somewhere?" Experimentally, people whose neural pleasure centers have been stimulated sometimes report that they still know about their headaches but they no longer care. Most people, I suppose, have had the experience of taking some "pain killer" which did not quite succeed in removing the headache but, nonetheless, caused them to lose interest in it. It is not my headache just because it is there. It is my headache because I am concerned about it. If, by psychological and physiological devices I might be caused to lose that concern, objects like pains do not reveal "me" to myself, though they help to do so when I am interested in them.

This is worth exploring in terms of at least one other example. There are things which are, in principle, more obviously "private" than pains, and which might form the contents of a preferred class of "special ob-

jects." It is easier to imagine that I might take on your pains than to imagine that I might take on your worries or, say, your feelings of sin. But
one should notice that it is not, apparently, the *object* which cannot be
taken over. If the Christian belief that Jesus assumed our sins were taken
to mean that what He did was to take over certain private feeling states in
our minds, the whole concept of sin would seem simply that of a special
kind of experience. I might actually do your worrying for you—leaving
you free for more productive things—but that could not mean that certain special states of your mind were transferred to me. It is the potential
confusion between my taking on some suitable activity which will relieve
you of the worry, and my taking on a state of your mind, which makes it
hard to imagine what is being proposed. What you need to know, to
understand yourself, is why you express your concerns *through* that state
of mind. If it was really true that to be a person was just to possess certain inner objects, life would be easy. One ought to be able to unload
one's sins—or one's worries—in the same way that one unloads one's
headaches with the proviso, of course, that, if persons are composed of
such objects, then one who unloads too many of them will cease to be.

5.2122   Clearly, something has gone quite wrong in all these examples.
The inspection of a peculiar set of objects does not reveal "me" to
myself, even if it is true that there are such peculiar inner objects. Much
less is it likely that such "objects" would reveal me to anyone else, even
if we were to imagine them not to be private. Suppose that God can be
directly aware of my pains, my feelings of sin, my worries, or whatever
you please. What does He now know? He does not know that I am *in*
pain—for I may be undergoing one of those experiments involving the
stimulation of the pleasure centres in my brain. He does not know that I
am a "sinner"—for the state of my mind may, after all, be wholly inappropriate. A pain, a feeling of sin or a worry has one significance in one
context, and a different one in a different context. Whatever it was that
Christians thought that God did, it was not, presumably, that he adopted
certain states of their minds.

5.2123   There are, to be sure, (as we suggested in our various discussions of
intentional objects, mental images and actions) states of affairs which
are internally related to personhood. Persons could be said to be
manifested through them. But none of these, it turned out, was the kind
of "object" which is a pseudo-thing, a kind of vaporous substitute for a
publicly recognizable thing. Rather, each of them revealed a kind of ac-

tivity through which persons manifested themselves. The person was always a term in the relation, and not simply assembled out of sets of such objects. Just how this is to be understood is at issue here.

5.22   It will help if we remind ourselves, briefly, of the kinds of "objects" which philosophers have sometimes supposed to exist in the world, and to see what happens when one tries to assemble a "person" out of them. The list is not very long: it includes ordinary things as they figure in perception, sense data, material objects, Platonic universals and—perhaps—minds. The point, however, is not to try to compile an exhaustive list but to reveal something about the consequence of supposing that a person is an object at all.

5.221   We have already seen that the consequence of regarding a person as an ordinary perceptual object is that we could not satisfy ourselves that anything was a person. For looking like a person is not a reasonable criterion for being one. A model of human behaviour—built, say, into a computer—is quite capable of achieving that, in principle if not in practice. And simulacra which were genuinely puzzling would simply force us to face the old mystery—how did *that* get to be a person?

We have also just seen that some slightly different objects of inner introspection to the list will not prove particularly rewarding either. The generalization of the view that the person is composed of a set of inner objects is, presumably, the view which Hume proposed but failed to find satisfaction in—that the person is a "bundle" of impressions and ideas. The difficulty, at the very least, is that, to be the person I am, I do not have to be able to introspect any particular impression or idea. There are no such objects which are either necessary or sufficient conditions for being a given person. It does not help particularly that it may well be a necessary condition for being a person at all that one be able to introspect some impressions and ideas. The person does the introspecting, not the object of the introspection, which is the subject matter of our concern. It is the relation between those impressions and ideas, and the person who is introspecting, which is revealing. At time T, two men may have in their "minds" only images composed of pictures from *Playboy,* but they may be utterly different persons for all that. We cannot say that what *would* tell us something about them is the sequence of impressions and ideas in their minds over a span of time, for to identify the sequence, we would have to know what it is that makes us say that the sequence belongs to the same person. And that property is not, as Hume pointed out, another impression or idea.

The force of this argument is that it reminds us, once again, that the problem with such analyses is not primarily that they purport to deal with persons as sets of objects to which there is only private access. The prior problem is that we cannot, in any case, generate the notion of person out of such objects.

5.222   Would these difficulties be overcome if we were to regard a person as a material object, or a set of material objects? Evidently, we would then not face either the privacy issue or the continuity issue. The criteria for the continuity of material objects are, at least, specifiable and public. Furthermore, we could then return to the notion that, so far as most of us know, persons are associated with quite ordinary material objects in the form of human bodies. Let us, for the sake of argument, assume that anyone who identifies a living human body is very likely to have to identify a human person, and that any errors he may make in the process can be allowed to lie within the normal margin of error permitted in human enquiries generally.

5.2221   There are two sorts of difficulties which will serve to illustrate the point I want to make here. One of them is parallel to the primary difficulty about impressions and ideas: Though we know what counts as bodily continuity, just what makes us decide that bodily and personal continuity run together? We have agreed to assume that one who has successfully identified a living human body has located *some* person, but we need to know, in addition, under what conditions we are prepared to agree that re-identifying the body is identifying the same person. The other basic problem is: Even if we grant all the premises, are we prepared to say that one who knows a body well knows a person well? I shall cope with these questions in turn.

The first problem begins with something which is not likely to occur to us at first glance. In principle, we could claim that a given body was a certain determinate collection of molecules, or even more basic physical particles. Or, we could claim that a given body was constituted by a characteristic set of structural features. In associating bodies with persons, we would, however, have to choose the latter position. The fact that I might be constituted entirely of physical particles which once constituted Napoleon would not make me Napoleon on any sensible view. Nor would the facts that a given object was made up in such a way that every particle in it was once part of Napoleon's body, and that no particle which constituted Napoleon's body was missing from mine, make it in the least likely. In any case, we do not claim that one person becomes another as a result of changes in his physical composition. Rather, it is a certain structure capable of a given set of functions which makes a set of particles a human body, and makes it reasonable to say that that body embodies a certain person. It is the form that counts.

But there is nothing about a given bodily form which makes it inconsistent to say that that form embodies one person rather than another. It may be factually false to predicate the personality of Russell upon the body of Churchill, but there is no formal inconsistency about it. In consequence, it is perfectly possible that the same body should embody, at different times, different persons. Religious persons frequently talk of being "born again"[1] and there is nothing formally wrong with their claims. They may be false or nonsense, but we do not refute such claims by showing bodily continuity. Nor is it clear that, if by organ transplants, we gradually replaced all of a man's body with another, we would have created a different person. However unlikely that is at present, it is, again, not a *formally* objectionable notion. It contains no inconsistency, no massive conceptual clash.

5.2222   Something other than knowledge of a man's body suggests that he is the same person. This difficulty merges naturally into the next one. If I knew all about the body of a certain man, would I be entitled to say that I "knew" him? I might know what he was likely to do under certain circumstances, for part of what I would know about him would be the electrical connections and storage patterns in his brain, which would be associated with many dispositions and pre-dispositions. I might even know much about his preferred vocabulary, for we might be able to associate much-used words with certain electrical patterns, and little-used words with other electrical patterns. But we should notice that all of these facts are compatible with being any number of different persons. They merely establish a set of restrictions within which a given person might express himself. The mistake involved here by one who claimed to know the man is, in fact, one which no one ordinarily is even tempted to make. It is as if an ecclesiastical historian were to make a long list of the properties which all the last eight Archbishops of Canterbury had in common and conclude from that that, since he knew the most recent Archbishop, he knew them all. No matter how long his list was, we would still think his claim silly. One simply does not get to know people in that way.

5.223   The structure of the first objection, however, may make us think that the natural place to turn for a better view of the kind of "object" which is a person is to the notion of form—perhaps to some special adaptation of a traditional Platonism.[2] For what seemed to be the case was that continuity of personhood amounted to continuity of form, rather than to continuity of a set of physical particles. Here, however, we simply meet the second difficulty about material objects anew. A given form is specified by a list of predicates expressing properties, each of which restricts the manner in which a personality might express itself; but no actual list of such properties specifies a particular person. The point is a logical one: Any number of persons can share a given property expressed as a *form* or any finite set of such properties. Yet, seemingly, persons are unique and are never, therefore, specified by such a list.

It is natural and tempting to argue that the postulate of uniqueness in persons is nothing more than a common prejudice to the effect that, if there are two persons, they are different in some respect. That is true, of course, *if* to be a person is to be an object, for objects are specifiable in that way. But few men would trade their wives for another "of the same specification." Is this because they habitually make some logical or epistemological mistake?

On the contrary, I would urge that the possibility of knowledge depends upon the notion that the postulate of uniqueness in persons can be sustained. I think what it means, in part, to be a person is that no act follows necessarily from any pre-existing specification. If this were not the case, nothing would count as sitting in independent judgment upon the evidence. If the act of coming to a conclusion depended necessarily upon a prior specification, it would be determined in advance. In that case, all claims to knowledge would be fraudulent, since all investigations would be trials before bought juries. Whatever it is that we claim to know, it cannot be that knowledge is impossible.

Now this is a rather abstract consideration, but it has immediate and concrete counterparts. Human beings—persons—enter characteristically into relationships in which such notions as trust, loyalty, love, friendship, and mutual concern play a continuous part. But none of them would make any sense in a world in which persons were interchangeable, or in which a given set of preconditions determined a given outcome.

All such relationships are, in a way, like knowledge and independent judgment. They have a meaning if freely entered into. They are illusions if they are simply predetermined. It makes no sense to order someone to love someone, or even to befriend someone. Genuine concerns can all be simulated, of course, and the fact that they can be is important and problematic. But if all cases were fraudulent or simulated, we should conclude that persons, in the ordinary sense, did not exist. And if all cases were simply the result of pre-existing states of affairs, none of these concepts would have any ordinary function. If a person can be known in terms of a set of specifications, it appears that all these notions are, indeed, empty. For then we could replace one lover by another of the same specification, one friend by another with the correct form, and so on.

What I would argue, in fact, is that to know someone is, indeed, in substantial measure, to know whether one or more of these conditions obtains. Basically, what is most wrong with all the proposals to consider persons as objects is that, if a person were an object, one would know by inspecting his sense data, his body, his structural form or whatever, whether he was one's friend, whether one should invest one's trust in him, whether one ought to be concerned about him, and so on. And this seems quite absurd.

5.224   It frequently seems that, when philosophers proceed through a list like this, they conclude that what is needed is a new kind of object. They are thus likely to turn to such notions as mind, ego, transcendental ego, and so on. It is difficult to deal with these cases because, as a rule, the concepts become impossibly vague.

What is it for two men to have the same or different minds? What is it like to have one ego—let alone one transcendental ego—rather than another? Here the problem is with individuation. It is all very well to distinguish one body from another, because bodies differ in their locations in space and time. But minds are traditionally said not to be located in that way. Should we distinguish them by their contents? If we do, we shall get either Hume's collection of impressions and ideas, or some other classification of "mental contents." But again, it seems clear that two physicists, say, might be thinking, at a given moment, of only the second law of thermo-dynamics, or of only the same *Playboy* centerfold, and yet we would not say that they had become the same person.

Suppose, then, we simply insist that everyone has a unique and differentiated ego which *is* him, and say that we cannot specify the properties of it for the obvious reason that we shall simply, then, get a list and fall into our old difficulties. Suppose, too, we just say that everyone has direct and immediate knowledge of his own ego and that, by analogy, he can infer that everyone else has one, too.

Have we not simply stated the postulate of human uniqueness, and covered it with a veil of mystery by postulating a special object of which there cannot be, in an adequate sense, knowledge?

We might, to be sure, cover ourselves by assigning a limited range of sufficiently vague, but intuitable, properties to the ego so as to make it an object of knowledge but not offend its uniqueness. It is by no means beyond the skill, imagination, and rational faculties of philosophers to fill this order.

Valuable as this might be in other contexts, it would be profitless here. For what we want to know, of course, is how personhood exhibits itself—how it enters into these crucial relations which we express as trust, love, loyalty, friendship, and concern. The more inaccessible we make the pure ego, the less helpful it is. Thus we might admit that there is such a thing—for there are persons, and they are unique. But it is not in its evasive loneliness as pure ego that we are interested—apart from the possible bearing a metaphysics which contained such entities might have on questions such as immortality. And even that evasive loneliness would not be established by a simple act of introspection, or a simple direct intuition. Such introspections and intuitions might reveal our convictions, but they could not, in principle, reveal our grounds for those convictions, simply because grounds imply principles and principles imply some investigation. I conclude, therefore, that no essay in the construction of peculiar entities will, by itself, actually solve the problem.

5.23   We can see the issues from a slightly different—and also revealing—perspective if we look at the methodologies traditionally recommended for finding knowledge. My contention in this section is that the puzzles about "knowledge of persons" stem substantially from the fact that these methodologies render it literally impossible that anyone should ever have the kind of knowledge which counts seriously as "knowing someone."

Philosophers have usually been (rather arbitrarily) divided by their commentators into two groups, rationalists and empiricists. Rationalists are those who believe that bona fide knowledge stems, somehow (there are many accounts of just how) from the correct application of reason. Empiricists are those who believe that it stems, somehow, from sensory experience.

5.231   While rationalism comes in many forms, it is probably true that there are two main species and many sub-species of it. Examination of either of the two main species seems mostly to re-enforce the intuitive sense of absurdity which comes to mind as one confronts the problem of "knowing someone" in these terms. I shall argue that the intrinsic absurdity is not so great as one might think but that, in grasping what might be said on behalf of the rationalist, one will discover crucial features of the issue.

One of the main species of rationalism proceeds from self-evident truths via some technique of formal deduction which guarantees that a set of theorems follows from the given axioms.

The other main species proceeds by attempting to show: (1) that reason plays a role in all knowledge finding; (2) that, for reason to function at all, a basic set of concepts is required; and (3) that only one or a limited number of worlds is consistent with the application of these concepts. Neither species, as a rule, contains on the primary level on which it functions, a validation of reason as such. But both lead to the view that effective criticism would require the application of reason, and that the validation of reason can be seen in the structure of challenges to the basic system.

5.2312   As we have seen in the preceding section, it would seem that the very possibility of being a person is inconsistent with the possibility that knowledge of persons, in the relevant sense, should meet the requirements of such a system. For persons are open-ended structures if they are the kinds of "entities" which might enter into relations such as trust, love, friendship, and concern. Spinoza, who was much concerned with such matters, attempts to produce within the structure of his system a general psychology—an account which will deal with emotion, with will, and even with the love of God. But he does not, of course, try to apply the system to show the necessity of the particular friendships which mattered so much to him; he is content to believe that they are necessary features of the world. Similarly, though Leibniz would dearly have loved to grasp the mind of the Elector of Hanover who disappointed him bitterly by becoming King of England and leaving him behind, he had to admit that the descriptions of the situation would be formed of apparently contingent propositions—propositions which, in his system, would require an infinity of other propositions to substantiate and which, therefore, are beyond human power to demonstrate. Rationalists of the second kind, Hegel for example, have generally sought to exhibit the workings of persons in the context of some more general structure which is open to rational formulation. Thus Hegel paints individuals as enmeshed in the

development of history, as features in the larger reality of a society, and
so on.

5.2313   That there is something in common between philosophers of
these two sorts can be seen if we reflect for a moment that Spinoza claimed that reason would lead to knowledge of at least one person, God. To
be sure, Spinoza's God is trans-personal—a person *and* much more. Yet,
for Spinoza, He is also the reality behind the appearance of the God of
the Judeo-Christian tradition.

5.2314   In this respect, Spinoza and Leibniz are exemplars of a very old
tradition in rational theology. God can be known by the application of
reason because God is perfect. Being perfect, God instantiates the
realities of pure reason. His love of us is, therefore, not an accident but a
necessary feature of his character.

Other persons, however, are imperfect—which is to say that they are
not quite, in themselves, real. For Spinoza, the one reality is God, the
cause of Himself, the embodiment of sufficient reason, the structure of
the world. In Leibniz's system, the individuality of monads is produced
by their varying degrees of clarity of perception. Only God, the chief
monad, perceives with perfect clarity; the unclear perceptions are a
derivative order of reality. In either case, what we think of as an individual human person is comprehensible only in a larger context. For
Spinoza, he is a set of modes of the attributes of thought and extension,
and for Leibniz he is a member of a set of hierarchical monads. Reality in
the former case is perfectly exhibited in the structure of the attributes
themselves; reality in the latter case is perfectly exhibited only in the set
of monads considered as such.

The individual, for Hegel, is intelligible in the context of history and
society. Completed history and the ideal society would, were they to occur, instantiate reality. Hence the individual person is not, really, an object of knowledge, for he is not real in the required sense.

5.2315   It would be tempting to speculate that such ideas are the deep
roots of Sartre's notion that man lies poised on the edge of non-being,
and Kierkegaard's final insistence on the irrationality of the human condition. Be that as it may, one can see that the rationalist stance forces one
to some such view *if* one concedes that persons ought to be *objects* of
knowledge. It is important to notice that Hegel comes very close to insisting that they are not objects of knowledge at all, for the

Phenomenology of Mind is an essay toward the demonstration of the proposition that all knowledge has a subjective as well as an objective side.[3] It is only when he comes to the Absolute that he seems unwittingly to allow the system to collapse to one pole of the dialectic—a collapse which explains something of the peculiarity of his social theory and his philosophy of history.

5.2316 Here, the issue is whether or not it would be tolerable to hold that what makes persons opaque to reason is their relative imperfection, their relative ontological distance from ultimate reality. It seems to me that this is not a tolerable position, for the states of affairs which we have associated with persons are by no means features of appearance which one might, with hope of success, attempt to analyze away.

We trust our techniques of knowledge finding because, and only because, we are able to believe in the reality of independent and considered judgment. If the person who must figure in such a judgment is a mere appearance, or *merely* a feature of some larger structure, then we have no reason whatever to believe in that independence of judgment. In that case, Spinoza's brilliant argument is, itself, mere facade. We shall accept or not, depending upon whether or not it is determined by our place in the system that we accept it. Spinoza is aware of this, of course, as reflecting his constant struggle to determine the conditions of human liberation. But, to succeed, he would have to abandon the notion of person as object.

5.232 Our earlier discussion suggests strongly that the empiricist will fare no better. For him, if persons are objects of knowledge, they are collections of sensory data known directly, or they are something else, and so known by inference from such data. We have seen that collections of sense data simply will not do as substitutes for persons as we know them. We have also seen that one cannot infer the nature of the person from any set of such data.

There is, however, a deeper issue which merits brief mention here. Russell, who liked to think of himself as an empiricist, divided knowledge into knowledge by acquaintance and knowledge by description. But he omitted to notice that knowledge by acquaintance also requires knowledge *of* acquaintance, and that knowledge by description also requires knowledge *of* descriptive process. I must know, that is, not merely that there is a red patch in my field of vision, but also that *I* am aware that there is such a patch. The alternative is the seemingly absurd notion that colored patches are aware of themselves, or that situations describe themselves. But this further knowledge cannot, itself, be translated into knowledge of a new set of objects. One might claim to be directly aware of the elusive "I" as a result of some immediate intuition. But then, what is it that is aware of the "I?" An infinite regress in this situation is clearly unprofitable, as Ryle pointed out.

The empiricist is, therefore, forced to accept the position that there is some kind of knowledge which is not analysable in terms of another postulated *object* of knowledge. And it is to this that we must now, at length, turn our attention.

5.24   The proposal I want to make is, indeed, simple enough. The difficulty is in relating it to a kind of knowledge which is not, per se, knowledge of an object.

In the ordinary way, we get to know people by talking, by the give and take of conversation. We also get to know ourselves by a process of articulation, not always in words, but always in some way which produces a context for reflection.

It is crucial to get some intelligible characterisation of these processes. What happens in a conversation is, assuming it does not consist of speeches made and responded to in a mechanical way, that we establish a community of meanings. The responses gradually come to make sense as we adjust to one another. An intelligible response is evidence that a portion of the original meaning "got across."

But what is going on is not simply an outpouring of some pre-existing, but hidden, state of affairs. Both participants are engaged in a process of self-exploration as well as in a process of learning about the other. The reality of the situation is in the created community of meaning.

Persons are not ready-made, fixed entities. They are, rather, entities revealed in the process of a constant and creative process of articulation. Everything one does tells one "something about oneself," provided only that it can be assigned a meaning.

5.241   We could not find out about ourselves in any other way. For, as we have seen, there is not a fixed object which *is* ourselves and only needs to be revealed by some suitable technique. Introspection, per se, reveals only emptiness. Try to think about yourself—not about what you think, do, say, and so on, but about *yourself.* There is nothing there to be found out. Yet as we develop articulate speech and behaviour, we gradually form a concept of ourselves and, as we undertake to converse with others, we gradually form concepts of them. Such concepts are always, in a sense, faulty—they are characterisations of what we have done, might do, or might imagine ourselves doing, and they all depend upon the likelihood that what we have been or have been able to imagine ourselves *as* being is what we are and shall be. They also depend upon our ability to associate ourselves with, and differentiate ourselves from, others. It is in the community of shared response that I get a sense of myself—that I form the self-concepts on which I can later reflect by myself.

Evidently, every act and every reflection changes the self which is being reflected upon. For each new meaning is itself part of that self. The nearest we can come to an "object" thus, always, trails behind the creation of the self. It is revealed through a creative situation but is never confined to that situation.

5.242   The basic point is that the methodology of self knowledge is, primarily, one of creation. It is by doing something, which is itself an articulation or which leads to an articulation, that such knowledge is developed.

It is for this reason that when we say we "know someone" we mean, primarily, that we share a community of meanings with that person. If we claim to "know him well" we claim, quite properly, that the community of shared meaning is substantial enough so that we can rely on our being able to continue it as some future time. If it is deep enough, we form the reasonable conviction that it will be sharable at any future time—though we know full well that every act in the life of a person is a change in that person.

5.243   But at least it is true that there is no purely passive knowledge of persons—there is no "knowing him as he would have been if I had never known him." The nearest we can come to that is in cases such as those of writers, whose articulation is to extensive that we can reconstruct the kinds of conversations we might have had with them, using their own words to fill in their side of the conversation. And every biographer who has tried to reconstruct his subject in that way knows full well just how difficult it is.

It is this process which distinguishes men and machines. Meanings are assigned by us and arise out of creative shared situations; machines may simulate the behaviour in question, but never originate such creations.

It is in the context of a shared community of meaning that such no-

tions as those we have discussed—trust, love, friendship, and concern—make sense. We trust someone because the community of meaning
we have established bears the weight of the necessary common concern. Friendship lies in that community of meaning in a very obvious
sense. Love, presumably, is a limiting condition—the case in which the
participants come to regard one another as inextricably involved in one
another's primary set of meaningful relations.

5.244 So far, perhaps, so good. But we still must confront the
hypothetical philosopher whose imaginary response opened this section.
He may well insist that all this is, in a sense, true; but it is the kind of
truth which is characteristic of the descriptions of illusions. The surface
behaviour which yields such "personal knowledge," he will say, really
has its explanation in objective matters of fact which will never emerge in
this way. The states of one's brain, the workings of one's sub-conscious
mind, the secretions of one's glands, all condition this surface behaviour
and make of it an illusion. The "person" really is the concern of the
biologist, neurologist, the depth psychologist.

His response rests on a confusion between necessary and sufficient
conditions. It is quite true that the creative acts which yield personal
knowledge are only possible if appropriate conditions are met.

5.245 We normally talk to one another in words, and we normally act in
ways which require the use of our bodies. There has to be interaction between persons and things—the kind of interaction which we discussed in
sections 4.6 and 4.7. Personality is always expressed through something.
Some set of such conditions includes the set of necessary conditions—though we do not know, of course, how wide that set is.

In consequence, our knowledge of biology, neuro-physiology,
linguistics, and psychology generally gives us some approximation to the
limits which circumscribe personality. But these things cannot supply the
sufficient conditions for expressions of personality because, as the long
discussion of objects of knowledge and methodologies for knowledge
finding show, no *object* will fill the bill. We cannot substitute the *general*
findings of depth psychology for knowledge of individuals and
psychoanalysts are surely right to insist that it is only through a patient
process of interaction between the analyst and his patient that any progress is likely, if the difficulty is associated with the creative process of expression itself. Certainly, many problems about that process will turn out
to have straightforward physical causes, and others will depend upon

whatever processes are intermingled with the creation and "storage" of the bases for shared meanings. A man's failures to make friends may be the result of a brain tumor, a speech defect or an Oedipus complex. But merely correcting those will not guarantee that his problem is solved.

5.246   Nothing that I am saying is intended, in fact, to degrade the importance of the various knowledge-finding enterprises which are institutionalised in the academic curriculum and enshrined in the establishment of learning. To assign things to their proper place is not to degrade them.

But we *are* in danger of forgetting that the way to get to know people is to talk to them and, hence, of abandoning the community of shared meanings for a set of abstractions which, by themselves, are helpless to yield personal knowledge. The opponents of this dehumanising process, however, are themselves frequently in danger of imagining a hopelessly hidden and unhelpful "inner self" of which, again, no knowledge is possible.

My suggestion does not entail that personal knowledge is somehow basically "irrational." On the contrary, the careful exercise of reason is a *sine qua non* of the creation of effective communities of meaning. Coherence, a sense of direction, careful analysis of what is said and intended, all have their roles to play. Nor is it by any means impossible (as most psychologists realise) to learn much about how such processes work. We must only remember that knowledge of persons is, in the end, an individual act of creation.

5.3 Knowing What One is Doing

5.31   One of the principal points of this book is to raise serious doubts about what has been called the traditional mental-physical dualism. For example, it was argued in 4.1 and 4.6 that the concepts of person and action would be unintelligible if one thought of a person as made up of a mental substance and a physical substance. I want to further that argument in this chapter by showing that on a traditional model, there is no way to understand how one knows what he is "doing." For instance, most adults have acquired the ability to tie their shoes and, on most occasions, when they do this they know full well what it is that they are doing. What I will argue is that common performances such as these become shrouded in mystery if one approaches them from the point of view of mental-physical dualism. My argument will have the structure of a *reductio ad absurdum:* there is nothing mysterious about performances such as these, so that any view that leads to the conclusion that there is must be defective. Once this is admitted, the possibilities of accepting an alternative account are increased.

5.32 I am concerned with investigating the epistemological consequences that flow from the metaphysical position of dualism.[1] The body is a physical thing, the mind is a mental thing, and a person is either predominantly one of these or the sum of both. Knowing what one is doing becomes the same kind of thing as knowing what is going on in one's surrounding environment. One observes, one takes note, one inspects. If one wants to know the speed and direction of a passing automobile, one observes it with stopwatch and compass. The same is true if one wants information about the movements of a friend or, for that matter, of oneself. What one has done, is doing, or will do are the operations of a substance that are governed by the laws of physics. Roughly, one determines what one has done on the basis of past observations, what one is doing on the basis of present observations; what one will do is a matter of prediction. If there is a single, outstanding defect of this model it has to do with the notion of agency. The idea has been turned on its head. One has become the spectator of, rather than the participator in, one's own activities. Ryle, for example, holds that "The sorts of things that I can find out about myself are the same as the sorts of things that I can find out about other people, and the methods of findings them out are much the same."[2] This is too narrow a view to be generally true. There are instances in which one finds out things about one's self and one's actions, and in these cases the method of finding out may be much the same as it is with other things. For example, I may discover that in buying that pack of cigarettes, I have spent my last dollar. I check out the wallet and find that it is empty. Being broke is, if you will, a public condition, so that its determination is roughly the same whether it is my condition or that of someone else. But not all conditions are like this. Intending to spend my last dollar is vastly different. I do not find out about something like this in the same way that I learn that I am flat broke. In fact I do not, in any ordinary sense, find out at all about my intentions.

5.33 I am going to concentrate my attention on the knowledge that I have of my present and future actions, and ignore the past. Knowledge of the past seems to me to raise very special problems connected with memory which would take me much too far afield.

5.331   The knowledge that one has of his present actions is, by and large, knowledge gained without observation. As such, it is distinct from the knowledge one has of things. To know that the sun is rising or the rain is falling, I must observe what is going on. The resulting claim that I make then rests on the information I have obtained. There is no parallel procedure which rests at the foundation of my claim to know what it is that I am doing; I have no evidence, and there is none required. The question "How do you know?" directed toward what I am presently doing has no answer analogous to the one directed toward what I say about the weather. I know that it is raining because I look out the window and find out. I know that I am now typing but *not* because I look and see the keys moving.

5.332   I center my argument for this account on a conception of "knowledge without observation" as it relates to the knowledge that one has of the position of his limbs.[3] My argument is that in normal circumstances one knows that, for example, his legs are crossed without recourse to the observation of anything. Specifically one does not observe such things as kinesthetic sensations *on the basis of which* one rests his claim about his legs. If one's legs had gone to sleep or had been anesthetized in some manner, then the tingling sensations might inform one as to the position of his legs. But one's legs are not normally asleep or anesthetized. When they are, then evidence that is obtained through observation—looking down and seeing or attending to how they feel—is appropriate; otherwise it is superfluous.

I want to make it clear that what I am denying is a bit of descriptive epistemology. So far as I know, I am not taking issue with any psychological doctrine of kinesthetic sensations. I am not denying that sensations may play an important role in our ability to determine the location of our limbs. If a child were kept selectively anesthetized for a number of years, he might not be able to tell if his legs were crossed or straight without looking. What I am denying is that normal people, under normal circumstances, must take note of something and then, on the basis of that, make their claim. Taking another example from Anscombe: most people who can write know what it is that they are writing even if they are blind-folded,[4] although their writing may be sloppy and illegible. In general, the observations that we make may guide or confirm our efforts in what we say or do, and they may be essential in allowing us to acquire the original skill, but they do not provide the foundation for the knowledge claim.

5.333   However, I am saying that this account can be extended to cover intentional actions, and that a vast number of those actions extend way beyond the mere position of our limbs. In the above example of writing while blind-folded, do I not have to observe in order to know that I am doing what I want to do? Perhaps the pen runs out of ink so that nothing at all appears on the paper. How can I tell that something of this sort is not happening if I make no observations?

5.34   In general, the answer to this question is that knowledge of one's own intentional actions is, in part, knowledge of what is going on in the world. As such, it must involve observation, as the above example with the pen shows. We are entangled in a conflict, but the way out has to do with the way in which observation is involved. In order for it to be possible for me to intend to write something with this pen, I must have learned what to expect from pens. In order for these expectations to be sensible, they must be founded in fact, which generally means that I have used and observed pens before. Now that I am equipped with this general knowledge of the way in which pens operate, it is possible for me to intend to do things with them. In other words, the knowledge that I acquire about the way in which things in the world operate is acquired through experience and observation. However, once I am in possession of this knowledge, the particular instance in which I know what it is that I am doing on this piece of paper with this pen is not based on observation. Of course what I am trying to do may not come off. For example, if the pen runs out of ink, and I do not notice it, I will not know that I am not signing my name. If I were then asked "What is it that you are doing?" and I reply "Signing a purchase agreement," what I have said is wrong. What this shows is that observation is useful and sometimes necessary, not to monitor oneself and one's doings but to check on the happenings in the world. The ordinary concept of action is an admixture of things happening in the world as well as the things that one does oneself. Whether or not the pen is full of ink and so whether or not the ink flows on to the page has to do with the condition of the pen rather than what it is that one is doing as an agent. Consequently, one needs to observe the behavior of the world so that one can make the necessary adjustments in one's own behavior. There is no way, without observation, to know that the pen has run out of ink, but it would be ridiculous to suppose that the pen's running out of ink was a part of one's doings and therefore something that one could be expected to know without observation. It is somewhat like returning someone's serve in tennis. One must keep his eye on the ball in order to have a fair chance of doing so. It would be foolish to argue that because the speed and direction of the ball figure significantly in my returning the serve I am committed to claim that they must be known without observation. All that I am committed to is the claim that I know what it is that I am doing without observing myself or my doings. This is not at all the same as saying that I know all or even most of what is true about my doings, as much of what is captured by that description will have to do with things that are happening in, around and about my actions.

5.341   The point that I am making can be clarified by understanding the difference between having an intention nullified, as opposed to contradicted. An intention may be nullified simply by its not happening; it is contradicted only by another intention. "I am going to sign my name" is nullified by anything that prevents it from happening, for example, "No, you are not. The pen is dry." It is contradicted only by something like "Oh, no, you are not. I am going to stop you." The nullifying claim relates to "I am going to sign my name" as evidence counter to a prediction. At issue is a future matter of fact, and the likelihood of its occurring. The reasonableness of the claim is directly related to the evidence. The facts are in command, so that a discrepancy between what is said and what goes on means that what is said has to be changed in order that things be set straight. It would be something of a joke to make what was said true by reaching out and emptying the ink from the pen. That is not the way in which the appropriateness of predictions is supported. But it is the way in which the appropriateness of an expression of intention is supported. If "I am going to sign my name" is countered with "No, you're not. I'm going to stop you," it would be most proper for me to try to make an honest proposition out of what I had said by emptying the ink from the pen.

Suppose that I have a shopping list, and go to the grocery store followed by a detective who has an interest in my behavior. The list serves me as a reminder of the things I intend to buy. I glance at it, go to the appropriate counter and pick up the item. The person behind me records what it is that I do. As I select a toothbrush he writes "toothbrush" on a piece of paper. At the end of the day, if all has gone well, his list and mine will have on them the same items. What is the relation between the two lists themselves, as well as to the items in the shopping cart?[5] I set out to make the facts correspond to the list, while the man following me tries to make his list correspond with the facts.

5.342 It would appear that a mistake had been made if an item on the list was not found in my shopping cart, though this must be qualified. If the list says "toothpaste" and the only thing that is in my cart that comes close to corresponding with that is toothpowder, there are several possibilities. They may have been out of toothpaste and/or I may have changed my mind. So a lack of correspondence between my list and the items in the cart is not sufficient to show that I made a mistake. However, lack of correspondence between his list and the items in my cart is sufficient to show that the man behind me has made a mistake. He is trying to record the facts, while I am trying to create them.

5.35 In section 4.6, I argued that Prichard's account of action, in terms of bodily movements preceded by an act of will, was inadequate. It is appropriate now to point out how that view distorts my knowledge of what it is that I am doing. The distortion occurs because of the nature of what it is that happens in the public realm, and because of the lack of connection between these events and what goes on in the mind. Prichard treats our body as just another material object. As such, its behavior is governed by the laws of nature. How these laws operate is a mystery; we know that changes occur, but we do not know how.

> And if we ask ourselves: "Is there such an activity as originating or causing a change in something else?", we have to answer that there is not. To say this, of course, is not to say that there is no such thing as causing something, but only to say that though the causing a change may require an activity, it is not itself an activity. If we then ask: "What is the kind of activity required when one body causes another to move?", we have to answer that we do not know . . . [6]

We can tabulate events as they happen, but that is as far as we can go. This is also the position that we find ourselves in with regard to our own actions. We observe, as best we can, an act of will and note that it is followed by certain occurrences. But there is no guarantee that what has happened in the past will continue in the future.

> We are thus left with the conclusion that where we think we have done some action, e.g., have raised our arm or written a word, what we willed was some change, e.g., some movement of our arm or some movement of ink to a certain place on a piece of paper in front of us. But we have to bear in mind that the change which we

willed may not have been the same as the change we think we effected. Thus, where I willed some movement of my second finger, I
may at least afterwards think that the change I effected was a
movement of my first finger, and, only too often, where I willed
the existence of a certain word on a piece of paper, I afterwards
find that what I caused was a different word.[7]

5.351   There are various problems here, all of which add up to the fact
that in many instances I really do not know what it is that I am doing until after it is done. To be certain of myself, I must wait and see what has
happened. The problem of connecting the particular act of will with the
hoped-for movement is apparently not an empty, theoretical one. At
least some of the time when what occurs is not what one wanted to happen, the reason will be either that the expected act of will resulted in an
unexpected movement or I initiated the wrong act of will. But the most
important thing to note is that what results from the act of will is not an
action, but merely a movement. This is what makes human activities a
species of natural ones. And it is this more than anything else that makes
us a spectator of our own actions. This means that to know what it is that
we are doing, it is necessary for us to gather evidence. It is not clear how
we gather information about individual acts of will, but there is no problem with how we become informed about our bodily movements. We
observe the pattern of their occurrences in much the same manner that
we observe the pattern of any events in nature. We look for regularities,
and make a note of any oddities. Prichard warns us not to expect that
such an enterprise will ever be entirely successful, but it seems to be the
only thing that we can do to fight off total uncertainty. However the
problem is not that such a project will be only partially successful. The
problem comes from viewing actions in such a fashion that it is deemed,
in all cases, appropriate. But, since all we have to deal with are
movements and events, this is the only thing that we have between us and
complete uncertainty.

Because we do initiate our own behavior, knowing what one is doing is
much different from knowing the behavior of something other than
oneself. The difference between my shopping list and the detective's list
is a real one. It is a joke to suggest that I (as opposed to the detective)
must wait and see what ends up in the cart in order to know what I have
been up to. Taking a cue from Prichard, we have to allow that things
may go wrong, and allow further that when they do, I may find out
about them by observation. However, that does not show that knowing

what I am about when things go as planned is a matter of having paid close attention to myself.

5.352 I am arguing that knowing what one is doing when one acts intentionally is never a matter of evidence and observation. Yet the fact remains that sometimes the things go wrong and when they do we can find this out in the normal way, that is, by observation. However, to see our way more clearly through this we need an example. Suppose that toothpaste is on my shopping list, toothpowder is what I end up with in my cart, and I have not changed my mind. There are two types of things that can explain this misfiring of events. One is an error in performance and the other is an error in information. Speaking very broadly, the first occurs when I foul up and the second happens when the world goes askew. In the first instance I am in a hurry, grab for an item, my hand slips, and knocks the wrong one into my cart. In the second instance I look carefully enough, but the item has been incorrectly packaged and so the wrong item goes into my cart. Surely we must use our senses and observe in order to know what is going on.

In the second instance we must and do make observations, but it is no counterexample to my claim because what we observe are not our own actions. The appearance of the toothpowder in the toothpaste carton is in no sense something that I am doing. It is not even an action let alone my action and so there is no reason to apply to it the doctrine of knowledge without observation. So, although we allow the application of observation we are not allowing its application to one's own action.

The fact of the matter is that there are a large number of things involved in one's actions that are crucially connected to their outcome. Because something happened which prevented one from achieving his goal does not show that what occurred was the action or a part of it. Essentially this is as appropriate in the second example as it was in the first. What one did was to reach out and grab for an item in a hurried and careless fashion with the result that the wrong item ended up in one's cart. My argument then is that the wrong item's ending up in the cart is the effect or result of what one did and thus not in itself what one did. It is something that happened because of the way in which one acted (carelessly), but it was not itself an action in the sense in which "grabbing for an item" was an action.

What is likely to cause confusion is the fact that one may still be culpable for the effects of what one does precisely because of the way in which one acted, that is, carelessly. To deny that it is a constituent of the action and to insist that it is the effect of what one has done is not necessarily to excuse oneself. Oftentimes under ordinary circumstances, we talk loosely about actions so as to include effects and consequences. It is quite proper that we do so because our interest is in those things that are important and subject to modification by our efforts. The effects of one's actions certainly fall into that category. We modify the world not only by our actions in the strict sense, but also by the things that we are able to make happen by our actions. However, from the point of view of the concept of knowledge without observation, it is important to distinguish actions in the strict sense from a more general sense that includes effects.

5.353   It would be a mistake now to argue that because we have ruled out as a foundation of knowledge the observation of the occurrence of external events that the proper foundation must be the observation of something internal. For example, it would be wrong to think, à la Prichard, that knowing what one is doing is a matter of properly identifying the act of will. Even if we abandon the *sui generis* act of will as a dead end, and instead speak of intentions, there is no workable sense in which we ground our knowledge of what we are doing on an observation of these as internal events. It is certainly true that one knows what one is doing by knowing what one intends. What is not true is that this knowledge is a kind of internal observation. In fact, much of the time when one is acting, one's attention cannot be directed inward. Think, for instance, what it is like to drive an automobile and how one's attention is directed toward the traffic, condition of the road, stop lights, weather and so on. One's ability to drive would be seriously endangered if in order to know what one was doing one had to divert his attention from the traffic to observe some alleged internal happenings. The fact that this knowledge is not founded on evidence does not mean that what goes on in the world plays no role in what I do. If the person with whom I am speaking does not understand what I am saying, then I might try to express it differently. Suppose someone challenges me and asks, "How do you know you are explaining to him how to get to Chagrin Falls?" If I were to reply that I had lived there for a number of years and so was familiar with the route, it would be a mistake to take this as evidence in support of my knowledge of what I was saying. It is true that it does support me, but it does so by certifying me as a person who is competent to give directions of this kind. Frequently, it is merely a matter of reassuring the person that I am in command of my faculties and that everything is normal. After all, how can one answer a question like "How do you know that you are talking?" "Because I am in possession of myself" is not so much an answer as it is an assurance that the question really need not be asked. It is simply a fact about people that as they mature, they gain mastery over themselves and their surroundings. However, one must not think that acting intentionally, or knowing what one is doing when one acts intentionally, are themselves skills. Having acquired the skill of speaking a foreign language, one may speak it intentionally. Particular skills such as this enable us to perform corresponding intentional acts. The development of these undoubtedly involves observation of evidence; the intentional practice of them does not. The latter is merely a matter of being a person.

Notes to Chapter 5

Notes to Section 5.1.

1. C.D. Broad, *Mind and its Place in Nature* (London: Routledge and Kegan Paul, Ltd., 1923), p. 186.

2. *Infra.*, sec. 2.32.

3. *Op. cit.*, p. 185.

4. F. Ebersole, *Things We Know* (University of Oregon Press, 1967), Chap. III. This is a particularly provocative way of dealing with the question.

5. A.J. Ayer, *The Problem of Knowledge* (MacMillan, 1958), p. 85.

6. *Op. cit.*, p. 88.

7. R.S. Hirst, *Encyclopedia of Philosophy*, ed. Paul Edwards (New York: Mac-Millan, 1967), Vol. 7, pp. 78-79.

8. Exactly what is meant by "directly given" is not ever very clearly, though at a later point Ayer talks about it as though it were to be defined in conjunction with "sense datum." *Foundations of Empirical Knowledge* (London: MacMillan, 1964), p. 60.

9. Note the expression " . . . object of . . . " What these cases really show is not that we do not perceive things, but that what we perceive is an intentional object. This does perhaps contradict some of these "common sense" philosophers (Austin?) who sometimes seem to argue that it is absurd to say that we perceive anything other than physical objects. Still, it does not lend support to skepticism.

It allows that, on occasions, things look other than they are, but this is something that naive realism can take into account.

10. *Infra.,* sec. 4.4.

11. Wittgenstein, *The Philosophical Investigations,* Pt. II, p. 193.

12. A.J. Ayer, *Language, Truth and Logic* (Dover, New York: 1952), p. 123; *Foundations of Empirical Knowledge,* p. 237.

13. G.E. Moore, "A Defense of Common Sense," *Philosophical Papers* (Allen and Unwin, 1959), Chap. II.

Notes to Section 5.2.

1. Indeed, amongst a large group of American fundamentalists, this notion has become the one which they regard as separating them from believers of other persuasions, and they now refer to themselves as "born again" Christians.

2. I am assuming a tradition which distinguishes what is loosely called "Platonism" from "neo-Platonism." The distinction, apparently, is between the notion that there are special entities with ontological priority, properly designated forms, and having a being independent of what is informed; and the notion that the world is not, finally, to be divided into bits and pieces, but to be regarded as a set of aspects which participate in a single, unifying guiding principle.

3. Though, indeed, one cannot reach the Absolute without knowing that knowledge has two sides, the duality must, finally disappear. See *The Phenomenology of Mind,* translated by J. B. Baillie (London: George Allen and Unwin, 1910), pp. 790-807.

Notes to Section 5.3.

1. For example, see Hume's statement of purpose in the "Introduction" to *A Treatise of Human Nature,* Selby-Bigge, ed. (Oxford: Clarendon Press, 1888), especially pp. xx-xxiii.

2. G. Ryle, *The Concept of Mind* (London: Hutchinson, 1949), p. 155. What might save this claim is a strict interpretation of the expression "finding out."

3. This expression and much of the following argument is taken from Anscombe's *Intention,* p. 49ff. See also "My Kinaesthetic Sensation Advise Me" by A.I. Melden, *Analysis,* Dec., 1957.

4. Anscombe, *Intention,* p. 53.

5. *Ibid.*, p. 56.

6. H.A. Prichard, "Acting, Willing, Desiring," *Moral Obligation* (Oxford: Clarendon Press, 1949), pp. 188-189.

7. *Ibid.,* p. 192.

Chapter 6

A Developing Thesis

The aim of our investigation was straightforward enough: the development of a conceptual scheme which would enable us to cope with a certain kind of experience—the experience which compels us to draw, maintain, and constantly update the demarcation between the "world within" and the apparent outer world. One can only do that, of course, if one forms some estimate of how one could best characterise that inner world. In its turn, that enterprise must compel us to characterise the outer world—at least clearly enough so as to establish a reasonable way of construing its relation to the inner world.

It was necessary, therefore, first of all to show that the problem was a genuine one; and it was necessary to look at serious attempts to dissolve the issue—to show that it depended on a false estimate of certain claims to knowledge, that it rested on a misuse of language, or that, given a different choice of conceptual frameworks, one would not be tempted to raise the questions with which we started. In the course of such investigations, one uncovers a large conceptual map whose component areas bear on one another in many ways. In the end, the most crucial problem turned out to be the construction of a conceptual system which would enable one to cope with these experiences without falling into the large logical difficulties of a traditional dualism, and without accepting the impoverishment which comes from adopting reductionist stances—whether they be those of a classical subjective idealism, or those of the recurrently popular reductive materialism.

The welter of argument which we turned up suggested very strongly that the most important and obtrusive notions of what may populate the world within almost uniformly turn out to be unintelligible, unless they can be seen to stand in clear and explicable relations to the outer world. Thus a classical dualism, which requires that the requisite intelligibility should be available independently, came to seem simply unworkable. For just the same reasons, however, it seemed that none of the available notions of reducibility would serve their purpose. If all our experience and every successful way of putting together a conceptual framework seems to take one across the line—if one can no more understand ordinary objects without the corresponding notions of encounter and perception than one can understand the notions of intention, image and will, without the corresponding notions of object—then we must somehow accept the fact that the solution can be neither ultimate duality, nor ultimate reduction.

The main body of the work is, in a sense, done: the concepts have been traced and delineated. The pictures it seems reasonable to form of the crucial transactions which go into the formation of the distinction between self and world seem to have been made.

In another sense, however, there is important work to be done in this concluding section. This work seems to divide, naturally, into two tasks. The first is to show that there is a comprehensible model of the whole conceptual structure—and that it is one which does not, in and of itself, do violence to notions about knowledge and experience which are, if anything, better sustained by rational analysis than our proposed conceptual structure. We could not, in other words, argue that our case was made if the price paid for it was that one could no longer find a place for claims which are themselves supported by strong reasons.

Essentially, this is the point of section 6.1—called "the dialectic of experience." The proposal is simply that we can well understand the various things said in earlier parts of the book if one sees our claims about experience and knowledge as ordered into a set of levels of reflection. We can begin with the ordinary knowledge of objects in the world and exhibit the rest of our normal claims as claims about analysis and construction which result from a series of acts of reflection. The claim is not, of course, that later levels somehow absorb the earlier ones—a claim sometimes made about and for the Hegelian dialectic. On the contrary, the claim is that the various levels maintain their intelligibility only by reference to one another. The distinction between the world within and the world outside is, then, maintained in terms of the relations which hold at these various levels, rather than in terms of different kinds of things.

This claim is simply that the system can be grasped in a unified way without conceptual disaster, and without disaster to other claims which, independently of what is in the book, sensible people are apt to want to make. It is not the claim that this way of arranging the results is the only possible one or that, indeed, there are overwhelming independent reasons for it. If one could make such a claim, it would require another and different book.

Once we have seen, however, that we have not worked ourselves into a hopeless situation, there remains something else to be done: we must re-examine the whole web of argument in order to determine how one argument bears upon another. It is not just that it is always desirable to have a summary. It is, rather, that failure to have a summary leaves one open to the possibility that, though the *conclusions* of the arguments form a consistent whole, the pattern in the arguments might actually produce serious conceptual conflict. One might, that is, have slipped considerations into argument A which are, somehow, inconsistent with considerations in argument B, and so on. One cannot, of course, review every detail of the argument. One can, though, look at the major elements in the most crucial arguments, and attempt to see what happens when they are put together.

The result we think, is that the argument hangs together. But that is for the reader to decide.

6.1 The Dialectic of Experience

Throughout the discussion, we have met two ordered sets of levels—one of experience and the other of knowledge. They represent different "levels" because, evidently, what occurs in experience as our ordinary experience of "material objects" is, in some sense, repeated when we try to understand talk about sense data, about systems of theoretical entities, about our reflections, and so on. They are also ordered in the sense that the arguments we have employed from time to time urged that (1) while it is possible and reasonable to move from level to level, it is not the case that one can move from any given level to any other at random, and (2) it seems to be true that there is a natural direction. (It is one thing to "analyze" one's experience of an Elephant into an experience consisting of sense data and another, evidently, to construct the experience of an elephant out of experience conceived as sets of sense data. There may be a sense in which one can suggest the way a given experience may be taken to be experience "of" a set of theoretical entities. That *might* be the way in which it is proper and reasonable to describe what goes on when one looks into the Wilson cloud chamber, and it *might* be the right way to describe one's transactions with an electron microscope. But one need not accept that description. And it does not seem that one could construct ordinary experience out of such specialized experiences with as much ease as one performs the analysis which leads one in the other direction.)

6.11 At any rate, there are comparative phenomena which one might describe as levels of experience and, somehow, we have to attempt this description; until we do, the role which *we* play in the matter remains unclear and, so long as that remains unclear, the distinction between the world within and the outer world must, to some extent, remain unclear. It should be noticed that, if there are levels of experience, then there are also levels of knowledge.

So far, however, we have simply made and exploited various distinctions. The function of this section is to bring them together preparatory to our attempt to assemble our conclusions. In one sense, nothing new enters into this discussion. In another sense, a whole different way of relating the data and organizing the argument arises.

I have called this relation a dialectic because it has to do with the way in which demands put on one mode of conceptualization break down that mode and force us to replace it with another mode in which the original concerns appear in a different guise. My claim is that it is the failure to grasp this process, more than anything else, which has led to a set of philosophical curiosities—the claim that ordinary objects are best viewed as "logical constructs" for which sense data provide the basis, the claim that theoretical entities in certain systems have a fundamental precedence over ordinary experiences, or even Hegel's claim that all reality is to be grasped as the unfolding of the Absolute in a fundamentally *logical*[1] process.

6.12 To some extent, I shall be drawing upon materials which Hegel himself developed in the *Phenomenology of Mind*. But, to an equally important extent, I shall be taking issue with him or, at least, insisting upon certain lessons which might be drawn from a close study of what happens in the *Phenomenology*. I think those lessons should be taken in a different way from that in which Hegel himself took them as he raced for the finish line of the *Phenomenology*.[2]

I shall try to establish conditions which would have to be met if various philosophical positions were to be sustained—thus establishing, hopefully, ways in which those who may disagree with our conclusions might start their arguments. It is vital, in any theory, to have some idea of what it would take to prove one wrong.

6.13   The most crucial enterprise is to try to determine what one is going to count as the primary mode of experience. Where does one start? And why?

The most fashionable view throughout most of the history of modern philosophy—since Descartes or, if you like, since Hume—has been that one starts by an attempt to find an *immediate* experience. Descartes tried to codify some species of self-awareness. (Despite the simplicity and forthrightness of his claim, its understanding remains a matter of dispute.) Hume sought that level of experience at which strictly *given* impressions become clear in all their original liveliness and vividness—undimmed by the mediating process through which we transform them into ideas.

It is interesting that Descartes believed that one could have immediate certainty of one's self-existence but that he doubted that one could have certainty about "a world" which belonged to the same level of experiential access. (Hence Descartes's "world" is a rational construction.) Hume believed that one could have immediate certainties only about essentially atomic impressions, and the cost of that—a cost which worried him—was that one knew oneself only as a collection of such impressions, which is to say that one does not *know* oneself at all. (Hence Hume treats self-knowledge as an unsatisfactory rational construct.) Both of them realized that there were other levels of knowledge and experience. Descartes was fully aware of the ordinary kinds of experience with which we all start, but believed that it does not, by itself, yield knowledge. In consequence of *that*, the levels of experience and knowledge part company in his system. Hume, too, is aware of the kinds of experience which precede the analysis he proposes—and which, to use his language, is to be "resolved" into impressions. He is also aware that, given his analysis, the levels of experience and knowledge do not mesh. What he calls "natural beliefs" function together with the ordinary kinds of "unresolved" experience, and are neither confirmed nor denied by the practice of analysis.

6.14   There are, you will notice, two curious and interesting facts here: one is the rival emphasis on subject and object, and the other is the tendency for various levels of experience and knowledge to part company with one another. For Hume, as for Descartes, there is an "order and connection of ideas"; but, while Descartes sees in this order the basis for the rational construction of a world, Hume does not see in it the basis for *any* rational construction which will yield knowledge that extends beyond its own connections.

It seems obvious that something rather curious is happening here. Hegel thought that it was both interesting and vitally important that the knowing situation involved both subject and object. The view which one takes of the objects of knowledge tends to determine the view one *must* take of the knowing subject. At the level of "sense certainty"—the level which seems to correspond to Hume's impressions—the "self" disappears.

Hegel's account of the matter at that level is, roughly, this: in order to achieve the necessary analysis of experience, one must both assert and deny self-knowledge. Hume was evidently right in supposing that one could, at most, be aware of a bundle of impressions and ideas. He was right because, at this level, no objects of knowledge are available which could do duty, in the ordinary way, for a "self." But one cannot quite do without a self, either. Hume began the *Treatise* with a set of descriptions of what enters into awareness. Sense certainty is not self-creating or self-sustaining and, indeed, Hume speaks of his self-awareness as a kind of constant but inexplicable companion.

6.141   The way in which Hegel develops this notion is interesting and important, but to follow all of its details, here, would lead us rather far astray. The simplest way of putting the matter, and one Hegel himself makes use of, is simply to notice that while the "self" is, in fact, thrust into the background and excluded, at this level, from the domain of objects of knowledge, it is nonetheless an essential ingredient in establishing the situation.[3] Hegel notices that the essence of sense is that it relies upon what is "here" and "now." The claim is that a certain reference frame renders immediate sensation or impression particularly important. But where does this reference frame come from? It does not appear as a sensation or an impression. Perhaps it is covertly asserted, an undisclosed feature which results from the focus of attention.

6.142   Hegel does not exploit the fact, but it seems plausible to think that one who dwelt on that situation would create what might be called the dialectical opposite of this scheme—one in which self-awareness is taken to be immediate, and sensations and impressions are all taken to be modifications of the self which figures in that awarness. This is an approximation to Descartes's scheme. Descartes claims that whatever is presented is always presented to a single designated observer. Early on, when he raises the hypothesis of the malign demon and, later, when he asks whether we can rely on the existence of a world of things in space and time, he speaks as though what is going on is that the malign demon or God is modifying the self (or consciousness) expressed as the original self-awareness. Sensations are ways in which consciousness manifests itself through its own activities, or as a result of outside interference. If Hume's problem is the covert intrusion of self-identity, Descartes's problem is the intrusion of objects which are not merely auto-biographical.

6.143   Hume and Descartes present rival conceptualizations of the same situation, and neither turns out to be perfectly consistent. Hume must cope with a self which is not a proper object of knowledge.[4] Descartes must cope with the possibility of entities independent of the self in a scheme in which nothing (experientially) counts as an example of such independence.

We could build a dialectic on this plan as, in effect, Hegel did. To choose a level of simple and immediate awareness is to choose a level on which either subject or object is repressed but still must function. The schemes are conflicting, but they have in common a reliance on immediate experience. However, immediate experience bifurcates itself annoyingly on either scheme. They both exclude a kind of reflective consciousness which provides a continuity over time, and provides for a domain of things within which, perhaps, the necessary distinctions can be made.

6.144   If we suppose these schemes to call attention to a real mode of experience—immediate awareness—but to be incomplete because they deny a kind of experience which will render them intelligible, we can construct the next level. Hegel does so in a way which is not too far distant from the process I have been suggesting. (The general rule for dialectical synthesis which I proposed in *Logic and Reality* is that it proceeds by creating a synthesis of the uniting property of the two preceding categories—here it seems to be immediate awareness—and the joint specific exclusion reference of those categories. It does not, of course, proceed by simply amalgamating the conflicting categories—a procedure which would produce a conceptual clash likely to issue in a formal contradiction.)[5]

6.145   We might, then, proceed with this story in a rather traditional way—drawing on the materials from modern philosophy in the period from Descartes to Hegel. But there seems to be something suspicious about it. The next level of the dialectic is one on which Hegel, in fact, seems to locate the domain of things and the mode of experience appropriate to the knowledge of things. But that, after all, is the level on which Hume started his analysis and on which it is not unfair to urge that Descartes started his. We would seem to be undertaking the reconstruction in analysis of the reverse order—but with the obvious difference that we would be generating the world of continuity and of things out of something like reflective consciousness. This would make our knowledge of ordinary things derivative, and that seems to be a mistake.

6.15   Is it not possible that there is another lesson to be learned from the breakdown of these analyses into immediate experience—the lesson that one cannot, after all, start there? We must see the problem in the context of the claim that there is, or may be, a natural dialectic of experience.

It will not quite do to say that one cannot start with Hume's impressions, Price's sense data, Russell's sensa, or Hegel's sense certainty just because the temporal development does not seem to be like that. As far as one can tell, it is true that experience starts in the richer mode of intentionality. The baby cries because it is dissatisfied with its sensations; it stops when it is satisfied. It no doubt begins to identify objects in a process which is inseparable from the development of its desires. No doubt, too, the growing development of subject and object—the basis of Hegel's dialectic—is a by-product of this same process: objects are distinguished from oneself at least because they are sometimes there and sometimes not, and one's intentional reaction must become differentiated through, and partially developed by, the patterned comings and goings of mothers, bottles, rattles, diapers, and what not.

6.151   This points out, once again, that the dissolution of either subject *or* object must render unintelligible the development of an understanding of such notions as intention, action, image, reflection, and dream. But, of course, it does not do justice to that distinguished body of philosophers whose theories are intermingled with accounts of the primacy of some level of experience which is not unlike Hegel's sense-certainty. They were not claiming to give a genetic account of primacy, but a logical account. They meant to say that the basis of experience, as a logical possibility which is conceptually independent of interpretation, must lie in some logically simple notion of the given.

6.152   If we are to attack the position that this level is primary amongst the levels of experience, we shall have to show that either (a) this notion of "logical primacy" will not function or (b) the notion of "logical primacy" will function, but what is logically primary is not what various "sensationalist" philosophers wanted to claim as primary.

First and foremost, it seems reasonable to question the notion of logical primacy itself, if what is meant is that experience without interpretation must lie on a more fundamental level than experience with interpretation. For the minimal notion of experience seems to involve the notion of awareness, and awareness seems to involve the notion of an experience frame. The notion of givenness involves a notion of here and now which Hegel claimed could not be explicated within the sensationalist framework itself. It is what one recognizes by some *criterion*. Even Hume felt himself forced to fall back on a notion of "vividness" as a sign of immediacy. But if immediacy requires a sign, it requires a criterion, and it is not logically prior to that criterion. Nor, for that matter, is the criterion, in any serious sense, logically prior to the given: they must come together.

6.153   One may feel that Hegel's insistence on "here and now"—which he uses to show that immediate experience forces one to a level *beyond* itself—relies rather heavily on his reading of some rather careless remarks by "sensationalist" philosophers of various sorts and periods. One may feel, as well, that Hume's vividness is a little feeble and that he might have done better if only he had tried a little harder. Ayer's basic propositions and Carnap's protocol sentences come to attention as attempts to make the criteria the logical form of utterances which are said to substantiate the most basic occurrences at the fundamental level of experience—to create, if possible, a logical situation in which what has to be verified can be verified on a single occasion. "Red, here now!" was sometimes thought to typify such a situation, but it does not matter what form of words one chooses. What does matter is that such schemes fall back on a potential minimal *act* of the observer which, if properly chosen, certifies or testifies to the existence of the appropriate level of experience.

The point I want to make is that it does not matter whether one talks of experience frames, characteristics of immediacy, or the logical form of the proposition: one is still in a situation in which, to get at the right level, one chooses amongst options. The element of intentionality is fundamental.

6.154   If one seeks the basic condition for experience which is minimally structured, that basic condition will have to make room for an act and an object. Whatever we know about child psychology suggests, surely, that there is an important point to that. The child demands something—even if all that he does is to scream. But he wants not just a set of "sensations"; he wants something which will nourish both factors in the demand. He wants to be assured of the efficacy of his own subjectivity just as much as he wants the warm feeling of milk in his stomach. Attempts to rear him without the affection of his mother or some tolerable surrogate do not produce good results. The more his self-assurance breaks down, the more his intentions will become curious, fragmented, unreliable, and undesirable. (If one must cite authorities for such propositions, can one do better than to cite Dr. Benjamin Spock, whose findings seem to have found a response in two generations of mothers not overly given to theoretical speculation?)

6.155   The simplest imaginable kind of experience which meets the obvious conditions is, after all, the kind of experience we quickly develop and generally sustain—the experience of a world of quite ordinary objects. It is possible to reduce this, in a sense, to the experience of sets of sensations. But to do that is just to find where subjectivity and the object meet—and that seems to be, logically, a derivative situation.

We might, that is, eventually teach the child who feels discomfort to concentrate on controlling the discomfort and to give up, for the moment, the attempt to match the intention that discomfort stimulates with some appropriate set of objects. He is hungry, but we are on a train without a dining car and there is nothing to be done about it for an hour. So we say, "I know you're hungry, but try to live with it for a while." At this point, he focusses clearly on his sensations. But the sensation is a mixture of the subjective and the objective. Partly, it is a wanting; partly, it is a gurgling in the stomach. But the two are not separate—the wanting is expressed *through* the gurgling of the stomach.

The red patch which is said to be beloved by philosophers of a "sensationalist" sort (the evidence for this love affair is a little weak) is the same kind of thing. It is not an object; it is not a manifestation of the subject. It is a point of intersection, the part of the object which impinges on self-awareness.

6.156   We *can* abstract the patch as the child *can* focus on his feelings so as to control them. But is it intelligible as a feature of experience without anything else? It is a patch and it is red; it therefore has some of the characteristics of things. But we have learned to manipulate those notions. Suppose there were only such surrogate objects, and that they came and went without orderly response to our attention and intention. How should we develop criteria for determining that something was red? Red is not just a proper name, but a common name for members of some organizable class. It gets its meaning from common transactions with such things. They have to stand still to be compared, reflected upon, ordered in sets from violet to orange, and so on, before we can use the notion in any satisfactory way. We have to develop a standard through reflection. We may use an "image" as our footrule—though the image, in its turn, will have to mesh with some specifiable criteria if we are to be able to use it.

Thus, the fundamental level of experience does seem to be the world of ordinary objects to which we are related by various states of attention and intention.

6.157 Corresponding to this level of experience is a certain sort of "knowledge," though the claim that it is "knowledge" is a little curious. It is the sort of complex relation of response to experience which constitutes, in fact, our ability to find our way around in the world. It enables intention and self-awareness to develop along with action, the awareness of reaction, and the notion of success and failure. It is the knowledge of the tourist guide, rather than the knowledge of the land-surveyor. It is not codified, though of course it can be explicated in various ways, one of the most obvious of which is that of explicating the rules-in-use for our ordinary language. We call a thing an automobile if it meets certain conditions—it must not just have a certain *look*; you must, if it is in running order, be able to drive it about. It must have a function as well as a description.

6.16 What is it, then, that leads us beyond this level? It is, of course, that we find subject and object inextricably mixed. The ordinary things in the ordinary world all have perceptual aspects—which is just to say that their common features all have connections to observers. They are all loaded with subjective responses and intentional reactions. The reaction I have to the mountains at the foot of which I grew up are not those of the geologists. For me, they carry overtones of mystery, they provoke feelings of exertion, they lure. I cannot think of them in their capacity as ordinary objects in any other way.

In this way I find myself in my reflections on the world or on other people. My earliest memories are of things charged with emotions. I am in them and I must think of myself through them.

6.161   The consequence of this is that the world falls, ultimately, into two parts. As I press the issue, I come to think of subject and of object—of the mountains as they might be without me, and of me as I now think of myself, wholly detachable from them. Yet the notion of a world of pure objects, or a world of pure objectivity, is unintelligible. If I dissolve everything into the world of objects, I cannot understand how I could have the knowledge or the experience which I do. If I dissolve the world into a world of pure subject, the notion becomes purely empty and formal—what am *I* without any of those objects through which, after all, I found myself?

The tension is always there. We feel it in our most ordinary transactions. It is only uneasily that we construe the ordinary world of perceptual objects burdened with intention; thus, there *is* a developing dialectic.

The two residue worlds—the world of pure subject and the world of pure object—have in common that they are univocal, determinate, and fixed. They are no longer laden with the ambiguities of ordinary objects. What they commonly exclude, however, is immediacy: each is an inference from the ordinary world, and a shaky one at that.

6.162   If one makes the dialectician's move (according to the principles of *my* dialectic anyhow), one puts together their uniting property—determinateness, unambiguity, and whatever goes with explicating those notions—with their joint specific exclusion reference, immediacy. We get what we expect: the world of sense data, impressions, sense certainty, or whatever. This is the level of experience which I would call immediate reflection. It is *not* the brute given; it is the outcome of a process. The fascinating beauty of this combination of properties has been seducing philosophers for a long time.

But if what I said a little earlier is correct, we now see just what was at issue: the truth about immediate reflection is that it brings us to the point of intersection of subject and object. It, too, will bifurcate, and this is the problem.

6.163   I do not think it can be seriously doubted that there *is* a kind of experience which might be called immediate reflection—though its characterization might be in doubt. I am also convinced that it is, in fact, derivative. It seems to me inevitable that it must, indeed, represent the intersection of subject and object as they appear in the original world of ordinary objects. No doubt, the notion that the synthesis involves the separation of the original worlds into two "residue worlds" is more controversial. In a way, those worlds are hollow shells, characterised mainly by negation.

They have their equivalents, in a sense, in Hegel's dialectic of experience, though their equivalents there appear in a different place in the system. Hegel's equivalents seem to arise in his discussion of the world of the Stoic philosophers—on the one side, the purely objective world of things governed by natural laws and, on the other, the world of pure subjectivity into which the self may withdraw. But I suspect that this is too rich a characterisation. What seems, more likely, to characterise the objective residue is an imagined world stripped of all the characterisations which mingle self-awareness and object. Familiar objects as they might be without regard to their perceptual aspects, without regard to intention, without regard to the influence process itself, make up its population. It is not like the immediate reflection which issues in sense data and is characterised by the intentional self turned on its direct objects. What are left are rather formal properties, and the effect is much like that of imagining the world as a mathematical system. But it seems to be a prelude, in experience, to immediate reflection because immediate reflection requires, first, the disengagement of the self from experience and, then, its re-engagement. The other residue world is simply the notion of selfhood in and of itself—as disengaged from the world. That, too, seems to be an act of imagination which is just the other side of the prelude to immediate reflection.

6.164 One might speculate as to the place these residue worlds play in knowledge. Is one of them the genesis of science, as the study of what is pure object, and the other that of mystical experiences? On the whole, I am inclined to doubt the first. The world of self, the world in which everything is reduced to the pure awareness of awareness, seems to correspond to what in *Logic and Reality* I called pure being—a category which cannot be long retained in experience, though it has elements in common with mystical experience. It simply is. But the residue world of objects is characterised by negations—it is the ordinary world *without* its ordinary elements, and it seems to be the experiential equivalent of what I called pure disjunction. Things can be imagined there, but every property one might want to assign them is gradually denied as it turns out that, one by one, the properties require the ordinary experiential situation to sustain them.

Indeed, that ordinary experiential situation is the domain in which we operate *before* we reflect. It is the ground of reflection and it does not, for that reason, turn up in the scheme of reflective categories which I discussed in *Logic and Reality*.

6.165   More likely—and here the "sensationalist" philosophers would join with me again, however briefly—the domain of scientific enquiry arises *in* immediate reflection, in an effort, somehow, to organize those reflections. Probably, experience will not rest in immediate reflection for the evident reason that the point of intersection it represents will yield neither ordinary objects nor the self of awareness. It, in its turn, breaks down.

Yet it provides a stance from which we can look at the world in a new light. We can regard the self of experience as fixed, and envisage the world as a kaleidoscope of sensory events. Since we have a point of intersection, that is, we can dissolve the experience and regard all the data as being "the world." In a way, this is the simplest scientific move. We simply look for pattern in the data and regard the world as that pattern and us as irrelevant to it.

6.166   It is worth noticing, though, that this device only works so long as we are willing to retain our attachment to the world of ordinary objects. We use the new level of experience as a device for giving us "hard data" but, to make sense of the data, we have to imagine the experience as being attached to reference points drawn from the original awareness of quite ordinary objects. This may be puzzling, but some ordinary examples perhaps will help to make it clear. The physicist looking into the Wilson cloud chamber is not interested in the cloud chamber as such. He concentrates his attention on the images discerned in it, and constructs a theoretical framework in which they figure as symptoms of certain kinds of particles. He never describes, in his theory, how the lab looks and feels, or whether the cloud chamber itself is fast approaching the status of an ancient piece of junk. But, without those quite ordinary reference points, the cloud chamber would not serve his purpose.

6.167   This point is important. Hegel sometimes seemed to suggest that the dialectic of experience represented an up-draught in which one was wafted toward the heaven of true knowledge—leaving all the lower and lesser kinds of experience behind. The truth seems to be that each level of experience enables one to put its predecessors in their context.

Immediate reflection, however, is only one focus of a level of experience. In it, one takes the point of intersection of subject and object and regards it as a set of discrete sensa. The other focus, of course, is that of the field of experience itself—the natural home of gestalt phenomena. Immediate reflection, in fact, gives us a system. If we attend to its components—as Hume did—we get a kind of determinate being in immediate experience. In this way, we regard the system as assembled out of its components, as defined by them. If we take the system as primary, however, experience becomes a systematic unity which has aspects rather than individual components. Our interest in immediate reflection most often inspires us to focus it as Hume did—it is this or that feature which we want to pick out and fasten on as a crucial sign or symptom. If, however, one tries in introspection to dissolve the world of ordinary objects into sensa, one finds that the field begins to take over and that the objects fade into a confusing background. We seldom bring this to our conscious attention but, of course, there are countless psychological experiments about perception which show clearly that what one sees is strongly influenced by the way in which the systematic character of the field affects the appearance of the data. Immediate reflection as a set of discrete objects is a somewhat difficult experience to sustain!

6.168 Just as immediate reflection in its guise as a collection of sensa *may* have its uses in conceptualizing some problems in physics, so, in its guise as the "field" of experience, it *may* have its uses in psychology. Perhaps by studying these field phenomena we can learn something about how experience is structured. It is evidently not the task of the philosopher to prescribe medicine for physicists or psychologists. It may be worth noticing, though, that, if the dialectical account holds, it would be foolish for anyone to try to muster an argument to show that one of these modes is *primary*. And we ought always to come back to the point that such notions are, anyhow, parasitical on the notion of ordinary experience.

6.17 It is vital to notice that, in immediate reflection, we really have neither a genuine object nor a genuine subject. We have experience turned in on itself and simply characterised as experience. The uneasy tension between its form as a set of *objects* (Russell's sensa) and its form as a field, the projection of a kind of gestalt self, forces us on to something else which one ought to call constructed reflection. Like its predecessor, it is a turning in of experience, but, this time, *beyond* the point of intersection of subject and object. Again, it absorbs what those categories exclude—deliberate construction, active intention, and all the things which go with activity as contrasted with passivity.

6.171 To block the constant dissolution of sensa into fields and fields into sensa, we try to construct a pattern which will hold experience constant. Such a move inevitably brings one to the process of experience itself—a process ignored in our ordinary transactions with the world in the first order of experience, disguised in the attempted objectivity of the residue worlds, suppressed in the immediacy of first order reflection. Thus, if we try to objectify the situation, we get the notion of a world in process being watched by a detached and stable self which does not figure in the system. If we convert our physics from a simple description of data in patterns to the notion of a dynamic system whose time lines are defined by *our* present, we get something of the picture. In fact, as physics develops from description to prediction, this is the process which develops.

6.172 It, too, has another side. If, instead of regarding the self as neutral observer, we regard the process of experience as taking place *in* the self, we get a kind of Bergsonian notion of pure process—an endless flow which is the flux of sensation. (Like Bergson, we shall not be able to hold that self to the notion of our own phenomenal selves, for those require, as usual, recourse to the distinction of an ordinary world of ordinary objects. We shall get, rather, the "deeper self" of *Time and Free Will*[6] or even the *élan vital* of *Creative Evolution,*[7] the unconfined self which exhibits itself through the flux of the data. Bergson had grasped, fairly obviously, a kind of experience which comes to one who releases the hold which constructive reflection usually puts on the data—of one who demands to see the data reflected *as* the process of self-awareness.

6.173 These "process" categories structure experience, nonetheless, in a way which accentuates the difficulty which is the central problem of this book: if we take a detached "observer's" view of a dynamic world, the inner world is essentially empty. It functions only as a reference point and that reference, itself, is increasingly hard to establish. Since the "observer" has no content, and everything which is to be *said* is to be said about the dynamics of the world, it is only because I carry over some residual notion of the self from some other mode of experience that I am able to form any self-conception at all. There is no doubt that the conceptual systems associated with "determinate process" have exercised a hold over important phases of our scientific systems. It is a commonplace of important phases of physics that one chooses to regard the observer as relevant for the determination of a temporal frame of reference, while every other feature of the "data" is ascribed to the "physical world." It is equally true, I suppose, that as the development of experience goes on, we sometimes perceive our situation as if we *were* detached observers looking at the universe through a cosmic peep-hole. But that does not, finally, make sense as a view of the world just because we are also aware that experience comes in other modes, and that our ability to structure our perceptions on the "peep-hole" model does depend upon our having carried something over from another mode of experience.

6.174 Similarly, the dialectical "twin" of this view, the kind of view which Bergson took in *Creative Evolution,* strikes a chord amongst reflective human beings. The idea that all one's experience is a continuous flow within which only arbitrary distinctions are to be made is one which goes back at least to Heraclitus, and it is not simply the invention of philosophers. The trouble, of course, is that it *is* a way of looking at the world and one which we can establish only by making contrasts. Since it requires effort and constant attention to maintain that view, we do not really obliterate the "self" which makes these contrasts. We simply let it lie in abeyance. But, although Bergson was not entirely unfair when, taking this stance, he painted intellectual activity as one which consisted of making distinctions in what might better be regarded as a continuity, there is an obvious sense in which this is like running a movie camera backwards.

   We can only come to the kind of experience he is calling attention to by deliberately subjecting the normal world of objects to analytical scrutiny. Once we have relaxed our conceptual hold on the ordinary things in the world, *then* we can regard those things as if they were arbitrary structures imposed upon a continuously flowing experience. If we think of this as an improvement, it is because we have a different conception of ourselves derived in a different way and kept, as it were, in control on one level of consciousness while we construct a new one. The resultant merging of self and world in experience is intelligible because, in short, we have other notions of self and world.

6.175   What all this amounts to is that the element of theorizing in experience grows as one moves from one level of experience to the next, and the intelligibility of each of these schemes depends more and more upon the possibility of mingling some immediate mode of experience with a continuing reference to constructed theoretical entities—the notions of self and objective world. The ideas of time and of appropriate frames of experience play an important part in the posssibility of shifting from one kind of experience to another but they are always held in the background. When we unveil experience in the various "process" modes, we become increasingly embroiled in such notions. To get a dynamic structure in physics, one needs not just reports of sensa, but theoretical constructions which give them structure. Bergson's "pure flow" ultimately involves theoretical notions of continuity which are deeply embedded in his conceptions of the *élan vital* and the "deeper self."

The successful establishment of these theoretical structures gives rise, of course, to knowledge in a different sense.

6.176   It is now knowledge in the sense of established universals. In the earliest modes of experience, the question does not really arise. In the world of ordinary objects, "each thing is what it is and not another thing" and knowledge is a matter of finding one's way about. The inner world is characterised by intention and response and, equally, the question is one about the way in which the world responds to one's intentions. When one first makes the distinction between self and world and tries to substantiate it, the "residue worlds" of "pure things" and "pure selves" are simple abstractions, and carry as much and as little weight as any abstraction. It is difficult to sustain those abstractions and the doubts thus begun may lead to the radical nominalism characteristic of the notions of immediate reflection which dissolve the world into impression, sense data, sensa or whatever.

If the conceptual collisions of that scheme force us to reconceptualize the world as a set of fields of experience which have overriding systematic structures, it is, nonetheless true that those systematic structures are themselves particulars. The system is just given *as* a field of experience. But, when we attempt to regard the world as a dynamic system and the self as detached observer, the question about universals becomes acute. It has to be the *same* observer—or an observer with the same function—who notices one thing at several times. But the internalized opposite in which everything is regarded as a single flow would pose new questions about identity.

6.177   The theoretical entities which we use to give shape to these structures have to be, in an important sense, universals. One electron has to have just the same properties as all the others, the *élan vital* has to have the same properties at many times.

We need to remind ourselves, here, that what we are concerned with is a kind of experience. If it has a place in what I have been calling the "dialectic" of experience, then it has, to be sure, a certain conceptual structure whose internal "logic" is the outcome of the conceptual structures which preceded it. But it must be true, also, that it is a mode of experience just as the original experience of a world of ordinary objects is a mode of experience, and just as the state of affairs which results from "resolving" experience into impressions is a kind of experience.

6.18   The "universals" problem is usually thought to arise at a rather remote level of abstraction and, indeed, it is most traditionally posed as, specifically, a problem of abstraction: it results from analysing one's accounts of things in a certain way. Essentially one adopts descriptive forms in which the properties of things are made to play a crucial role. One then asks what it means to say that a single property characterises more than one thing or can be "predicated" of many things. As such, it is not evidently a problem about "experience," but a problem which arises out of certain ways of characterising that experience. It should be noticed, though, that even in such a form, it only makes sense as a problem if there is a certain kind of experience to be characterised.

6.181   At the point, for instance, at which one questions the world of ordinary objects and seeks to break that world down so that some of its properties can be properly attached to an "objective" world and others to the knowing subject, that division itself seems to give rise to the problem. One would think that there must be some general charcteristic which distinguishes the two realms and attaches, in a suitable way, to each and every item in the domain which it marks out. That separation, however, turns out to be impossible for the obvious reason that each and every property can be assigned with equal ease to either world. I can take the approach of the subjective idealist and attach every property to the knowing self or I can, as we saw in the early discussions in this book, take every property and assign it to the objective world as the reductive materialist does. The arguments we presented suggested that such schemes turn out to be empty in the sense that the assignments of properties do not, surely, do anything to make experience intelligible. Indeed, though the experience of thinking that the world is what the subjective idealist or the reductive materialist says it is *is* an experience, our ordinary encounters tend to make it transitory. The inner logic of the conceptual structure forces on us such notions as sense data, or fields of experience. The form of the universals problem which arises there accordingly seems to turn out to be spurious. Berkeley was right in pointing out that one scarcely can imagine the abstract universal—the universal simply as real property characterising a number of disparate things. I can say what it is to be a horse, but if I am asked to characterise the experience of "horseness" as opposed to the experience of a particular horse, I have nothing to say. The problem, rather, is a symptom of the wrongheaded way of taking reality to be one of the "residue" worlds which result simply from the original separation of subject and object.

6.182   The association of empiricism and nominalism results, again, from taking the primary mode of experience to be the mode of sense data, impressions, or "sense certainties." We get the simplicities of that mode of experience precisely by adopting a conceptual structure in which there is no room for anything but particulars. Hence, the universals problem seems to disappear. In a world of immediacy, the primary mode of associating words and things is, as philosophers as recent as Russell insisted, the mode of reference. There are simply givens to be pointed at, referred to, in the most basic kind of way. The association is necessarily arbitrary, and even the language of "universals" seems absurd.

6.183   It is not surprising that when philosophers—including Moore and Wittgenstein—began to be interested in the original experience of the world of objects which they thought of as the ordinary world of common sense, they discovered that the association of words and things has, there, a very different pattern. Wittgenstein noticed that the association has to do with the way in which we carry out, in use, the ordinarily understood rules for that association. If we put this in the way which appeals most to me, it is that we develop the meaning of words through the process by which we find our way around in that world. Object, intention, and action are not readily separable in such transactions. Here, again, we do not have the universals problem, because the issue is about the ways in which the actions are grouped so as to enable us to find our way around, and not about the ways in which abstract properties attach to things. But we do have a problem about the self and is relation to the experience of objects, intentions and actions.

6.184 If we then regard the self as some thing which has these experiences, we have again, an empty, unstructured self—a mere observer.
But if we regard it *as* these experiences it becomes a Heraclitean flux. We
cannot get a grip, in either case, on such notions as selfhood or, really,
on metaphysical notions like Bergson's *élan vital.* They remain unex-
plicated notions associated with a kind of experience. In short,
something more than the *particular* experience is demanded, but nothing
is forthcoming. We can build pictures of the world—whether they are
pictures in the physical garb of atoms and their parts, or pictures in the
metaphysical garb of Bergson's directional process. We can *use* those
pictures to make predictions, or as attitudes towards the world, but they
seem to outrun any experience which we do or could have. If we use them
as conditioning agents to modify the stance we take toward the world of
ordinary objects, we can get them "into" experience, but we cannot then
separate our attitudes from our perceptions.

6.185 These schemes both demand and exclude an effective notion of
universality. They demand it because they can only be rendered intelligible by introducing notions which go beyond experience; but they exclude
it because they are founded upon a direct experience of a world in process which is given, still, as a set of particular experiences.

Yet, all along, it has been evident that what is happening is something
rather simple. We grasped the self of experience in the most basic kinds
of experience. Successive kinds of reflection tend to empty it out by
assigning all the properties to a world of objects, or inundate it by assigning all the properties to it. Successive reflections issue in a series of
models, all of which collapse just because of the way in which they shape
experience—though each gives us a different way in which to grasp
ourselves and the world.

6.186 In turning in on itself, consciousness has, in effect, stripped off
the notions of action and intention which colored the original world.
Successive modes of reflective experience are characterised by successive
attempts to construct the world out of the experience of immediacy. The
abstractions open various interesting vistas to inspection, but they all collapse because they are missing whatever it is that would render the
original experience intelligible. Our original experience does not present
either the self or the world as a set of immediate particulars, given fields,
or pure ongoing processes. The original experience, rather, structures
both subject and object as continuous developments through which we

gradually develop our self-identity and create a background of objects.

6.187   There are two ways in which one can look at what is missing. One is to regard the developing self as assembled out of sets of actions, intentions, and reflections. The other is to regard it as a universal which gradually reveals itself through its actions. Similarly, we can regard objects in the world as something we assemble from facets of experience which gradually reveal themselves to us.

In either case, if we now demand knowledge of things which is not just the original set of accounts of how to find one's way around in the world, not just correlations of the appearance of things, and not just the assembly of arbitrary universals which have pragmatic value, we need to attend to a different kind of experience—which develops naturally as our reflections go on.

One obvious feature of the reflective experience which I have been trying to disentangle is that the self of consciousness invariably outruns the schemes with which it is presented. We can trace it through all the stages, but we cannot capture it in any of them. Everyone is capable of—and at times finds himself confronting—all the experience modes I have been talking about; everyone finds himself reflecting on the ordinary world of objects, confronting the data of his immediate sensations, feeling himself pulled by the Heraclitean flux of experience, and so on. Were it not for that, it would be hard to imagine that philosophers who have undertaken elaborate explications of these modes of experience would have succeeded in striking a response in their readers.

"Consciousness," literally, is the bringing together of a diversity of objects in some focus of attention. Once reflection is possible, it *must* be the case that the scope of consciousness invariably outruns any one instance of itself. For we can always reflect on whatever we can establish as the focus of attention—creating still another mode of experience along with the new level of reflection. And reflection is possible because it is a feature of the relations between intention, awareness and object, which constitute the most basic level of experience.

It is inevitable, therefore, that consciousness should seem both to be assembled from the experiences that we have, *and* that the experience we have should be seen as a development of it. Consciousness can be seen either as a constructed universal which develops through this process, or as a universal which is always there and unwinds itself through the process.

6.188   Hegel had envisaged the possibility that we might, finally, reach the limit of its development in the sense that we would understand consciousness through an object which was, finally, its adequate object—the state of affairs which he called the Absolute. We can regard both subject and object as the unfolding of the Absolute through the dialectic of experience. The Absolute might, then, be regarded as a single, concrete universal whose development turned out to be the world.

There is nothing very mysterious about the notion of the Absolute in this sense—it is simply whatever it is that is not relative to anything else, every other "object" is relative to the corresponding notion of subject at a given level of the dialectic. Nor is there anything particularly odd about such a notion of the "concrete universal." The doctrine is simple enough. We might regard the concept of "horse" as explicated by reference to that set of developments which would constitute the systematic development of all the possibilities for "horseness"—so that the proper "idea" of "horseness" is given by the objective existence of horses in a suitable context. But that would require the development of a suitable environment for horses, and so on until we had the world as a single system.

Universals become embedded in our discourse through the development of notions of system; and the system comes, ultimately, to be interconnected in some way.

6.189   The proposed final unity of subject and object seems to involve us in a subtle mistake: we know that consciousness in this sense simply outruns whatever objects are presented to it. We cannot turn around and capture it because it is *not* an object. Rather, it exhibits itself through objects.

Hegel's 'dialectic ultimately comes down on the side of the object—however special and complete it is. Hegel is right in supposing that the demand for systematic knowledge is the outcome of the fact that consciousness—since it is a reflective process within which experience comes to be structured in a variety of ways—can only be explicated by exhibiting the various ordered structures which can be discerned in experience.

It is, after all, the dialectic of self and world which gives substance to both notions. The more extensive the systematising of experience—the more the contents of experience can be exhibited as a set of universals which explicate themselves through sets of instances—the more constructive reflection becomes, and the more we can say that we know what consciousness is capable of.

Hegel is thus right to argue against attempts to establish a pure reflective consciousness which might be the object of a final self-awareness.

What we would probably call knowledge in its most sophisticated sense is the exhibition of the structure of experience as a system of universals whose unfolding has a necessary relation to data which experience encounters. (An extension, if you like, of the ideal of the hypothetico-deductive method would give us the notion of the world as unified system, and would do so in terms of universals whose meanings consisted in orderly instances revealed in experience.) The natural counterpart of this knowledge is an appropriate experience of self-activity, the self-activity which is involved both in constructing such systems and in developing the insight which reveals the logical connections.

6.19   Yet, there is a limit to such systematising. It depends, first of all, upon the experience which runs through the whole dialectic; however pretty the constructed system, the corresponding self-awareness is still tied to the original world of ordinary objects. In experience, the self-awareness of one engaged in such splendid intellectual activities will be that of a man amid ordinary objects—his laboratory, his telescope, his typewriter, or whatever. He will also realize that he cannot confine himself to the system he has constructed. The perfection of the system is, in fact, matched by a growing openness of the consciousness which is involved in its construction—for it has required the gradual freeing of that consciousness from its common sense concepts, a growing mastery of the data, a growing freedom to cope with various ways of organizing it.

6.191   One cannot lose that consciousness in the constructed system. And one cannot turn it into an object, either. Though, as we construct such systems, there seems to be a growing "objectivity" (in the literal sense of the structuring of the world into a set of precisely delineated objects), there is a paradoxical increase in the importance of subjectivity as well. For one has passed from the passivity of sensa data theories, the passivity of Bergson's intuition, and so on, to a very clear notion of constructed reflection. The mere ordering of sense data—the level at which, perhaps, theorizing begins—gradually gives way to elaborate systematising in which none of the data is simply taken at its face value. Rather, it is given the reading which will make of experience the most systematic structure.

6.192 In periods of human thought and experience such as ours—or such as the one which confronted reflective intellectuals in the thirteenth century—the paradox usually stretches credibility to the point at which it breaks down. The momentary reaction to the rather complex physical cosmologies of our time has produced, for us, a marked interest in world views which emphasise subjectivity—a revival of interest in some kinds of eastern philosophy, attempts to exploit the subjective elements in the cultures of American Indians, a variety of urges to assert one's individuality. In the thirteenth century, the theological systematising produced a movement which runs through Duns Scotus and William of Ockham to Nicholas of Autrecourt, ending in a set of subjectivist claims and a demand to return to the most basic elements in the structure of experience. The reaction need not be that severe. It may only, as happened a little earlier in western philosophy, lead to a return of interest in the original modes of experience or, as was the case with the ordinary language philosophers, to a return of concern about ordinary modes of talking.

6.193 Unless, like Hegel, one believes that the self of consciousness might finally disappear into the "super system," one is left in something of an impasse. We could seek the way out by moving back down the dialectical spiral. We could seek refuge, once again, in an empty and hopeless subjectivity.

The argument I suggested in Chapter 5, of course, is that one should do none of those things—that the reality of self-awareness is to be sought by attending to the specifications for knowledge of persons. If the "inner self" is not an object, but becomes explicable through objects, then we shall need the notions of orderly system combined with a return to the specifications of individuality. But, we can begin with experience.

There is an experience which enables us to establish our own individuality by establishing its relations to that of others; this is the process of coming to know oneself through others. The argument in section 5.3 was that such relations are provided, finally, by talking to people. The ordering of experience through language, the use of universals as devices for creating language, the possibility of structuring experience so as to be able to structure and focus it, all have their place in the ordinary processes by which we establish communities of meaning.

6.194 The self which, in ordinary experience, is inextricably mixed up with the objects through which intentions are expressed, and perceptions rendered explicable, fades from view as we retreat into the original attempt to separate subject and object. It becomes a kind of irreducible surd in our descriptions of the world as sensation. It becomes a mere reference point in our attempts to describe dynamic experience, or hides as "the deeper self" in a kind of pure Bergsonian process. It is elided into its expressions as knowledge when we talk about the systematic structures of constructive reflection. But it remains to haunt us.

All of those processes, however, go into building up the structure of, and mastery over, language in a variety of guises; and that language forms the background for the kind of knowledge we obtain of ourselves through others.

In the most basic kinds of experience, the personalising of everything evidently confuses knowledge of ourselves and of others. Primitive peoples project personality onto objects of all sorts—natural phenomena, animals, plants. Whatever enters into their experience is an object shaped by their own intentionality. The retreat from this picture into a series of pictures of the world in various guises impedes, in one sense, the development of personal awareness; but, in another sense, it creates the mastery over language and experience which makes possible, in the end, a different view.

6.195   This is not to say that we move out of the object-world of the original experience—just that we use it differently.

None of this settles the ancient metaphysical dispute as to the level of experience which best exemplifies reality—though there is a strong suggestion that the charcterisation of reality must take account of all the levels and modes of experience. The point, here, is just that the self-and-world problem persists throughout all the levels. The denial of one side or the other leads to absurdity as, indeed, does the attempt to freeze the process at one level.

In one sense, the problem of marking out the world within comes from the mislocation or mis-characterization of what is intelligible on one level by attempting to assimilate it to another level. The mistakes, if you like, are category mistakes. Reality, perhaps, *is* the point at which self-awareness emerges into the light of day as we learn to discover ourselves through others. But, even if that is true, reality evidently requires expression through the long and rich characterisation of experience in *all* levels. That process is most likely more complex than this sketch has suggested. It is, at least, not simpler.

6.2 The Structure of a Conclusion

There are three aspects to the theory we have been trying to develop. One has to do with the *kinds* of true propositions which one needs to develop an account of the problem, and the experiences which give rise to and validate the distinction between "the world within" and "the world outside." I shall seek to show that these are general conditions which apply to discourse about any world which can be discussed intelligibly. Because they have to do with the *kinds* of true propositions and because these kinds of propositions are distinguished by matters of propositional form, I shall call them "formal" conditions. Another aspect has to do with the kinds of knowledge which are required to cope with the experience involved. These I shall call the "epistemological" conditions. The third has to do with the things which a reasonable man would believe if he understood the first two and acquired the minimal essential specimens of the kinds of knowledge involved. These I shall call the "factual" conditions for the soundness of the theory.

I shall discuss each of them in a separate section. I shall begin each section with an account of the propositions which figure crucially in that section. Each list will be followed with brief summaries of the appropriate arguments and with additional arguments where those are needed to bring out the bearing of the propositions upon each other. The only *new* arguments here relate the propositions to one another.

6.21   The Basic Conditions:

1. Some first person propositions are true.
2. Some of the true first person propositions are of such a kind that they cannot be reduced, without change of meaning or loss of certainty, to propositions of another type or form.
3. Some true propositions are not first person propositions.
4. Every true first person proposition entails the truth of at least one proposition which is not a first person proposition.
5. Every true proposition which is not a first person proposition entails the truth of at least one first person proposition.
6. Every true proposition refers to or entails a reference to at least one particular.
7. Every true proposition refers to or entails a reference to at least one universal of indeterminate application.

These propositions arise, in their own context, in sections 3.1 and 3.2. What mainly needs to be brought out here is their relation to the epistemological conditions which will occupy us in 6.22, their specific relations to each other, and some of the logical and quasi-logical concerns which stem from their structure and from the use of such expressions as "entails."

6.211   Primarily, propositions 1 and 2 meet a basic condition for there being knowledge. A first person proposition is one whose truth clearly hinges upon a special condition arising from the occurrence within it of expressions like "I." A non-reducible first person proposition is one in which such expressions cannot be removed without loss of certainty or meaning. Its epistemological function stems from the fact that such a proposition embodies the necessary form for reporting encounters and judgments. If *no* such propositions were true, no one would have correctly reported either an original encounter or an assessment of the evidence. Then, obviously, nothing would count as "knowing," for "to know" is to have applied whatever criteria happen to be adequate for determining what is an original encounter, or what is an adequate assessment of the evidence. If *all* such propositions were reducible to propositions which did not include expressions which function like "I," then all such "first person reports" would be devoid of the special information which makes them epistemologically relevant.

This might not be blindingly obvious: it has sometimes been said that the epistemological consequences of the fact that physical theories depend upon reports which include references to non-physical entities, observers, can be overcome simply by noticing that what are "really" being reported are physical states—meter readings, the physical states of measuring rods, and so on. But every attorney knows that, for instance, if the cross-examination of the policeman passes from an enquiry into the reading recorded on his speed measuring device to an enquiry into whether or not the policeman can testify as to its accuracy, the going becomes quite different. Someone has to know what the criteria are and whether or not they were correctly applied; the application of criteria is an act of judgment. If the court cannot find out whose act of judgment it was and cannot bring that person to testify, the whole case may break down. The production of a non-reducible first-person statement is, indeed, crucial.

Propositions 1 and 2 begin: "Some . . . are", the plural form indicating that there must be at least two of them. The alternative would be solipsism. It has sometimes been argued that solipsism is the natural outcome of any system which includes non-reducible first person propositions as an ingredient in the most fundamental kinds of knowledge. The argument is obvious. If some first person proposition enters into every bona fide claim to knowledge, then any claim to knowledge I make involves such a proposition. Every claim to knowledge about myself involves a first person proposition which only I have the means of validating; every claim to knowledge which I make is a claim about myself and therefore is an instance of such knowledge. But this involves a series of misunderstandings. The most profound involves the supposition that I could operate the "first person pronoun" without being able to identify anyone else. But how do I determine when "I" am making a judgment and when it is simply "being made?" It is only in an elaborate world within which distinctions have been made that the first person pronoun has any meaning. If I cannot recognize at least one other user of it, I have no criteria for using it myself.

The minimum set of such users seems to be two. It should also be noticed that it was only by assuming that there might be a use for the first person pronoun while there were no criteria for it that it could be said, legitimately, that every piece of knowledge I have is also a piece of self-knowledge. Such a claim supposes that everything that I can refer to is, in some sense, a state of myself. But suppose I say "I know that the Roman Republic broke down and was replaced by the Roman Empire." Is it not true that I am both saying something about myself—that I know something, and about the Roman Empire—that it broke down? True, but all that I am saying "about myself" is that I judge certain criteria to have been fulfilled, and *that* is a judgment about criteria and about their fulfillment. The fact that the first person pronoun is not reducible is not to be confused with the different proposition that the information is irreducibly about its subject. If there are criteria for identifying that subject, then they will sometimes be fulfilled and sometimes not, and the proposition will not be rendered true or false by substituting a "self" which meets one set of such criteria for a self which meets another. Two of fifty of us, in short, may well know that the Roman Republic broke down.

But if there were not at least two of us, there would be no criteria for using the first person pronoun and, therefore, no criteria for ascertaining whether or not the utterer of the proposition met the essential conditions (whatever they are) for knowing what is in question.

6.212   We may now pass to proposition 3, the justification for which is that, for there to be knowledge, there must be assessors, criteria, and something assessed. The use for the first person proposition disappears if there do not exist criteria and subject matters. And the existence of both is, in any case, a necessary condition for the identifiable existence of the "I" who utters the first person proposition. Thus, if I know that the Roman Republic broke down, there is a true proposition of the form "there was a Roman Republic"—and so on. Again, there will have to be at least two subject matters. If there is only one, we cannot distinguish the "I" from what it passes judgment upon.

We ought to be careful to notice, however, that what is at issue is the relation of propositions of one form to propositions of another. They are necessary conditions for one another, not only in that the truth values of one imply equivalent truth values of the other, but also in that the intelligibility of one depends on the intelligibility of the other; this intelligibility depends on an actual context of use.

6.213   Propositions 4 and 5 raise another kind of logical relation, one which will hold in case some first person proposition is true, or in case some proposition of another form is true. We have already seen that a true first person proposition entails a true proposition of another form, because the criteria for first person reference cannot be fulfilled only by first person references. But is the obverse of this true? It is true if the policeman example represents the right reaction on the part of the court. For a proposition of the form "Smith was travelling at eighty miles an hour" or "the later Roman Empire was characterised by corruption" implies that someone has developed the appropriate criteria, and applied them and would affirm them. It may be argued, of course, that there are true propositions which are not like this. "Time travels backwards in black holes" is a typical example of what may be a proposition which is non-confirmable in its essential nature. If one could find a black hole and enter it, one could never communicate the result since, by definition, no signals can escape from black holes. But this is to misunderstand the situation. The words "time," "backwards," "black hole," and so on all have their uses—or else we should not be able to understand them. One who utters the sentence is saying, first of all, that it represents a possible combination of these uses—that the sentence either expresses a proposition which is true or false, or that it expresses something else to which some alternate values may be attached. Thus we may be making one of several judgments—we surmise it to be true, we surmise it to be false but find it amusing, we imagine that it is what someone would say if

he were there. Any one of these still entails the truth of a first person proposition.

The only remaining possibility is that we may want to say that the proposition would be true even if no one had ever asserted it or imagined
that it might be asserted. But this doctrine entails the "reality" of
unasserted and unimagined propositions. If one says that a proposition is
a kind of logical entity, that it is "what a sentence expresses" or "what
an assertion asserts," this possibility does not seem so very far-fetched.
One may want to be a logical "realist," at least to the extent of holding
that reality does have a structure which may be said to "have a logic."
What is wrong with the notion of unasserted propositions, however, is
simply the implied relation to truth.

If part of what we mean by a "proposition" is "whatever it is that is
either true or false" then it is, evidently, a mistake to suppose that there
are unasserted propositions. For, then, truth is one of the properties "of
the world" and not something "about the world." In that case, we shall
have to have other propositions which express the truth *about* those propositions which are features of the world, and the two sets of propositions will not be true in the same sense. Whatever one's theory of truth, it
seems to defeat the purpose to make truth a property *of* the world. But if
it is not, then truth requires a judgment and, in that case, there are true
propositions if and only if there are true first person propositions—that
is, if and only if someone has correctly identified and applied the appropriate criteria.

There are, to be sure, more dramatic arguments for propositions 4 and
5. Much of the argument in section 4.7, for instance, was to the effect
that the neutrality of things stems from their ability to bear meanings,
and that these meanings acquire the appropriate independence in the
context of the dialectic of experience discussed in section 6.1, or in the
context of the establishment of the appropriate relation of object and intention discussed in section 4.9.

6.214 Propositions 6 and 7 involve still another kind of logical relation.
They have to do with restrictions on the sorts of values which can be ex-
changed for the variables in the propositional forms. One of them asserts
that "every true proposition refers to or entails a reference to at least one
particular," and the other asserts that "every true proposition refers to
or entails a reference to at least one universal of indeterminate application." Crucially for our purpose, these propositions state conditions for
identification—the links, in effect, between the formal and the
epistemological conditions.

A proposition which neither referred directly to a particular, nor entailed a reference to one, would be indeterminate—we would not know what proposition it was. Obviously, many true propositions do not directly refer to any particulars: "In any standard spectrum, red and blue appear at opposite ends" is true and refers to no particular. But it *entails* a number of such references. If nothing counted as an example of a standard spectrum, the criteria for determining its meaning would not be forthcoming. If it could not be expressed, it would also not be true. But its expression must take a determinate, particular form. Here, of course, it is best to use some expression which does not suggest a simple logical relation between truth values, for the relation is not between truth values but between the propositional form and what must "go with it" to give it meaning. In the case of first person propositions, the relation may well be more complex still. "I am now seeing a red patch" is a simple enough example in which we would not want to say (following 4.9) that the "I" literally refers to a particular, or that the blue patch (perhaps an intentional object) is, itself, necessarily a particular. But it must be entailed that some account of a particular which will give body to the situation will be forthcoming.

6.215   The truth of proposition 7 simply fills in the remainder of the necessary conditions for being a proposition. On the one hand, a proposition must entail localizing conditions which will enable us to locate it. On the other, it must transcend those conditions in order to *be* a proposition and not simply a state of affairs—which would be meaningless in itself apart from any meanings assigned to it. It must signify something beyond itself if it is not to be simply a mound of ink, an arrangement of space and time, or whatever. But it can only do that if one or more of its references is to something indeterminate, in the sense of being applicable to more than one situation—of being, in short, a universal of indeterminate application. Thus the classical "red, here, now" fails to express a proposition unless the words are more than proper names, unless they refer to more than one possible occasion.

What is most important about all this, of course, is that universals of indeterminate application are bound inseparably to intentionality. They obtain determinateness from their function, since they do not have it in their form. Particulars, on the other hand, are fixed and determinate but may obtain indeterminateness from their function—they may function as references for propositions, bearers of meanings, or whatever is demanded. If true propositions invariably involve both, then every true proposition has built into it a duality of perspective. This duality contains the elements of the distinction between the world within and the outer world. This primitive basis develops its structure in the distinction between first person propositions and other propositions. It neither intrudes on the independence of things—which, as the argument of 4.3 suggested, is an independence of meaning, nor upon the possibility of escaping from the ego-centric predicament—which, as the argument above suggested, depends simply upon a misunderstanding of meaning conditions. But it does mean that no account of the world can be constructed which does not make a place for a world within.

Every form of reductionism fails, if this argument is correct, simply on logical grounds. And every attempt to describe the world in a way in which the boundaries cannot be understood fails on the same ground.

6.22   The Epistemological Conditions:

1. Knowledge of particulars requires criteria which are applicable to immediate experience.
2. Knowledge of universals of indeterminate application proceeds *through* their application.
3. Knowledge of things proceeds through the development of meanings which transcend autobiographical applications.
4. Knowledge of persons is constructed or created through an interchange of meanings.
5. First order experience, experience in encounter, does not yield knowledge, but knowledge depends upon first order experience.
6. First order knowledge is, therefore, associated with second order experience—immediate reflection.
7. First order knowledge is an analysis of experience in reflection.
8. First order knowledge is intelligible if, and only if, there are other orders of knowledge.

6.221   Little that is new needs to be added here. Particulars, in context, are simply confronted, but they are known only if we can order them through criteria. The criteria must, therefore, be applicable to experience, but meet certain requirements of order.

All this means is that traditional kinds of empiricism and rationalism stem from certain very obvious considerations, but tend to derive their apparent force from a confusion of the levels of knowledge and experience; that is, they confuse the boundary between the "world within" and the "outer world."

The empiricist insists that there is no knowledge without particulars and that particulars are found in experience. The rationalist points out that particulars do not *yield* knowledge; they simply are what they are. Knowledge begins with the development of criteria, with the coming of generality, with freedom from the particular.

The empiricist paints the person as trapped by his confrontation even—in Hume's terms—seemingly reducible to those confrontations if he attempts to substantiate his self-knowledge. The rationalist paints the person as the mere bearer of general principles, sharing in the eternality of the universe just in so far as he acquires significance by transcending the particular.

The notion of an individual person becomes, in either case, a notion which cannot be cashed, a curious reflection of nothing. The rationalist, furthermore, finds the empiricist prey to any passing delusion, while the empiricist finds the rationalist a prisoner of the fantasies of reason. Faced with these choices, as bizarre as they are unintelligible, a reasonable man might well seek safety in a lunatic asylum. One of the aims of this book, accordingly, has been to show that these choices are founded on very basic misunderstandings.

The criteria which permit knowledge of particulars must be applicable to the particulars of experience—by definition. But they are not and cannot be, of course, derived from those particulars. We ask of our language that it should have an intelligible use, not that we should be able to derive its meaning from simple reference to particulars. Thus, the choice for meaningful discourse is not between traditional rationalism and traditional empiricism. Propositions do not simply "correspond" to confronted particulars—how could they?—nor do they express a truth measured simply by logical considerations of coherence. Rather, they organize the data in a way which renders that data intelligible, which enables us to find our way from one datum to another by way of a chain of questions and answers.

6.222 Thought adds to this process open-textured universals—universals of indefinite application. They are not denizens of some Platonic heaven wholly unrelated to particulars and they are not, either, assemblies of particulars, Humean "ideas." Rather, they turn out to be what we expect: we call classes of things "doors" or "mountains," "bears" or "alligators," because we can create patterns with a certain unity. We learn "about them" or "acquire knowledge of them" in the course of their application. Each application of such names extends the pattern, just as each legal decision extends the rule under which it is classified. Excessive richness leads to new subclasses—we may distinguish kangaroos and wallabies, or horses and zebras, for some purposes and not for others.

Such universals may take many forms. Some of them are literally objects of experience—mental images, for instance—while others are expressed in words as rules. Still others may be expressed as images or as rules. They all have about them a certain aspect of intentionality: there is a point to the pattern, and a direction of assimilation of new cases. This is not to say that we make them up as we please for they are controlled by the cases they ingest, and they will take one form or another depending upon the cases we insist on ingesting or the cases the existing pattern tends to favor.

They are the best clue to the "inner life," for the things we most closely associated with the inner life—images, intentions, meanings, and so on—are all composed of them and, in seeing how they develop, we see the inner life at work. To understand the inner life of another is to see the growth and pattern of his universals of indefinite application plotted against the terrain which we take for him as a person. Their expression in words, in art, in the association of behaviour and policy, is a public process, one no more hidden *in principle* than is our own private world. For our own private world needs to be expressed to become intelligible, too, though we always have the option of expressing our own private life to ourselves in a manner on which others may not eavesdrop. But even that is an oversimplification, as the summary below will attempt, once more, to explain.

This association of a certain sort of universal with the private life, and of the subject matter with which it interacts with a public world, is, itself, suspect. It is not just, as the last paragraph suggested, that the expression of such universals is potentially public; it is also that there are no ultimately pure universals about which we might learn in some way which brought out their pristine purity. And there is not "a world" of pure particulars.

We can see this in any example. We might think, say, of the distinction between meanings and the physical expression of words as a distinction between "pure particulars" and the kinds of universals we are thinking about. The meanings bring together the physical expressions in a certain pattern. Whether or not the pattern embraces, say, both "night" and "nite" is a question of whether one works for the *Chicago Tribune* or the *Oxford English Dictionary*. It involves a decision which one may make one way or another. But we make a different kind of decision when we decide to call these "marks on paper." When we present them for a decision which depends on a certain context we are, of course, deploying yet another universal. We are not confronted with them *as* "marks on paper"; we are simply confronted with a certain experience. It is only at a given level of reflection that the inter-relation which presents them for decision arises. We can only get the contrast between the universal and the particular it embraces by presenting the situation in a context. The context is a direct response to the question which we happen to want answered.

The universal-particular distinction, like the "inner outer" distinction itself, belongs to a specified level of analysis. Contexts can always be provided which render a given universal a particular, and vice-versa. It is as if one started out to make the distinction in a large library between the books as particulars and the classifications of them as universals. But we can choose to regard the classifications as actual clusters of books on the shelves. Or, we can choose to regard the individual books as simply manifestations of "real books" of which there are many appearances or instances. The physical pages and their ink marks can be regarded as curious sorts of particulars, but they can also be regarded as instances of certain ways of organizing experience. And so on, indefinitely.

The point is that it is only in a certain interplay of components in a context that the distinction arises. It is required that there should be confrontations and interpretations, but confrontation is not, by itself, a superior sort of "knowledge." It is not, indeed, knowledge. It simply is, and is itself only intelligible by contrast with the possibility of interpretation in a given context. Interpretation must start with something, and we can always shift the context so that what was confrontation is taken as interpretation—as when we shift from taking the "marks on paper" as what we are confronted with, to asking why we regard that sort of experience as "marks on paper." Knowledge is the process of establishing contexts and working interpretations.

Our sense of there being a "reality" to cope with is given, of course, not by the fact that there is some ultimate context wholly free from possible interpretation and intention, but by the fact that, though we can shift levels, contexts, and interpretations, we must still deal with what is there. We are like the literary critic who can choose the meanings to put on the words but must, somehow, cope with what is there to be coped with. He will, if he is wise, choose the reading which makes most sense, though he can never simply be "objective." He can never escape the duality which corresponds to the "inner" and the "outer" worlds, the duality of confrontation and interpretation. He could choose, indeed, to thumb the dictionary giving each word its most absurd interpretation (some seem to do just that) and thus expose the thing as a tissue of nonsense. We, too, in general, could always choose to cope with what we confront in any context by giving the most absurd reading possible—thus showing that no "knowledge" is possible; indeed, some philosophers may be suspected of adopting just this technique. The chance of there being the closest thing to "objective" knowledge in the larger sense is exactly the chance that there is some ultimate reason for supposing that it is best to choose the reading which makes most sense. That question deserves to be dealt with in its own right—as the central question of epistemology. The problem of this book is simply to show that, on any reading, absurd or sensible, the duality of inner and outer will remain.

6.223   We can, however, elaborate in another dimension the distinction between knowledge of things and knowledge of persons, and so develop another perspective on the distinction between the "inner" and the "outer" world.

The belief that there are "things" is, essentially, the belief that there are object-situations whose meanings transcend the limits of anyone's autobiography. The knowledge that this is so is, therefore, the knowledge that certain situations cannot be confined to personal contexts.

The traditional distinction is that between the "knowledge" that a man suffering from delirium tremens has of the crawling black things on the wall, and the "knowledge" that a civil engineer has of a bridge under construction. The first of these seems, reasonably, to be merely autobiographical knowledge, knowledge of one of the states of one's mind which has, somehow, become confused with knowledge of an external thing. The second seems to entail knowledge of a bona fide "thing." The traditional assault on the distinction is predicated on the fact that one can make a claim for the proposition that, in each case, the actual "object" of direct awareness is a set of sense data.

A significant part of the burden of this book has been to point out, in a variety of ways, that there is much that is suspicious about such "shifts." One set of suspicions has centered around the problem that one who undertakes such a shift also, without seemingly noticing what he is doing, demolishes the basis of his own proposition. For, by making both statements autobiographical, he has made autobiography impossible. How, now, are we to give meaning to the "I?" How are we to give meaning to any first person propositions if we have *only* first person propositions? This quasi-logical difficulty belongs to the conditions which we have called "formal."

Another set of suspicions centers around the problem which arises if one uncritically allows the change suggested in the orders of experience and analysis. For one who manipulates his experience changes it.

We start with a problem which belongs to levels involving interpretation and analysis; we shift uncritically to what is taken to be a neutral "first order" experience. But this shift really involves a transfer to another kind of reflection and analysis—that kind over which statements about "sense data" arise. We find this alternative analysis to be "neutral," although it is not, of course, genuinely so. For we have given it a structure.

Neither of the characters in our stories about delirium and bridge building was actually concerned about sense data. One man was frightened by crawling black things, and the other built a bridge. There is something just a little odd about being *frightened* of sense data or about *building* collections of them. The intentional relations do not carry over well.

The fact is that we start out with a context in which interpretation and confrontation are given some status, and in which there are criteria for distinguishing the two. If we did not, *no* knowledge would be possible. The man who sees crawling black things on the wall is simply the victim of a situation in which the ordinary criteria have misled him. The solution, in that context, has to be provided by the rules appropriate to that context. If no such solution is forthcoming, then we abandon the context or the rules. But we would not abandon any context *a priori*.

In fact, a solution is normally forthcoming. The fact that others do not see the crawling black things, though they do see the bridge, is a symptom that something is awry. What is awry is that, in the ordinary way, no knowledge of the crawling black things is forthcoming. Furthermore, as a rule, odd states of affairs are discovered by those who investigate the physiology of the victim. It is learned that he consumed a quart of gin daily for eleven months. His unusual experiences have an explanation in that context, in which the crawling black things form, precisely, a part of his autobiography.

The bridge is not *merely* part of the autobiography of the engineer. If it falls down, it will be possible to apply the ordinary legal criteria for determining whether or not an action can be brought against him by the man whose new Buick received an unexpected dunking; we cannot imagine the victim of delirium tremens being sued for negligence in controlling his bugs. The test, in a given context, is whether the knowledge appropriate for the application of a specified range of concepts is forthcoming.

The reasonble conclusion is that a shift to analysis in terms of "sense data" would fail to reveal a number of interesting things—why one man might be sued and another not, why the fears of one man are best quieted by tranquilizers. We could not explain why these various sets of concepts work and function unless we accepted that, within the normal rubrics, claims to knowledge about "things" are validated in a certain way. It is a fact that the concepts function, though it may always be doubted in any particular case whether or not they have been correctly applied. Conceptual functioning is evidence that there is something which potentially counts as a correct conclusion. The skeptic cannot trade on the proposition that any particular case may lead to a mistake and he cannot, evidently, simply shift levels of analysis at his pleasure.

The distinction between the purely autobiographical and that which transcends the limits of autobiography is a real one—necessitated by the logic of the demand for intelligibility, and borne out in practice by at least the central cases in which the distinction arises.

6.224   This does suggest, however, that the knowledge of persons and the knowledge of things are really quite different. If they were not, there would be nothing special about autobiography. The burden of the argument for this occupied section 5.2. A little more of its significance can be brought out here by relating the contexts more directly.

Knowledge of persons has invariably seemed problematic. If one tries to locate "persons" amongst the likely objects of knowledge, the result usually turns out to be unsatisfactory, if not downright paradoxical. How would one finally cope with knowledge of "persons" if, say, he thought that the ultimate objects of knowledge were Platonic forms? The mediaeval debate over universals was triggered, in part, by the possibility that there might be just one "form" of humanity, of which each of us was an instantiation. The alternative that there might be a separate and ultimate "form" for each individual did not appear much more satisfactory. Knowing a person is not, seemingly, much or at all like knowing a form. At the opposite extreme if, as Hume thought, claims to knowledge derived from claims to be acquainted with sensory impressions, the outcome would be equally implausible. "Do you know Smith?" does seem like a question which one could answer one way or the other on the basis of a producible list of sense data. Of course, where there are persons, it seems very likely that there *will* be knowledge of universals in some sense and that there will be sensations associated with them. If one resists these rather traditional rival claims, one might expect to find, as a variety of contemporary philosophers have, that knowledge of persons can be associated with knowledge of "things" in a quite ordinary sense. Persons are ordinarily embodied, and bodies are things. But the attempt to associate knowledge of persons with knowledge of bodies is, again, somewhat forced at best. A surgeon may be very well acquainted, professionally, with your body and yet, when asked at a party if he knows you, may reply honestly that he does not. Conversely, I might, from an extended study of his writings, claim to know Thomas Jefferson quite well, without having the least idea of what his body was like.

This list of difficulties is not simply random. Amongst the things philosophers have claimed as preferred "objects" of knowledge, Platonic forms, sense data and ordinary "things" rank rather high. But the list could, of course, be refined and extended indefinitely. The point is that "persons" do not seem, in the required sense, to be "objects" of knowledge *at all*. To know someone is to have entered, with him, into a co-operative effort which is essentially creative in kind, and in which the more obvious kinds of subject-object distinction disappear. If I claim to know Jefferson through his writings it is because I have, somehow, entered into the pattern of his thought, shared it, made it partly, at least, mine.

We can make this point better if we turn from "objects" of knowledge to the methodologies for knowledge-finding which philosophers have traditionally recommended. Could one get to "know" someone by assembling empirical data—pages of statistics, tables of measurements, accurate photographic sightings, maps and charts of movements? After reading such information, could someone claim to know him? Not, surely, without qualification. One might claim to know "about him." Or one might claim that, having read the "facts" on him, one had entered into some process of imaginative construction which enabled one to come to feel that it was "as if" he knew him. But the "as if" would have to be put to the test in some actual face-to-face encounter. Even my claim to "know" Jefferson is, of course, suspect, as the authors of all the rival biographies know full well. I come close to knowing him because, given his formal writings, his letters, his notebooks and so on, I can well imagine a conversation with him and I can fill in his part pretty much with his own words.

Would one fare better by employing the techniques classically favoured by rationalists? It does seem absurd, on the face of it, to think that one might acquire knowledge of persons by formal deduction from self-evident premises, or by any modification of rationalist techniques which might seem to make them more palatable. The rationalist might reply, naturally, that it is because persons are both imperfect and imperfectly real that such techniques seem so laughable. They might well argue, and, indeed, they have argued, that for perfect persons one may proceed in this way very satisfactorily. That is what rational theology appears to be about.

But, then, even if rational theology finally does its job, its job is rather like that of "making the book" on a person by providing all the charts and diagrams. The theologian may quite properly claim to know much "about" divine attributes; yet, it is left to the saints to "know" God.

It is important, here, to call attention to matters which occupied section 5.2 because they relate so closely to the attempt we have made throughout this book to dissolve certain central paradoxes about the world within and the outside world, and because they enable us, here, to attack the problem of relating our claims about persons to our claims about things. Knowledge of persons cannot be knowledge of another *kind* of object, or knowledge obtained by any of the methodologies so appropriate for knowledge of things—whether those things be the structure of natural theology, the topology of distant stars, or the mundane inner workings of motorcars—or even, if you please, the functioning of human brains. For that knowledge is obtained by creating the appropriate contexts in which confrontation and interpretation, or the developing dialectic of experience, can be handled. There is always left the residue of action which is required to make the necessary moves. And that residue cannot be remanufactured into a new set of objects without simply starting the whole process again.

Persons have to be handled quite differently, in short, on pain of defeating the whole logic of the enterprise. But we need to be very careful about this. As we refine away the classes of objects which are not persons, and as we refine away the methodologies which must fail us in these enterprises, we may be tempted to construct vaporous notions of person and vapid methodologies which simply fail to come to grips with anything.

From finding that the "self" fails to meet the criteria for given kinds of objects of knowledge, it is an easy jump to the notion that the "self" is a very peculiar object of knowledge which, as it happens, meets no criteria except those governing immediate intuition. It should be obvious as a point of logic that the emptier one makes one's concept of the self or subject of consciousness, the easier it will be to defend whatever claims one wishes to make to the effect that the criteria for its discovery have been met. In the extreme cases, if there are no such criteria, there is nothing to be fulfilled.

In consequence, one may easily embellish one's philosophical system with talk about the transcendental ego, the pure and individual self, and so on. Such embellishments, if the concept is thin enough, impose few or no new demands on the system. But they satisfy no one either.

If the real point is that the self or subject is not, properly speaking, an object at all, the choice cannot be between asserting it to have a very thin existence and no existence at all; rather, the choice is between its having a very different mode of existence or no existence at all. The second of these choices evidently is not open to us, for the world inside surely fades into mere illusion and misunderstanding if there is *no* self or subject on which it may be predicated. We are therefore forced to the view that its status in knowledge is not that of an object but, nonetheless, it *does* have a status.

6.225   We have tried to illustrate this in a number of ways. In the discussion of action, the core of the argument was that the notion of action and its correlates—acting and actors—must be preserved, but that the ephemeral "Prichardian" will was not a bona fide object of knowledge. Indeed, Prichard's will turned out not to be merely an undemanding embellishment like its running mate, the pure ego; but since it could not be effectively connected to action, it would ultimately destroy the possibility of any rational understanding of the situation.

The actor in this case is, in fact, comprehensible through his actions. Knowledge of the actor is exactly (not more than and not less than) knowledge of the possibility of construing a given occasion as one of human action, rather than as one of mechanical causality. The self, in this case, is known *through* its actions. It is a shape and pattern given to events, and is not more ephemeral than the action itself; it is not *another* object, for it is known through the understanding of the situation.

In our discussion of things, it turned out that the self is not known apart from the environment in which it plays a part. Rather, any understanding of the context in which things are identified also reveals the self at work in establishing that context. It is exhibited first through the intelligibility of a given context and, then, through the plain and simple fact that there are envisionable alternatives to any specified context.

Ultimately, the self or subject is revealed in the orders and levels of experience and knowledge. It is because there are many levels at work that we are convinced that there is a self, and so an inner life corresponding to every delineation of the outer life and vice-versa.

If one asks *what* the self is, the answer must be given by reference to the way in which it reveals itself in the various orders, levels and contexts. What is resisted is the notion that it has some additional ghostly existence apart from *any* of these situations. To demand *that* would be to make of it a special kind of object.

Admittedly, to say *only* this would be to admit to a rather unsatisfying situation, as if the self were rather like a kind of phantom movie projector which popped up here and there. From what it projected and the occasions on which it showed itself, we might attempt to infer its purpose, but we would persist in trying to track it down and confront it directly.

It turns out, as the beginning of this discussion and the whole of section 5.2 were meant to point out, that one can meet the problem head on but that the result is not the revelation of a new kind of object, but of a new dimension to the other objects.

The self is mostly revealed in the assignment of meanings. It is because we can give meanings to contexts, because we can give meaning to the contrast between contexts, and so on, that we find the intelligible process which we might well call self-manifestation is actually going on.

When we say we *know* someone, we mean that we have established a community of meanings with him. It is that community of meanings which provides the structure of knowledge of ourselves and of others. But it is not a new set of objects. Words are a set of "natural objects" with meanings. Symbols are objects in their own right and symbolize *for* someone. No ghostly pseudo-object intrudes, but a new dimension of objects is discovered when one finds out that symbols have meanings. Much more strongly, what was simply a human body takes on a new significance when one finds out that it is associated with a source of meanings.

The "source" is not established by a ghost in the machine. Nevertheless, all possible objects have an inner side as well as an outer side, an aspect of intelligibility and significance as well as an aspect of objective order, and this makes for ambiguity.

What we might properly call the core of "the world within" is established by creating situations in which the significance is wholly autobiographical in principle. When I say that Professor Bartlett has mental images which I do not and cannot share, the statement is ambiguous. Of course, as *images* they have a significance for him that they could not possibly have for me, and an "image" is not possible without some assignment of significance—it must be "of something." But the object which properly bears that significance *might* be perfectly public in principle. After all, we may, one day, be able to associate suitable brain wave patterns with appropriate image-objects and develop a machine, not unlike a television set, which would translate those signals into "pictures." But they would not be *his* images, for as images they are, as we have suggested, universals of indefinite application; if they are determinate pictures, that is an accidental feature. The reason that this hypothetical machine seems an unlikely piece of future hardware is that, given what mental images actually are, there is no reason at all to think that, in case Professor Bartlett and I are both imaging the same thing, we are using the same carrier object. The essential point is that the carrier-object is not the image. The image is the significance *given to* a carrier-object. Just as "nite" and "night" will both do for the same thought, so any carrier objects will do for the same image. Uncovering the carrier object is a possible enterprise; for the image is associated with its own significance; uncovering the image is not.

6.226   The "world within" is, thus, quite safe from encroachment not because it represents an ethereal object set which is hard to get at, but because it represents, literally, no object set at all. It is made up, ultimately, of elements of meaning, significance, and intentionality.

The kind of knowledge which is crucial here, therefore, is the knowledge which depends upon the exchange of meanings. Knowledge of things is interpretative, starting, in a given context, with confrontation and developing into the organization of that context through the application of appropriate criteria. Knowledge of persons is creative, beginning with established contexts and meanings, but proceeding through the development of a community of meaning.

The interplay of these factors yields the distinction between the world within and the outer world as a kind of developing dialectic. First order experience is simply immediate confrontation. It is an essential precondition of knowledge, but it does not yield knowledge itself, for knowledge is the product of an activity.

Second order experience is immediate reflection—the attempt to turn the knowing process inwards. It is here that we find the primary level at which questions about knowledge naturally arise, and meet those "certainties" which result simply from turning the reflective process inwards on itself. The dependence of this reflective process on the original confrontation, and the dependence of the confrontation itself on the appropriate contexts—linguistic, perspectival, and so on—restricts these "certainties." Thus one who associates first order knowledge with, say, sense data, achieves his goal by choosing a certain way of speaking, a certain segment of the reflective process, and a certain context for his endeavours.

At each stage of this process there are, as well, two orders of meanings—those which derive from the objects of confrontation, interpretation, and reflection, and those which derive from the order, structure, and the process itself. When they seem to merge, as in the second order experience of immediate reflection, it is, evidently, because the process has been turned inward on one of its own segments. (Hume's dilemma about the "self" thus has a perfectly natural explanation, as does Descartes's claim that one cannot doubt one's own existence; but each of them is, substantially, a by-product of a chosen context, and the conclusions cannot be carried beyond that context.)

6.227 The natural epistemological conclusion, therefore, is that the knowledge of immediate reflection is only intelligible given that there are other orders of knowledge. Knowledge in a more serious sense derives from further reflection on the relations between the original confrontation and the process of reflection. It is here that the significance, if any, of the immediate confrontations and the immediate reflections begins to emerge. Second order knowledge is not constructed, as the logical positivists supposed, literally "out of" immediate cognitions, but out of the relations between immediate reflection and the original confrontation.

The double parallelism of the orders of knowledge and orders of meaning, of course, creates a situation of great complexity and one which, on traditional theories, has proved consistently baffling. At each level, there is knowledge of an object and the knowledge of the process itself which yields the sense of a self, of a center of consciousness, and of inter-personal understanding. There is the immediate self-awareness which is a feature of every confrontation, the second order self-awareness which results from turning the process in on itself, and the constructed sense of continuing self-hood which parallels explanation and theory. But there is the awareness of others which comes from confrontations which do not present themselves in a simple autobiographical context. We meet actions and feelings which are clearly not ours. The awareness of others in immediate reflection gives structure to the emotions, sensations, and the occasion of reflection itself. The community of meanings comes from acting on those reflections so as to create an intelligible interchange.

The conditions for anything which can legitimately be claimed as knowledge involve aspects of all these features. Thus the epistemological conditions which seem to be most general and pervasive involve a significantly richer structure than most traditional theories of knowledge seem to have envisaged.

6.23   If the general theory we have been offering is true, a number of factual conditions must obtain. They follow, of course, if and only if one can meet the epistemological conditions stated in the last section and interpret them in the light of the basic conditions stated in the section which preceded that. In a sense, this amounts to applying the epistemological procedures, and then applying the modes of analysis urged in the statement of the formal aspect of the basic conditions. But this may well be too grand a series of announcements. The epistemological conditions were intended to give an account of what could be claimed as knowledge in various situations—what *ought* to count given what we know about the results of taking various views about human experience and reason. We have tried to make sense not just of human experience, but of the suggestions which have been provoked in the minds of philosophers from several traditions—empiricists of the early modern period, Hegelians, some phenomenologists, and some of the analytic philosophers who represent the currents set in motion by the common sense of Moore, and by the linguistic analyses of Wittgenstein. We have not tried to accommodate the conclusions of all these philosophers in some new but dire eclecticism. Rather, we have tried to unveil the situation which provoked their conclusions, to make sense of their concerns and to add concerns of our own. Thus we have not really been confronting experience "in the raw," if only because no one knows just what that would mean. It is through the investigation of rival concerns that the insufficiency of rival solutions must emerge if it is to emerge at all.

If all this is so, it is just a little naive to treat our epistemological conditions as though they were independent of the likelihood of their being fulfilled. It is convenient to make the distinction but no sensible person would, certainly, advocate a theory of knowledge which he thought to have no outcome. (Philosophers have, admittedly, as A. J. Ayer once suggested, not infrequently amused themselves by setting conditions for knowledge which cannot be met, and then expressing mock astonishment at the fact that nothing meets them. We have tried to avoid this device and to get our amusement in other, hopefully more satisfying, ways.)

What is left as the task of this chapter is a summary of the factual outcomes, and a statement of the sense in which they are to be understood. This last is rather important, for we have argued throughout that the orders of levels of experience, knowledge, and meaning are crucial and that much gross misunderstanding results from a failure to grasp the distinctions.

The "facts" we are about to announce, then, belong to a rather rarefied level—to a level beyond the description of immediate reflection and, indeed, beyond the level on which one unites reflection and confrontation in hypothesis and explanation. To *that* union belong, of course, statements in physics such as "bodies attract one another directly as their mass and inversely as the square of the distance between them." To it, also, belong hypotheses about human behaviour, such as "gentlemen prefer blondes," or "men try to buy cheaply and sell dearly." There are other books to be written (perhaps not by us) about how these two sets of statements must be logically different if the distinctions between persons and things maintained here is correct, and those books would be devoted to a different sort of philosophical problem. But here the "factual" conclusions are philosophical statements such as "there are things" and "there are persons" (and some a good bit more complicated), which are essentially interpretations of the results of meeting the epistemological conditions. The simple fact of meeting those conditions yields statements which may belong to the physical sciences, the social sciences, or just to common sense. The interpretation of them in an attempt to see what minimal conditions must obtain in any possible world in which the relevant knowledge exists is a species of philosophical analysis. It is potentially, but not quite actually, metaphysics in the traditional sense. For it says something about the world, but what it says is that the world contains the minimal conditions for the appropriate functioning of certain concepts. "There are things" means *at least* that the concept of "thing" can be used and cashed. "There are persons" means that the concept of person functions similarly; for one who denies that there are persons is committed to the view that, wherever it occurs, the concept of person can be replaced by some other concept or set of concepts. It is not literally metaphysics in the traditional sense for, to get to that, one would have to complete the analysis of various relations which hold say, between the concept of things and that of material object, between the concept of person and that of mind—relations which we have opened to some light but not pursued to their ultimate end. And one would have to relate all these concepts to the most basic ontological notions, whatever those might turn out to be—being, existence, reality, nothingness, and so on. Our concern in this book has just been with the examination of a crucial cutting edge in human experience, and with the determination of the range of notions which one needs in order to deal with it.

The relation between these sets of questions may, however, be important here. For one might think that if only one had the right understanding of nothing-ness or of being, one would not say any of the things we are inclined to say here. But this seems an implausible contention. A Berkeleyean idealist, for instance, is committed to the belief that there are no material substances, but that does not commit him to the view that there is no function for the concept of motorcar. Similarly, one may ultimately come to the view that true being is not analysable in a way which gives independent existence to sets of material objects. But that would not lead one to reject the notion of "thing" which we have been using here, or to reject the sense in which we have urged that things have an aspect which is their "material." For the argument has been only that certain distinctions must be preserved in the understanding of human experience.

This is not to say that what we have said in this book has no bearing on these ultimate questions, for indeed it does. It rules out many simplistic attempts to elide everything into a single lump. The ultimately real might be Plotinus's One but, if so, then the One will have to have a suitable complexity of manifestation, and the appropriate metaphysic will have a corresponding complexity of structure. Similarly, our argument, if sound, rules out a certain kind of materialism, the kind which holds that all statements about components of the world are reducible to statements about material objects. It does not, as such, rule out the possibility that everything which is ultimately real has an aspect which is its association with material objects, although it suggests strongly that knowledge of persons is not, *as such,* knowledge of material states. (Our argument suggests a certain sort of independence; it does not claim to settle all the questions which would result from the delineation of that independence.)

Nothing here suggests either the foolishness of these further questions, or that they can actually be settled. One who believes these questions to be vapid and in principle unsettleable, or one who believes he has settled them, cannot simply appeal to this book for confirmation. We do suggest to him, though, that he *will*, like anyone else, find that he has to take account of the distinctions we have been trying to make.

That said, let us proceed, as in the past sections, to a list of the propositions to be defended here:

1. There are things.
2. Things have a continuant-occurrent aspect.
3. Things have a perceptual aspect.
4. Persons are related to things in their continuant-occurrent aspect by external relations.
5. Persons are related to things in their perceptual aspects by internal relations.
6. There are intentional objects.
7. Intentional objects are neither things nor grammatical devices, but universals of indeterminate application.
8. Intentional objects are related to persons by internal relations.
9. The thing or state of affairs which corresponds to an intentional object is a determinate form of that intentional object.
10. Images are universals of indeterminate application, but are characterised by having encounterable particulars as their determinates.
11. Persons are related to images by internal relations.
12. A person is defined by a set of internal relations whose other terms are universals of indeterminate application.
13. The thing-world is determinate.
14. Persons are not wholly determinate.
15. Action is the rendering determinate of a universal of indeterminate application.
16. Physical change is the replacement of one determinate state of affairs by another.
17. The world within is a coherent subset of aspects of the world.
18. The world outside is the context within which those aspects become intelligible.

6.231   The first five of these propositions deal with things and their relation to persons. There are things just in case there are criteria for identifying things and those criteria are sometimes met. The argument which we have used in many ways throughout this book is simply that the most direct level of human experience, the experience of encounter, becomes intelligible through the contrast with reflection and yields knowledge as propositions which reconcile the encounters with the experiences are developed.

Things in their primary meaning are those reference points in encounter which make it possible for us to render our experiences intelligible to ourselves and to others. They are inherently social phenomena, a fact revealed by the rules for discourse about them in the common ordinary language. They are distinguished from other reference points—as the discussion of the epistemological conditions suggested—by the quite simple fact that discourse about them cannot be rendered autobiographical without either failing to reconcile encounter or reflection, or rendering vast tracts of ordinary, quite functional, language inoperative.

To say that there *are* things, in this sense, is just to say that the necessary operations frequently are carried out by human beings in such a way as to render the concept of thing functional. Its deeper "ontological" meaning is just that certain basic distinctions will have to be accounted for, whatever one's ultimate metaphysics.

Yet this still gives rise, of course, to questions about the relations between persons and things. Things, we noticed, have both a perceptual aspect and a continuant-occurrent aspect. There is nothing very mysterious about this. Things enter into our affairs as objects of encounter. When the process of encounter and reflection is completed, they are said to be perceived—that is, to enter into experience as entities identified as having a place in a context.

For this to be possible, it has to be the case that something counts as identification and re-identification. As items in an experience, they are occurrents. As items which spread through a series of experiences so as to be re-identified and classified, they are continuants. It is this aspect of them which makes us say that statements about them are not merely autobiographical. They are, in this sense, externally related to persons. That is to say, there is a core of statements about them which is true independently of any relation which they happen to have to any given percipient.

But this relation, equally, is not possible without the perceptual aspect of things which turn up in the set of facts we describe as "how the thing looks to Smith when he views it from a particular perspective." Distant things look small, close things look large, things reflected in distorting mirrors look distorted, and so on. To say that a thing has "a look about it" is to say that it *is* seen. And that look is not divorceable, ultimately, from the perspective of the experiencer. Notice that it is a mark of a genuine thing that it responds to the rules about perspective in a standard way, so that statements about its observation by x can be translated into statements about how it would normally look to y.

Every particular statement about a perceptual aspect represents a property which is internally related to a given observer. That property would not occur were not the individual where he is and doing what he is doing.

If it makes no sense, as we urged, to talk about things as though all statements about them might be rendered autobiographical, it equally makes no sense to talk about them as if they were not to be perceived at all. The occasion for talking about them arises just from the fact that encounter and reflection yield a context for that talk.

We could examine the debate between realists and subjective idealists and attempt to show that each of them falls into the trap of trying to exploit one of the aspects of things at the expense of the other. But our point is somewhat different. It is simply that the world-outside/world-within distinction emerges in sharp focus at this point; there are two aspects of things, they differ in their characteristic relations to persons and, given that the criteria for the identification of things are ever fulfilled (and it seems evident that they *are*), we have a situation in which both worlds are instantiated in our commerce with things as much as in our commerce with ourselves and with persons in general.

Our point follows unless someone wants to say (1) the criteria for thing identification are *never* fulfilled; (2) there is a genuine and meaningful discourse about things which does not entail reference to the non-autobiographical aspects of things; or (3) there is a genuine and meaningful discourse about things which does not entail reference to the perceptual aspect of things.

6.232   The next five propositions have to do with the direct contrast to the world of things—the basic contents of the world within, intentional objects and images. The argument is meant to be parallel. Intentional objects and images are defined by a set of meanings which are, essentially, both autobiographical and internally related to the knowing subject. But they are not merely subjective. One cannot intend what could have no conceivable place in the world; one cannot image what could in no sense be encountered. Furthermore, these meanings are associated with carriers of the meanings, themselves things which can be talked about and identified after the manner of things.

As a consequence, intentional objects are not things or pseudo-things—not surrogate objects—but universals of indeterminate application which, once rendered determinate, are, of course, things or states of affairs in the ordinary sense. They are not just grammatical devices, for a grasp of them is as essential to understanding things in their perceptual aspect as it is to understanding the stance of the person who makes perception intelligible. One who could not be said to be intending something could not be perceiving an object, an ordinary thing. For then he would be simply regarding his perception as an immediate reflection, and be caught in the trap of one who finds that all his perceptions are simply sense data. But that there are intentional objects is a fact which depends upon the fact that there are things. Otherwise, it would not make sense to maintain that one was intending *something*—that one's intention was a relation which carried one, prospectively at least, into the world.

The same analysis holds for images, as we saw in the discussion in 6.225. One has an image *of* something. The image itself, however, is not a surrogate thing but a universal capable of appropriate determination when it is cashed in outward experience. Hence, it does not follow that my image of my ideal house on a misty island either has or has not six front windows, or has or has not a thick oak door. Nor does the island have to be or not be in the *Thousand Islands*. It gets its power from its ability to be *in*determinate with respect to some properties, and thus to capture the intended region of potential experience.

Presumably, if we had no mental images at all, many crucial kinds of identification would become impossible; but, because they are not literally things, they need not be in one space or another, involved in one causal system or another. In the literal sense of being "images of" they might not exist if there were no things. But there could be no things if nothing could be imaged, either, for then, the public aspect of things, the aspect in which things are a social phenomenon, could not be delineated. We could not, that is, form a context which would yield the continuant-occurrent aspect of things were there no basis for that context. And that basis lies in our perceptual ability to strike and delimit contexts. That, in turn, depends upon our ability to imagine alternatives. But the imagining (as the earlier argument showed) is associated with the kind of imaging which has reference to universals, which can be rendered determinate in one way or another.

The claims to conceptual understanding which make knowledge possible, in short, yield claims to know the existence of at least a limited range of intentional objects and images. If there are things then there are intentional objects and images, and statements about them cannot simply be reduced to statements about things.

The argument, once again, is simply that reasonable traffic with knowledge and experience yields, if it is intelligible at all, specimens which meet the criteria for these denizens of the inner world. Yet they are not ghostly or pale copies of things in the world. Rather, they are features of a conceptual situation which is part and parcel of our ability to make sense of, to manipulate, to understand the world of ordinary things.

6.233   The twelfth proposition simply attempts to give some notion of the central features of the concept of person—to provide some access to the claim that there *are* persons. A person is the other term of the relation which characteristically defines intentional objects, mental images, perceptions, thoughts, feelings, and so on. The complete set of these relations defines the person. But the person is the thing manifested in them. The fact that a person is a distinct term in these relations has given rise, as we saw in parts of the discussion summarised in 6.22, to the notion that a person is a special kind of thing, an object of an unusual kind. The fact is, of course, that an intention is an intention because it exhibits a person intending, an image is an image because someone images (in the relevant sense), and so on.

It is for this reason (as we saw originally in section 5.2) that knowledge of persons is unique. The point, here, is to notice what must happen if one denies, in fact, that there are persons. He must then hold that certain of these crucial relations—intending, imaging, and perceiving amongst them—are intelligible through an analysis of only one of their terms. He will then end by making intentional objects, mental images, and perceptions into pseudo-things, for if he can analyze the relations intelligibly into one of their terms, he would have to hold that that term was externally related to the other term. Having done this, the penalty would be that these very odd "things" would have to be given very odd properties, made opaque to understanding and knowledge—rendered, ultimately, so vague as to be mere objects of intuition. But the self or person, cut off from its relation to the objects which normally define it, would also become dim, vaporous and merely intuited.

One who thinks there are persons but doubts there are things is, therefore, advised to move with care. The relation between them is made intelligible by a reasonable analysis of the components of the "inner life," but the whole edifice stands or falls together.

Descartes intuited the vast web of connections which makes every judgment involved, to one degree or another, with claims about selfhood. But he was wrong to think that one might be assured, in isolation, of the existence of personhood. For the roads that lead to it lead away from it as well, and the remaking of them into one-way streets breeds endless paradox.

We can, of course, translate G. E. Moore's classical remark into this context. He is supposed to have said he had no doubt that there were material objects; what he doubted was that he had the correct analysis of the expression. Similarly, we can see that to doubt that there are persons would be difficult. But it is easy to doubt any particular analysis of the concept—including, naturally, the limited one we have attempted here. But is it so easy to doubt that one must make one's concept of person work by relating it to the structure of our transactions with *both* the inner world and the world outside? It does seem virtually certain that any such failure would collapse the conceptual analysis of both worlds.

6.234 Propositions 13 through 16 merely reinforce these conclusions, taking account of our analyses of action and causality.

Little new needs to be said about them here. The world of things is fixed and determinate. It consists of the kinds of things one *encounters*. The world within consists primarily of universals which can be rendered more or less determinate. The person, considered as the author of actions, is not a set of cogs and wheels, metaphorical engines and drive shafts. Rather, he is what is manifested through the significance of his actions. He is indeterminate in the two obvious senses: he is not the sum of his present and past acts, and he can always be manifest in more than one way. Professor Bartlett is "not himself" if he begins to talk and act just like Martin Heidegger, but there is a wide range of things he can do which are wholly consistent with his remaining Bartlett. In acting, he determines himself—he renders precise and formed what existed only as a universal of indeterminate application. In the determination of the person through action he remains, precisely, himself. He is not replaced by a "new" self when he takes on a new task, role, function, or activity. Rather, those tasks, roles, functions, and activities render determinate and explicit what existed as his "potentiality."

Continuity of personhood is not, to be sure, inevitable. But when it ceases, it does so in ways which are intelligible in their own terms, and not in the terms appropriate to things. Professor Bartlett might cease to be "himself" and become a surrogate Martin Heidegger. But, if so, that is because what is lacking is the continuity of intention and imagination. It is, in short, because the actions through which he is manifested no longer hang together, no longer manifest a continuous person. The end of a physical process, by contrast, is marked simply by the failure of those occurrences which bind a set of perceptual aspects to a set of interpretations. The unity of the thing as continuant is no longer suggested. Once New York has been atom bombed, its future will be resolved into the future of its atomic and sub-atomic components. The continuant "Grand Central Station" will have been dissolved in a single occurrence.

Thus the conditions for personal integrity are quite different from the conditions for the integrity of things. But this is not problematic unless persons are reduced to pseudo-things.

6.235   The remaining two propositions simply summarize our final conclusion. The inner world is a coherent sub-set of aspects of the world, while the world outside provides the conditions under which those aspects become intelligible. It is not that there are "two worlds," one of things and one of pseudo-things. It is, rather, that there is an inner side and another side to things. The outer world is a set of determinate states whose determinables (to use some terminology from W. E. Johnson) figure as the structures of the inner world. There are different kinds of relations—there are particulars and universals of indeterminate application, there are bearers of meanings and there are meanings themselves.

The problem with which we started—of the individual faced with the task of orienting himself in the face of an inner and an outer world—thus becomes the problem of understanding that the individual's task is to use the levels of experience, meaning, and knowledge to create an intelligible and coherent experience. He must render the world a coherent context in order to grasp himself, and he must order the structure of his own experience in order to grasp the world.

There is, thus, no simple solution to his problems, no end to the process of the orientation of self and world, no psychological trick by which all our problems might disappear. At the same time, there is no unresponsive world of bare, brute things which renders all our activities meaningless. The machine-monster world of the reductive materialists is a conceptual misunderstanding. But so is the dream of the subjective idealist—the dream of a world which depends solely upon our own private reflection. Private reflections there are, but they are only intelligible as reflections on a public world. A public world there is, but it is only intelligible as a social phenomenon—a by-product, in *part*, of our language, our choice of contexts, our conceptual schemes. There may be a deeper domain of the ultimately real but, if so, we shall only find it by making, first, our peace with the immediacy of confrontation and reflection.

Notes on Chapter 6

Notes to Section 6.1.

1.   My quarrel, here, is not with the concept of the Absolute or with Hegel's notion of logic, but simply with the implications of some of Hegel's proposals for our account of the way in which reality is grasped. I argue, indeed in *Logic and Reality* (Assen and New York: Royal Van Gorcum and the Humanities Press, 1972) that a balance carefully maintained by Hegel is allowed to dissolve at the end of the *Science of Logic* and that the basic notion of dialectical individuality is lost. See *Logic and Reality,* Chap. 6, and *Science of Logic,* translated by W.H. Johnston and L.G. Struthers (London: George Allen and Unwin, 1929, Vol. II), p. 466ff.

2.   The discussion of the Absolute in the *Phenomenology of Mind* (translated by J.B. Baillie, London: George Allen and Unwin, 1910) occupies only about two percent of the text. Hegel claims in a letter to Schelling that he finished the book quickly (and not very satisfactorily) because he was working on the eve of Napoleon's attack on Jena. Baillie, in his introduction, blames the problem on Hegel's arrangement with the publisher.

3.   *Ibid.,* pp. 149-160.

4.   See Hume's own account of his worries about this matter in the appendix to his *Treatise of Human Nature,* ed. Selby-Bigge (Oxford: The Clarendon Press), p. 634ff.

5.   *Logic and Reality* (see note 1 to Section 6.1 above), Chap. 3.

6.   Henri Bergson, *Time and Free Will,* translated by F.L. Pogson (London: George Allen, 1913).

7.   Henri Bergson, *Creative Evolution,* translated by Arthur Mitchell (New York: Henry Holt, 1911).